RESEARCH IN THE HISTORY OF ECONOMIC THOUGHT AND METHODOLOGY

RESEARCH IN THE HISTORY OF ECONOMIC THOUGHT AND METHODOLOGY

Founding Editor: Warren J. Samuels (1933–2011)

Series Editors: Luca Fiorito, Scott Scheall and Carlos Eduardo Suprinyak

Recent Volumes:

EDITORIAL BOARD

RESEARCH IN THE HISTORY OF ECONOMIC THOUGHT
AND METHODOLOGY   VOLUME 41B

RESEARCH IN THE HISTORY OF ECONOMIC THOUGHT AND METHODOLOGY: INCLUDING A SELECTION OF PAPERS PRESENTED AT THE FIRST HISTORY OF ECONOMICS DIVERSITY CAUCUS CONFERENCE

EDITED BY

LUCA FIORITO
University of Palermo, Italy

SCOTT SCHEALL
Arizona State University, USA

AND

CARLOS EDUARDO SUPRINYAK
American University of Paris, France

United Kingdom – North America – Japan
India – Malaysia – China

Emerald Publishing Limited
Emerald Publishing, Floor 5, Northspring, 21-23 Wellington Street, Leeds LS1 4DL.

First edition 2023

Editorial matter and selection © 2023 Luca Fiorito, Scott Scheall, and Carlos Eduardo
Suprinyak. Published under exclusive licence by Emerald Publishing Limited.
Individual chapters © 2023 Emerald Publishing Limited.

Reprints and permissions service
Contact: www.copyright.com

British Library Cataloguing in Publication Data
A catalogue record for this book is available from the British Library

ISBN: 978-1-80455-983-3 (Print)
ISBN: 978-1-80455-982-6 (Online)
ISBN: 978-1-80455-984-0 (Epub)

ISSN: 0743-4154 (Series)

INVESTOR IN PEOPLE

CONTENTS

ABOUT THE EDITORS

Luca Fiorito received his PhD in Economics from the New School for Social Research in New York and is currently Professor at the University of Palermo. His main area of interest is the history of American economic thought in the Progressive Era and the interwar years. He has published many works on the contributions of the institutionalists and on the relationship between economics and eugenics.

Scott Scheall is Assistant Professor in the Faculty of Social Science in Arizona State University's College of Integrative Sciences and Arts. He has published extensively on topics related to the history and philosophy of the Austrian School of Economics. Scott is the Author of *F. A. Hayek and the Epistemology of Politics: The Curious Task of Economics* (Routledge, 2020) and *Dialogues concerning Natural Politics: A Modern Philosophical Dialogue about Policymaker Ignorance* (Substack, 2023).

Carlos Eduardo Suprinyak is Associate Professor of Economics at the American University of Paris. He specializes in the history of political economy, exploring the intersections between economics and politics in different historical contexts, from early modern England to Cold War Latin America. Besides numerous papers in peer-reviewed journals, he is also Co-editor of *The Political Economy of Latin American Independence* (Routledge, 2017) and *Political Economy and International Order in Interwar Europe* (Palgrave, 2020).

LIST OF CONTRIBUTORS

Tiago Camarinha Lopes	Universidade Federal de Goiás, Goiás, Brazil
Valentina Erasmo	Università G. d'Annunzio, Chieti-Pescara, Italy
Luca Fiorito	University of Palermo, Palermo, Italy
Rafael Galvão de Almeida	Universidade Federal de Minas Gerais, Belo Horizonte, Brazil
Micha Gartz	American Institute for Economic Research, Great Barrington, MA, USA
Eli Goldstein	Ashkelon Academic College, Ashkelon, Israel
Cynthia Hawkinson	Arizona State University Polytechnic Campus, Mesa, AZ, USA
Vibha Kapuria-Foreman	Colorado College, Colorado Springs, CO, USA
Phillip Magness	American Institute for Economic Research, Great Barrington, MA, USA
Charles R. McCann, Jr	Independent Scholar, Pittsburgh, PA, USA
Nadeera Rajapakse	PHARE, Université Paris 1, Panthéon-Sorbonne, Paris, France
Roger J Sandilands	University of Strathclyde, Glasgow, UK
Scott Scheall	Arizona State University Polytechnic Campus, Mesa, AZ, USA
Daniel Schiffman	Ariel University, Ariel, Israel
Harley Silva	Universidade Federal do Pará, Belém, Brazil
Carlos Eduardo Suprinyak	American University of Paris, Paris, France
Jaqueline Vilas Boas Talga	Universidade Federal de Goiás, Goiás, Brazil
Toru Yamamori	Doshisha University, Kyoto, Japan

VOLUME INTRODUCTION

Volume 41B of *Research in the History of Economic Thought and Methodology* features a selection of papers presented at the First History of Economics Diversity Caucus Conference, held online in the summer of 2021. The selection of papers was collectively edited by the Diversity Caucus itself and, in keeping with the Caucus's mission and the conference theme, features an array of papers diversified in terms of authors, topics, and methods. Nadeera Rajapakse, Jaqueline Vilas Boas Talga and Tiago Camarinha Lopes, Rafael Galvão de Almeida and Harley Silva, Valentina Erasmo, Cynthia Hawkinson, Vibha Kapuria-Foreman and Charles R. McCann, Jr, and Toru Yamamori contribute to the selection of papers.

The volume also includes new research essays from Roger Sandilands on Albert Hirschman, Lauchlin Currie, and Paul Rosenstein Rodan, and from Daniel Schiffman and Eli Goldstein on Marion Clawson and Israeli agricultural policy in the mid-1950s. The volume closes with an interview of Francis Wilson conducted by Phil Magness and Micha Gartz.

The Editors of *Research in the History of Economic Thought and Methodology*
Luca Fiorito
Scott Scheall
Carlos Eduardo Suprinyak

PART I

A SELECTION OF PAPERS
PRESENTED AT THE FIRST
HISTORY OF ECONOMICS
DIVERSITY CAUCUS
CONFERENCE

CHAPTER 1

WOMEN MIGRANT WORKERS AND MARKET FORCES: TOWARD AN INTER-DISCIPLINARY REPRESENTATION OF FEMALE LABOR MIGRATION

Nadeera Rajapakse

ABSTRACT

The economic literature on labor migration has incorporated insights from various disciplines with regard to content and method, although the representation of migrants has not fully moved away from the neoliberal, market-dominated framework. This paper addresses the issue of women migrant workers using the particular example of Sri Lankan migrant women workers to the Middle East. It aims to highlight the need for more diversity in economic research without which conceptual representation, as well as empirical reach, is limited.

After a brief overview of the representation of migrants in economic literature, I develop the concept of vulnerability. I refer to qualitative and quantitative analyses on Sri Lankan migrant women workers to the Middle East from a variety of disciplines in order to differentiate the "vulnerable," that is, the workers in need of protection, from the "vulnerabilities." The latter concept refers to the debilitating effects on workers, produced by market forces, which are often perpetuated by underlying assumptions, as well as policies. A broader, inter-disciplinary perspective, which considers the agency of women, can go a long way toward removing some of the limitations and preconceptions

Research in the History of Economic Thought and Methodology: Including a Selection of Papers Presented at the First History of Economics Diversity Caucus Conference
Research in the History of Economic Thought and Methodology, Volume 41B, 3–25
ISSN: 0743-4154/doi:10.1108/S0743-41542023000041B001

*ingrained in most economic representation. This in turn could help to improve
the protection of the vulnerable and empower them to better face market forces.*

Keywords: Agency; domestic work; gender; inter-disciplinary
representation; migrant workers; vulnerability

INTRODUCTION

Michele Gamburd wrote that "money makes the world go round and makes
women go around the world" (Gamburd, 2005, p. 75), referring to Sri Lankan
women migrant workers, who are the highest source of foreign exchange earners
for the country. Macro analyses of female labor migration and its overall economic results are glowing. However, when the spotlight narrows and individual
stories are sought, the narrative offers a different picture. There are stories of hor-
rendous abuse, even death, exploitation, and ill effects on families, especially on
children left behind. Even in the official national discourse on the subject, women
migrant workers are portrayed with mixed feelings. It took many years for the
government to decide to call them "rata viru," national heroes.[1] This paper discusses the representation of migrants in economic literature as a way of explaining the demeaning influence it has had, by using the particular example of Sri
Lankan women migrant workers.

As quoted above, money is a key lens through which the reasons for and the
effects of migration are analyzed. It is, nonetheless, only one, among many sali-
ent factors, and as the author of the quote has shown, understanding migration
requires an inter-disciplinary approach. The money perspective has been captured by the economic literature – dominated by the neoclassical framework –
in labor economics, migration studies and development economics, to name a
few of the strands. The purpose of this paper is to emphasize the need for inter-
disciplinary studies diverse in both content and method, going beyond the focus
on money and economic factors in representing migrants. I pinpoint "vulnerabilities," which are created by neoliberal free markets and by the commodification of low-skilled labor. I also discuss how migration policy and governance
are ineffective without proper understanding and consideration of the agency
of women.

Since Ravenstein (1885) proposed the first "laws of migration," there is a
prevailing assumption that people move from low- to high-income places (De
Haas, 2010). Lewis (1970) presented the disparities of labor as the underlying
theoretical explanation of migration. It then led to analyses based on push-pull
factors (Todaro, 1969), cost-benefit comparisons, wage and skills disparities, etc.
These analyses have a strong focus on the individual migrant, allowing for human
agency to play a central role in the decision to migrate. Following criticisms of the
narrow focus on households and neglect of the reality that migrants do not have
access to complete and accurate information, criticisms addressed by Marxist-
structuralist theoreticians, a more historical, structural approach was endorsed,
although this did not address migration theory directly.

The New Economics of Labour Migration (NELM) was developed in the 1980s by Oded Stark and David Bloom, presenting the motivation for migrating as a collective decision taken at the household level. Migration is viewed as a "rational way of hedging against risk in a world characterized by incompleteness of information and incomplete markets" (Abreu, 2010, p. 58). In this theory, remittances play a big role in influencing the decision to migrate. NELM was presented as a synthesis of the neoclassical and historical-structural approaches. However, it ultimately attempts to explain migration through economically motivated decisions at either the individual- or household level and ignores how even the opportunity to make these decisions is dictated and constrained by broader policies, politics, and interactions.

Economic theory has, in more recent times, also borrowed from sociological and anthropological research on migration to include cultural underpinnings, diaspora and community influences, and gender perspectives. Diaspora knowledge networks – associations of highly skilled expatriates, willing to contribute to the development of their origin countries – emerged in the 1990s (Leclerc & Meyer, 2007). For migration studies, this meant a shift in the existing emphasis on brain drain toward a perspective on brain gain. In addition, instead of focusing on the physical return of people, it considers that origin countries can benefit through these connections. Integrative approaches, which mix various levels of analyses, migration flows, and historical and contemporary processes, include the NELM, the network theory (Boyd, 1989; Massey & España, 1987), cumulative causation theory, and institutional theory (Massey et al., 1993).

While the original neo-liberal economics explored the theoretical foundations for the reasons for migration and its economic impact, the later literature stemming from gender economics explores two key areas: first, the type of jobs and industries that women, both migrant or otherwise, traditionally work in, along with the conditions (monetary and non-monetary) of work. Second, it deals with family-related issues that arise due to women's empowerment or lack thereof. This shapes, for example, the sphere of intra-household bargaining and the ability to overcome social norms which govern the division of work within a family, and the role of women as mothers. As documented in a comprehensive review by Priya, Venkatesh, and Shukla (2021), there is a long and distinguished discourse conceptualizing and measuring women's empowerment that goes well beyond the ability to earn and access economic resources, either in the home or host country.

This paper incorporates key contributions made by gender studies and anthropology, notably, in discussing migration. Migration in anthropological studies has been studied through the angle of kinship and family networks (Collier & Yanagisako, 1987; Gamburd, 1995). Anthropologists explore the interconnected social relations which enable people to move and settle and the cultural understandings that are part of all processes of movement and settling. Gender analysis has made a crucial contribution to understanding the institutions that structure migration processes. Gender is seen as "an essential tool for unpicking the migration process" (Sinclair, 1998; Wright, 1995). There is now more emphasis on differential migration responses by men and women (themselves context-dependent), gender discrimination in returns to migrant labor, and the differences in perception of men and women migrants by the greater community. Ncube and Mkwananzi (2020) view the contribution of migration to development as surpassing economic measures. They provide a human development-informed capability approach, cutting across political, economic, cultural, and social spheres. A number of studies have used the Capability Approach to look at gender (Nussbaum, 2011) as well as migration (Ncube & Mkwananzi, 2020).

Despite the ever-expanding diversity of approaches, research issues, methods, and results with regard to migration studies, the neoliberal, market-oriented approach remains the dominant framework (Haug, 2008, p. 586). The more recent research linking migration, trade, and development (Hollified, 2007; Ratha, Mohapatra, Vijayalakshmi, & Xu, 2007; Wickramasekera, 2009; Jayet & Rapoport, 2010), despite its diverging analyses and conclusions, also remains embedded in this framework.[2] Most research has acknowledged that global labor markets are characterized by neoliberalism (Wimmer & Schiller, 2003). Hollified (2007) specifies that while trade and finance have been founded on neoliberal regimes, migration, apart from the exception of refugees, has not seen an international liberal regime. This paper notes that the neoliberal regime in place for trade and finance has impacted global labor markets. As such, labor markets are deregulated, the forces of demand and supply for global labor determining wages and the terms on which global labor is employed, and experienced. As I will elaborate, labor in general (i.e., both migrant and non-migrant) has been subjected to the downgrading of standards through the loss of traditional union rights, which is attributed to the spread of neoliberalism (Castles, 2009) and economic globalization characterized by the "race to the bottom" in the search for cheaper labor (Piper, 2008).

Sri Lankan Women Migrant Domestic Workers (SLWMDW)

The oil boom of the early 1970s in the Persian Gulf region triggered a surge of migration flows to the Middle East, which accelerated from the early 1990s onwards following an increase in the demand for domestic servants and female migration from Sri Lanka. Sri Lanka's labor migration since the 1970s has been concentrated in low-skilled categories, although recent policies and global trends have given a greater impulse toward male migration. Housemaids belong to this category, which comprised 73% of migrants in 2007 (Wickramasekera, 2010, p. 9). Sri Lanka is the only country in South Asia where women make up more than half of total migrants, although the declining number of female migrants in recent years is a clear trend. Most women migrants are low-skilled domestic workers and belong to one of the most vulnerable categories in destination countries, especially Persian Gulf countries.[3] This paper refers to women migrant domestic workers who are low-skilled temporary (or contract-based) female migrants (whether regular or irregular), mainly working in the Persian Gulf countries.[4]

Neoliberal Market Forces

Liberalized labor markets have had the strongest influence on the experience of women migrant workers. Although the deregulation of labor markets has created new kinds of job opportunities for migrant workers, it has also resulted in an erosion of employment standards and an increase in contract labor (Chant & Pedwell, 2008). Research shows how greater labor market flexibility has helped create conditions that maximize the potential for the exploitation of migrants, predominantly in the most disadvantaged segments of the market (Phillips, LeBaron, & Wallin, 2018). There is also a growing body of work revealing "unfree labour," where some migrants (e.g., day laborers and domestic workers) get trapped in exploitative labor relations. Methods of control include disciplining by employers, debt bondage, and the use or threat of violence (Phillips et al., 2018). Research has also revealed the liberal paradox:

> Receiving states are likely to remain trapped in what Hollifield called a liberal paradox for decades to come—the economic logic for migration is one of openness, while the political and legal logic is one of closure. (Hollifield, 2007, p. 7)

These issues afflict SLWMDW, and in keeping with the studies that point to highly exploitative conditions of work in industries, which promote flexible labor practices in order to compete internationally, the need for the protection of migrant workers becomes paramount.

Then there is the issue of gender inequalities that spill over into and grow even bigger in international labor markets. Gender discrimination is hardly confined to the private domain of the home (Kabeer, 2008). It also operates through the institutionalized norms and practices of public institutions of state, markets, and society, so that private and public inequalities serve to reinforce each other. As we will see, women who are active in wage labor face markets that have become increasingly deregulated, with labor reduced to the status of a commodity.

Section 1 will serve to interpret, in this context, the statement that money makes the world go round. I will discuss this by focusing on the predominantly economic measures that determine value with regard to low-skilled labour. The economic gain is pushed to the foreground, using remittances as an indicator. After analyzing the problems arising from this narrow indicator, I will develop "vulnerability," and explain how economic measures have contributed toward creating the low social perception of low-skilled labor. In Section 2, I will talk about how women go around the world: The case of SLWMDW will enable us to discuss policy measures and governance, by examining two key issues: protecting women migrant workers and ensuring the well-being of children left behind. I analyze policy documents such as the Family Background Report to reveal how they reflect the money focus of standard economic analyses, thus, failing to take the agency of women into account.

SECTION 1 – BEYOND REMITTANCES: MEASURING THE SOCIAL VALUE OF LOW-SKILLED LABOR

1.1 Predominant Focus on Remittances

The Sri Lankan government's promotion of women's participation in the labor-export programmes is based on the distinct economic advantages in women working overseas. Earnings can be remitted to alleviate poverty. As a source of foreign currency, remittances can assist in addressing external balance problems and can also constitute a source of funds to contribute to economic development (Taylor, 2007, p. 201, in Hollifield, 2007).

Often in economic literature, labor migration is analyzed through the lens of remittances, the money sent back to their home country by migrant workers (Ratha et al., 2007).[5] Remittances are defined by the International Labour Organization as the portion of international migrant workers' earnings sent back from the country of employment to the country of origin. This viewpoint has enabled authors to illustrate the connection – to varying degrees – between migration and development and also migration and poverty alleviation (Ratha et al., 2007; Wickramasekera, 2010). The well-being stemming from migration has mostly been studied as a financial gain, via remittances. In the representation of SLWMDW, there is almost no analysis that does not mention the importance of the remittances they send back. Remittances are the key indicator, the main measure of success or failure of labor migration (Rosewarne, 2012). This paper brings out the discrepancy between high levels of remittances and low levels of effective protection that arises because of this predominant indicator. Even more, I argue that the narrow focus on remittances tends to accentuate the vulnerabilities that these women face.

Remittances have indeed secured Sri Lankan women migrant workers' place on the podium as the highest foreign exchange earner for the Sri Lankan national economy which is estimated to be 8% of gross domestic product (Sri Lanka Ministry of Foreign Employment, 2015). While undeniably important when studying migration, the focus on remittances has overshadowed many limits and shortcomings of these analyses.

1.1.1 Internal Limits of Remittances

Starting with internal analytical limits, studies have shown that a calculation of monetary benefits, combined with the post migration economic status of migrants, reveals, in the majority of cases, that migrants' earnings are insignificant (Abeyasekera & Jayasundere, 2014). Sri Lankan women domestic migrant workers remain small income earners without any significant improvement in their investment capacity. Few migrants are able to pay back their initial debt with one work contract. Even fewer are actually able to save money (Jayatissa & Wickramage, 2015, p. 2). However, in aggregate, they are major contributors to foreign earnings and to the national economy in terms of GDP and export earnings. Despite the divergence between the micro and macroeconomic results, analysts and policy-makers have mostly highlighted the benefits to the home country from remittances (Athukorala, 1992; Puri & Ritzema, 1999; Wickramasekara, 2015). As for individual migrants, they have been, for the most part, led to renew their temporary contracts, or seek new contracts and depart again in order to earn enough to cover their migration costs, reimburse debt, and manage to save. Repeat migration, also described as contract labor, has become the trend, with only a handful of migrants returning home permanently after one contract. When studying remittances, it is, therefore, essential to look beyond the macroeconomic gain and to fully evaluate the financial impact on individual migrants.

Second, it is important to consider the cost of remittances. Money transfer companies structure their fees to make profit. According to Dilip Ratha et al. (2007), one of the reasons for remittances being sent through informal channels is the high cost of transferring money, as well as foreign currency restrictions.

A third factor that limits the salience of remittances as a measure of the migration impact is the phenomenon of "leakages." When migrants opt to send money through informal channels[6] instead of using official money transfer services (Western Union is the biggest money transfer service in Sri Lanka, with the Sri Lanka Post office, state and private banks, and other companies also providing the service), the money is said to be "leaking" from official channels (Athukorala & Rajapatirana, 2003). Consequently, it is difficult to get an accurate estimate of the actual volume of remittances.

1.1.2 External Limits of Remittances

Turning next to the external limits of using remittance as a key measure, the question arises as to whether migration is valued because it provides capabilities for more choice, for a good life, or, for itself. Instead of seeing it as solely a means of gaining remittances, increasing income, or bettering oneself, it could be seen as a goal in itself. Labor migrants may reap more than material benefits (Rosewarne, 2012, p. 83). When turning to multidisciplinary viewpoints, sociologists and anthropologists have focused on how migration can also be a strategy for gaining better recognition in gender roles, for escaping abusive, violent partners, and homes (Kottegoda, Jayasundere, Perera, & Atapattu, 2013). These are capabilities that are very rarely discussed in economics, but can be seen as important, because they are what people value (Sen, 1999).[7]

Secondly, remittances are not only financial in nature, nor are they limited to financial gain. Whether we see remittances as a development panacea or as a way for states to shift responsibility for solving structural problems to migrants, economics does not provide the whole story. Sociologists have coined the term social remittances to call attention to the fact that migrants send home more than money (Levitt, 2001). Social remittances – defined as ideas, know-how, practices, and skills – flow both ways: They shape encounters with and integration into their host societies. Migrants also send back social remittances that have an impact on development and on lives in their countries of origin. Thirdly, economic gains may come at the cost of some other areas of well-being. In the case of labor migration, migrants' rights, their working conditions, are aspects that could outweigh the positive financial gains of migration.[8]

I now turn to the concept of vulnerability and propose an analysis of the various problems that accentuate vulnerabilities and make migrants more vulnerable. Here I differentiate the migrants, who may be "vulnerable," from the circumstances that enhance this situation. These circumstances are referred to as the "vulnerabilities" in so far as they tend to exacerbate the precarious, unequal and exploitative situation faced by domestic migrant workers.

1.2 Neoliberal Markets Creating Vulnerabilities

Guilmoto and de Loenzien (2014) highlight how migration places young women in a different environment and makes them especially vulnerable. "By vulnerability landscape we mean different contexts in which young women operate and the diversity of corresponding risks they face" (Guilmoto & de Loenzien, 2014, p. 28). In this analysis, the concept of vulnerability is seen as a multidimensional measure of the exposure of individuals to various sources of "external stress, ranging from economic downturns to environmental changes and political unrest" (Guilmoto & de Loenzien, 2014, p. 27).

This is a relevant framework for this paper, where labor markets can be seen as vulnerability landscapes. I follow this approach where

> vulnerability emerges as a salient dimension in this assessment, along with better-known contextual factors of migration, such as poverty, employment opportunities, wage differentials, and the presence of migratory networks. (Guilmoto & de Loenzien, p. 29)

Migration is a phenomenon that, by its very nature, creates vulnerabilities. It renders migrants vulnerable through the very act of moving from the home country, the known, the familiar, to the host country, unknown, different, and foreign. I will present three categories of vulnerabilities, relating to labor, the labor market, and migration.

This discussion takes place within a gendered perspective, following the idea that gender-segregated job markets in some host countries influence women migrants' experiences. Their employment opportunities, earnings, and threats of exploitation are strongly linked to the gendered aspect of the labor market (Boyd, 2006). Furthermore, temporary contract migration schemes are the trend that applies to SLWMDW, since they allow destination countries to adjust their workforce to the cyclical nature of economies without further commitments (turning migrants into what political economists would refer to as "disposable labour"), while ensuring a steady flow of remittances on which many countries of origin depend (Piper, 2008).

1.2.1 Vulnerability Related to Low-skilled Labor

Labor migration is broken down into various categories: skilled, low-skilled, permanent, temporary, and return migration. These categories are useful in economics and help bring out differences in wages, types of employment, access to employment, and working conditions, and help ensure that specificities relating to each category are taken into account in theories and policy-making. At the same time, there are judgments and negative perceptions linked especially to the low-skilled category discussed here. Low-skilled temporary labor is the direst category in terms of protection from vulnerabilities and social perception, and this creates a vicious cycle. Low-skilled labor is under-valued.

Individual workers earn little, they have few qualifications that enable them to earn money. But, these economic considerations have blurred the capabilities of these individuals.

Promoting skilled labor is a key objective of the Sri Lankan government (National Policy for Migration of Labour). However, there is obvious demand for low-skilled labor as well as an enormous pool of low-skilled workers. The government's strategy, taking this reality on the market into account, is relatively weak.[9] While it is commendable and greatly desirable to promote skills for everyone, there is also a need to acknowledge the vast numbers of low-skilled women who also deserve opportunities for decent work. Until they are given the opportunity to acquire better skills, a great deal of thought and action are essential to empower them, and secure their rights.

Low-skilled workers, who represent low-income classes, are also seen as undermining the state's aspirations to be a "progressive" and "modern" economy (Abeyasekera & Jayasundere, 2014, p. 13). The reality of the state's dependence on remittances from low-skilled workers damages the image the state wants to portray. Therefore, the government's rhetoric places greater value on high-skilled labor because it is associated with middle-class ideology, to the detriment of low-skilled labor, often the target of contempt.

Low-skilled workers are paid less, with all the negative consequences that follow. However, if we look at low-skilled work from other perspectives, we see much higher measures. Beginning with economic factors, there is more demand from host countries for low-skilled labor than for high-skilled labor. Demand for low-skilled labor is driven by temporary migration schemes, which could be partially interpreted as a co-product of the neo-liberal deregulations of the 1980s–1990s (Castles, 2006). The macro-micro discrepancy mentioned earlier does not change the fact that, as a whole, low-skilled migrants contribute more in terms of total remittances.

There are more low-skilled migrants going from South Asia, including from Sri Lanka, to the Middle East. Job opportunities are more numerous. It is also easier to find low-skilled than skilled jobs. However, considerable resilience among low-skilled migrants to the Middle East is required. In light of the harsh and exploitative working conditions that many women migrant workers face, the commitment and effort put in by low-skilled domestic workers is no doubt greater, compared to what is required from skilled workers.

Finally, low-skilled migrant labor makes a considerable contribution to the general economy. Amartya Sen (2001) has illustrated that domestic work performed (mostly) by women in their homes, for their families, is unpaid labor not included in GDP, though it is fundamental. The entire social structure, including skilled labor, could not be maintained without such low-skilled domestic work. By drawing parallels between the work they perform in their own homes and the jobs they do in the Middle East, we become aware of the enormous contribution they make to their households by becoming bread winners, providing hope for betterment, as well as their contribution to the country as a whole. Once again, it is important to highlight that this contribution is not limited to financial remittances, but is also a matter of shifting the burden of poverty alleviation and unemployment from the state to migrant workers. Moreover, they contribute to their household's ability to invest in education and advance their social standing. Having a member working abroad gives some families more power, voice, and recognition in their communities.

Ciupijus (2010) has pointed out that in contrast to forced migration, which always has had a recognizable ethical dimension in terms of the universal right to asylum, temporary labor migration has tended to be viewed as an exclusively economic and thus ethically neutral phenomenon. The absence of ethical interrogation with regard to temporary labor migration has exacerbated the negative social perception.[10] This social perception is shaped by opinions held by their families and Sri Lankan society in general, but also by their employers. "Many migrants complain that their remittances 'burn like oil', disappearing without a trace" (Gamburd, 2004, p. 167). Indeed, a major share of their earnings is spent on daily consumption without always leaving enough for significant investment. However, as Gamburd points out, this notion is also connected to the moral and cultural logic of how money is earned. Migrants agree that they toil very hard, – it is indeed a fact acknowledged, if not lauded, by all – and honest, hard work "guarantees that wages will thrive for the worker" (Gamburd, 2004, p. 176). In the case of temporary, low-skilled migrant labor, nevertheless, there is another determining factor: "Housemaids argue that their employers dislike them" and this negative emotion causes money to disappear, "burn," without "thriving" (Gamburd, 2004, p. 177).

> Many returnees, when speaking about their working life abroad, remember first not the amounts earned but about the workload, how they were treated by their employers, the gifts they received and the experiences they had. (Kottegoda et al., 2013, p. 38)

In this case, the positive non-material aspect seems to override the negative non-material impact. Migrants' narratives reveal the surprising fact that despite harsh working conditions and unbearable workloads, it is moments of kindness and generosity that seem to be deeper instilled in their memory.

> Yet when these workers have been treated kindly, where affection, humaneness and generosity has been shown, the details of the work is not a litany but a mere statements of facts. (Kottegoda et al., 2013, p. 38)

These accounts reveal that although self-perceptions and social perceptions may not always be aligned – they are complex, sometimes contradictory – they wield an enormous influence on the experience. Transforming low-skilled domestic labor into a positive factor, recognising its social value and contribution in both monetary and non-monetary terms can reduce the effect of the vulnerabilities. Removing the negative perceptions is essential, and a first step could be to move away from merely financial considerations. This might help economics recognize the social value of low-skilled labor. Sending countries will acknowledge and appreciate it better, and might negotiate better on behalf of these workers, thus reducing the vulnerabilities.

1.2.2 Vulnerability Related to the Labor Market

The supply of low-skilled labor is greater than the demand for it. From the point of view of market theory, this means that wages are driven down, but migrants are vulnerable for reasons other than low wages. Migrant labor is driven by market forces of asymmetric influence. The workers, especially women, are powerless, while employers abroad see individual workers as expendable. Low-skilled temporary migrants are victims of "commodification of labour," where workers are mostly valued for their skills and productive capacity (Cox, 1997). This tendency toward commodification may have taken precedence over the state's duty to protect the rights of migrant workers.

The governments of source countries give primacy to remittances and employment situations over workers' rights, all the more because claiming rights and protection may be seen as diminishing the appeal of workers in competitive labor markets. In other words, markets are competitive and in order to maintain the attractiveness of migrant labor, or its comparative advantage, governments may be reluctant to insist on better working conditions and ensuring workers' rights. Women migrant workers are subject to the dictates of profit, which concern for their well-being could undermine.

There is no justifiable reason why the rights of unskilled workers should be given less importance than those of skilled workers. Furthermore, the harsh working conditions, reports of harassment and abuse[11] suggest that they need more protection than skilled workers. To avoid a race to the bottom, it is necessary to improve the rights of the low-skilled to match, if not surpass, those of skilled workers.

However, there appears to be little effort by the government to pressure receiving countries to adhere to international laws protecting migrant workers. The Sri Lankan authorities emphasize the protection of migrants' children over the protection of migrant women themselves. Consequently, there has been more discourse about and measures aimed at protecting children, by restricting the choices open to potential migrant women. This issue will be discussed in Section 2. The International Organization for Migration (and the United Nations) has stated that government policies and public sentiment regarding migrant domestic workers can exacerbate, as they can attenuate, the vulnerabilities migrants face. Restrictive domestic employment and recruitment policies can make migrant women more vulnerable to marginalization and abuse. Gamburd describes Sri Lankan state measures to be "anaemic" compared to those of the Philippines (2009, p. 61). As mentioned earlier, Sri Lankan officials were confronted with the necessity of protecting a fragile market position that it could not afford to undermine by protecting workers. Sri Lanka's economy, like the Philippines', has grown heavily reliant on exporting labor.

1.2.3 Vulnerabilities Related to Migration

Vulnerabilities arise from the massive cost that migration entails, especially for low-skilled migrants. The financial costs, both the debt burden and comparative costs for those who earn less, are much higher, as discussed above. In addition, there are deeply ingrained mentalities that affect migrants' well-being. The way society judges migrant workers, especially low-skilled workers, who leave the protection of their families, their kin and communities, generates a great deal of mixed feelings.

The social and cultural perception of migrant work complicates the evaluation of costs and benefits.

> The local cultural logic includes a moral component concerning how money is earned and exchanged. It also includes a social component concerning the relative positions in society of the actors involved in the exchange, and the emotions they feel toward one another. (Gamburd, 2004, p. 168)

The moral component is related to negative social perceptions regarding women's jobs as domestic workers abroad. In some instances, leaving the family enclave and venturing overseas is considered morally questionable.

In Sri Lanka, migrant women workers are considered transgressive according to conventional values, where women are symbolically equated to the nation (de Costa, 2022). They are expected to conform to the "heteronormative roles of docile daughter, chaste wife, nurturing mother, or sagacious grandmother" (de Alwis, 2002 quoted in de Costa, 2022). Women who do not stay within the boundaries of these stereotypical categories, such as migrant workers, workers in free trade zones, war widows and feminists, are subjected to vilification and marginalization.

These vulnerabilities obviously overlap and tend to magnify the effects. If migration is looked down upon, the nature of domestic work, which is seen as "(...) to most observers, an occupation of low social status and little economic importance" (Cox, 1997, p. 60), only makes things worse for poor women. The structural, political patterns underlying liberal global labor markets create these vulnerabilities. As mentioned earlier, home countries acknowledge these vulnerabilities and state the need to "protect" workers from them. However, as I will discuss in Section 2, the way protection is carried out undermines the ability of workers to exert agency to face these conditions.[12]

A multi-dimensional framework is needed to balance temporary migrant workers' vulnerability with their agency and resilience. Emphasizing the threats faced by Sri Lankan women migrant workers, for example, could reinforce the one-dimensional stereotype of migrants as powerless temporary laborers. Hence it is necessary to acknowledge migrant workers' agency without downplaying the conditions of exploitation at work and the violations of their rights. In other words, protection needs to be effective against vulnerabilities.

SECTION 2 – INEFFECTIVE POLICY MEASURES WITHOUT AGENCY AND EMPOWERMENT

The vulnerabilities mentioned above are further affected by the gendered dimension. As Boyd (2006) noted, migration is not gender-blind nor gender-neutral, but gender-sensitive. The socialization and often patriarchal nature of migrants' home countries create challenges for them to cope and adapt in their host countries. The societal attitude, along with the official, national discourse on women migrant workers is also gender-influenced. While Rosewarne (2012) has pointed out that governments in Sri Lanka, Philippines, and Indonesia have used colorful language to praise migrant workers' contributions to the national economy, in Sri Lanka, such praise has long been withheld.

The very nature of the temporary work contract discussed earlier, coupled with the gendered nature of domestic work, guarantees remittances:

> Although never explicitly articulated, the restrictive employment practices that confront migrant workers employed in low-skilled occupations are thus vital to the success of the labour-export and remittance policy agendas. The expectation that female labour migration will generate remittances is the fundamental rationale that defines the labour-export policies of the Philippines, Sri Lanka and Indonesia, and the sanctioning of foreign domestic worker employment is the foundation of their export-revenue generating policies. (Rosewarne, 2012, p. 86)

This section highlights two issues that are symptomatic of the dilemma that women's labor migration seems to have created in Sri Lanka. Because of the vulnerabilities enumerated in Section 1, Sri Lankan women migrant domestic workers have faced conditions of exploitation, suffered abuse and even death at the hands of their employers in the Middle East. Secondly, studies have revealed the ill effects that have befallen the children left behind, as a result of female labor migration. While these two problems are not the only adverse consequences arising from female migrant labor, the Sri Lankan case has spotlighted the both the limits and successes of institutional responses. These responses are carried out by the government, regulatory bodies (ILO, IOM), NGOs, and other activist organizations. It is most significant to focus on governmental and multi-lateral responses, because, in keeping with the argument put forward in this paper, they appear to be most influenced by the neoclassical discourse and its belief in neo-liberal market forces. This section will highlight that effective protection requires a prior understanding of women's agency and an acknowledgement of the need for meaningful empowerment.

Kabeer's (2008) discussion of agency and empowerment can be pertinently related to migration. Empowerment is defined as "the expansion in the ability to make strategic choices by those who have been denied this ability" (p. 19), such as women migrant workers who had no alternative options to earn a living. Agency is one of the three dimensions of strategic choice, along with resources and achievements.

> It refers to the capacity to define one's goals and to act on them. It goes beyond observable behaviour to encompass the meanings, motivations, skills and purpose that people bring to their actions, their "sense of agency." Agency is thus closely bound up with human capability. (Kabeer, 2008, p. 20)

2.1 Protection Through Restriction

Most of the measures implemented by the government to protect workers are of a restrictive nature. In the late 1990s, women made up 75% of Sri Lanka's migrant labor force (UN Sri Lanka, 2015, p. 9), whereas, by 2008, the rate was below 50%. This can be attributed in the main to the policies and measures taken to reduce the number of female migrants and encourage more male migration. Although the policy measures have been successful in decreasing the share of female departures, their effectiveness in actually protecting low-skilled women migrants is limited.

On the one hand, Sri Lanka has ratified the International Convention on the Protection of all Migrant Workers and their Families, and this has provided the normative framework for national migration policy. In 2008, the Ministry of Foreign Employment, and then the Ministry of Foreign Employment Promotion and Welfare drafted the first National Labour Migration policy, which was approved by the Cabinet in 2009, and has since been governing the migration process. The three main objectives of the national policy are governance and regulation, protection and empowerment of workers, and development benefits (Government of Sri Lanka, 2009).

On the other hand, there appears to be little effort by the government to pressure host countries to adhere to international laws protecting migrant workers. The International Bill of Rights, which identifies the family as the fundamental unit of society, is complemented by three specialized conventions of particular relevance to the protection of migrant workers and their families.[13] The ratification of such laws in host countries should be a necessary condition for migration. Instead, it is a cause for alarm that many host countries have not done so.

> Thus, the UN committee on Migrant Workers has commented that the fact that many countries employing Sri Lankan migrant workers are not yet parties to the ICRMW is an obstacle to the enjoyment by those workers of their rights under the Convention. (quoted in UN Sri Lanka, 2015, p. 593. Concluding Observations: Sri Lanka, ICRMW, *supra* note 37)

As mentioned earlier, Sri Lanka, as a source country, may overlook such legal forms of protection due to the fear of becoming less attractive as a labor-supplying nation. Whatever the reasons, the objective of protecting women migrants cannot be wholly effective if host countries are not party to the international treaties on the protection of migrants. Indeed, even other measures undertaken in Sri Lanka are rendered inefficient in this regard if host countries do not follow international laws.

At the same time, this asymmetric situation between home and host countries may explain why Sri Lanka is imposing restrictive domestic laws to avoid the problem. Since tackling the actual problem – in this case, requiring host countries to ratify international law – is difficult, or even undesirable from a competitive labor perspective, restricting the freedom and choices of migrants appears to be an easier alternative. Sri Lankan women have been drawn into highly gendered and segmented global labor markets. The participation of women in the global domain would not have been as "significant as it has been were it not for the active engagement of their governments in developing the labour migration programmes that have submitted workers to the force of unregulated labour markets" (Rosewarne, 2012, p. 88).

There is a conflict of values between acknowledging the importance of remittances to the national economy and addressing the negative impact of women's absence from home. As said earlier, the promotion of female labor-export programmes relies on women being drawn into the global economy on terms that institutionalize their subordination. The majority of women domestic migrant workers are employed on terms that, compared with most other waged work, are subject to very few forms of labor protection, and the capacity of these workers to resist exploitative and abusive conditions of employment is limited by the isolated nature of the work (Samarasinghe, 1998). Accepting the distinctive character of gendered labor-export programmes is essential in order to understand the barriers to ensuring effective protection for these workers. The gendered character may also explain why protective policies are not effective enough. The government seems torn in their objectives. Much of their initiatives regarding protecting migrant workers lean toward reducing, limiting, and sometimes even banning migration, with the objective of reducing the risks and vulnerabilities women migrants face.[14]

Restrictions, while deflecting attention from the kinds of interventions that are needed to protect the rights of migrant women workers, are often also counterproductive. Restrictions and bans impel prospective migrants to turn to informal and illegal channels, thus increasing their vulnerability in the hands of unauthorized agents. The fact that women migrants still seek to travel illegally (Weeraratne, 2021) implies that their agency is overlooked in policy-making. Kabeer (2008) explains how agency and empowerment should allow for greater freedom in decision-making, access to resources and paid work. Allowing for their agency here means giving migrant women workers the opportunity to make informed choices about whether to migrate or not. Removing this choice forces them into illegal channels.

2.2 The Responsibility of Child-Care

The second issue, that of the safety and well-being of children left behind, is seen as the responsibility of women migrants (Jayasuriya & Opeskin, 2015). The division of labor in domestic chores and childcare is rarely renegotiated across genders. Therefore, even when absent, mothers bear the burden of childcare. It can hardly be said, in all fairness, that migrant mothers abandon their children. Instead they mostly adapt their mothering role after migration. This is true among other migrant communities where the role of caregiving continues to fall on women's shoulders even after migration (Ukwatte, 2010).

The statistics in Sri Lanka are dismal: two out of five left behind children in Sri Lanka have mental disorders and behavioral problems (Jayatissa & Wickramage, 2015). Two angles of discussion, both with heavy gender bias, are presented here: the restrictive measures of protection implemented by the government and the gender roles characterizing social perceptions.

Until July 2022, Sri Lankan women migrant workers were subject to a requirement called the Family Background Report (FBR). Introduced in 2013 and amended several times, the report served to ascertain whether potential migrant women, leaving for domestic work, have children who are younger than five years old. The FBR requirement was implemented by the Sri Lanka Bureau of Foreign Employment with the intention of reducing the adverse psychosocial implications of children left behind as a result of the migration of mothers. Thus, females with children under the age of five years were not recommended for foreign employment, while females with children above five years could only be recommended for migration if satisfactory alternative care arrangements were in place to ensure the protection of children.

With the FBR requirement, the state gained control over women's decisions to migrate for domestic employment with the pretext of maintaining the best interest of their children. Many studies showed that the FBR was supported by gender-based assumptions (Abeyasekera & Jayasundere, 2014; Jayatissa & Wickramage, 2015; UN Sri Lanka, 2015; Weeraratne, 2021). Firstly, the association of low skills and poverty implies that poverty is a result of underdeveloped skills and not, for instance, subordination. The idea that women may be poor because they do not possess much freedom and cannot exercise control over their lives is left out of the discourse. This is especially relevant in the case of traditional, patriarchal societies in the South Asian context (Sen, 2001).

Next, the policy implied that low-skilled workers are particularly vulnerable and that they are inadequately prepared, mentally and psychologically, to face the challenges of their job. This is all the more striking when considering that poor migrants are also perceived as being unable to make rational decisions. Promoting skilled labor is therefore a key objective. However, considering the fact, discussed in Section 1, that there is an obvious demand for low-skilled labor as well an enormous pool of low-skilled workers, the government strategy is ineffective and ill-defined.[15] Until low-skilled workers can acquire skills, they need protection from exploitative working conditions in both home and host countries.

Low-skilled labor being associated with poverty, it is interesting to note that the FBR specifically targeted poor women who migrate for domestic labor. The discourse suggests that poor women are incapable of making the right choices for their children and families.

> The circular suggests that *poor women* often do not understand the importance of protecting their children and do not prioritise the welfare of their families, whereas women from a middle or upper-class background who migrate overseas for professional work or higher education are capable of protecting their children and the well-being of their families. (Abeyasekera & Jayasundere, 2014, p. 9)

The FBR seemed to imply that most of the social ills attributed to female migration (breakdown of families, children's suffering, disintegration of kinship networks, etc.) are almost exclusively borne by poor families.

Furthermore, it is understood that the State's role is to empower women by protecting them, suggesting that, without such protection, women would not be empowered. While it is evident that the state can help by protecting women through legislation and governance – especially by resisting the unequal, exploitative market forces in the global domain, it undermines the capabilities of women who have the power to overcome difficult circumstances. Gamburd (2020) has compared the effects of the FBR in restricting mobility to the threat of deportation, whereby they are two forms of oppression exerted on migrants.

Finally, the discourse underlying the FBR disregards the principle of gender equality included in the National Policy. The FBR breached women's inalienable right to employment, emphasizing instead their stereotyped role as primarily responsible for family welfare. This is especially evident with regard to the perception the state seems to have of the well-being of migrant families.

> By regulating women, and not men, the policy places the responsibility of childcare in particular and the well-being of the family squarely on the woman's shoulders, and disregards the role of the father and the consequences the absence of the father has on the well-being of children and families. (UN, 2015, p. 24)

The FBR contradicts constitutional provisions on equality in terms of employment.

Social and economic reality is such that despite the existence of two main governance tools – national policy and the FBR – it is the latter that appeared more powerful in terms of influencing outbound migration. In a working paper studying the impact of the FBR ban, Weeraratne (2021, p. 13) shows that the introduction of the FBR policy reduced the numbers of low-skilled workers' departures, while facilitating migration of higher-skilled workers. Her conclusions confirm that "the FBR policy has inadvertently created an impetus for informal and illegal activities among lower-skilled female migrant workers through their attempts to circumvent the policy" (Weeraratne, 2021, p. 14). The lack of employment and livelihood alternatives pushes women to forge documents in order to qualify to migrate. In summary, the government rhetoric focusing on the stereotypical role of women, which has the effect of restricting women's choices, passes greater muster than the discourse of gender equality and women's rights.

2.3 Gender Roles in Their Cultural and Moral Context

This brings us to the issue of gender roles in influencing social perceptions, as well as actual policies.

> Women bore the responsibility of disciplining the family and regulating household finances; village discourse held the wife largely responsible for any misadventures that might befall her husband during her stay abroad. (Gamburd, 1995, p. 57)

Ironically, from the migrants' perspective, as many anthropological and sociological studies reveal, many complaints fall on husbands who fail to fulfill their responsibilities in the absence of the mother.

There is also disappointment when family and community members fail to show gratitude and respect for the migrants and their contributions to family well-being. Gamburd (1995, p. 49) summarizes one of the most influential factors:

> Several case studies reveal the extent to which men have not taken over tasks such as childcare and household chores. In all-male drinking groups, unemployed husbands reassert their masculinity in the face of their wives' new role as breadwinner. The values of the drinking community stand in implicit opposition to values channelling family resources towards "getting developed" (*diyunu venawaa*), the dominant village idiom of successful migration.

Therefore, many cultural and moral obstacles prevent low-skilled female migrants receiving widespread approbation and encouragement.

In such a context, where complex social, cultural, moral and economic norms interact in shaping migrant behaviour, decisions based on a narrow economic framework become irrelevant (Bonfanti, 2014). Indeed using that framework alone leads to erroneous conclusions. For one, economic value has been the main indicator driving evaluations and considerations relating to low-skilled domestic work, leading to low wages being equated with low-value. Consequently, the various vulnerabilities discussed in this paper support the actual social value of low-skilled work. Adopting a more pluralistic perspective that includes empowerment, agency, capabilities, and gender, reveals even higher social value. I have further argued that considering only the low economic value, that is, the commodification of low-skilled labor, has resulted in ineffective protection. Instead, if low-skilled labor is accorded greater social value, as it is rightly due, wages would not be the main indicator. Home countries could demand better working conditions from host countries that might prohibit enslavement, exploitation, and harassment. In addition, acknowledging migrants' agency would remove the mistaken assumption that migrants are unable to manage their finances. Another mistaken idea is that migrants are unable to decide what is good for their children and their family. Without an inter-disciplinary perspective, prescriptions are offered – sometimes restrictions imposed – which do not protect women migrants, let alone improve their well-being.

Women's empowerment, understood as the combination of agency, resources and outcomes (Kabeer, 2008) needs to make its way into social perceptions, just as they need to be incorporated into policy and governance measures. Migration offers a window of opportunity for women to improve their lives and break the glass ceiling imposed by the gendered nature of society. While empowering women economically, migration can also increase their independence, improve their self-esteem and general well-being (Bachan, 2018). Even specific forms of forced migration of women, for example, migration resulting from conflict, can benefit women by modifying existing gender roles. Conversely, migration can also embed traditional roles and disparities, and expose women to new vulnerabilities that result from their precarious legal status, exclusion, and segregation (Ncube & Mkwananzi, 2020). I have dealt with two specific instances in which traditional forms of discrimination are aggravated by restrictive migration policies. Their ineffectiveness can be explained by the fact that they do not take women's agency into account. On the contrary, these measures ignore their agency and resilience, which, ironically, force them to be yet more resilient as a result. One of the messages of this paper is that policies can be created which ensure that women migrants do not have to be so resilient.

CONCLUDING REMARKS

Combining a money-centred, that is, remittance-centred, economic analysis with narratives from gender studies and the other social sciences is a step toward improved understanding of the complexities of migrant labor, and the specificities of female temporary migrant labor. Understanding female labor migration on a theoretical level and implementing effective measures on a policy level require analyses that go beyond economics to include comprehensive people-centred and gendered perspectives. One of the biggest obstacles to recognising the true social value of low-skilled labor is an excessive focus on narrow financial measures. The mixed feelings stirred by current social perceptions, with heavy gender biases, can also be positively influenced by changing the tendency to commodify low-skilled labor.

On a governance level, migration policies are currently embedded in the neo-liberal paradigm that views migrants as agents in need of protection, leading to restrictive measures. By taking into account women's agency, I have pointed out the ineffectiveness of restrictive measures in actually protecting women. Instead, by regulating market forces and reducing the vulnerabilities they create, women migrants can be better empowered to go around the world and make more money. Incorporating integrative theoretical and governance approaches can set the ball rolling: market forces can be tamed; women migrants, whether skilled or low-skilled, can enjoy decent working conditions and have their work given its due value on economic, social, and cultural levels.

NOTES

1. The term "rata viru" has a strong connotation in the Sri Lankan context, given the 30-year long ethnic conflict, which ended in 2009, with bloody wars between the separatist militant Tamils, the LTTE, and the government, where government soldiers were the given the title of "viru," heroes in the patriotic, nationalist discourse.

2. It does, however, point to the very important role played by institutions, as compared to openness to trade or geographic disparities (e.g., Osang, 2007, in Hollifield, 2007).

3. The Gulf Cooperation Council countries dominate the destination countries of Sri Lankan women migrant workers (86%) and according to Wickramasekera, this is consistent with the situation in South Asia, where most countries "rely on the Gulf as the major destination for their migrant workers" (2010, p. 11). He also comments on this "high dependence" on the Gulf countries as another issue of Sri Lankan migration.

4. "There are many different potential systems for categorizing international migrants; one system organizes migrants into categories of distinct groups. These are temporary labor, irregular, illegal or undocumented, highly skilled and business associates, refugees, return migrants, family members and long-term, low-skilled migrants. Migrants can typically also be divided into two large groups which are permanent and temporary. Permanent migrants intend to establish their permanent residence in a new country and possibly obtain that country's citizenship. Temporary migrants intend only to stay for a limited period of time; perhaps until the end of a particular program of study or for the duration of their work contract or a certain work season. Whether temporary or permanent, international migration has a profound effect on the society and economy of both the host country and the home country of migrants" (OECD International Migration Outlook, 2007, p. 40).

5. "Sri Lanka finds that children of remittance-recipient households have a lower school dropout rate and that these households spend more on private tuition for their children. In Sri Lanka, the children in remittance-receiving households have higher birth weight, reflecting that remittances enable households to afford better health care. Several studies also show that remittances provide capital to small entrepreneurs, reduce credit constraints, and increase entrepreneurship" (Ratha et al., 2007, p. 178; Hollifield, 2007).

6. "Under the *hundi, hawala, padala, fei-chien,* and other informal remittance systems, no money need cross national borders immediately to have remittances paid to beneficiaries" (Martin, 2007, p. 18, in Hollifield, 2007).

7. According to Amartya Sen, capabilities can be explained as the opportunities and freedoms open to a person to achieve functionings, which are the "various things a person may value doing or being" (Sen, 1999, p. 75). Capabilities are thus the various combinations of functionings that a person can achieve and that make up a person's well-being.

8. Newspaper reports, petitions, and cases filed by NGOs and women's rights groups recount the physical, mental, and sexual abuse inflicted upon women migrant workers, some of which have resulted in their death at the hands of their employers. "After several years of official and popular protests in Sri Lanka, 24-year-old Rizana Nafeek was beheaded by sword in public near Riyadh in 2013 for the murder eight years earlier of a baby in her care" (Ireland, 2014, p. 26).

9. "The State recognizes the importance of ensuring the safety and protection of low-skilled workers while setting in place a process of promoting skilled migrant workers. The State aims to promote the migration of skilled workers by securing employment opportunities for skilled workers in safe and regulated work environments, and by providing accessible and widespread opportunities for prospective migrant workers to become skilled workers" (National Policy for Migration of Labour, p. 21).

10. "The prohibition of outside employment for women can sometimes be brutally executed in an explicit and fierce way (as, for example, in contemporary Afghanistan). In other cases, the prohibition may work more implicitly through the power of convention and conformity. Sometimes there may not even be, in any clear sense, a ban on women's seeking employment, and yet women reared with traditional values may be quite afraid to break with the tradition and to shock others. The prevailing perceptions of 'normality' and 'appropriateness' are quite central to this question" (Sen, 2001, p. 115).

11. "After several years of official and popular protests in Sri Lanka, 24-year-old Rizana Nafeek was beheaded by sword in public near Riyadh in 2013 for the murder eight years earlier of a baby in her care. The woman had protested her innocence, and the Sri Lankan president had made repeated appeals for clemency. The Asian Human Rights Commission nonetheless blamed him for Ms. Nafeek's execution, declaring that his government 'did nothing, except issuing valueless statements' (Ghosh, 2013). An opposition member of parliament, Ranjan Ramanayake, complained that the state had a financial incentive not to complain too forcefully to the Saudis (Jayasekera, 2013)" (Ireland, 2014, p. 26).

12. For a long time, Sri Lankan officials more readily referred to WMDWs as victims. "While Philippine mobile phone companies were treating 'heroic' overseas Filipino workers to yuletide celebrations in receiving countries across Asia (Globe treats, 2011), their Sri Lankan counterparts were partnering with the government to deliver special SIM cards as an emergency service to 'vulnerable' FMDWs" (Ireland, 2014, p. 26). In the past few years, however, Sri Lankan authorities have started extolling male and female migrants as "Rata Viruwo" ("foreign employee heroes") and "heroic earners of foreign exchange" (Attygalle 2012 in Ireland, 2014, p. 26).

13. The Convention on the Elimination of All Forms of Discrimination Against Women (1979), the CEDAW, the Convention on the Rights of the Child (1989), CRC, and the International Convention on the Protection of the Rights of All Migrant Workers and Members of their Families (1990), the ICRMW.

14. Do arguments in favour of restrictions confuse a problem of exploitation with a problem about movement? A protectionist approach derives from social norms, which inhibit women's mobility and treat marriage as the appropriate means of protecting women. The gender norm as an expression of power relations is elaborated through marital control over women's sexuality, which is weakened by mobility. This would explain why support for restrictions gets more vocal when the vulnerability of women to sexual abuse and trafficking is highlighted (Kodoth & Varghese, 2012).

15. "The State recognizes the importance of ensuring the safety and protection of low-skilled workers while setting in place a process of promoting skilled migrant workers. The State aims to promote the migration of skilled workers by securing employment opportunities for skilled workers in safe and regulated work environments, and by providing accessible and widespread opportunities for prospective migrant workers to become skilled workers" (National Policy for Migration of Labour, p. 21).

REFERENCES

Abeyasekera, A., & Jayasundere, R. (2014). Migrant mothers, family breakdown, and the modern state: an analysis of state policies regulating women migrating overseas for domestic work in Sri Lanka. *South Asianist, 4*(1), 1–24.

Abreu, A. (2010). The new economics of labor migration: Beware of neoclassicals bearing gifts. Forum for Social Economic, *42*(1), 46–67 https://doi.org/10.1007/s12143-010-9077-2.

Athukorala, P. (1992). The use of migrant remittances in development: Lessons from the Asian experience. *Journal of International Development, 4*(5), 511–529.

Athukorala, P., & Rajapatirana, S. (2003). Capital inflows and the real exchange rate: A comparative study of Asia and Latin America. *The World Economy, 26*(4), 613–637.

Bachan, A. (2018). An exploration of the gender–migration–development nexus the impact of labor migration on women's empowerment. Consilience, *20*, 1–22.

Bonfanti, S. (2014). Towards a migrant-centred perspective on international migration: The contribution of Amartya Sen's capability approach. *Social Work and Society, 12*(2). Retrieved from https://www.socwork.net/sws/article/view/411

Boyd, M. (1989). Family and personal networks in international migration: Recent developments and new agendas. *The International Migration Review, 23*(3), 638–670. doi:10.2307/2546433.

Castles, S. (2006). *Back to the future? Can Europe meet its labour needs through temporary migration?* Working Paper No. 1. International Migration Institute, Oxford.

Castles, S. (2009). Development and migration–migration and development: What comes first? Global Perspective and African Experiences. *Theoria, 56*(121), 1–31. 10.3167/th.2009.5512102

Chant, S., & Pedwell, C. (2008). *Women, gender and the informal economy: An assessment of ILO research and suggested ways forward.* Geneva: International Labour Organization.

Ciupijus, Z. (2010). Ethical pitfalls of temporary labour migration: A critical review of issues. *Journal of Business Ethics, 97*(Suppl. 1: Mind the Gap), 9–18.

Collier, J, & Yanagisako, S, (1987). *Gender and kinship: Essays toward a unified analysis.* Stanford, CA: Stanford University Press.

Costin, A. (2021). A literature review on left-behind children. *Journal Plus Education, XXVIII*(1), 89–98.

Cox, D. (1997). The vulnerability of Asian women migrant workers to a lack of protection and to violence. *Asian and Pacific Migration Journal, 6*(1), 59–75.

de Costa, N. (2022). Representation of migrant women workers and their negotiations with the nation: A study of selected Sri Lankan English fiction. *New Literaria-An International Journal of Interdisciplinary Studies in Humanities, 3*(2), 86–99. doi: https://dx.doi.org/10.48189/nl.2022.v03i2.011.

De Haas, H. (2010). Migration and development: A theoretical perspective. *International Migration Review, 44*(1), 227–264. doi: 10.1111/j.1747-7379.2009.00804.x

Freeman, G. (1992). Migration policy and politics in the receiving states. *The International Migration Review, 26*(4, Winter), 1144–1167.

Gamburd, M. R. (1995). Sri Lanka's army of housemaids: Control of remittances and gender transformations. *Anthropologica, 37*(1), 49–88.

Gamburd, M. R. (2000). *The kitchen spoon's handle, transnationalism and Sri Lanka's migrant housemaids.* Ithaca, NY: Cornell University Press.

Gamburd, M. R. (2004). Money that burns like oil: A Sri Lankan cultural logic of morality and agency. *Ethnology, 43*(2), 167–184.

Gamburd, M. R. (2009). Advocating for Sri Lankan migrant workers: Obstacles and challenges. *Critical Asian Studies, 49*(1), 61–88. doi: https://pdxscholar.library.pdx.edu/anth_fac/39.

Government of Sri Lanka. (2009). *Sri Lanka National Labour Migration Policy, 2009.* Sri Lanka: Ministry of Foreign Employment Promotion and Welfare. Retrieved from http://www.ilo.org/colombo/whatwedo/publications/WCMS_114003/lang-en/index.htm

Guilmoto, C., & de Loenzien, M. (2014). Shifts in vulnerability landscapes: Young women and internal migration in Vietnam. *Genus, 70*(1), 27–56.

Haug, S. (2008). Migration networks and migration decision-making. *Journal of Ethnic and Migration Studies, 34*(4), 585–605, doi: 10.1080/13691830801961605.

Hollified. (Ed.). (2007). *Migration, trade, and development*. Federal Reserve Bank of Dallas; The Tower Center for Political Studies, Southern Methodist University; Department of Economics at Southern Methodist University; Jno E. Owens Foundation. Retrieved from http://scholar.smu. edu/ebooks/3

Ireland, P. (2018). The limits of sending-state power: The Philippines, Sri Lanka, and female migrant domestic workers. *International Political Science Review, 39*(3), 322–337.

Jayasuriya, R., & Opeskin, B. (2015). The migration of women domestic workers from Sri Lanka: Protecting the rights of children left behind. *Cornell International, 48*(3), 579–638.

Jayatissa, R., & Wickramage, K. (2015). What effect does international migration have on the nutritional status and child care practices of children left behind? *International Journal of Environmental Research and Public Health, 15*(2), 218.

Jayet, H., & Rapoport, H. (2010). Migration and development: New insights. *Annals of Economics and Statistics, 97/98*, 5–12.

Kabeer, N. (2008). *Paid work, women's empowerment and gender justice: Critical pathways of social change. Pathways of Empowerment working papers* (3). Brighton: Institute of Development Studies.

Kodoth, P., & Varghese, V. J. (2012). Protecting women or endangering the emigration process: Emigrant women domestic workers, gender and state policy. *Economic and Political Weekly, 47*(43), 56–66. http://www.jstor.org/stable/41720301

Kottegoda, S., Jayasundere, R., Perera, S., & Atapattu, P. (2013). *Transforming lives. Listening to Sri Lankan returnee women migrant workers*. Colombo: Women and Media Collective.

Lansink, A. (2009). Migration and development: The contribution of women migrant workers to poverty alleviation. *Agenda: Empowering Women for Gender Equity, 23*(81), 126–136.

Leclerc, E., & Meyer, J. B. (2007). Knowledge diasporas for development. *Asian Population Studies, 3*(2), 153–168. doi:10.1080/17441730701500004

Levitt, P. (2001). *The transnational villagers*. Berkeley, CA: University of California Press.

Massey, D. S., Arango, J., Graeme, H., Kouaouci, A., Pellegrino, A., & Taylor, J. E. (1993). Theories of international migration: A review and appraisal. *Population and Development Review, 19*, 431–466.

Massey, D. S., & España, F. G. (1987). The social process of international migration. *Science, 237*(4816), 733–738.

Ncube, A., & Mkwananzi, F. (2020). Gendered Labour migration in South Africa: A capability approach lens. In F. K. Seiger, C. Timmerman, N. B. Salazar, & J. Wets (Eds.), *Migration at work. aspirations, imaginaries & structures of mobility*. Leuven: Leuven University Press.

Nussbaum, M. (2011). *Creating capabilities*. Cambridge, MA: Harvard University Press. Retrieved from http://www.jstor.org/stable/j.ctt2jbt31. Accessed on May 15, 2021,

Phillips, N., LeBaron, G., & Wallin, S. (2018). *Mapping and measuring the effectiveness of labour-related, disclosure requirements for global supply chains*. Geneva, ILO: Research Department Working Paper No. 32.

Piper, N. (2008). Feminisation of migration and the social dimensions of development: The Asian case. *Third World Quarterly, 29*(7), 1287–1303. doi:10.1080/01436590802386427

Priya, P., Venkatesh, A., & Shukla, A. (2021). Two decades of theorising and measuring women's empowerment: Literature review and future research agenda. *Women's Studies International Forum, 87*. https://doi.org/10.1016/j.wsif.2021.102495

Puri, S., & Ritzema, T. (1999). *Migrant worker remittances, micro-finance and the informal economy: Prospects and issues*. Social Finance Working Paper No. 21. Social Finance Unit, Enterprise and Cooperative Development Department, International Labour Office.

Ratha, D., Mohapatra, S., Vijayalakshmi, K. M., & Xu, Z. (2007). *2007 Remittance Trends*. Migration and Development Brief 3, Development Prospects Group.

Rosewarne, S. (2012). Trading on gender: The perversity of Asian labour exports as an economic development strategy. *Work Organisation, Labour & Globalisation, 6*(1), 81–102.

Samarasinghe, V. (1998). The feminization of foreign currency earnings: Women's labor in Sri Lanka. *Journal of Developing Areas, 32*(3, Spring), 303–326.

Sen, A. (1980). Equality of what. In S. M. McMurrin (Ed.), *The Tanner lectures on human value* (pp. 195–220). Salt Lake City, UT: University of Utah Press.

Sen, A. (1999). *Commodities and capabilities*. New Delhi: Oxford University Press.

Sen, A. (2001). *Development as freedom*. New Delhi: Oxford University Press.

Sinclair, M. (1998). Community, identity and gender in migrant societies of Southern Africa: Emerging epistemological challenges. *International Affairs, 7*(2), 339–353.

Sri Lanka Bureau of Foreign Employment (SLBFE). (1997–2014). *Statistical hand book on foreign employment*. Colombo: Research and Development Division.

Sri Lanka Ministry of Foreign Employment. (2015). *Annual statistical report of foreign employment 1996–2015*. Colombo: MOFE Publications.

Ukwatte, S. (2010). Sri Lankan female domestic workers overseas: Mothering their children from a distance. *Journal of Population Research, 27*(2), 107–131.

UN Sri Lanka. (2015). Sri Lankan migrant domestic workers. The impact of Sri Lankan policies on workers' right to freely access employment. Retrieved from www.un.lk

Weeraratne, B. (2021). *Ban on female migrant workers. Skills-differentiated evidence from Sri Lanka*. WIDER Working Paper 2021/44. Helsinki: UNUWIDER. https:// doi. org/ 10. 35188/ UNU-WIDER/ 2021/ 982-2

Wickramasekera, P. (2010). *International migration and employment in the post-reforms economy of Sri Lanka*. Technical Report, International Migration Papers No. 107. Geneva: ILO.

Wickramasekara, P. (2015). *Mainstreaming Migration in Development Agendas: Assessment of South Asian Countries*. Working Paper No. 2015/02, Working Papers in Trade and Development, Arndt-Corden Department of Economics, Crawford School of Public Policy, ANU College of Asia and the Pacific, Australian National University, Canberra. Retrieved from https://ssrn.com/abstract=2563454 or http://dx.doi.org/10.2139/ssrn.2563454

Wimmer, A., & Schiller, N. (2003). Methodological nationalism, the social sciences, and the study of migration: An essay in historical epistemology. *The International Migration Review, 37*(3), 576–610.

Wright, C. (1995). Gender awareness in migration theory: Synthesizing actor and structure in Southern Africa. *Development and Change, 26*(4), 771–792.

CHAPTER 2

PAUL SINGER'S SOLIDARITY ECONOMY: A PRACTICAL EXPERIENCE WITH A RECYCLING COOPERATIVE IN GOIÁS, BRAZIL

Jaqueline Vilas Boas Talga and Tiago Camarinha Lopes

ABSTRACT

The paper presents the concept of Solidarity Economy proposed by the Austrian-Brazilian economist and professor Paul Singer who passed away in 2018 at age 86 years in his home in São Paulo. Singer arrived at the concept of Solidarity Economy by mixing utopian socialist thought originated in Europe during the Industrial Revolution with the wisdom of Latin American working people to find alternative paths to the capitalist economic system. Following the teachings of Paul Singer, we, as practitioners and academics, report the first stage of the formation of a popular cooperative in the sector of recycling that occurred between 2019 and 2021 in the Town of Goiás, Goiás, Brazil. Our analysis of this collective endeavour leads to two main lessons: first, Solidarity Economy is an even broader proposal of an alternative to the capitalist economy than Paul Singer imagined, because its roots are not restricted to the European cooperativism of the nineteenth century, and second, economics must be taught in more popular way because the most urgent economic problems affect primarily the working people.

Keywords: Solidarity economy; self-management; Paul Singer; cooperativism; alternative economics; popular economics

Research in the History of Economic Thought and Methodology: Including a Selection of Papers Presented at the First History of Economics Diversity Caucus Conference
Research in the History of Economic Thought and Methodology, Volume 41B, 27–47
ISSN: 0743-4154/doi:10.1108/S0743-41542023000041B002

1 INTRODUCTION

We present the economic thought of Paul Singer (1932–2018) based on our support to the formation of a workers cooperative in the sector of recycling in the city of Goiás, GO, Brazil. To support the foundation and development of a popular cooperative is an educational endeavour and it directly affects dozens of people (workers, public agents and teachers). This cooperative is part of the local program to regulate the adequate disposal of solid waste and to close the irregular dumping waste, and we, as academics and practitioners, have been mediating the relations between these workers and the municipal government so as to facilitate the implementation of this social and environmental public policy. The practical aspect of the Solidarity Economy is a distinguishing characteristic in comparison to most variants of economic thinking and a systematic presentation of how to relate its abstract principles with concrete measures to change reality is provided by Nunes (2009).

Paul Singer was an economist, professor and intellectual who became an important reference for the critical economic thought in Brazil, especially in the context of neoliberalism. After emigrating with his Jewish family from Austria in the context of World War 2, Paul Singer developed a trajectory as an urban worker and academic in São Paulo. He was involved in relevant strikes in Brazil's most industrialised area and contributed to spreading an alternative thinking about the economy. He was an eminent student and teacher of Marx's Political Economy and a critical observer of Soviet socialism. After the fall of the USSR, he opened a collective discussion about alternative paths towards socialism to counter the Washington consensus in the 1990s. Against the usual notion that creativity is an exclusivity of the young, Paul Singer at around 60 years old launched an original thesis for changing society and the economy.[1] Inspired by the European revolutionary cooperativism movement of the early nineteenth century, he coined the expression Solidarity Economy to refer to a kind of economic system that pops up everywhere as a defensive force of working people against the attacks of financialised capitalism. According to his view, the popular cooperatives are germinating points of an alternative economic system that is based on social values such as solidarity, self-management, collective action, non-alienated work, shared income, horizontal democracy and critical pedagogy.

The cooperative of recycling waste pickers that we incubate needs a philosophy that is adequate to its mission of social inclusion and environment protection. So, it must be an economic enterprise of Solidarity Economy. It is not a capitalist firm, but an economic enterprise without the logic of profit above all. Paul Singer's oeuvre has helped us in that reeducation process of all people involved with the solid waste program in the city of Goiás, GO, Brazil. We have noticed that the standard thinking in economics didn't indicate how to deal with the challenges and tasks of that program. According to our analysis, this is so because the standard way to think about the economy adapts itself to replicate and reinforce the status quo of economic reality. So, to imagine and build a non-capitalist economy that follows the principles of human and nature care requires another type of economic thinking and so the economics of Solidarity Economy has proved to be a much more useful theory for the success of that program.

The paper presents in session 2 Paul Singer's intellectual and political biography. Then we develop in session 3 the concept of Solidarity Economy based on four characteristics that show how the economic thought of humanity can be plural, diverse, inclusive and caring. In session 4, the most relevant in terms of the union between theory and practice, we report the history of the constitution of the cooperative of waste pickers and manual recyclers of the Cidade de Goiás. This session is specially important because Paul Singer's thought cannot be adequately presented without a practical experience: all principles of Solidarity Economy are grounded on real attempts to change reality and so they are not simply an abstract catalogue of principles of good intentions. Utopianism is indeed a strong feature in his writings, but in a very narrow sense that this perspective is fundamentally attached to a consistent intervention in reality.

In session 5, we make final remarks to close the paper with two main conclusions that derive from our critical analysis of Paul Singer's thought and our appraisal of the incubation of this workers cooperative of waste pickers. The first one is that the Solidarity Economy should be viewed as a mode of production and living not restricted to nineteenth century Europe, but as an economic system that is present in many human societies throughout history, ranging from indigenous peoples to peripheral spots of contemporary metropoles. The second one is that the organic intellectual in the sense of the Italian Marxist philosopher Antonio Gramsci, especially in the area of economics, has a huge potential to contribute to the transformation of reality in the direction of an inclusive and solidarity society, and so, the teaching of economics must be based on a more popular and practical approach.

2 PAUL SINGER AS AN EXAMPLE OF THE CREATIVITY OF THE ELDERLY

Paul Singer was born in Austria in 1932 and he moved as a child to Brazil with his family because of the Second World War (Mantega & Rego, 1999). The Singer family was of Jewish origin and had a small business in the worker's neighbourhoods in the city of Vienna (Vannuchi & Spina, 2005). São Paulo was a safe new starting point for many people from this community, and Brazil became Paul Singer's homeland in the 1940s. During his youth, he was trained as an electrotechnician in the Escola Técnica Getúlio Vargas (Technical School Getúlio Vargas) and worked as such in the 1950s. He joined the Sindicato dos Metalúrgicos de São Paulo (Metalurgic Workers Trade Union of São Paulo) and he was one of the leaders of an important strike in 1953 in the metropolitan area of São Paulo (Globo, 2018), known as the strike of the 300 thousand (Mori, 2004; Singer, 1953).

Paul Singer's actions were also related to his political party affiliation; at that time he was active in the Partido Socialista Brasileiro (PSB) (Brazilian Socialist Party). As a trade unionist and political organisator, Paul Singer began a self-education in economics (Vannuchi & Spina, 2005). He read Karl Marx, Friedrich

Engels and Rosa Luxemburg and in the second half of the 1950s, he took classes of economics at the University of São Paulo (USP), obtaining an undergraduate degree in 1959. In the 1960s, Paul Singer began to lecture at USP and continued his postgraduate studies. His line of research was focused on urban development and the critical analysis of capitalism. His intellectual and political contributions were relevant for bridging the gap between the Brazilian Marxist intelligentsia and the organised working class of São Paulo.

In the 1970s, Paul Singer was compulsorily retired due to the oppression of the military government when he joined the CEBRAP (Centro Brasileiro de Pesquisa e Planejamento), a non-governmental institution of research and analysis about the demographic and economic dynamics of Brazil, which was created by intellectuals and professors that had been purged from their original workplaces in the State universities (Vannuchi & Spina, 2005). During this period, he published works interpreting the reality of the labour market and the economic performance in Brazil, calling attention to the terrible effects of the crisis and of the increasing inequality.

If we consider his intellectual output up to this point, we would classify Paul Singer as yet another radical economist, strongly influenced by orthodox Marxism and engaged with writing didactical works on Political Economy, who analysed the concrete problems of capitalist underdevelopment as they revealed themselves in the debates about urbanisation, planning and economic policy. However, as Costa-Filho (2001) also reported, there came a new phase in which he embarked on a critical revision of his own way of seeing things, due to the challenges of a new epoch of the world economy. The following table displays Paul Singer's major books chronologically so as to show that the Solidarity Economy does not represent a break with his past, but the peak of a longstanding construction, evolution and maturation of his thinking about capitalism, economics and education in which creativity is enthusiastically exercised as an elderly.[2]

In our interpretation, Solidarity Economy as a concept synthesises Paul Singer's intellectual and practical oeuvre, and so, all his previous work that does not deal directly with Solidarity Economy, must be viewed as foundational steps of education and activism leading to this concept.

The idea of Solidarity Economy begins to appear more evidently in the 1980s, when Paul Singer resumes his activities as a professor at PUC-SP (Pontifícia Universidade Católica de São Paulo [Catholic University of São Paulo]) and he joins the Partido dos Trabalhadores (PT) [Workers Party]. At that time, he became close to Luiz Inácio Lula da Silva and was active in shaping the economic programs of the candidates of Partido dos Trabalhadores, specially in São Paulo (Vannuchi & Spina, 2005). The political mobilisation in Brazil at this period was centred at ending the military dictatorship established in 1964 by imperialist forces and forging the necessary democracy to match the challenges of the new time.

One of these challenges had to do with the strategy of social reform. After the fall of the Berlin Wall in 1989 and the neoliberal offensive in Latin America, the socialist project had to be revised. Singer always accompanied with a critical eye the historical and political development of the Soviet Union and East Europe after the Second World War, and he became a severe critic of Stalinism (Andrada &

Table 1. Paul Singer's Main Books from Groundwork to Solidarity Economy

Groundwork	*Economic Development and Urban Evolution* (Singer, 1969)
	Population Dynamics and Development (Singer, 1970)
	Political Economy of Urbanisation (Singer, 1973)
	Political Economy of Labour (Singer, 1977)
	What is socialism today? (Singer, 1980a)
	A people's guide to inflation (Singer, 1980b)
	Domination and inequality: class structure and income division in Brazil (Singer, 1981)
	Learning Economics (Singer, 1983)
	The formation of the wage working class (Singer, 1985)
	Income Division: rich and poor under the military regime (Singer, 1986)
	Capitalism: its evolution, its logic and its dynamics (Singer, 1987)
	São Paulo's Master Plan, 1989–1992: the politics of urban space (Singer, 1993)
	Social exclusion in Brazil (Singer, 1997)
	What is the Economy? (Singer, 1998a)
	Globalisation and Unemployment: diagnoses and alternatives (Singer, 1998b)
	Brazil in the crisis: dangers and opportunities (Singer, 1999)
	Understanding the financial world (Singer, 2000)
Solidarity Economy	*An activist utopia* (Singer, 1998c)
	Introduction to Solidarity Economy (Singer, 2002)

Esteves, 2018), although he never classified himself as a Trotskyst (Vannuchi & Spina, 2005)). Paul Singer always thought that the road to communism is marked with real challenges and that concrete experiences are valid as long as we can learn from them. With the aim to debate these lessons, Paul Singer was invited by sociologist and intellectual Antonio Candido who had been asked by the leader of Partido dos Trabalhadores (PT) Lula to organise a series of seminars about the socialist economy (Lula da Silva, 2000). The purpose was to think about global geopolitics and conceive new ways towards socialism (Tavares & Lopes, 2018).

Various people with different backgrounds took part in these meetings. There were students, academics, workers and civilians engaged in the progressive development of democracy in Brazil after the end of the Brazilian Military Government installed through a coup in 1964. This was a rich, diverse and pluralistic approach to the problem of socialist construction. So, Paul Singer, an elderly activist and scholar in his 60s created a new concept capable of embracing all currents in favour of an economic system other than capitalism. The wish to surpass capitalism was vivid and strong, but socialism had to be conceived in a more flexible and open way. Accepting a suggestion from a party colleague, Aloizio Mercadante (Andrada & Esteves, 2018; Souza, 2018), he named this new concept "Solidarity Economy" [Economia Solidária] and presented it more systematically in two books: *Uma utopia militante* (Singer, 1998c) [An activist utopia] and *Introdução à Economia Solidária* (São Paulo, Perseu Abramo, 2002) [Introduction to Solidarity Economy].

The concept of Solidarity Economy is, therefore, closely related to the idea of the construction of socialism. According to our reading, it is a gradualist vision of transition, not because there are certain stages that need to be developed, but in the sense that there must be an accumulation of organisation and people's power through a day-to-day work of political, econom(ic) and philosophical education. The Solidarity Economy is neither simply an economic nor a political system. Also, it is not a philosophy separated from the material world. In our own terms, the Solidarity Economy is a cosmovision of the material reproduction of human beings in harmony with each other and with nature (Silva & Lopes, 2018).

According to our interpretation of Paul Singer, a revolutionary process based only on taking over the State is not able to complete the transition to a non-capitalist society. Namely, such a transition also requires a systemic change in the way people interact outside the economic sphere. These new social relations depend on a new kind of social education. The line to which Paul Singer's political thought can be ascribed is the one which thinks that the traditional scheme of the Russian Revolution led by the Bolshevik Party does not apply to the concrete circumstances of Latin America of the late twentieth century. The main critique to that scheme is the lack of a more autonomous organisation of the working class, and a lack of confidence in the popular initiatives that arise in different forms as anticapitalist actions within capitalism. The concept of Solidarity Economy recovers the humanist values of the socialist movement without abandoning the profound theory developed by Karl Marx. As we understand it, Paul Singer's Solidarity Economy is a proposal of communication between Marxism and other socialist currents, rooted in the foundations of the critical pedagogy of Brazilian educator and philosopher Paulo Freire.[3]

Many believe that only young people are capable of being creative, while the elderly would not have the same capacity for invention. Against this common sense, Paul Singer, after more than a half century of a productive intellectual and political life, showed that we are not condemned to repeat previous thoughts. We are able to envision the future, being creative even as elderly. That is the context in which he profoundly revises the history of the socialist movement, recovering the contribution of radical cooperativism.

In his book Introduction to Solidarity Economy (Singer, 2002), he argues that the first organisations of the working class under capitalism were initiatives for founding cooperatives in the first half of the nineteenth century in Europe. Some of these cooperatives exerted strong intellectual and ideological influence over society and they contributed to consolidate the movement later known as utopian socialism. One of the exponents of this philosophical approach to economics was Robert Owen, an industrial owner and radical thinker. Robert Owen experimented with his own enterprises, putting self-managing to praxis in factories and highlighting the importance of education. These are some of the best examples of what Paul Singer calls revolutionary cooperativism. Revolutionary cooperativism is related to a kind of organisation of the economy based on moral and ethical values that are different from these values of capitalism. Equality and humanisation are two features of the cooperativist ethos that confront individuality and self-interest, for example. Paul Singer (2002) argued that this current of cooperativism, that wanted to break with the capitalist order, lost power as capitalism developed further during the nineteenth century, because monopolisation makes competition ferocious against cooperatives that put human beings above profits.

By transferring the ideas of European revolutionary cooperativism from the early and mid nineteenth century to Latin Americans oppressed by neoliberalism of the 1990s, Paul Singer argues that similar popular initiatives emerge as a method of facing the deficiencies of capitalism, such as its incapacity to generate full employment. According to him, such initiatives have the potential to develop networks of mutual aid, so that their dependency on the capitalist market would be over. Ideally, this development would break with the capitalist system and open the way to a new kind of transition.

This is, very briefly, how Paul Singer envisages the construction of socialism in the beginning of the twenty-first century. As theory and practice always remained together in his life, Paul Singer was extremely active as a supporter, educator and mobiliser of all groups that initiated an economic organisation around the principles of Solidarity Economy until his death at 86. Functions of leadership were assigned to him to promote Solidarity Economy in Brazil through the Secretaria Nacional de Economia Solidária (National Secretariat for Solidarity Economy), a federal institution created and consolidated in the governments of Lula and Dilma Rousseff. This had a positive effect on the income of Brazilian workers from the 2000s to the mid 2010s, due to the synergy stemming from bottom-up initiatives of popular cooperatives and solidarity economies and top-down public policies directed by the government. Unfortunately, after the parliamentary coup of 2016, this entire network was broken and the Solidarity Economy ceased to be a national institutionalised economic policy. Together with the tragic effects of the world capitalist crisis, this contributed to aggravating the economic, political and social situation in Brazil.[4]

3 SOLIDARITY ECONOMY: PRINCIPLES OF HUMANE ECONOMY

From this brief overlook in Paul Singer's biography, we notice that the concept of Solidarity Economy is what distinguishes him, not only from mainstream economists, but also from other Latin American critical thinkers within the Marxist tradition. Paul Singer's critique of capitalism was based both on his praxis as a trade unionist and teacher. So, his analysis of inequality, underdevelopment and poverty was not restricted to denouncing what was wrong with the capitalist economy, but also tried to propose an alternative. In that sense, even though it is correct to say he didn't like capitalism, it is much more precise to state that his negation of capitalism was accompanied by a sharp understanding and admission about the power and flexibility of that system.

Although we praise Paul Singer and consider ourselves as followers of his work, we also have learned to understand his limitations and errors. Our main critique to Paul Singer is that he seems to rely too much on the European origins of socialist thinking. For him, the origins of Solidarity Economy lie in the revolutionary cooperativism movement of the first half of the 19th century (Singer, 2002, p. 35). As we understand it, the Solidarity Economy is much more than just the model of European cooperative enterprises. In other words, in our view, there is no intellectual father of the concept of Solidarity Economy, because it has been rediscovered or reinvented over and over in many places in many epochs.

We think that the Solidarity Economy of which Paul Singer talks about is a specific form of a more broader notion. The cooperatives based on utopian socialism are the European version of what we may call a humane economy. That is, the Solidarity Economy is essentially an economic organisation based on humanitarian principles. For that reason, the literature employs different expressions to name such models of organising production and distribution, as for example "Social and Solidarity Economy," "Popular Economy," "Sustainable and Circular Economy," "Economia Social y Solidaria" (in Spanish), etc.[5] All these expressions refer to a model of economy which is centred on the human being, considering the plurality of human culture across the world and the harmonious relation of humans with nature. Plurality, diversity, inclusiveness and protection are all fundamental features of Solidarity Economy. For our purposes, we will highlight four main points that we think capture the essentials of Paul Singer's thought and which we believe are also present in all modalities of that humane way to produce and reproduce the material conditions that sustain and promote a good life.

3.1 Self-Management and the End of Exploitation

The first element that we identify in Paul Singer's work is the wish to end exploitation by improving the conditions of political participation at the firm. Exploitation is the standard case in every class society, where there is a clear separation between those who decide/think and those who obey/work. In a capitalist society, the mode of how workers are exploited is quite complex in comparison to other societies. Departing from this Marxist standpoint, Paul Singer asks how we can overcome exploitation without falling into the trap of erecting yet another social exploitation system (Singer, 1998c). In the universe of the Solidarity Economy, besides solidarity (Singer, 2002, pp. 7–11), there is another element without which it is impossible to advance towards the desired system. That is self-management of the firm (Singer, 2002, p. 16). Self-management is a method of organising social labour that differs radically from the method to which we are all used in all hierarchical enterprises.

In all class societies, the division of labour follows a logic of rigid hierarchy. There is someone or something at the top of that structure that symbolises absolute power. At the base, we find everyone else who behaves as servants. The latter have no right to participate in decision-making processes about how economic and social matters are to be carried out. Their function is only to work, to execute manual tasks without thinking. There is no room to think about how society works and about the possibilities of its configuration. The separation between manual and intellectual labour is a strong feature in firms hierarchically organised. This style resembles military structures and Paul Singer (2002, p. 16), calls them "heterogestão" (alien-management, hierarchical management) in opposition to "autogestão" (self-management, democratic management).

According to Paul Singer, the Solidarity Economy aims at dissolving such a situation. Here, there is no previous determination about how the tasks should be fulfilled or who should be responsible for them. Ideally, everything would be democratically discussed, and the decisions collectively made. Everybody has the right to say and to vote, so that an image of radical democracy inside the firm emerges.[6] Self-management is not, however, just joy. It is very demanding, in a salutary way. To avoid confusion and wrong decisions, self-management requires that all participants be intensively engaged and interested in the matters under discussion. This is a real challenge, because everybody should know as much as possible about a large quantity of subjects. Every worker must comprehend the relation between their daily tasks and the overall aims of the enterprise. They must know how the firm is positioned in the sector and the (inter)national economy, as well as understand the reports about its economic performance.

According to Paul Singer, the main enemy of the Solidarity Economy is not an external entity, but a lack of interest on the topics that demand collective deliberation (Singer, 2002, p. 19). Self-management is at the same time fundamental for the end of exploitation because it is the starting point to overcome alienation, and extremely difficult to implement. Many cooperative enterprises which try to apply the principles of Solidarity Economy find it hard to reconcile democratic decision-making with high financial performance, and so we have a trade-off that requires careful study: the stronger self-management, the weaker the impetus of competition and reckless pursuit for monetary profit. In contrast, the stronger alien-management, the stronger the drive towards money, capital accumulation and thus the higher material economic results. Paul Singer dedicated much attention to this challenge pointing that

> The danger of self-management practice degeneration comes, mostly, from insufficient democratic education among the participants. Self-management's main strength is not economic efficiency (which is necessary), but the human development it provides to participants. To take part in the discussions and collective decisions, in which one is involved, educates and raises awareness, making the person more accomplished, self-confident and self-assured. Solidarity economy is worth it. (Singer, 2002, p. 21, our translation)

3.2 Non-Violent Solution to Contradictions and Conflicts

A second aspect of Paul Singer's thought is the search for non-violent solutions. Human history is filled with violent episodes and aggression of humans against humans is not rare. Class societies have a structural organisation of institutionalised violence, which is the State. So, violence is too often a tool used to settle questions when there are groups or individuals with conflicting interests. In general, we can say that violence is the least humane way to solve conflicts between humans.

The conflicts to which we refer here are not only related to those systemic divergences of class struggle. We refer to conflicts that may occur within the same class and minor conflicts that arise in a community. For example, suppose a community has to decide whether it builds a soccer field or a theatre stage and it cannot make a decision because there are supporters to both projects. It is precisely in this situation where the principles of non-violent solution of Solidarity Economy apply (Singer, 2002, p. 19). According to the Marxian doctrine (Lenin, 1917), material conflicts of opposed social classes may not be entirely solved through non-violent means, and so, in our view, the Solidarity Economy is not the adequate framework to approach class struggle so directly. We see it is an auxiliary tool to improve the position of the working class, helping it to accumulate strength for the more broad war.

In the Solidarity Economy, the construction of self-management always generates episodes of conflicts. This is because, since everyone is free to defend their position, there are always moments in which opinions diverge. On these occasions, they have to convince the majority that their proposal or standpoint is the best for the whole collective. The solution to these divergences requires dialogue, understanding and sympathy towards the other (Singer, 2002, p. 19), precisely because everyone is on the same side in the struggle for a new society and economy. In this context, all divergence can be settled with organised study, debate and voting. Search for the truth based on science, in alignment with the values of revolutionary humanism, guides the decision-making processes of which Paul Singer talks about. In the economic enterprises of Solidarity Economy, each participant has the same right and power of vote. That is not the case in capitalist enterprises where the shareholders have different voting powers according to their share in total capital. This contrast is intensively developed by Singer (Singer, 2002, pp. 39–40, 62, 90).

He also highlights that all episodes of conflicts surrounding the construction of Solidarity Economy are rich moments of learning, mutual recognition and strengthening of the value of equality, justice and self-esteem, especially among a large part of the population living in poverty (Singer, 2002, p. 112). Everyone who participates in the democratic assemblies experiences an emotional educational process. The Solidarity Economy dissolves tensions through open debate based on the maxim that everyone is an apprentice and a teacher depending on the subject under consideration. So, the Solidarity Economy expels violence and aggression and includes everybody in revolutionary education, as systematised by Freire ([1968] 2007).

3.3 Overcoming Capitalism Through Education

As presented, the concept of Solidarity Economy of Paul Singer can be interpreted as a synthesis of his evolving view about the overcoming of the capitalist economy. One of Paul Singer's most polemical thesis is the idea that Solidarity Economy is a complete mode of production in the sense that it is a full economic system, independent and self-sustained.[7] This thesis is controversial not only because it opposes the neoliberal discourse that "there is no alternative," but also because there is no agreement among the critics about how capitalism should be surpassed or even if this is possible in the first place. Specially, Paul Singer's argument is criticised at this point because practically all real experiences of Solidarity Economy are related to economic unities that are born and develop inside the capitalist economic system and are frequently dependent on the dynamics of the capitalist market.

Indeed, the cooperatives founded in the nineteenth century based on an anti-individualist and pro-collectivist philosophy operated within the borders of the capitalist market. The reality of the twentieth century is not so different, because capitalism continued to be the prevailing economic system in the West. So, Paul Singer acknowledges that the Solidarity Economy is born within capitalism (Singer, 2002, p. 24). The twenty-first century presents a similar development and it is worth to speculate about the future in order to show the details about the thesis of Solidarity Economy as a project to overcome the macrosystem of capitalism.

Because of the various problems created by capital, such as unemployment, wealth concentration, pollution, material and spiritual poverty, the workers mobilise to defend themselves and to improve their life conditions. However, the capitalist labour market cannot absorb all working people and so many remain outside the system. Throughout the world, there is a growing population that is excluded from the formal dynamics of capitalism. This prevents the organisation of trade unions of a great part of the working class, which survives in the so-called informal sector. In some occasions, groups of mutual aid are formed to work, produce, sell and generate income. In these opportunities, cooperatives can be founded.

Such a cooperative operates inside the market, which is dominated by capitalist macrologic. The cooperative needs to produce and sell, in the normal process of competition. Accordingly, even if it was founded to be an alternative to the capitalist model, the cooperative is entirely surrounded by capitalism and the dynamics of competition and self-interest, which necessarily produce a minority of "winners" and a majority of "losers" (Singer, 2002, pp. 7–10). The necessity to transform output in kind into money is the gateway to the world of capital. For that reason, even though this cooperative has a different philosophy of business, it is constantly contaminated with the profit-seeking ethos through the relations it maintains with the capitalist world. Individualist and self-interested behaviour are permanently replicated due to this. The Solidarity Economy is born within capitalism and depends on it to breathe and to eat, in the same way a baby depends on their mother. In the same way, however, the newer generations repeat the patterns of the older generations, there is room for a change.

According to our understanding of Paul Singer's teaching, if an educational process takes place and the various cooperatives establish a network, the Solidarity Economy sector may become strong enough not to depend on the capitalist market anymore. In that case, all transactions and economic relations could be done between solidarity economic units. The bigger such a sector becomes, the greater the number of people it employs and so the weaker capitalism becomes. At the end of the process, capitalism would have been surpassed and a major part of the economy would operate according to the principles of Solidarity Economy. Money would be used, however the process of its permanent and uncontrolled transformation into capital is abolished.[8]

3.4 Political Revolution Based on Daily Micro Transformation Through Education

The fourth element we highlight to present the essentials of Paul Singer's thought is the notion that the transformation of the political order is not the result of a previously written program which is to be implemented by a distinguished group of leaders. This means that political and social changes are the outcome of day-to-day activities at the micro level, that is, activities of politicisation that occur in the process of fulfilling regular tasks of work and organisation. So, the role of the educator is central for the political revolution that Paul Singer defends.

This kind of action is close to the methodology of education developed by Paulo Freire ([1968] 2007). In brief, this methodology is based on promoting and incentivizing interactions and analysis about a subject of interest of the individuals organised in groups. So, there emerges a self-managing dynamics of learning which triggers the first steps of politicisation. In the next stages, each new challenge of organisation presents new opportunities of learning and understanding the relation between things. By expanding and continuing this process, the apprentices begin to grasp how their lives are conditioned by the current political and economic order. In the case of a cooperative, the participants learn how their economic activity relates to the economy of their city, of their region of their country. In the end, ideally, it is possible to reach a global analysis of world political and economic affairs.

Accordingly, the microactions of education within the solidarity economic units lead to a coordinated political action between all these units. There is an upward movement of politicisation, beginning with basic tasks of humanisation and recovering human dignity. Next, the cultural and civilian values are developed in order to restore and strengthen the self-esteem of the participants who have been rejected by capitalism as it is in the real world. In the end, the creation of a network of self-managed and solidarity economic units would open the way to overcome capitalism. The following illustrations represent our reading of Paul Singer's thesis of how the Solidarity Economy may contribute to the overcoming of capitalism:

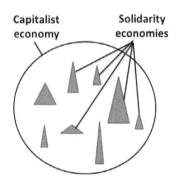

Fig 1.   Solidarity Economy Unities Inside the Capitalist Economy.

Figure 1 shows the diverse initiatives of Solidarity Economy as triangles. These are the popular economies that pop up within the capitalist system as reactions against exclusion and exploitation. Though small and pulverised, they have the potential to connect with each other and this connection depends on their organisation and politicisation, which is represented in the following figure.

Figure 2 indicates that the process of political organisation for overcoming the capitalist economy begins at the base of the Solidarity Economy. The first step is to reestablish the human dignity of the individuals who were excluded, do not possess any means of production and cannot find paid work. These are the so-called "losers" of which Paul Singer (2002, pp. 7–10), talks about. The next steps advance upwards, and the self-organisation of the work contributes to the cultural creativity and self-esteem of all involved. The politised and self-managed unity of Solidarity Economy reaches the top when all members become conscious that, even it is small in comparison to the outer system of capitalism, it can become very strong when connected to the other unities of Solidarity Economy that have appeared in other places of the capitalist macrosystem. The connection of these various points would have, according to Paul Singer, the capacity to overcome capitalism.

Within the Marxist tradition, there are robust critiques against Paul Singer's proposal of an overcoming of capitalism through the expansion and growth of the sector of Solidarity Economy. Wellen (2008, 2012), for example, argued with a large amount of empirical data that the initiatives of solidarity economy and popular cooperatives are too weak and small to be able to confront capitalism, not to mention that they are always subordinated to the logics of market and money and thus unreliable to break with the fundamentals of the capital order.[9] However, we think that the debate about the relevance of the Solidarity Economy

Fig 2. Politicisation Within the Solidarity Economy.

is not restricted to a scholastic discussion about whether it is capable or not of overcoming capitalism. The relevance of Solidarity Economy, as of anything else, must be judged by its capacity to contribute to the education and political capacitation of all agents who make History. With regard to that, all experiences of constructing popular and solidarity economic enterprises are successful in the sense that every praxis to increase the conscience about exploitation helps the overcoming of the condition of exploitation.

4 HOW TO INCUBATE A WORKERS COOPERATIVE OF WASTE PICKERS

It is important to highlight that the practical aspect of Solidarity Economy is not an appendix of its theory, but the real guide to the systematisation of all knowledge. Let us look at a concrete case to understand how the organisation of an economic enterprise may benefit from this alternative way of thinking about the economy. The episode we report here is the history of foundation and initial development of a workers cooperative of waste pickers in the Town of Goiás, Goiás, Brazil, a city founded in 1729 during the Brazilian Gold Rush, with a population of 24.727 (IBGE, 2010) and located 300 km from Brasília, the federal capital of Brazil. After the end of this period when the town grew and concentrated much power, it decayed economically and, due to the model of mining through slavery, it became one of the most unequal and underdeveloped locations of the region during the twentieth century.[10]

The background of the foundation of this cooperative is the National Policy of Solid Waste Management, established by the federal law 12.305 in 2010. This law makes it obligatory that every city in Brazil organise the sustainable management of solid wastes, so as to protect the environment and diminish the pollution generated by industry. Solid wastes are all materials that are discarded after consumption and are not gases or liquids. One of the main steps for recycling these materials is to separate those materials that are more easily decomposed in nature (organic wastes, etc.) and must be placed in the regularised landfills from the materials that can be reused in the production circuit (recyclables).

The municipal solid waste management first began in large cities and today there is a great effort to implement this policy in medium and smaller cities. Due to its past, the city is a location of historical and cultural value, and the town's historical centre became in 2002 a UNESCO World Heritage Site (Delgado, 2005; UNESCO, 2010). The city holds an annual movie and documentary festival about the environment and in 2018, in August, as part of the festival programme, we organised a roundtable about the National Policy of Solid Waste. There were many participants from various areas and the discussion generated a fruitful change of ideas and experiences.

This defined our methodological approach: horizontal rounds of discussion with all interested in improving the relation with the environment in the city. The economic functioning of the partnership between the cooperative enterprise and the State would be discussed in meetings where we all involved studied the principles of Solidarity Economy as previously described. So, while some of us already had read and studied Paul Singer's work, others were engaging with those matters for the first time. The principles of Solidarity Economy were not simply taught in a standard way, where we, as teachers, speak and write on a board and the listeners try to memorise everything. We discussed the principles as they appeared in the day-to-day struggle to constitute the cooperative and to consolidate the waste management program.

Having defined our methodological approach, we knew that the town of Goiás could wait no longer to solve its waste management problem. After all, all waste generated in the urban area was being deployed in a nearby area for approximately 30 years, polluting the soil, the air and the water. Besides, as it happens in extremely unequal economies such as in Brazil, around 20 families survived by picking up and selling the recycling materials from this site, and their health was obviously in danger.

These are the local waste pickers, who found in all that mountain of trash the materials that the industry buys as input. The dynamics here described is essentially the same as that operating in the global capitalist economy. As energy costs became more and more relevant and the environmental movement expanded, a capitalist industry of recycling evolved in the 1960s and 1970s (Strasser, 1999). So, the waste pickers, by collecting these items and organising their separated disposal in large bags, sell to private agents in the recycling industry and generate their income. This is a special kind of labour because it cleans and diminishes the effects of capitalist pollution.

The challenge was the following: according to the Brazilian Law 12.305/2010, the municipality manager, the mayor, is obliged to close the irregular dumping waste. This means that the site must be closed and no person is allowed to enter it. People are not allowed to stay or work there because it is dangerous and unhealthy. But where would these people now work to survive? And how could their contribution to the environment continue?

It was necessary to found a workers cooperative that could operate inside a proper warehouse, so that the workers could continue separating the recyclables and preparing them for the sale to the recycling industry. Such materials would come to the warehouse through the selective waste collection, a scheduled public program to collect in all neighbourhoods the previously separated items like glass, paper, plastics, etc.

In 2019, we formed a team of what we call incubators, to assist the workers. These are the educators responsible for helping all the organising process of the workers and facilitating their relations with the State agency. They are university professors, students, religious authorities, liberal professionals from accounting, advocacy and communication. The group is called Coletivo Recicla Goiás [Recycle Goiás Collective]. That name highlights the importance of collective work, because complex problems require union and teamwork. After many meetings and analyses, including a public audience at the municipal legislative house in the end of 2019, which marked the official support of the deputies towards the project of activating the municipal waste management in the Town of Goiás, the waste pickers gathered in an assembly in February 2020 to found the Cooperativa de Catadores e Catadoras da Cidade de Goiás [Cooperative of Waste Pickers of the Town of Goiás], shortened name: Recicla Tudo [Recycle it All].[11]

Along that, the Municipal Government initiated the selective waste collection, under the auspices of the Municipal Secretary of Environment and the Municipal Secretary of Education. And so, the recyclable items began to arrive at the workplace of the cooperative and for the first time, these waste pickers were working as an enterprise outside the dumping waste. Initially, the cooperative worked in a temporary place, a public house with a small area to manage the items. In its first year of activities, the cooperative faced the challenges of the COVID-19 pandemic in 2020, which negatively affected the dynamics of the meetings with the incubators. Still, there was strong mobilisation so that all bureaucratic tasks were finalised and the cooperative began to work inside the public local warehouse for material sorting in September 2020, which had been until then irregularly occupied by a private agent.

In 2021 the cooperative counted on nine members that divided all the tasks among themselves. They have a regular meeting with the incubator team, when various themes are discussed. Some of the members do not read or write and the incubator collective initiated in 2022 a weekly special class. This has been enthusiastically approved by the participants. The truck used to collect the recycling materials in the residential areas is being rented by the cooperative, but the municipal government has acquired a new and much more adequate vehicle which will be put to use and thus liberate the cooperative from this financial burden. The service of driving and picking up the material put in front of the houses in the scheduled days by the population is paid to the cooperative by the government of the Town of Goiás. This was the first formal contract that Recicla Tudo signed and it represented an important step. In the first weeks, sorting the materials inside the warehouse was done on a rather precarious workstation assembled with two adapted and large wooden tables. Later, the workers managed to build a much stronger platform with metal plates that had been discarded. Many relevant means of production are still lacking, such as bobcats, and there is a high volume of manual heavy labour to be done. Recently, a local industrial owner donated a machine press to compact the sorted materials, but it has not yet been installed. This will be the first capital item to be listed in the enterprise's accounting as its property. The individual equipment of safety (gloves, boots, etc.) was offered by the municipal government until recently, but now the cooperative has the financial means to acquire them. As of April 2021, the cooperative is generating a monthly income of more than one minimum wage on average for each member. This shows that the enterprise is economically viable, a fact reinforced by the huge demand of local workers to be part of the cooperative, given that the local capitalist economy is not capable of employing all the working population.[12]

The economic success of Recicla Tudo is not, however, the greatest achievement from the standpoint of Solidarity Economy. In our view, economic sustainability is of course important, but it must be subordinated to the humanisation and education process occurring during the formation of the cooperative. There were many moments of tension, misunderstanding, conflict and dispute among the workers during the formation of this cooperative. On all these occasions, the principles of Solidarity Economy described by Paul Singer guided us and we can ensure that this was what allowed the continuation of the project.

5. FINAL REMARKS

Paul Singer is considered an influential economic thinker in Brazil, but above all, he is widely acknowledged as an outstanding teacher. Our project of incubation of a workers cooperative of waste pickers in a region suffering from poverty and high inequality indicators has benefited greatly from his ideas, especially from his contribution to systematise the concept of Solidarity Economy. This shows that practice and theory belong together, which points to the power of economic philosophy over the real world. We draw two main conclusions from this research.

First, in contrast to how Paul Singer presents it, the Solidarity Economy should not be understood only as a model of management of production and distribution based on the European cooperativism movement of the nineteenth century. As we see it, the Solidarity Economy is just another name for a broader idea that exists in all epochs and places. This is the idea of a humane economy, which puts the human being at the centre. Such a notion is present in human societies throughout history on all continents. This is the reason why Paul Singer is not the only name related to this concept. There are various economists and thinkers who propose an analysis of the economic system based on the fundamental values of humanism, may it be related to the Enlightenment or to other epochs and philosophical systems that praise harmony between humans and their environmental surroundings.

Second, in economics, the influence and power of the intellectual are very strong. This is so because economics connects various fields of knowledge and deals directly with material interests. Here, society, history, culture and nature are mixed to describe how we, humans, live and transform our world, our home, our oikos, the Earth. In that sense, the organic intellectual as conceived by Gramsci (2004) has much to offer in discussions about the economy of the future.[13] If economics remains a discipline taught only to a minority, there will be no positive changes. Initiative to bridge the gap between intellectuals and manual workers, especially in areas dealing directly with matters such as accounting, management and financial planning of enterprises, should thus be encouraged.

Considering that economic thought today still is dominated by the ideology of financial neoliberalism, despite the great crisis of 2007–2008, it is necessary that professional economists and academics get to know who Paul Singer was. Although he has been criticised as an utopian and even a dreamer, which may have diminished his influence over public policy definition, it is consensual that Paul Singer was humble to admit that "learning economics" (as one of his books, Singer (1983), is titled) is not something restricted to the scholarly and members of the leading elite. To learn and teach economics is to be part of the struggle of workers in all sectors, from education to waste picking, from industry to the services sector, from the urban to the rural areas. The twenty-first century is look-ing for real novelties in economic thinking and Paul Singer's Solidarity Economy may be an interesting starting point.

ACKNOWLEDGEMENTS

We are thankful for the comments from the anonymous referees, which helped us in developing the final version of our work. All text is our responsibility.

NOTES

1. Not to confuse with the Prebisch-Singer hypothesis or thesis about the deterioration of terms of trade against producers of primary goods, which involves German-born Brit-ish economist Hans Singer, and not Austrian-born Brazilian teacher and economist Paul Singer.

2. This is a representative selection of full published books. With the exception of Singer (1993, 1997), which are published in English, these are our own translations of the titles in Portuguese. According to Costa-Filho (2001), Paul Singer had written between 1961 and 2001 around 20 scientific reports and 150 published works, including books and arti-cles. A good part of Paul Singer's work was also recorded in non-written media: besides academic written works, didactical pieces and political analysis in the press, there is an enormous volume of oral output, much of which has been recorded and is widely used as educational tools specially in recent years. On YouTube there are many audiovisual record-ings of interviews, roundtables and documentary presentations related to Paul Singer and his concept of Solidarity Economy. Most of it is in Portuguese. For an interview subti-tled in German and produced by Rosa Luxemburg Stiftung, see https://www.youtube.com/watch?v=i7J7Pehpdlc&t=6s. Editing the complete works of Paul Singer and translating it to English will be an important endeavour for his followers in decades to come. For national initiatives to compile Paul Singer's work and archive his intellectual legacy, see: https://paulsinger.com.br/, https://institutopaulsinger.org.br/, https://editoraunesp.com.br/blog/colecao-com-obras-de-paul-singer-ganha-primeiro-volume-

3. For another, parallel proposal to relate Marxism and Solidarity Economy, based on a partial reconciliation of Marxism with anarchism, see Wright (2021). On the influence of Paulo Freire's thought over Paul Singer, see Schiochet (2018) and Nascimento and Santos (2019).

4. On Brazilian president Dilma Rousseff's impeachment and its relation to interna-tional imperialism, see Moniz Bandeira (2016). On the creation and decline of the Sec-retaria Nacional de Economia Solidária (National Secretariat for Solidarity Economy), see Arcanjo and Oliveira (2017). The Brazilian official public policy supporting Solidar-ity Economy disappeared during the years 2017 and 2022. With the election of Lula as president on 30 october 2022, it is hoped that this fundamental tool will return from 2023 onwards to contribute with poverty alleviation and income redistribution in Brazil. Aline Sousa, a waste picker and member of the National Waste Picker's Movement, one of the strongest social and workers movements supporting Solidarity Economy, placed the presi-dential sash on Lula's shoulder at the presidential inauguration ceremony on 1 January 2023 along with other representatives of the Brazilian people (Aliança Internacional de Catadores, 2023; Agência Brasil EBC, 2023).

5. See, for instance, the Wikipedia entry for Solidarity Economy and notice the broad scope of definition, including the variants in other languages. For a presentation of the various conceptual approaches to Solidarity Economy based on the experiences of South and North America, see Gaiger (2017).

6. For a critical assessment of Paul Singer's notion of self-management, related to the difference between the ideal of the maxim "1 worker = 1 vote" and reality, see Cornelian (2006), pp. 63–66.

7. For a summary of the polemics around Singer's definition of Solidarity Economy as a mode of production, which is a significant concept of Marxian Political Economy, see Cornelian (2006, chs. 1 and 3).

8. This is a profound theoretical discussion that should be done elsewhere. For an introduction to the distinction between money and capital as it was originally discussed between Marx and Proudhon, see Camarinha Lopes (2022, p. 74). This line of investigation, in the context of Solidarity Economy, may depart from Hanke and Winck (2010), whose paper proposes a very courageous and coherent research on the role of the Solidarity Economy in the overcoming of the law of value.

9. Other representatives of this line of critique are Germer (2006), Castro (2009) and França (2013). For a systematic review of the literature for and against Solidarity Economy, see Dardengo (2013). Our approach to that controversy is to develop a clever relation between utopian and scientific socialism (Marxism), based on the foundations of praxis as the guidance factor to theoretical development. We believe this approach is a strong feature of Paul Singer's mature work and it is coherent with the thought and action of Paulo Freire, Antonio Gramsci and Rosa Luxemburg.

10. For a presentation of the plurality and singularity of the local abolitionist movement in the 1880s, see Sant'Anna (2013).

11. For a detailed report and visual documentation of this experience of incubation led by Coletivo Recicla Goiás, see https://www.instagram.com/reciclagoias/, https://essafilmes.com/recicla-tudo/ and https://www.habitaracidade.com/recicla.

12. In 2010, the working population was 12.283 people but only 4.329 people were formally employed (IBGE, 2010). In 2020, an emergencial program of income transfer was implemented by the Brazilian Federal Government to aid the population without income during the COVID-19 crisis. The amount was about US$37,00 per month, for 3 months which did not prevent starvation in Brazil. Half of the Brazilian population received this aid. In the Town of Goiás, 67.46% of the population (16.680 people) received this aid. This is one of the highest percentages of participation in the State of Goiás, indicating that poverty and unemployment in the Town of Goiás is extremely high (http://www.portal-transparencia.gov.br/beneficios?ano=2020).

13. The concept of organic intellectual, coined by Gramsci refers to someone who has social recognition as an expert and is also class conscious. Thus, the organic intellectual participates in the class struggle at the ideological level and, being a member of the working class, he/she is able to fight the hegemony of bourgeois intelligentsia. For presentations on that concept, see Semeraro (2006), Kiernan (1991) and Mayo (1999).

REFERENCES

Aliança Internacional de Catadores (2023). Presidente Lula recebe faixa presidencial pelas mãos de Aline Sousa, catadora e representante do MNCR (Movimento Nacional dos Catadores de Materiais Recicláveis). Janeiro, 02, 2023. *Aliança Internacional de Catadores*. Retrieved from https://globalrec.org/pt-br/2023/01/02/presidente-lula-recebe-faixa-presidencial-pelas-maos-de-catadora/

Agência Brasil EBC (2023). *Learn the people who handed Lula his presidential sash are*. Published on January 2nd 2023 by Pedro Rafael Vilela, Brasília. *Agência Brasil EBC*. Retrieved from https://agenciabrasil.ebc.com.br/en/politica/noticia/2023-01/know-who-are-people-who-delivered-presidential-sash-lula

Andrada, C., & Esteves, E. (2018). Paul Singer: uma vida de luta e de trabalho pelo socialismo e pela participação democrática. *Estudos Avançados, 32*(93). doi:10.5935/0103-4014.20180051.

Arcanjo, M. A. S., & Oliveira, A. L. M. (2017). A criação da Secretaria Nacional de Economia Solidária: avanços e retrocessos. *Perseu: História, Memória e Política, 17*, pp. 231–249. Retrieved from https://revistaperseu.fpabramo.org.br/index.php/revista-perseu/article/view/127.

Brazilian Law (2010). *Política Nacional de Resíduos Sólidos*. Lei 12.305 de 02 de Agosto de 2010. Retrieved from http://www.mma.gov.br/port/conama/legiabre.cfm?codlegi=636.

Castro, B. (2009). A economia solidária de Paul Singer: A construção de um projeto político. *Dissertação de mestrado em Ciência Política*. Unicamp, Campinas, SP, Brasil.

Cornelian, A. R. (2006). *A concepção de "Economia Solidária" em Paul Singer: descompassos, contradições e perspectivas*. Dissertação de Mestrado, Programa de Pós-Graduação em Sociologia, UNESP, Araraquara, SP. Retrieved from https://repositorio.unesp.br/handle/11449/99005

Costa-Filho, A. (2001). Paul Israel Singer. *Estudos Avançados*, *15*(43), 363–374. Retrieved from https://www.revistas.usp.br/eav/article/view/9842/11414

Dardengo, A. M. (2013). *A panaceia econômico-solidária: uma sistematização dos discursos apologéticos e críticos da economia solidária no Brasil. Dissertação de Mestrado em Política Social*, Universidade Federal do Espírito Santo, Vitória.

Delgado, A. F. (2005). Goiás: a invenção da cidade "Patrimônio da Humanidade". *Horizontes Antropológicos*, ano *11*(23), 113–143. doi: 10.1590/S0104-71832005000100007

França, F. P. (2013). Economia de Mercado e Economia Solidária: Duas faces de uma mesma moeda. 182f. *Dissertação (Mestrado em serviço social)*, Universidade Federal da Paraíba, João Pessoa.

Freire, P. ([1968] 2007). *Pedagogy of the oppressed*. New York: Continuum.

Gaiger, L. I. (2017). The solidarity economy in South and North America: converging experiences. *Brazilian Political Science Review*, *11*(3). doi: 10.1590/1981-3821201700030002

Germer, C. M. (2006). A 'economia solidária': uma crítica marxista. *Outubro* (São Paulo), *14*, pp. 193–214.

Gramsci, A. (2004). *Cadernos do Cárcere*. (3rd ed.) Rio de Janeiro: Civilização Brasileira.

Hanke, D., & Winck, B. R. (2010). A economia solidária e a necessidade da superação da lei do valor. *Revista Espaço Acadêmico*, *10*(114). Retrieved from http://www.periodicos.uem.br/ojs/index.php/EspacoAcademico/article/view/10974.

IBGE (2010). Panorama Cidades. *Instituto Brasileiro de Geografia e Estatística*. Retrieved from https://cidades.ibge.gov.br/brasil/go/goias/panorama

Kiernan, V. G. (1991). Intellectuals. In T. Bottomore, L. Harris, V. G. Kiernan; R. Miliband (eds.). *The dictionary of marxist thought* (2nd ed., p. 259). Blackwell Publishers Ltd.

Lenin, V. I. (2017). The state and revolution. *Collected Works*, *25*, 381–492. Retrieved from https://www.marxists.org/archive/lenin/works/1917/staterev/

Lopes, T. C. (2022). *Law of Value and Theories of Value: Symmetrical Critical of Classical and Neoclassical Political Economy*. Leiden: Brill.

Lula da Silva, L. I. (2000). Apresentação. In P. Singer & J. Machado (2000). *Economia Socialista*. São Paulo: Fundação Perseu Abramo.

Mantega, G., & Rego, J. M. (Org.) (1999). Paul Singer (entrevista). *Conversas com economistas brasileiros II*. São Paulo: Editora 34.

Mayo, P. (1999) *Gramsci, Freire and Adult Education. Possibilities for transformative education*. London: Zed Books.

Moniz Bandeira, L. A. (2016). O golpe contra Dilma insere-se no xadrez da política internacional. *Revista Princípios*, Edição no. 145, novembro/dezembro 2016. Retrieved from http://www.revistaprincipios.com.br/artigos/145/brasil/261/entrevista-com-moniz-bandeira-.html.

Mori, K. (2004). Greve dos 300 mil foi escola de sindicalismo. *Folha de S. Paulo*, 6th January 2004. Retrieved from https://www1.folha.uol.com.br/fsp/cotidian/ff0601200405.htm

Nascimento, C., & Santos, A. M. (2019). Paul Singer e a pedagogia da autogestão na Economia Solidária. *Trabalho Necessário*, *17*(34). doi:10.22409/tn.17i34.p38048

Nunes, D. (2009). *Incubação de empreendimentos de economia solidária. Uma aplicação da pedagogia da participação*. São Paulo: Annablume.

Globo, O. (2018). Morre Paul Singer, um dos fundadores do PT. *O Globo*, 16 April 2018. Retrieved from https://oglobo.globo.com/politica/morre-paul-singer-um-dos-fundadores-do-pt-22598799

Sant'Anna, T. F. (2013). Os abolicionismos na cidade de Goiás: pluralidades e singularidades nos anos 1880. *Élisée, Rev. Geo. UEG*, Anápolis, *2*(2), 92–107.

Schiochet, V. (2018). Memórias de uma experiência aprendente. *P2P & Inovação*, *5*. doi:10.21721/p2p.2018v5n0.p53-60

Semeraro, G. (2006). Intelectuais "orgânicos" em tempos de pós-modernidade. *Cadernos CEDES*, Campinas, *26*(70), 373–391.

Silva, M. A. S., & Lopes, T. C. (2018). A educação para além do mercado: do individualismo no lixão à solidariedade na cooperativa. *Anais da VI Conferência Internacional de Pesquisa sobre Economia Social e Solidária - CIRIEC "Economia Social e Solidária, Sustentabilidade e Inovação: enfrentando os velhos e os novos problemas sociais."* Manaus, AM, Brasil. Retrieved from https://www.even3.com.br/anais/ciriec/59479-a-educacao-para-alem-do-mercado-do-individualismo-no-lixao-a-solidariedade-na-cooperativa/

Singer, P. (1953). A greve dos metalúrgicos, *Página Sindical*, Ano V, p. 5, n. 1 (05/06/1953); n. 2 (05/07/1953); n.3 (20/07/1953). In Centro de Documentação e Memória da Unesp (CEDEM/ UNESP).

Singer, P. (1969). *Desenvolvimento Econômico e Evolução Urbana*. São Paulo: Editora Nacional.

Singer, P. (1970). *Dinâmica Populacional e Desenvolvimento*. São Paulo: Hucitec.

Singer, P. (1973). *Economia Política da Urbanização*. São Paulo: Brasiliense.

Singer, P. (1977). *Economia Política do Trabalho*. São Paulo: Hucitec.

Singer, P. (1980a). *O que é socialismo hoje*. Petrópolis: Vozes.

Singer, P. (1980b). *Guia da inflação para o povo*. Petrópolis: Vozes.

Singer, P. (1981). *Dominação e desigualdade: estrutura de classes e repartição de renda no Brasil*. Rio de Janeiro: Paz e Terra.

Singer, P. (1983). *Aprender Economia*. São Paulo: Brasiliense.

Singer, P. (1985). *A formação da classe operária*. São Paulo: Atual.

Singer, P. (1986). *Repartição de Renda - ricos e pobres sob o regime militar*. Rio de Janeiro: Zahar.

Singer, P. (1987). *O Capitalismo - sua evolução, sua lógica e sua dinâmica*. São Paulo: Moderna.

Singer, P. (1993). *São Paulo's Master Plan, 1989-1992: the politics of urban space*. Washington, D.C.: Woodrow Wilson International Center for Scholars.

Singer, P. (1997). *Social exclusion in Brazil*. Geneva: International Institute for Labour Studies.

Singer, P. (1998a). *O que é Economia*. São Paulo: Brasiliense.

Singer, P. (1998b). *Globalização e Desemprego: diagnósticos e alternativas*. São Paulo: Contexto.

Singer, P. (1998c). *Uma utopia militante: repensando o socialismo*. São Paulo: Vozes.

Singer, P. (2000). *O Brasil na crise: perigos e oportunidades*. São Paulo: Contexto, 1999. 128p. *Para entender o mundo financeiro*. São Paulo: Contexto

Singer, P. (2001). Economia Solidária versus economia capitalista. *Sociedade e Estado*. *16*(1-2), Brasília. Retrieved from http://www.scielo.br/scielo.php?script=sci_arttext&pid=S0102-69922001000100005

Singer, P. (2002). *Introdução à Economia Solidária*. São Paulo: Fundação Perseu Abramo.

Singer, P. (2008). Economia Solidária (entrevista a Paulo de Salles Oliveira). *Estudos Avançados*, *22*(62), São Paulo. Retrieved from http://www.scielo.br/scielo.php?script=sci_arttext&pid=S0103-40142008000100020

Souza, A. R. (2018). Professor Paul Singer e a economia solidária. *P2P & Inovação, 5*. doi: 10.21721/p2p.2018v5n0.p43-52

Strasser, S. (1999). *Waste and want: A social history of trash*. New York, NY: Metropolitan Books.

Tavares, A. G., & Lopes, T. C. (2018). Nunca é tarde para acreditar: Paul Singer e a Economia Solidária como renovação da revolução socialista. In Roris, M. S. (Ed.). *Economia Solidária em Debate. Relatos do Encontro Goiano de Economia Solidária*. Goiânia: Editora da UFG.

UNESCO (2010). Historic centre of the town of Goiás. *World Heritage List*, UNESCO. Retrieved from https://whc.unesco.org/en/list/993/

Vannuchi, P., & Spina, R. (2005). Paul Singer. *Teoria e Debate*, edição 62. https://teoriaedebate.org.br/2005/04/10/paul-singer/

Wellen, H. (2008). Contribuição à Crítica da Economia Solidária. *Katálysis*, *11*(1). Retrieved from http://www.scielo.br/scielo.php?script=sci_arttext&pid=S1414-49802008000100010

Wellen H. (2012). *Para a Crítica da Economia Solidária*. São Paulo: Expressão Popular.

Wright, C. (2021) Marxism and the solidarity economy: Toward a new theory of revolution. *Class, Race and Corporate Power*, *9*(1), Article 2. doi: 10.25148/CRCP.9.1.009647

CHAPTER 3

THE ENTREPRENEUR BETWEEN TWO CIRCUITS: THE CRITICAL CONTRIBUTION OF MILTON SANTOS TO ENTREPRENEURSHIP STUDIES

Rafael Galvão de Almeida and Harley Silva

ABSTRACT

This article delves into the contributions of Milton Santos (1926–2001) to the economic study of entrepreneurship. Santos made contributions to spatial economics, urbanization, and planning theories, being an important author to the field of regional and urban economics. His most famous idea is the "two circuits" of the urban economy. According to this approach, the urban economies in peripheral countries create two economic-urban circuits that are both distinct and connected. The superior circuit comes from the technological modernization and cultivates international relationships. High-value goods and networks and new technologies circulate through it. The inferior circuit works outside these networks. It consists of low-dimension activities from local populations. Santos elaborated this theory to understand urbanization in peripheral countries and to give voice to the ones left behind by the development process. He did not write directly on entrepreneurship. We argue, however, that his thoughts can be important to entrepreneurship studies. The entrepreneurship discourse, that had in Schumpeter one of its main sources, assumes that the entrepreneur has traits related to the superior circuit, such as access to

Research in the History of Economic Thought and Methodology: Including a Selection of Papers Presented at the First History of Economics Diversity Caucus Conference
Research in the History of Economic Thought and Methodology, Volume 41B, 49–66
ISSN: 0743-4154/doi:10.1108/S0743-41542023000041B003

resources and networks, which would not be available to entrepreneurs in the inferior circuit. We argue that Santos' contributions can inform economic thought in entrepreneurship by calling attention to how literature can approach structural problems and contribute to making economics a more diverse discipline.

Keywords: Milton Santos; entrepreneurship; urbanization; Global South; economic geography; economic-urban circuits

JEL classifications: B29; L26; R11

1. INTRODUCTION

Ever since Joseph Schumpeter wrote his *Theory of Economic Development*, the entrepreneur is seen as a fundamental character of the economic development process. They are the person who finds new ways to combine means of production, using the available credit in the best way they can. The failure of a project is merely a mishap, because, in the overall, their efforts will eventually contribute to the development process (Schumpeter, [1934] 1949, pp. 74–94). Although Schumpeter is more known for being pessimistic in relation to the role of the entrepreneur, due to the automation of the innovation process (Schumpeter, [1943] 2002), his apparently impersonal definition allows that any person, independent of gender, social class, religion or ethnicity to be identified with the entrepreneur. This makes entrepreneurship one of the most potentially diverse fields in economics.

The definition of the entrepreneur has changed a lot since Schumpeter. While there are alternative definitions (Kirzner, 1973; Redlich, 1957), Schumpeter stands out because he transcended academic barriers, being one of the few prestigious economists recognized in other disciplines. In entrepreneurship literature from 1970 to 1989, he was the most-cited author by economists, the fifth most-cited author by business scholars, and second in other fields (Ländstrom, 2020, p. 123). He helped to turn what was once a relatively obscure academic topic and, even today, outside the main economic journals, into a fundamental public policy concern (Burgin, 2018). As Ländstrom (2020, p. 115) wrote,

> In the 1980s many pioneering studies on entrepreneurship and small businesses emerged that focused on (1) the discovery of this "new" phenomenon, (2) differentiating it from mainstream disciplines, and (3) making entrepreneurship and small businesses more visible, not least to policy makers and politicians.

In the words of Burgin (2018, p. 174), "Schumpeter's chiliastic vision thereby began to evolve into the relentlessly optimistic discourse of entrepreneurship that has pervaded business education ever since." Thus, an *entrepreneurship discourse* is born.

After ascending as a public policy target, many countries started to promote this discourse. A report from the World Bank emphasized that all modern entrepreneurship hubs had a set of fruitful government policies as part of their success (Lerner, 2014). Therefore, governments rushed to promote entrepreneurship, including in poorer communities. The idea is that more entrepreneurs can help achieving development by expanding the limits in the lower strata of society, creating value through satisfaction of demands, and creation of new opportunities of consumption, independent of class (Holcombe, 2021). This is reflected in one of the questions that Banerjee and Duflo (2007, p. 162) proposed to answer: "why are so many poor entrepreneurs?" Schumpeter, however, had in mind a specific person as the creative entrepreneur: the one that discovers new combinations of factors, advancing the technological level.

Entrepreneurship, in reality, has many meanings. One of the most common procedures, however, is to equate entrepreneurship with self-employment and to treat an increase in self-employment as a sign of an entrepreneurial economy (Bögenhold, 2021). Baumol (1990), upon separating entrepreneurship into "productive" – the one that makes economic agents apply their creativity to find new ways to combine and expand production – and "unproductive" – the one whose creativity is used to find rent-seeking or illegal profits – made an important reminder that the *context* of entrepreneurship matters (Bögenhold, 2021, p. 24). Are a corporate CEO and a peddler selling counterfeit goods in the street entrepreneurs? Even in spite of their massively different contexts, they are both called "entrepreneurs" by different settings of literature. Bögenhold (2021, p. 29) argued that economies with a high rate of self-employment are not healthy ones, because they tend to present high levels of unemployment and deficient safety nets. Thus, the superoptimism of the entrepreneurship discourse should be seen with reservations, since many politicians seem to treat entrepreneurship as a "magic bullet" (Shane, 2009).

In order to give a new perspective to this issue, we recur to the thought of Brazilian geographer Milton Almeida dos Santos (1926–2001). Santos was a scholar recognized by his work on the organization of the urban space and a prolific researcher.[1] In 1994, he was awarded the Vautrin Lud Prize, which is considered the most important award in Geography and was a public intellectual in Brazil (Teramatsu, 2018). His main contribution is *The shared space: the two circuits of the urban economy in underdeveloped countries* (Santos, [1979] 2004).[2] In this book, Santos divided the urban space between two circuits that are both distinct and connected: in one side, we have the superior circuit, which is the one that is connected to the vanguard of the national and international technology, with the industry captains, who are already established and have the control of the means of production; the inferior circuit, on the other side, is associated with small-scale production, possibly informal, centered in a lower income context.

In spite of Santos not being an economist, his works are studied in courses of urban economics and economic geography because he adopted an interdisciplinary approach. Santos had extensive descriptions and discussions on the state of the inferior circuit entrepreneur in the peripheral countries, even if he did not make any direct contribution to the entrepreneurship literature. Due to the scope of the article, we adopt the identification of entrepreneur with the self-employed person, even though we are aware of its limitations (Bögenhold, 2021). While entrepreneurs from the inferior circuit also seek to enterprise, they do not have the same privileges as the ones from the superior circuit. To understand this is to understand how the diversity of entrepreneurial and economic experiences can be manifested.

2. THE ENTREPRENEUR DISCOURSE IN ECONOMIC THOUGHT

In *A History of Entrepreneurship* economic thought, Hérbert and Link (2009, pp. xviii, 100–101) listed constant themes in the writings of the economists that influenced the discipline most. They focused on the entrepreneur as an active force, taking risks, innovating, managing and providing resources to the public.

They focused on authors that wrote not necessarily on the encompassing economic reality, but in a context of a developed economy. Therefore, these views imply taking the entrepreneur as an individual that possesses a set of privileged personal and structural conditions for their undertakings, although these conditions are not explicitly considered. These traits are more common in the ones Schumpeter had in mind.

2.1. Schumpeter and the Formation of the Entrepreneurship Discourse

In the first edition of his *Theory of Economic Development*, Schumpeter ([1912] 2003, p. 64) emphasized that

> the behavior of the entrepreneur differs substantially from that of other economic agents, who fit into the scheme devised by static theory to account for the economic activities of people.

They are capable of "channeling" the economy in new directions. Saying the development process does not need entrepreneurs is the same as saying the clay does not need a potter to become a vase; "the economy does not grow into higher forms by itself" (Schumpeter, [1912] 2003, p. 75).

His 1926's German edition, which translation is the most known version (Schumpeter, [1934] 1949) had many suppressed passages. Schumpeter wanted a greater focus on economic issues. Sociological and psychological discussions of the entrepreneur would be a distraction (Peukert, 2003; van Meerhague, 2003). Even so, traces of his original thought remain. In a well-known passage, he wrote on the "will to conquer: the impulse to fight, to prove oneself superior to others, to succeed for the sake, not of the fruits of success, but of success itself" (Schumpeter, [1934] 1949, p. 93). The entrepreneur does not only have a desire for profit, but also to attain a greater social status and self-realization. Compare with the first edition, in which Schumpeter wrote on how the entrepreneur gains "political and social power," becoming the subject of "arts and literature" just like the medieval knight; a lifestyle is built around them (Schumpeter, [1912] 2003, p. 99).

The entrepreneur, then, becomes an ideal type of citizen. Their qualities are coveted by the common people. "The joy of creating, of getting things done, or simply of exercising one's energy and ingenuity" (Schumpeter, [1943] 1949, p. 93) defines their character. At this point, Schumpeter had a romantic view of the entrepreneur, but that apparently faded away as he got older. The entrepreneur is a transient phenomenon. Although their image is immortalized in stories, the entrepreneur gives their place away to the R&D department of great corporations (Schumpeter, [1943] 2002). Schumpeter's legacy is known in evolutionary economics and the Neoschumpeterian School, which emphasize technological innovation instead of entrepreneurship. His understanding of the economy as a social and dynamic process influenced many authors, among them Santos, who referenced him on social and technological change (Santos, 2003, pp. 138, 187).

The romantic remnants are present in later works (Peukert, 2003; van Meerhague, 2003). Besides, Guichardaz and Pénin (2021) argued that Schumpeter always subscribed to the "Great Men" view of history,[3] being directly influenced by iconoclast authors such as Friedrich Nietzsche and Henri Bergson. Friedrich Wieser also influenced him through his theories on masses and leaders, where the leaders are identified with entrepreneurs (Peukert, 2003, p. 228). Schumpeter never considered entrepreneurial failure seriously because, for him, it was not important for them as "great men" (Redlich, 1955). Medearis (2009, pp. 68–72) considered Schumpeter a conservative and antidemocrat thinker because he believed the traditional elites should lead the innovation process and their absence is one of the causes of capitalist decline. In the words of Guichardaz and Pénin (2021, p. 25), "entrepreneurial activity is made of an extra-rationalist aspect, or 'extra-logical functions' [...], that is found ultimately in the 'energetic surplus' of some rare individuals" and this fades away with the advance of capitalism.

Considering together the Schumpeterian perspective and the existence of the two circuits of the urban economy in the periphery of capitalism, the entrepreneur appears as an individual from the superior circuit through a network effect. Although Schumpeter admitted the possibility of class mobility, he hardly considered the possibility of deeper contextual differences among entrepreneurs. The majority of the innovations is first available to a nation's elite and the lower classes have to wait until prices become accessible. They receive passively the blessings created by superior entrepreneurs in the form of lower prices (Schumpeter, [1912] 2003, p. 84). The capitalist might even get confused with the hostility received, because they consider they are working for all classes of society (Schumpeter, [1943] 2003, pp. 143–144).

In spite of this, Schumpeter created a framework of analysis of the entrepreneur, that is, for Hérbert and Link (2009, p. 76), simple and powerful; unforgettable, as Redlich (1955) would add. The entrepreneur becomes an indispensable force of change in a healthy economy. There is an appeal to the ego of his audience, the idea that they also can become as "special" as the entrepreneur of the book's pages – especially when he writes on how the entrepreneur can be object of adulation and emulation. It might not have been Schumpeter's intention, but a *discourse* emerges from his writings.

The focus on an entrepreneurial elite is also present in other authors. Fritz Redlich, who had been Schumpeter's colleague in Harvard, also wrote extensively on the entrepreneur (Redlich, 1955, 1957) and, in his own words, always had a "bias for aristocracy" (Poettinger, 2018, p. 6). The entrepreneur in Kirzner (1973) is someone without a defined social class, because entrepreneurship is not just an economic action, but also a human one. However, Ramoglu (2021), among his critiques to Kirzner, argued that the Kirznerian system tolerates and might even promote an increasing economic inequality.

The transformation of the academic research in entrepreneurship into the popular discourse intensified in the 1980s, following the transformation of the managerial economy into an entrepreneurial one. The model of great corporations with stable careers started to weaken after the late 1960s–early 1970s, with the end of cheap oil and Bretton Woods (Harvey, 1989). Instead of being "gobbled up" by the large corporations, studies started to verify many cases where small companies outperformed in many markets, with the ascension of startups, and business colleges popularizing technological incubators (Burgin, 2018; Harwood, 1979; Ländstrom, 2020). There was an identification between the figures of the entrepreneur and the small business owner (Carland, Hoy, Boulton, & Carland, 1984). Businessmen, who had hobby shops, started being called "entrepreneurs." Although this identification was first applied to small and wealthy business owners, soon it was used to refer to poor entrepreneurs as well. In the Brazilian legislation, for example, the figure of the individual micro-entrepreneur (*microempreendedor individual*) emerged as a way to formalize small entrepreneurs (Oliveira, 2013).

And so, the word "entrepreneur" became more and more diluted in relation to its original meaning. "Stay on the top of your game," "we are all entrepreneurs," "live the hustle," among others, became popular idioms. Any bookstore has self-help and entrepreneurship books side to side. The entrepreneurship discourse becomes, then, an important part of the professional self-realization process, what Boudreaux, Elert, Henrekson, and Lucas (2022) associated with the *eudaimonia*, the good living of Greek philosophy – entrepreneurship as a way to reach *eudaimonia*. The extension of the definition of entrepreneur beyond the one imagined by Schumpeter is a consequence of the entrepreneurial economy expanding the number of people that can be identified as entrepreneurs.

Reality, however, shows issues. The majority of the low-income entrepreneurs that work "independently" for companies of the sharing economy (Uber, DoorDash, etc.) – who in theory would be some of the greatest winners of the economy in constant transition (Thurik, Stam, & Audrestch, 2013) – are being afflicted more and more by precarization, in terms of working conditions and mental health (Forsyth, 2020; Gariau, 2019; Uchôa de Oliveira, 2020). Liberalization processes that started in the 1980s, instead of improving the economic environment, only made the small entrepreneurs even more vulnerable by removing social safety nets (Vogel, 2022). These issues call into question the "magic bullet" of entrepreneurship and can be included in Santos' critique of technocratic solutions.

2.2. Attempts to Break With the Hegemonic View of the Entrepreneurship Discourse

In spite of this discourse, economists have tried to study how different entrepreneurs in low-income contexts are. Theodore Schultz, in his Nobel Memorial Prize lecture, argued that the poor are not different from other economic agents, not even the richest ones; on the contrary, they are also entrepreneurs and use their resources rationally (Schultz, 1979). They, however, do not have the same access to the resources as the rich, being limited or incapable of doing simple operations in the economic logic, such as seeking cheaper resources to sell for a better price, which erodes profits and savings (Banerjee & Duflo, 2007). The "barefoot entrepreneur" (Imas, Wilson, & Weston, 2012) has nothing of the Schumpeterian *glamour* because they need to enterprise to survive.

Among the ones who studied the poor entrepreneur is the economist and diplomat Hernando de Soto (2000), author of *The mystery of capital*. De Soto argued that the lack of property titles and clear laws were the greatest obstacles to the development of peripheral nations. He also recognized that the majority of the entrepreneurs in these places need to enterprise to survive. Even so, there is a lot of wealth in the poorest regions of the world, what he called "dead capital." It is dead because it cannot benefit from a structure of property rights. Upon defining property rights, de Soto argued that the "mystery" of the capital is solved and an environment of friendly exchanges can be built. As an example, he attributed the defeated of the Peruvian terrorist group *Sendero Luminoso* to the rural property titling scheme developed along with his *Instituto de Libertad y Democracia*.

The problem with de Soto's argument is the same as the entrepreneurship discourse criticized by Shane (2009): it is a magic bullet. His book is aimed at policymakers that want a low-cost political solution. Titling is a visible process, that generates direct personal results, but many question its real efficacy, especially in Peru (Gilbert, 2002; Mitchell, 2009).[4] This ends up being a process imposed topdown. It is, therefore, possible to derive a critique to de Soto's project, because, upon focusing on the existence or not of property rights, de Soto ignores social questions of the inferior circuit and of alternative forms of property organization.

Almost a decade after de Soto (2000), Abhijit Banerjee and Esther Duflo wrote *Poor Economics* (Banerjee & Duflo, 2011). The book also attempts to find strategies against poverty and became equally popular. They need to remember in the preface that it is a wrong idea that "because the poor possess very little, it is assumed that there is nothing interesting about their economic existence." This indicates that, even after 30 years after Schultz's plea, this has been an issue that has not received the due attention.

In one of the most vivid cases of their book, they met an entrepreneur from Udaipur, India, with depression because he lost his camel, his only capital. When they asked him if he had done something about – like seeking a therapist, something any person from the superior circuit would have done – he replied, "I lost the camel. It's obvious I'm sad. There's nothing to be done." Banerjee and Duflo recognized they were naïve. The contexts of entrepreneurship are different.

Banerjee and Duflo argue that, in spite of these barriers, there is a lot of entrepreneurial activity in the periphery: the poor has many occupations in their attempt to generate a surplus; since there is no space to specialize, their enterprises cannot grow. Because of their small scale, there are no incentives to increase the diversity of products and services in the peripheral regions. The poor still prefers stability to risk and tends to abandon risky enterprises in exchange for safe jobs in places like the government.

The problems with Banerjee and Duflo are similar to de Soto's. Just as de Soto (2000) is a showcase for titling, Banerjee and Duflo (2011) is a showcase for randomized controlled trials (RCTs), in which great economic experiments involving entire communities can hope to find the economic variables that "work."[5] Reddy (2012) argued that many results from Banerjee and Duflo are exaggerated and are based in a technocratic posture that define what is "better" to the peripheral populations independent of what they want. Both present the Western bias of the entrepreneurship discourse of the literature, that they should stop acting like themselves and act more like their Western teachers (Gamage & Wickramasinghe, 2012).

Even so, de Soto, Banerjee, and Duflo are important for having called the attention to the fact entrepreneurship in peripheral regions is different from the central ones. One of the critiques Santos made against economists was that they were not interested in doing "field economics" (Santos, 2000, p. 23). Thus, we see an attempt to break up with the hegemonic discourse and an increasing interest in seeing and analyzing poverty in first person. An anti-poverty strategy will only work if it incorporates the poor in them, something Santos always made sure to emphasize.

3. MILTON SANTOS: INTELLECTUAL OF THE GLOBAL SOUTH

Milton Santos' thought has a great influence in Brazil, especially in geography and urban economics. His texts are studied along with mainstream regional economists and New Economic Geography authors, such as Walter Isard and Paul Krugman[6] (Braga, 2008). His works focus on themes of critical geography, nature of space and calls to alternative globalizations that may truly incorporate the poor in the world system. His thought was influenced by many different approaches, from the Latin-American structuralist school to the French critical geography, after his exile imposed by the civic-military dictatorship of 1964 (Lima, 2018). He was also an important Black intellectual, which is relevant in a society as unequal as the Brazilian one (Cirqueira, 2016). In the words of Hecht (2021, p. 1):

> His intellectual ties to French analyses of regional development and American critical geography did much to transform those fields, from their somewhat parochial perspectives to perspectives more engaged in both theory and practice "from the South." Santos helped transform the understandings of development and provided a robust critique of development planning as it unfolded in the 1960s and 1970s, while simultaneously forging new methods and practices for the transformation of communities, as well as new understandings of how nature, history, and the complexities of lived life produced citizenship, rights, and the formations of urban and rural life.

Santos' research always attempted to include elements that were not present in analyses made in developed countries. He criticized mainstream economics for being ethnocentric – merely importing strategies built in developed countries would be fruitless without critical analysis; the peripheral countries do not just belong to "a world in development, but an underdeveloped world" (Santos, [1979] 2004, p. 19). During his career, he was associated with the Economic Commission for Latin America and the Caribbean (ECLAC) and the dependency theory, but, as a geographer, he is usually ignored in the history of economic thought, in spite of being part of the network of Latin-American structuralist economists[7] (Ferretti & Pedrosa, 2018; Linhares, 2009).

In the field of Brazilian regional and urban economics, Santos' work has considerable influence, especially on economists that work with economic geography and regional planning.[8] He approached economic themes in works related to urbanization and organization of the territory (Santos & Silveira, 2001). Santos' influence is relevant in the spatial treatment of the economic phenomena and in the investigation of economic particularities of peripheral regions of the Brazilian economy (Castriota & Tonucci, 2018; Linhares, 2009; Monte-Mór & Castriota, 2018).

Again, Santos did not write directly on entrepreneurship. However, in his works, we find constant concerns with the situation of entrepreneurs in the inferior circuit. His work analyzed the conditions in which these agents conducted their businesses and how they used their resources in creative ways. Among the problems pointed by Santos are the lack of property rights, difficult access to credit, accumulation of unsanitary conditions, among other restrictive aspects. Cases like the Udaipur entrepreneur, in Banerjee and Duflo (2011), are a daily occurrence in the inferior circuit because of the problems Santos exposed. In his final years, he denounced globalization as being only focused in the interests of the large corporations, harming peripheral countries (Santos, 2001). Even if his focus was on the problems of organization of the urban space, Santos considered the economic practices understood as entrepreneurship as having an important urban dimension.

Observing the urban growth in peripheral countries and debates on formal and informal economies started by economists J. H. Boeke and W. Arthur Lewis (Regitz, 2012), Santos proposed that the urbanization process creates two "circuits" in the urban economy: the first of them is the superior one, which has its origins in the technological modernization of the economy and space. In its structure, the elites have access to the latest gadgets, fruits of the fashionable technological apparatchik created in high-tech centers. Therefore, the spread of technology happens unevenly through sectors, which is one of the most important sources of inequality in the economy. Thus, its members are connected with the international networks of goods and services.

In contrast, the inferior circuit is practically its opposite; the scale of operation is much smaller, because they are related to poorer populations and regional networks (Santos, [1979] 2004, p. 22). It is not just a "geographical" periphery, but also a "socioeconomic" one, which concentrates the "marginalized places by the development process and, above all, the people rejected by growth" (Santos, 2003, p. 82). Both have the same economic needs, but people in the inferior circuit cannot satisfy them as they wish to; they have to go through less modern means, maybe even illegal ones (Santos, [1978] 1979, p. 37). The superior circuit has greater access to different ways of funding their enterprises – credit, bank preferences and, more recently, cryptocurrency – while the inferior one has access only to paper money (Santos, 1999, p. 10). Thus, the inferior circuit has "its own organization and its own operational laws and evolution" (Santos,

[1978] 1979, p. 37), including entrepreneurial ones. Table 1 summarizes the differences between the two circuits.

There is also a productive conflict between these two circuits. On one hand, the superior circuit expands, with its members becoming "world citizens," through access to international urban networks. Cities are the focus of capital reproduction "thanks to the presence of industrial complexes and services that guarantee the financial and technological multiplication" (Santos, 2003, p. 149). But, because they absorb the rural populational surplus, that migrate because of technological unemployment or in search of better life conditions, soon they reach their limits and slums proliferate (Santos, 2003, p. 152). And these spaces might be rebuilt at the discretion of the superior circuit. Santos mentioned the example of the Kariakoo commercial center in Dar-es-Salam, Tanzania (Santos, 2003, pp. 193–196), in which a traditional market was demolished to give place to a modern economic complex. The traditional sector had in Kariakoo a well-established communication system between the urban and rural sectors, allowing entrepreneurs to conduct business in their houses. With the renovation, financed by the World Bank, the people who lived there for decades are expelled to peripheral areas, thus increasing their distance from the city's central networks, and increasing the domination of the superior circuit over the inferior one.

Table 1.   Differences Between the Inferior and the Superior Circuit.

	Superior Circuit	Inferior Circuit
Technology	Intensive use of capital	Intensive use of labor
Organization	Bureaucratic, focus on efficiency	Primitive, not structured
Capital	Important	Scarce
Workforce	Limited	Abundant
Regular wages	Usual	Not required
Inventory	Large quantities	Small quantities
Prices	Fixed (generally)	Negotiable between buyer and seller (bargain)
Credit	From institutional banks	Personal, not institutional (recent use of microcredit)
Profit margin	Small per unit, but compensated with business volume (e.g., luxury goods)	Large per unit, but small in relation to the business volume
Relationship with customers	Impersonal	Direct, personalized
Fixed costs	Important	Negligible
Advertisement	Necessary	None or limited in scale
Reuse of goods	None (waste)	Frequent
Reserve capital	Essential	Non-essential
Government help	Important	None or almost none
Insertion in foreign markets	Oriented for external markets	Small or none

Source: Santos (2003, p. 127, adapted).

The project which is being executed is a typical case of "short-circuit" of the economy's inferior circuit ..., but, in the same way, it also implies the short-circuit of the politic-economic general project of the government. (Santos, 2003, p. 195)

Thus, due to this dependency from foreign paradigms and technology, most of the sectors that control peripheral countries is "neocolonized" (Cerqueira-Neto & Santos, 2017, p. 222; Santos, 2001).

Considering Santos' definition, we can say that the entrepreneurship discourse privileges the superior circuit, because this is the part that moves more money, from where innovation comes from. It is also the discourse members of the superior circuit would like to emulate from central countries, both in academic and popular literature. Santos openly criticized orthodox economists because they were only interested in the "mechanisms of the modern economy" (Santos, 2003, p. 81). This critique can be extended to the hegemonic entrepreneurship discourse.

In the usual terms, when the entrepreneur fails, their defeat would not be different from a sports match, like in soccer or chess. Frank Knight, who defined the entrepreneur as the one that faces uncertainty and the risk of losing money while seeking profit, considered entrepreneurship as a "game" (Emmet, 2010). The result is unpredictable and it is responsibility of the entrepreneur to restrict their consumption and spend time evaluating risks before investing. "If you are not willing to have any 'skin in the game,' then you are not an entrepreneur" (Emmet, 2010, p. 1143). The use of the game metaphor implies a friendly process, gentlemanly even. The entrepreneur tends to continue his relationships with the ones who "defeated" them in the competitive market. They still have open access to the networks that allow them to acquire new data, to be used in another opportunity, with greater chances of success.

If we consider the conditions imposed to the entrepreneur of the inferior circuit, however, these privileges do not exist. The access to credit is limited and they do not have access to high-value networks. They need to be embedded in the local networks that are always suffering with infrastructure problems and being forgotten by the government, which tends to be controlled by the superior circuit. In the most extreme cases, the entrepreneur of the inferior circuit is a survivor (Imas et al., 2012; Montiel, Novelo, Ávila, & Sierra, 2020). A failure in selling their product can be the difference between going to sleep with an empty stomach or not. In contrast, the superior circuit entrepreneurs contribute in Santos' view, for an "'a priori' justification for recourse to foreign capital and experts" (Santos, 1977, p. 88) that deepens inequalities because, once again, the resources are not produced indigenously neither for the entire population.

One of the most important differences between the two entrepreneurs is the abyss between discourse and reality. Different from the hegemonic entrepreneurship discourse, many times the entrepreneurial journey in the inferior circuit does not end with a "happy ending." The reward is just to survive another day.[9] In the words of Santos ([1979] 2004, p. 241): "if some people, in small numbers, borrow to increase their wealth, the large part of the population in the cities borrow simply to consume."

In addition to these problems, there is a process of stigmatization of the poor, in which, at the same time they are encouraged (or coerced) by the entrepreneurship discourse to escape poverty using their own efforts,[10] they are criticized and stigmatized for demanding better life conditions and seek help from anti-poverty programs (Eufrásio, 2019; Pinker, 2017). Santos ([1979] 2004, p. 47) argued that this stigma is many times encouraged by the government,[11] because it justifies the elimination of social programs that would combat the structural problems in the inferior circuit, to free (even more) resources to projects relevant to the superior circuit.

Due to these inequalities, Santos criticized the "growth ideology" that can only create "pseudodevelopment" (Santos, [1979] 2004, p. 25). The volume of resources in the superior circuit can more than compensate any worsening of life conditions in the inferior circuit, in a strict utilitarian way, justifying neglect. With an accumulation of power and resources, the hegemonic discourse of glorification of "great men" and stigmatization of the poor becomes stronger. In reality, safe entrepreneurship is also a *privilege*. To treat entrepreneurship as a "game" is, in a certain way, lack consideration, because the metaphor is not associated with a game in which more than money is lost.[12]

Santos' critique of mainstream economics becomes relevant at this point, because of its "top-down" strategy (Imas et al., 2012; Santos, 1977). Many of these changes ignore the culture and institutions of the inferior circuit. They need to go away in exchange for better imported cultures – just like what happened in Kariakoo, according to Santos. In reality, while the superior circuit stays with the "creative" part of the term "creative destruction," the inferior circuit stays with the "destruction" part. Santos ([1979] 2004, p. 255) wrote: "It is not because it is thrilling that activities change throughout a year, or even a week, or even a day, but because it is necessary to quickly adapt to a demand that is very sensitive to changes in the conjuncture."

The constant change is seen as something positive and desirable by the hegemonic discourse (Holcombe, 2021; Thurik et al., 2013;), but it also creates uncertainty and social disintegration – the unhealthy economy that Bögenhold (2021) warned about. The liberal historian Bertrand de Jouvenel, against his colleagues who saw with excitement a society ruled by creative destruction, alerted that a society incapable to see something wrong with this process is a society deeply alienated, with social relations and families destroyed (Anderson, 2001, p. 99). If the economic result is better, any cost should be acceptable, even if it is against the wishes and well-being of those who bear most of the cost – the inferior circuit. The entrepreneur becomes an object, no different from his creations, lacking the self-realization the discourse promises (Ericsson, 2021).

While the entrepreneurship discourse emphasizes that it is the people who must adequate to changes, to "become" mobile Labor and give up social security (Thurik et al., 2013), Jouvenel's concerns find echo in Santos, who saw the inferior circuit as "the structure that holds the people who were expelled from the rural areas; it appears, therefore, with an undeniable social and economic role" as the social dampening device of the migratory shocks and even economic growth itself (Santos, [1979] 2004, p. 368). Poverty is accepted as a feature of a competitive society, as the deserved punishment of the inefficient, thus there is no real effort to eliminate it (Santos, [1978] 1979). Rather, the poor are still asked to sacrifice the little they have in name of this discourse. And this is one of the main conclusions of Santos' *oeuvre*: there is a *dependency relationship* between the two circuits – in other words, the superior circuit can afford its dominance over society by keeping the inferior circuit subordinate to itself, economic and culturally. This creates a rigidity in the inferior circuit because, as the dependency relationship increases, the members of the inferior circuit have to further depend on how the members of the superior one manage the economy. This, then, leads to the segregation of the space in the urban economy and the denial of options to the poor.

For that reason, public policies aimed to tackle problems in the inferior circuit will not be as effective if they are not followed by attempts to modernize it in its own terms, because there is a series of networks and institutions created by its inhabitants to cope with their situation. Or else it might "short-circuit" the inferior circuit. Santos (1977) criticized economic planning because it did not consider these issues. Most planning projects of his time, from both capitalist and socialist blocs, followed the "illusion" that Hirschman (1967, p. 23) observed, in which "'experts' have already found all the answers to the problems and that all that is needed is faithful "implementation" of these multifarious recommendations."

The purely economic logic would not be enough, because it does not recognize this dependency relationship. The inferior circuit and poverty will not disappear with just more money poured or "raw" entrepreneurship discourse. Santos ([1979] 2004, p. 371) argued that society needs to replace the idea of "economic productivity" by "social productivity," so that technology – one of the main sources of inequality – can be subordinated to humanity. Only with indigenous production the peripheral countries can join the world system as equals and not as subordinated to the central countries (Cerqueira-Neto & Santos, 2017). And, thus, also the entrepreneurs from the inferior circuit can be recognized as just as important for theory and practice. In his words: "the ideal, evidently, would be that the inferior circuit became less inferior, but that would only happen if the superior circuit became less superior" (Santos, [1978] 1979, p. 58).

Santos saw the entrepreneur of the inferior circuit as someone embedded in their community. Imas et al. (2012) related stories of barefoot entrepreneurs: beggars, waste pickers, fix-it-alls, tragic protagonists when compared to the Schumpeterian entrepreneur. Are not they using their resources as the best as they can to find new combinations and to generate a surplus as well? Santos wanted to call attention to these people as well.

Therefore, although Boudreaux et al. (2022) have a point in emphasizing the *eudaimonia* as entrepreneurial self-realization, Santos would say there should be something further, other types of satisfaction from entrepreneurship. An alternative would be the *buen vivir* – name given to a South American philosophy that also emphasizes the social and environmental satisfaction (Villalba, 2013) – that tries to avoid the "development ideology" of growth as an end in itself. The idea of "frugal innovations," low-cost products that are adapted to low-technology regions (Hossain, 2018), would also be an alternative in the spirit of Santos' writings; he criticized the idea that poverty can be fought off with consumerism, through emulation the consumption patterns of the superior circuit, because of the dependency relationship between the two circuits (Santos, [1978] 1979). Entrepreneurs that can explore frugal innovations should become more relevant as they can bridge the two circuits with less consumerism-focused products.

4. CONCLUSION

In theory, entrepreneurship is one of the most diverse fields of economics. Even if it was not Schumpeter's intention, he did open the possibility that anyone could be identified with the entrepreneur. In its widest definition, any person that is good in organizing productive resources in an innovative way and supply the population's demands can be an entrepreneur. However, the economic theory and its history show that the entrepreneur is a limited person, more than it seems. Its discourse, in spite of it, is so attractive that reality surpassed theory.

From individual micro-entrepreneurs to the industry captains, the term "entrepreneur" has been used to label them. This shows the ubiquity of the entrepreneurship discourse in the economy and its "magic bullet" problem. Therefore, theory must catch up with reality so that the economics of entrepreneurship can understand better its object of study.

Thus, Milton Santos' contribution is relevant. Some parts of his writings are outdated. For example, he wrote in a time when microcredit or marketing aimed at the poor did not exist in a widespread way. But, by emphasizing the different contexts between superior and inferior circuits, Santos called the attention to entirely different life experiences that both economic theory and entrepreneurship discourse may not give the due attention. He also called his readers to think critically the economic discourse, and this extends to the entrepreneurship one. There is still a lot of potential in bringing Santos to the international economic dialogue, in the analysis of the shared economy, its relationship with technology, entrepreneurship and the two circuits, among other topics. One of Santos' main objectives was that people from the inferior circuit, including its entrepreneurs, could be respected. A more diverse economics and entrepreneurship studies must incorporate this respect.

NOTES

1. His curriculum at his memorial site has 87 pages: https://www.miltonsantos.com.br/site/miltonsantos_curriculum.pdf

2. The book was originally published in French, as *L'Espace Partagé*, in 1975, during his exile. An English translation was published by Methuen (1979), and a new edition by Routledge, in 2017. We are following the Portuguese edition.

3. According to Burke (2001), the "Great Men theory," inspired by Leopold Ranke, dominated historical research until the end of Second World War. Such paradigm limited history to the actions of great figures, creating an incomplete and biased history.

4. Mitchell (2009, pp. 393 and 398) wrote that the *Instituto de Libertad y Democracia* lost favor with the Peruvian political elite due to lack of results in the 2000s. His popularity only was kept afloat because of his ample network, being a member of the Peruvian superior circuit.

5. It should be noted that de Soto (2000) and Banerjee and Duflo (2011) are scientific divulgation works that are based on academic research. They helped to disseminate academic

ideas in popular language and increase their visibility, providing a bridge between academic ideas and the entrepreneurship discourse. De Soto won the Global Award for Entrepreneurship Research in 2017 and Banerjee and Duflo won the Nobel Memorial Prize in 2019.

6. See Rahman and Dimand (2021) for a history of geographical economics.

7. Maria da Conceição Tavares wrote the preface to Santos (2001), praising his multidisciplinary approach and his concern in promoting a more inclusive approach. Santos (1995, p. 99) called Celso Furtado "my good friend." For a history of the dependency theory, see Bresser-Pereira (2005).

8. Santos was member of the National Association of Graduate Schools and Research in Urban and Regional Planning (ANPUR), being its president during 1991–1993. He is also patron of the Milton Santos Prize, conceded starting from 2011. ANPUR has an important role in promoting the discipline in Brazil and being a community for economists that do not fully subscribe to the mainstream economics. Santos (2000) had a negative opinion of mainstream economics, that its imperialism would make social sciences as whole poorer.

9. According to Bertand et al. (2006), the poor consumer has little incentive to save because they need to consume in the short run just to fulfill their basic needs. Unable to consistently save, they are subject to worse long-term conditions.

10. This is called "magical voluntarism". According to Gunn and Cloud (2010), magical voluntarism is the idea, recurrent in self-help books, that all one person needs to leave poverty is entrepreneurial willpower. This allows the discourse to ignore and exempt itself from society's structural problems.

11. A recent example comes from the former Brazilian President Jair Bolsonaro. Commenting on the deaths caused by floods in the end of January 2022, he said they only having themselves to blame, because they lacked "future vision" for living in risky areas (Behnke, 2022). Another example is former Australian Prime Minister Scott Morrison saying that help will only be available to people wanting to buy homes, renters would not be entitled to reliefs (Gould, 2022). These attitudes punish the poor for being poor and assume all that lacks to them is willpower. On one hand, reactionary governments claim to help the poor, using the "magic bullet" of the entrepreneurship discourse; on the other, they enact policies that make their situation worse, such as limiting their access of programs of additional income that would lessen the pressure on them (Eufrásio, 2019; Vogel, 2022).

12. The 2021 South Korean series *Squid Game* is a better metaphor for the obstacles poor entrepreneurs have to face than any other game.

REFERENCES

Anderson, B. C. (2001). Bertrand de Jouvenel's melancholy liberalism. *Public Interest*, *143*, 87–103.

Banerjee, A. V., & Duflo, E. (2007). The economic lives of the poor. *Journal of Economic Literature*, *21*(1), 141–167.

Banerjee, A. V., & Duflo, E. (2011). *Poor economics*. New York, NY: Public Affairs. Ebook.

Baumol, W. T. (1990). Entrepreneurship: Productive, unproductive and destructive. *Journal of Political Economy*, *98*(5), 893–921.

Behnke, E. (2022). Bolsonaro diz que 'faltou visão de futuro' a vítimas em SP. *Poder360*, February 1. Retrieved from https://www.poder360.com.br/governo/bolsonaro-diz-que-faltou-visao-de-futuro-a-vitimas-em-sp/

Bertrand, M., Mullainathan, S., & Shafir, S. (2006). Behavioral economics and marketing in aid of decision making among the poor. *Journal of Public Policy and Marketing*, *25*(1), 8–23.

Bögenhold, D. (2021). Self-employment and entrepreneurship: productive, unproductive or destructive? In O. Anders (Ed.), *Against entrepreneurship* (pp. 19–36). London: Palgrave.

Boudreaux, C. J., Elert, N., Henrekson, M., & Lucas, D. S. (2022). Entrepreneurial accessibility, eudaimonic well-being, and inequality. *Small Business Economics*, *59*, 1061–10799. doi:10.1007/s11187-021-00569-3

Braga, R. M. (2008). Tendências e perspectivas das teorias locacionais no capitalismo contemporâneo. *Geografares*, *6*, 167–179.

Bresser-Pereira, L. C. (2005). *From ECLAC and ISEB to dependency theory*. Retrieved from https://www.bresserpereira.org.br/papers/2005/05.6-ISEB-CEPAL-DependencyTheory.i.pdf. [Originally published in *Intelectuais e política no Brasil: a experiência do ISEB*, organized by Caio Navarro de Toledo, 201-232. São Paulo: Revan.]

Burke, P. (2001). Overture. The new history: Its past and its future. In B. Peter (Ed.), *New perspectives on historical writing* (pp. 1–24). University Park, PA: Pennsylvania University Press.

Burgin, A. (2018). The reinvention of entrepreneurship. In H. Raymond & H. Andrew (Eds.), *American labyrinth: Intellectual history for complicated times* (pp. 163–182). Ithaca, NY: Cornell University Press.

Carland, J. W., Hoy, F., Boulton, W. R., & Carland, J. C. (1984). Differentiating entrepreneurs from small business owners: A conceptualization. *Academy of Management, 9*(2), 54–59.

Castriota, R., & Tonucci, J. (2018). Extended urbanization in and from Brazil. *Environment and Planning D: Society and Space, 36*(3), 512–528.

Cerqueira-Neto, S., & Santos, C. J. d. (2017). A ciência e a tecnologia na visão de Milton Santos. *GeoTextos, 13*(2), 209–225.

Cirqueira, D. M. (2016). Milton Santos: um corpo estranho no paraíso. In S. Chalhoub & A. F. M. Pinto (Eds.), *Pensadores negros – Pensadoras negras* (pp. 405–428). Belo Horizonte: Fino Traço.

De Soto, H. (2000). *The mystery of capital: Why capitalism triumphs in the West and fails everywhere else*. New York, NY: Basic Books.

Emmett, R. B. (2010). Frank H. Knight on the "entrepreneurial function" in modern enterprise. *Seattle University Law Review, 34*, 1139–1154.

Ericsson, D. 2021. Notes on a fetishistic war machine. In Ö. Anders (Ed.), *Against entrepreneurship* (pp. 37–56). London: Palgrave.

Eufrásio, A. (2019). *Expressões do conservadorismo moral na atualidade: A culpabilização de famílias beneficiárias do Programa Bolsa Família*. PhD thesis. Pontifícia Universidade Católica de São Paulo.

Ferretti, F. B., & Pedrosa, V. (2018). Inventing critical development: A Brazilian geographer and his Northern networks. *Transactions of the Institute of British Geographies, 43*(4), 703–717.

Forsyth, A. (2020). Playing catch-up but falling short: Regulating work in the gig economy in Australia. *King's Law Journal, 31*(2), 287–300.

Gamage, H. R., & Wickramasinghe, A. (2012). Development in the Western ideology of entrepreneurialism and their (mis)applications in the context of non-Western cultures. *Corporate Ownership and Control, 10*(1), 421–433.

Gauriau, R. (2019). Precarização e direito do trabalho: *Quid novi?*" *Revista do Tribunal Superior do Trabalho, 85*(4), 116–137.

Gilbert, A. (2002). On the mystery of capital and the myths of hernando de Soto: What difference does legal title make?" *International Development Planning Review, 24*(1), 1–19.

Gould, C. (2022). *Scott Morrison says renters should buy a house if they want relief*. News.com.au, March 30. Retrieved from https://www.news.com.au/finance/economy/federal-budget/scott-morrison-and-ally-langdon-clash-over-rent-relief-after-federal-budget-delivered/news-story/2e8208699dddcdfd9dc383d38e5055e7

Guichardaz, R., & Pénin. J. (2021). *Entrepreneurs "from within"? Schumpeter and the challenge of endogenizing novelty*. Document de Travail N° 2021-41. Bureau d'Économie Théorique et Appliquée, Strasbourg.

Gunn, J., & Cloud, D. L. (2010). Agentic orientation as magical voluntarism. *Communication Theory, 20*, 50–78.

Harvey, D. G. (1989). From managerialism to entrepreneurialism: The transformation of urban governance in the late capitalism. *Geografiska Annaler Series B, Human Geography, 71*(1), 3–17.

Hecht, S. (2021). Introduction: Milton Santos: Rebel of the backlands, insurgent academic, prescient scholar. In M. Santos (Ed.), *The nature of space* (pp. 1–9). Durham, NC: Duke University Press.

Hirschman, A. O. (1967). *Development projects observed*. Washington: Brookings Institution.

Holcombe, R. G. (2021). Entrepreneurial economies. *Economies, 9*(123), 1–12. doi:10.3390/economies903012.

Hossain, M. (2018). Frugal innovation: A review and research agenda. *Journal of Cleaner Production, 182*, 926–936.

Imas, J. M., Wilson, N., & Weston, A. (2012). Barefoot entrepreneurs. *Organizations, 19*, 563–585.

Kirzner, I. M. (1973). *Competition and entrepreneurship*. Chicago, IL: University of Chicago Press.

Ländstrom, H. (2020). The evolution of entrepreneurship as a scholarly field. *Foundations and Trends in Entrepreneurship, 16*(2), 65–243.

Lerner, J. (2014). *Entrepreneurship, public policy and cities*. Policy Research Working Paper No. 6880. World Bank, Washington, DC.

de Lima, T. M. (2018). Um intelectual na mira da repressão: Milton Santos e o golpe de 1964. *Revista de História* (177). doi:10.11606/issn.2316-9141.rh.2018.137230

Linhares, L. (2009). O (sub) desenvolvimento na teoria e na política: um possível diálogo contemporâneo entre Celso Furtado e Milton Santos acerca dos novos arranjos produtivos. *Ensaios FEE, 30*(1), 57–86.

Medearis, J. (2009). *Joseph A. Schumpeter*. New York: Continuum.

Mitchell, T. (2009). How neoliberalism makes its world: The urban property rights project in Peru. In M. Philip & P. Dieter (Eds.), *The road from Mont Pèlerin: The making of the neoliberal collective thought* (pp. 386–416). Cambridge: Harvard University Press.

Monte-Mór, R., & Castriota, R. (2018). Extended urbanization: Implications for urban and regional theory. In P. Anssi, H. John, & J. Martin (Eds.), *Handbook on the geographies of regions and territories* (pp. 332–345). Cheltenham: Edward Elgar.

Montiel, M. O. J., Novelo, A. F., Ávila, E., & Sierra, M. S. J. (2021). "Tengo que sobrevivir": relato de vida de tres jóvenes microemprendedores bajo COVID-19. *Telos, 23*(1), 68–81.

de Oliveira, J. M. (2013). Empreendedor individual: ampliação da base formal ou substituição do emprego? *Radar: tecnologia, produção e comércio exterior, 25*, 161–180.

Peukert, H. (2003). The missing chapter in Schumpeter's *Theory of Economic Development*. In J. Backhaus (Ed.), *Joseph Alois Schumpeter: Entrepreneurship, style and vision* (pp. 221–232). New York, NY: Kluwer.

Pinker, R. (2017). Stigma and social welfare. In O. John & P. Robert (Eds.), *Social policy and welfare pluralism* (pp. 61–68). Bristol: Policy Press.

Poettinger, M. (2018). An actor of change: The entrepreneur of Fritz Redlich. *In Proceedings of the 22nd annual ESHET conference*, June 7–9, Madrid.

Rahman, J., & Dimand, R. W. (2021). The emergence of geographical economics: at the contested boundaries of economics, geography, and regional science. *Journal of the History of Economic Thought, 43*(2), 241–261.

Ramoglu, S. (2021). Why do disequilibria exist? An ontological study of Kirznerian economics. *Cambridge Journal of Economics, 45*(4), 833–856.

Reddy, S. G. (2012). Randomise this! On poor economics. *Review of Agrarian Studies, 2*(2), 60–73.

Redlich, F. (1955). Entrepreneurship in the initial stages of industrialization (with special reference to Germany). *Weltwirtschaftliches Archiv, 75*, 59–106.

Redlich, F. (1957). A program for entrepreneurial research. *Weltwirtschaftliches Archiv, 78*, 47–66.

Regitz, M. M. (2012). A teoria dos circuitos da economia urbana de Milton Santos: de seu surgimento à sua atualização. *Revista Geográfica Venezolana, 53*(1), 147–164.

Santos, M. (1977). Underdevelopment, geography and planning. *Antipode, 9*(3), 86–98.

Santos, M. ([1978] 1979). *Pobreza urbana*. São Paulo: Hucitec.

Santos, M. (1995). O futuro do nordeste: Da racionalidade à contrafinalidade. In F. S. Gaudêncio & M. Formiga (Eds.), *Era da esperança: teoria e política no pensamento de Celso Furtado* (pp. 99–107). Rio de Janeiro: Paz e Terra.

Santos, M. (1999). O dinheiro e o território. *GEOgraphia, 1*(1), 7–13.

Santos, M. (2000). A grande crise já se instalou. In C. Benjamin & L. A. Elias (Eds.), *Brasil: crise e destino* (pp. 21–33). São Paulo: Expressão Popular.

Santos, M. (2001). *Por uma outra globalização*. Rio de Janeiro: Record.

Santos, M. (2003). *Economia espacial: críticas e alternativas*. São Paulo: EdUSP.

Santos, M. ([1979] 2004). *O espaço dividido: Os dois circuitos da economia urbana dos países subdesenvolvidos*. São Paulo: EdUSP.

Santos, M. ([2006] 2021). *The nature of space*. Durham, NC: Duke University Press.

Santos, M, & Silveira, M. L. (2001). *O Brasil: Território e sociedade no início do século XXI*. Rio de Janeiro: Record.

Schumpeter, J. A. ([1934] 1949). *Theory of economic development*. Cambridge: Harvard University Press. Retrieved from https://archive.org/details/in.ernet.dli.2015.187354/.

Schumpeter, J. A. ([1943] 2002). *Capitalism, socialism and democracy*. London: Routledge.

Schumpeter, J. A. [1912] 2003). The theory of economic development In J. Backhaus (Ed.), U. Backhaus (Trans.), *Joseph Alois Schumpeter: Entrepreneurship, style and vision* (pp. 61–116). New York, NY: Kluwer.

Schultz, T. W. (1979). *The economics of being poor*. Lecture to the memory of Alfred Nobel, December 8. Retrieved from https://www.nobelprize.org/prizes/economic-sciences/1979/schultz/lecture/

Shane, S. (2009). Why encouraging more people to become entrepreneurs is bad public policy. *Small Business Economics, 33*, 141–149.

Teramatsu, G. (2018). Milton Santos: do Vautrin-Lud ao Google Doodle. *Blog da Associação dos Geógrafos Brasileiros, Seção Campinas*, 10 de fevereiro de 2018. Retrieved from http://agb-campinas.com.br/site/2018/milton-santos-google-doodle-e-vautrin-lud/

Thurik, A. R., Stam, E. & Audrestch, D. B. (2013). The rise of the entrepreneurial economy and the future of dynamic capitalism. *Technovation, 33*, 302–310.

Uchôa de Oliveira, F. M. (2020). Saúde do trabalhador e o aprofundamento da uberização do trabalho em tempos de pandemia. *Revista Brasileira de Saúde Ocupacional, 45*, e22.

van Meerhaege, Marcel A. G. (2003). The lost chapter of Schumpeter's 'economic development'. In J. Backhaus (Ed.), *Joseph Alois Schumpeter: Entrepreneurship, style and vision* (pp. 233–244). New York, NY: Kluwer.

Villalba, U. (2013). *Buen vivir* vs. development: A paradigm shift in the Andes? *Third World Quarterly, 34*(8), 1427–1442.

Vogel, S. K. (2022). Neoliberal ideology and the myth of the self-made entrepreneur. In R. N. Ebehart, M. Lounsbury, & H. E. Aldrich (Eds.), *Entrepreneurialism and society: New theoretical perspectives (Research on Sociology of Organizations*, v. 81), (pp. 77–99). Bingley: Emerald Publishing. doi:10.1108/S0733-558X20220000081005

CHAPTER 4

"MY WELL-BEING IS (NOT) AS IMPORTANT AS YOURS": SELF-SACRIFICE AS FURTHER ECONOMIC MOTIVE IN AMARTYA SEN'S THOUGHT

Valentina Erasmo

ABSTRACT

This paper shows that Amartya Sen admitted self-sacrifice as an opposite motive to self-interest. Between the eighties and the nineties, in his works on development economics, Sen often referred to the conditions of women in less developed countries, because these are areas where gender inequality is more pronounced, and women's well-being is worsened by behavior motivated by self-sacrifice. But these women were affected by a perception bias that made them unable to understand their deprived condition. Perception bias made it harder to improve their freedom and reduce inequality. Sen offered a more complex analysis of economic behavior as compared to his contemporaries. Selfishness and public discussion might be identified as the ideal methods of improving individual well-being when inequality and perception bias leads people to self-sacrifice.

Keywords: Gender inequality; perception bias; self-interest; self-sacrifice; well-being; women

Research in the History of Economic Thought and Methodology: Including a Selection of Papers Presented at the First History of Economics Diversity Caucus Conference
Research in the History of Economic Thought and Methodology, Volume 41B, 67–81
Copyright © 2023 by Valentina Erasmo
ISSN: 0743-4154/doi:10.1108/S0743-41542023000041B004

1. INTRODUCTION

According to Overvold (1980), self-interest and self-sacrifice seem to be two opposite economic motives, but their conceptual borders are nuanced. At first glance, self-interest implies an improvement of individual welfare, while self-sacrifice implies a significant loss in individual welfare. But this loss in individual welfare is not a sufficient condition for determining that a certain behavior has arisen from self-sacrifice.

In the philosophy of welfare, self-sacrifice is generally defined by the following conditions:

> I. the loss of welfare is expected or anticipated [...]; II. the act is voluntary [...] III. There is at least one other alternative open to the agent at the time of the act which is such that (a) if the consequences of the alternative had been as the agent expected them to be, then the alternative would have been more in the agent's self-interest than the act he actually did perform, and (b) if the agent had chosen to perform the alternative act, then his act would have been more in his self-interest, objectively, than the act which he actually did perform. (Overvold, 1980, pp. 113–114)

Given this definition, Overvold argues that it is logically impossible to simultaneously satisfy all these conditions. In particular, he claims that every act that satisfies conditions I and II is in accordance with self-interest (Brandt, 1982), but that, when these two conditions are satisfied, condition III cannot be satisfied too, given a standard and unrestricted preferentist theory of welfare. So, it follows that self-sacrifice is also conceptually impossible. Many scholars agree. Brandt (1982), Carson (2000), Darwall (2002), and Griffin (1986) all conclude that genuine self-sacrifice behavior does not exist at all. Sumner (1996) argues that Sen (1977) foreshadows Overvold in charging the desire theory with "definitional egoism" (Heathwood, 2011). Thus, Sumner includes Sen among the scholars who share the idea that self-sacrifice is conceptually impossible.

Against this view, this paper will show that Sen admitted self-sacrifice as an opposite motive to self-interest. Sen (1983, 1987, 1989, 1990a, 1990b), Dréze and Sen (1989), and Kynch and Sen (1983) analyzed self-sacrifice in their development economics' works written during the eighties and the nineties, not in their criticisms of social choice theory (Sen, 1977, 1985). This might explain the origins of Sumner's misunderstanding. But we should proceed gradually.

In his works on development economics, Sen specifically referred to the conditions of women in less developed countries, because these are areas where gender inequality is more pronounced, and women's well-being is worsened by behavior motivated by self-sacrifice. In this economic analysis, Sen also referred to some anthropological studies about the conditions of women in India (Kapur, 1999). When interviewers asked these women whether they felt deprived, they said "no." Sen argued that these women "didn't understand the question. They were talking about family welfare rather than their own individual welfare" (Kapur, 1999).

Such women identified themselves with their families and self-sacrifice might be considered as their prevailing economic motive, because they were focused on family welfare. However, these women were affected by a perception bias that made them unable to understand their deprived conditions. Sen explored self-sacrifice and its origins in depth, especially through the analysis of gender inequality and the perception bias that affects economic agents' behavior, and which leads them to self-sacrifice. Given this broad exploration, Sen concluded that selfishness and public discussion might be considered among the ideal methods of improving individual well-being when inequality and perception bias lead people to self-sacrifice.

This point is doubly interesting. On one hand, Sen's distinction between self-sacrifice and self-interest contradicts Sumner (1996). On the other hand, Sen advocated selfishness in these rare extreme cases, though self-interest had been the economic motive that he had always criticized in his criticisms of standard rational choice theory and its *homo economicus* assumption (Giovanola, 2009). Thus, the analysis of self-sacrifice showed Sen to be offering a more complex understanding of economic behavior as compared to standard rational choice theory. To see this important point, it is necessary to consider not only Sen's works on rational choice theory of the seventies and eighties, but also his writings on development economics of the eighties and nineties.

The paper proceeds as follows. In Section 2, I explore Sen's understanding of economic motives, especially sympathy and commitment, explaining how they can influence individual privateness. Then, in Section 3, I provide an overview of self-sacrifice as another economic behavior. In Section 4, I introduced gender inequality from a capability approach perspective in order to show the heterogeneity of voices about this issue. In Section 5, I analyze self-sacrifice through its relationship with gender inequality, perception bias, and cooperative conflicts. In Section 6, I show that self-sacrifice can affect personal identity, referring to false consciousness and the weakness of those ties that individuals establish in some intra-household contexts. In Section 7, I argue that Sen suggested self-interest and public discussions to be among the ideal routes against self-sacrifice. In the concluding section, I argue that Sen challenged rational choice theory through his analysis of self-sacrifice and discuss those elements that Sen believed might contribute to a female revolution.

2. AN OVERVIEW OF SEN'S UNDERSTANDING OF ECONOMIC BEHAVIOR

In his works about rational choice theory of the seventies and eighties, Sen (1977, 1985) considered three rational motives in economic decision-making: self-interest, sympathy, and commitment. Commitment and sympathy represented a significant extension as compared to rational choice theory. Broadly speaking, Sen suggested that sympathy, "corresponds to the case in which the concern for others directly affects one's own welfare." Thus, "if the knowledge of torture of others makes you sick, it is a case of sympathy." However, "if it does not make you feel personally worse off, but you think it is wrong and you are ready to do something to stop it, it is a case of commitment" (Sen, 1977, p. 326).

More carefully, sympathy has a psychological and egoistic connotation. Indeed, on one hand, "when a person's sense of well-being is psychologically dependent on someone else's welfare, it is a case of sympathy" (Sen, 1977, p. 328). On the other hand,

> behaviour based on sympathy is in an important sense egoistic, for one is oneself pleased at oth-
> ers' pleasure and pained at others' pain, and the pursuit of one's own utility may thus be helped
> by sympathetic action. (Sen, 1977, p. 326)

Sympathy contributes to a maximization of individual utility, hidden behind apparently unselfish preferences, to improve individual well-being. Thus, Sen believed that sympathy is an intermediate motive between neoclassical self-interest and unselfish altruism.

Commitment is a more complex notion in Sen (1977, 1985). It has ethical and political values. On one hand, commitment is a form of recognition of the injustice underlying certain behaviors. On the other hand, in turn, commitment involves a sense of duty to stop them. But this recognition of injustice and the sense of duty to stop unjust behaviors is not limited to the public sphere, since commitment might also influence behavior in family group contexts. Furthermore, Sen defined commitment "in terms of a person choosing an act that he believes will yield a lower level of personal welfare to him than an alternative that is also available to him" (Sen, 1977, p. 327). According to Sen (1985), contrary to standard rational choice theory, individuals do not lose their rationality even when commitment harms their individual welfare. In addition to the possibility of such harm, commitment makes individuals independent from other persons' welfare. This independence implies that others are not considered as "means" for improving individual welfare.

All these economic motives have significant effects on individual decision-making. Sen (1985) analyzed how economic motives may influence what he defined as "three different kinds of 'privateness' for an agent' preference ordering," such as "self-centered welfare, self-welfare goal and self-goal choice" (Hédoin, 2016, p. 6). Sen (2002) defined these kinds of privateness as follows:

> self-centered welfare: a person's welfare depends only on her own consumption and other
> features of the richness of her life (without any sympathy or antipathy toward others, and
> without any procedural concern). *Self-welfare goal:* a person's only goal is to maximize her
> own welfare. *Self-goal choice:* a person's choices must be based entirely on the pursuit of her
> own goals. (pp. 33–34)

These kinds of privateness are also three aspects of the self that might be mixed in different ways, given that they are independent of each other (Davis, 2007). When self-interested and self-regarding motives are adopted, for example, these three criteria are all satisfied (Hédoin, 2016). Where the individual ignores any public or social dimensions, the behavior equates with the maximum of privateness. In such cases, individuals are totally focused on the maximization of their welfare. In contrast, sympathy violates self-centered welfare because the former refers to how individual welfare is affected by the positions of others. Commitment can violate self-welfare goal and self-goal choice because it considers others' goals or choices in decision-making. Thus, commitment is the only economic motive that erases individual privateness, because it orients individuals toward others.

But commitment also has a reflexive value that leads individuals to self-scrutiny. Davis (2007) defined self-scrutiny as the fourth aspect of the self that refers to individuals' capacity to reflect on themselves and their lives with others. Self-scrutiny is a uniquely human trait. Other creatures are not able to reflect on what they desire to do or desire to be in their lives (Mahieu, 2016). The distinguishing mark of self-scrutiny is reflexivity that enables a virtuous dialogue between the above-named aspects of the self and a proper development of personal identity.[1]

It is important to emphasize that reflexivity is considered irrational in standard rational choice theory, not for the activity itself, but for its effects on individual decision-making. Indeed, when commitment prevails, individuals may accept a worsening of their own welfare. However, when commitment does not prevail in decision-making, there is a breakdown, as compared to a proper development of personal identity caused by a lack of reflexivity (Davis, 2007).

3. SELF-SACRIFICE AS ANOTHER ECONOMIC MOTIVE: AN INTRODUCTION

Sen introduced the notion of self-sacrifice in his writings on development economics. In these works, Sen mostly analyzed the socioeconomic conditions of less developed countries. These realities have always been characterized by poverty, high fertility rates, and social backwardness about basic education (especially, female education), health care systems, and life expectancy (Sen, 1997). In this regard, Sen made pivotal contributions to the early literature about gender bias in South Asia (Klasen & Wink, 2003), exploring questions like the allocation of resources, health outcomes, and nutrition, with significant empirical and theoretical results (Kynch & Sen, 1983; Sen, 1990a; Sen & Sengupta, 1983), the abnormally high sex ratios and their worsening in India,[2] as well as gender biases in mortality and high sex ratios in developing countries (like China, the Middle East, North Africa and South Asia).

In the analysis of less developed countries, for instance, Sen also focused on the conditions of women, because gender inequality is pronounced, and behavior motivated by self-sacrifice worsens their well-being. Self-sacrifice differs from Sen's other economic motives because it is oriented neither to individual welfare, like self-interest and sympathy, nor to collective welfare, like commitment. Rather, self-sacrifice is oriented to family welfare only. In this sense, family welfare can be considered a third dimension in addition to individual and collective welfare. This total focus on family welfare leads individuals (mostly, but not exclusively, women) to degrade their individual well-being, differently from sympathetic and self-interested behaviors, although they do not recognize their deprivations. Furthermore, these deprived people neither participate nor have the authority in public fields to stop injustice, as happens thanks to commitment. On the contrary, they suffer injustice, but they do not have a sense of their personal or social identity, because individuals inspired by self-sacrifice identify themselves with their families only. Thus, family identity become their own identity.

In this respect, Sen claimed that "there was a sense for a while that development was a very hard process, and that people had to sacrifice. There was a lot of blood, sweat, and tears involved," despite "the early, classical writings in development you find that it was always assumed that economic development was a benign process, in the interest of the people" (Kapur, 1999). In less developed countries, development is certainly a bloody process. Over the years, Sen continued, "development is not quite as harsh as it used to be" (Kapur, 1999), but significant problems remained, especially those related to gender inequality. For example, Indian's women are still dreadfully deprived.

Referring to some anthropological studies about the conditions of women in India, Sen emphasized that when interviewers asked them whether they felt deprived, the women answered "no." Directly quoting Sen, a typical rural Indian woman

> would find the question unintelligible, and if she is able to reply, she may answer the question in terms of her reading of the welfare of her family. The idea of personal welfare may itself be unviable in such a context. (Sen, 1987, pp. 6–7)

This answer might be explained through what Sen (1983) and Kynch and Sen (1983) described as "perception bias." But before exploring the relationship between gender inequality and perception bias, as compared to self-sacrifice, a preliminary analysis of gender inequality from a capability approach perspective is required.

4. GENDER INEQUALITY FROM A CAPABILITY APPROACH PERSPECTIVE

Although this paper is not related to Sen's capability approach, we should briefly mention how Sen and other scholars addressed gender inequality from a capability approach perspective. In his recent memoir, Sen (2021) pointed out that he considered "himself as a leftist, given his major commitment to the reduction of poverty and inequalities" (Baujard, 2022, p. 1007), including gender inequality. Among the strengths of the capability approach, there is the acknowledgment of "human diversity, such as race, age, ethnicity, gender, sexuality, and geographical location as well as whether people are handicapped, pregnant, or have caring responsibilities" (Robeyns, 2003, p. 66). Given these premises, Sen (1992) argued that gender inequality might be understood "much better by comparing those things that intrinsically matter (such as functionings and capabilities), rather than just the means [to achieve them]" (p. 125).

This confirms Sen's rejection of John Rawls' focus on primary goods for reducing inequality (Sen, 1980), including those concerning gender. It also shows his will to provide only a "general framework, and not a fully fleshed-out theory" (Robeyns, 2003, p. 62) through his capability approach. Sen did not define the relevant capabilities for assessing inequality, because he was not a capability theorist and his capability approach is mostly of heuristic value for his idea of justice (Baujard & Gilardone, 2017). Some feminist economists concretely applied the capabilities approach to gender inequality, though their arguments differed. Alkire and Black (1997) and Nussbaum (1995, 2000, 2003), for example, elaborated a universal list of capabilities that might also be applied to gender inequality. Robeyns (2003) formulated a specific list of capabilities to estimate gender inequality in Western countries.

This point suggests that not only gender but also geographical context, might influence the capabilities that should be considered as part of an analysis of the achieved capabilities (or freedoms) of women. Robeyns (2003) stressed that Sen endorsed the idea that a "list of capabilities must be context dependent, where the context is both the geographical area to which it applies, and the sort of evaluation that is to be done" (p. 68), although he never elaborated a list of well-defined capabilities. So, geography is considered in some capability approach perspectives, including the specific analysis of gender inequality.

If gender and geographical context can partially (but significantly) explain rising inequality and influence the list of capabilities that enhance the conditions of women, these elements alone cannot explain why individuals, especially women in less developed countries, might adopt economic behavior inspired by self-sacrifice. We should also consider the phenomenon of "perception bias."

5. GENDER INEQUALITY, PERCEPTION BIAS, AND COOPERATIVE CONFLICTS: A PHENOMENOLOGY OF SELF-SACRIFICE

In his analysis of gender inequality, Sen explored the role of basic capabilities in the context of family distribution (Kynch & Sen, 1983; Sen, 1983). In particular, Sen pointed out that not all family members have the same access to basic capabilities, especially in those countries where inequalities also occur in intra-family distribution. However, in many cases, the disadvantage of a certain group (or individual) is not perceived, although this deprivation exists (Gilardone, 2021). This is "perception bias." a phenomenon that might explain why Indian women answered "no" when the interviewers asked if they felt deprived, as previously discussed.

Gilardone (2021) identified three possible causes of perception bias: (i) a "magnification of the needs of the males in general and the head of the household in particular" (Kynch & Sen, 1983, p. 364); (ii) a biased perception of the respective contributions to family prosperity in terms of gender (Dréze & Sen, 1989); (iii) the perception of individual self-interest might be biased by the norms and values of society and (Sen, 1989). Among these causes of perception bias, the first two are those that can potentially lead women to self-sacrifice. They lead women to believe that males' needs are more important because males either are heads of households or contribute more to family prosperity. In order to better describe family economics, Sen (1989) and Drèze and Sen (1989) introduced a new perspective, the so-called "cooperative conflict" (Gilardone, 2021). According to this idea, when mutual gains occur in cooperation elements of conflict can nevertheless arise. Sen (1990a) explored cooperative conflict in his analysis of gender divisions.[3]

It suffices to know that Sen acknowledged a coexistence between cooperation and conflict in gender divisions. In particular, the division "of fruits of joint
activities" may "sometimes [sustain] inequalities in the commodities consumed
in relation to needs (e.g., of food in poorer economies)," while "the nature of the
co-operative arrangements implicitly influences the distributional parameters and
the household's response to conflicts of interests" (Sen, 1987, p. 15). In his broad
analysis of gender and cooperative conflicts, Sen focused on gender divisions
inside and outside the family. In this space, there are ambiguities in the perception
of interests and about what is "deserved" among family members.

According to Sen (1990a), these ambiguities are partially influenced by the
diffusion of social technology that has almost confined women to the domestic
sphere. Thus, social technology legitimizes the established order inside and outside the family (Gilardone, 2008). Although social technology might be one of the
most important causes of this ambiguity, the effect is always the same. Perception
bias principally affects the understanding of the "interests of the others in the
family that apply particularly to women in traditional societies" (Sen, 1987,
p. 24). This misunderstanding, which mostly affects women, leads them to adopt
self-sacrifice in their decision-making. A woman "may get a worse deal in the col-
lusive solution if […] her perceived interest takes little note of […] her own well-
being" (Sen, 1987, p. 24). This neglect of individual well-being is a distinguishing
feature of self-sacrifice.

This analysis of the causes of perception bias is limited to Sen's works and does
not exhaust all the possible cases. We should also consider that, on the one hand,
men might also adopt self-sacrifice as a motivation in their economic behavior.
On the other hand, perception bias is not limited to certain geographical areas,
though it is more common among women in less developed countries.

Regarding men and self-sacrifice, there is a poignant episode recently narrated
by Sen (2021) that undoubtedly should be mentioned. When he was a child, Sen
witnessed a man almost dying from a stab wound in his garden. Kader Mia was a
Muslim man. Despite the dangerous tensions between the communities in India,
he was formally free to stay home or to go and work in the Hindu area. As a
father, his desire to feed his family more than anything else, including his own
security, almost got him killed (Baujard, 2022, p. 1008).

> This example effectively shows that men are also willing to self-sacrifice for the improvement of
> their family's well-being, especially in countries where deprivation is most severe.

6. FROM FALSE CONSCIOUSNESS TO THE WEAKNESS OF WEAK TIES: HOW SELF-SACRIFICE AFFECTS PERSONAL IDENTITY

Perception bias is more than a reason why self-sacrifice is adopted as an economic
motive in decision-making. It mirrors the injustice individuals experience in certain contexts and is also connected to a lack of awareness of their deprivations.
This lack is due to what Marx (1978) would have defined as "false consciousness." According to Sen (2002), false consciousness concerns the "ways in which

injustices persist because of a tendency of 'making allies out of the deprived'" (Sen, 2002, p. 474; quoted in Qizilbash, 2016, p. 1212).

Given this acknowledgment of how false consciousness operates in the deprived, Sen privileged the study of those adaptive strategies that obscure the inequalities deprived individuals experience in society (or in the family). In this sense, it seems like perception bias follows from false consciousness, while perception bias encourages self-sacrificing behavior among the most deprived people. In light of these elements, Sen did not believe that deprived persons freely choose to focus on their family welfare only because of self-sacrifice. In family-centered societies, like India, "the family identity may exert such a strong influence on [their] perceptions that [they] may not find it easy to formulate any clear notion or [their] individual welfare" (Sen, 1987, p. 6). In this way, perception bias does not enable a proper understanding of either their goals, choices, or individual well-being, though they were affected by inequalities due to society and family.

This failure to understand might be explained through another difference between commitment and self-sacrifice, as compared to personal identity. As previously stated, commitment enables a virtuous dialogue between the four constitutive aspects of the self and a proper development of personal identity through an adequate balance between individuality and sociality. Conversely, self-sacrifice produces a self-identification with the family group, causing, in turn, an improper development of personal identity. This improper balance between individuality and sociality is due to that excessive focus on family well-being derived from identifying too closely with one's family.

This self-identification with the family might be further explained by Granovetter's (1973, 1983) notion of dangerous "strong ties." According to Granovetter (1973, 1983), strong ties are those relationships that exist *within* groups, like families, friendships, and romantic relationships. These are the most intense relationships that an individual can establish with others. Conversely, weak ties are those relationships that exist *between groups*. Granovetter emphasized that weak ties are better than strong ties because the former favor the exchange of instrumental resources (which is useful, e.g., in labor markets), while the latter worsen individual vulnerabilities and welfare. These negative consequences derive from cultural, economic, environmental, and social contexts where strong ties usually emerge, for example, in less developed countries (Erasmo, 2020).

According to Granovetter (1973, 1983), the risk of increasing individual vulnerabilities can be avoided through weak ties that enable the creation of bridges between different home communities. In less developed countries, women mostly have strong ties, while weaker ties, like those with the broader society, are totally hindered. Strong ties may become extremely harmful to individual well-being. Identification with the family may cause the disappearance of one's self into the group. When this sacrifice occurs, individuals lose their personal identity because they do not understand themselves either as "individuals" or as "member[s] of a wider, social community." Self-sacrifice has been idealized, idolized, and praised by Indian culture, but this "heroism" does not help these women to improve their well-being, but inhibits their achievement of an acceptable array of basic capabilities.

7. SELF-INTEREST AND PUBLIC DISCUSSION AS THE IDEAL ROUTES AGAINST SELF-SACRIFICE

At the beginning of the nineties, Sen introduced the concept of "missing women," stressing that more than 100 million women were missing from less developed countries (Sen, 1990b), especially China, and countries in southern and western Asia. The ratio of women to men is lower than expected compared to European and North American data. This phenomenon might be explained through gender inequalities concerning the allocation of survival-related goods that hinder women's survival (Erasmo, 2021).

"Gender inequality is not one homogeneous phenomenon, but a collection of disparate and inter-linked problems" (Sen, 2001, p. 466). Among these problems, Sen focused on natal inequality, emphasizing that

> given the preference for boys over girls that characterizes many male-dominated societies, gender inequality can manifest itself in the form of parents' wanting a baby to be a boy rather than a girl. (p. 466)

Given the availability of technical and medical opportunities to discover the gender of a fetus in utero, the awful practice of sex-selective abortion has become popular in many countries. China, India, South Korea, Singapore and Taiwan, are among the countries where sex-selective abortion is most common (Sen, 2001). Sen studied South Asia, the so-called Indian subcontinent. In his empirical analysis of gender inequality, focused principally on inequalities in births and deaths.

This example is representative and suggests the need to recognize that some regions are more affected by gender inequality than others. However, Sen (2001) warned his readers

> against the smugness of thinking that the United States and Western Europe are free from gender bias simply because some of the empirical generalizations that can be made about other regions of the world would not hold in the West. Given the many faces of gender inequality, much depends on which face we look. (p. 469)

But, if we consider inequalities of births and deaths as specific kinds of gender inequality, then these two kinds of gender inequality are more common on the subcontinent than in other areas.

In this regard, Sen (2001) showed that the ratio of females to males in the population under the age of six fell from 94.5 to 92.7 females per 100 males in the decade between 1991 and 2001. This decline in female births was evident especially in Gujarat, Haryana, Maharashtra, and Punjab, but not in Kerala, which represented a notable exception to this trend. This fall in the female birth rate was mostly (but not exclusively) connected to sex-selective abortion. The Indian government banned the use of sex-determination techniques, except when necessary for medical purposes, but the law has unfortunately been frequently violated.

Thus, the issue of missing women is very complex and includes issues regarding both what others do to women and what women do to themselves, having been trained to self-sacrifice by their families. This is not always a conscious decision to self-sacrifice by focusing exclusively on family well-being. So, not only are these women missing, as shown by their higher death rates, but also due to their involuntary complicity, which we have previously connected with perception bias. Self-sacrifice is rarely a conscious decision. In this regard, when families encourage self-sacrifice, other household members are acting self-interestedly and commitment is forgotten, because no one is trying to prevent or mitigate these inequalities.

What are the ideal routes against self-sacrifice to improve individual well-being? It is hard to define how to improve the well-being of both deprived individuals and the societies in which they live. However, Sen suggested two alternatives that might proceed side by side for this purpose: on the one hand, at a macroeconomic level, public discussion; on the other hand, at a microeconomic level, self-interest against self-sacrifice.

In his works on development economics, Sen mostly focused on the analysis of gender inequality, but without entering into details about policies suitable for improving the conditions of deprived people. In more recent writings, Sen (2009) has further elaborated his ideas about inequality and injustice, assigning a more relevant role to public reasoning. Sen (2009) suggested that institutions play a decisive role in enhancing collective capabilities because policies may concretely reduce inequality and poverty, but personal conditions might also be improved by overcoming perception bias and false consciousness. Without the awareness of deprivations, institutions are not capable of improving individual conditions. But this awareness can be reached through public discussion and public reasoning that offers the opportunity to better scrutinize individual conditions.

Public discussion and public reasoning might create conditions to acknowledge the improper relationship that deprived individuals establish with themselves and their societies, focusing on the family group only. Given such acknowledgement, a proper development of personal identity might be realized through an adequate balance between the individual and social dimensions. This proper development of personal identity can contribute to the extension of capabilities that will improve, in turn, individual freedom and well-being. In this regard, Sen (2001) introduced that notion of "women's conscious agency." This consciousness is important for women to overcome perception bias, but this awareness contributes

> to the lives of men as well as women, children as well as adults: [...] the greater empowerment of women tends to reduce child neglect and mortality, to decrease fertility and overcrowding, and more generally to broaden social concern and care. (Sen, 2001, p. 474)

Improving the conditions of women means improving the conditions of the whole society.

In addition to this consciousness, Sen argued that, when self-sacrifice prevails, "this is one of those contexts in which being more self-interested may do the world a lot more good" (Kapur, 1999). Sen suggested that self-interest might be one of the ideal methods of improving individual's conditions, albeit only within those specific contexts, until a more humane condition is achieved through public discussion. Oddly enough, self-interest is the economic motive that Sen had often criticized for its part in the mainstream *homo economicus* assumption of standard rational choice theory (Giovanola, 2009). However, Sen carefully clarified that self-interest is admitted and useful for improving individual well-being only when severe deprivations occur. Indian women are deprived, and self-interest is oriented only toward improving their individual well-being that will enable them to live dignified lives.

8. CONCLUDING REMARKS

This paper has shown how self-sacrifice might be considered a fourth economic motive in Sen's analysis of decision-making. Self-sacrifice differs from self-interest and better represents the diversity of economic behavior. Sen's analysis was developed in the context of development economics that also takes into account, for example, the impact of gender inequality. The consideration about how gender could influence economic behavior was very relevant during the nineties.

By the eighties, rational choice theory had infected disciplines like anthropology, history, political science and sociology as a tool for explaining several forms of collective action, for example, altruism, the growth of organizations, protest behavior, state formation and voting behavior, just to name a few. However, many scholars began to criticize standard rational choice theory principally for its inability to take into account individual heterogeneity. Rational choice theory aimed to be part of a wider universal theory of social phenomena, but its excessive generality ignored the impact of history and geography on socio-economic systems (Hodgson, 2012).

In this respect, economic geographers were divided about standard rational choice theory. For instance, Miller (1992) accepted rational choice theory, while Barnes (1988, 1989), Barnes and Sheppard (1992) and Sayer (1984) refused *homo economicus* and its methodological individualism. This refusal concerned standard rational choice theory's omission of the influence of interactions, place, and space on human behavior. At the same time, these scholars rejected *homo economicus* focus on strategic rationality, according to which collective action is understood through a single economic motive, self-interest.[4] In a nutshell, the standard rational choice theory seemed ineffective as a representation of the real-world complexity of individual behavior, where inequality and poverty often prevail.

In this context, Sen was offering an extension compared to standard rational choice theory that included further motives beyond self-interest, like commitment, sympathy and self-sacrifice. The acknowledgment of self-sacrifice enables a better representation of the diversity of economic behavior. At the same time, this acknowledgement contradicts Sumner (1996) perspective according to which Sen considered all self-sacrifice behaviors as selfish. On the contrary, self-sacrifice is a different motive than self-interest, which, indeed, Sen considered a possible route to overcoming self-sacrifice. Certainly, this advocacy of self-interest represents a significant exception to Sen's analysis of economic behavior in his works on rational choice theory, but it might be useful only to improve women's well-being in less developed countries and dangerous where inequality is less pronounced. So, Sen's analysis of economic decision-making criticizes rational choice theory for its emphasis on maximizing behaviors but also admits exceptions to this criticism, supporting self-interested behavior in well-defined contexts.

How might a "female revolution" concretely develop on the basis of self-interest in opposition to self-sacrifice? Firstly, fertility rates need to be reduced. Sen (1996) advocated improved female education. Higher fertility rates, for example, are common where female literacy and employment rates are lower. Improving female education enables the enhancement of employment opportunities and encourages smaller families. In turn, fertility rates ought to be reduced, given that children are considered a source of economic security (Abrams, 1997). Voluntary birth control might be encouraged (Sen, 1994), pointing out the positive relationship between women's capacity to make decisions about fertility and their own well-being. Given a decline in fertility rates, development might improve women's conditions, as occurred in Kerala, expanding their capabilities thanks to higher employment rates and smaller family sizes. In turn, the gender inequality gap might progressively diminish.

This perspective on the consequences of population growth is partially borrowed by Condorcet (1795): high birth rates lead to a diminution of happiness, because of falling living standards, not only increasing food scarcity, as Malthus (1798) claimed. Conversely, when birth rates fall, the quality of female lives improves thanks to the greater opportunities deriving from improved education, and greater participation in employment and politics. In addition, a decline in the birth rate causes a reduction of death rate, in particular, of children, and an improvement in economic security, especially for elder family members. Finally, lower fertility rates, deriving from higher female literacy rates, could be considered a product of "selfish" behavior, rather than of self-sacrifice, indicating an improvement of female well-being.

ACKNOWLEDGMENT

Previous versions of this paper were presented at the YSI Webinar Session on Heterodox Economics and History of Economic Thought, July 2020, and at the first History of Economic Thought Diversity Caucus Annual Conference, May 2021. I would like to thank the editors, John Bryan Davis, Luis Angel Monroy-Gomez-Franco, Scott Scheall and the two anonymous referees for their valuable comments and suggestions on earlier drafts of this paper.

NOTES

1. Personal identity concerns both individuality and sociality. It refers to "how the person sees himself or herself" (Sen, 1985, p. 348), and also to how persons see themselves with others. In this respect, Sen (2000, 2006) stated that personal identity is also "plural" because it is associated with the different social groups to which an individual belongs, establishing a sense of identity with these groups. Given these group identifications, duties towards members of these groups arise and might be explained through economic behaviour inspired by commitment. An adequate development of personal identity refers to how individuals "are individuated or hold together single beings and how they can be reidentified through change and do not disappear into social aggregates" (Davis, 2010, p. 234). Thus, Sen referred to a conception of individuals balanced between individuality

and sociality when individuals are inspired by commitment. In this sense, individuals have duties towards others, but they do not lose their individuality. On the contrary, this happens when individuals are inspired by self-sacrifice. They feel duties toward others to the point of losing their own individuality.

2. Among the causes of sex-bias, there was mainly, but not exclusively, undernourishment of female children (Sen, 1984), as well as sex selective abortion, as we will better see below.

3. For a complete overview on the determinants of the outcomes of cooperative conflicts, see Gilardone (2021). An extended analysis of gender divisions is beyond the scope of this paper.

4. I will not enter into further details on *homo economicus* assumed rationality because this would go beyond the aim of this paper. I prefer to explore this criticism of rational choice theory as exclusively based on self-interest.

REFERENCES

Abrams, P. (1997). Population control and sustainability: It's the same old song but with a different meaning. *Environmental Law, 27*(4), 1111–1135.
Alkire, S., & Rufus, B. (1997). A practical reasoning theory of development ethics: Furthering the capabilities approach. *Journal of International Development, 9*(2), 263–279.
Barnes, T. (1988). Rationality and relativism in economic geography. *Progress in Human Geography, 4*, 473–496.
Barnes, T. (1989). Place, space, and theories of economic value: Contextualism and essentialism in economic geography. *Transactions of the Institute of British Geographers, 14*, 299–314.
Barnes, T. J., & Sheppard, E. (1992). Is there a place for the rational actor? A geographical critique of the rational choice paradigm. *Economic Geography, 68*, 1–21.
Baujard, A. (2022). Home in the world: A memoir. By "Amartya Sen" book review. *History of Political Economy, 54*(5), 1005–1010.
Baujard, A., & Gilardone, M. (2017). Sen is not a capability theorist. *Journal of Economic Methodology, 24*(1), 1–19.
Brandt, R. B. (1982). Two concept of utility. In H. B. Miller & W. H. Williams (Eds.), *The limits of utilitarianism*. Minneapolis, MN: University of Minnesota Press.
Carson, T. L. (2000). *Value and the good life*. Notre Dame, IN: University of Notre Dame Press.
Condorcet, M. d. (1795). *Esquisse d'un tableau historique des progrès de l'esprit humain*.
Darwall, S. (2002). *Welfare and rational care*. Princeton, NJ: Princeton University Press.
Davis, J. B. (2007). Identity and commitment: Sen's fourth aspect of the self. In F. Peter & H. Berhard (Eds.), *Rationality and commitment* (pp. 313–335). Oxford: Oxford University Press.
Davis, J. B. (2010). *Individuals and identity in economics*. Cambridge: Cambridge University Press.
Drèze, J., & Sen, A. (1989). *Hunger and public action*. Oxford: Clarendon Press.
Erasmo, V. (2020). Oltre le specificità di genere. Cura e diritti nella prospettiva relazionale di Amartya Sen e Martha Nussbaum. *Società Mutamento Politica, 11*(22), 151–161.
Erasmo, V. (2021). *Female economists and philosophers' role in Amartya Sen's thought: His colleagues and his scholars*. Working paper, Female economists and philosophers' role in Amartya Sen's thought: His colleagues and his scholars – Munich Personal RePEc Archive (uni-muenchen.de).
Gilardone, M. (2008). Dobb, Dasgupta et Tagore: Trois sources méconnues de la pensée d'Amartya Sen. *Storia del Pensiero Economico, 2*, 1–25.
Gilardone, M. (2021). The Influence of Sen's applied economics on his non-welfarist approach to justice: Agency at the core of public action for removing injustices. In R. Backhouse, A. Baujard, & T. Nishizawa (Eds.), *Welfare theory, public action, and ethical values. Revisiting the History of Welfare Economics*. Cambridge: Cambridge University Press.
Giovanola, B. (2009). Re-thinking the anthropological and ethical foundation of economics and business: Human richness and capabilities enhancement. *Journal of Business Ethics, 88*, 431–444.
Granovetter, M. S. (1973). The strength of weak ties. *The American Journal of Sociology, 78*(6), 1360–1380.

Granovetter, M. S. (1983). The strength of weak ties. A network theory revisited. *Sociological Theory*, *1*, 201–233.

Griffin, J. (1986). *Well-being*. Oxford: Oxford University Press.

Heathwood, C. (2011). Preferentism and self-sacrifice. *Pacific Philosophical Quarterly*, *92*, 18–38.

Hédoin, C. (2016). Sen's criticism of revealed preference theory and its 'neo-samuelsonian critique': A methodological and theoretical assessment. *Journal of Economic Methodology*, *23*(4), 349–373.

Kapur, A. (1999). Human development: An interview with Amartya Sen. *The Atlantic Online*, December 15.

Klasen, S., & Wink, C. (2003). Missing women: Revisiting the debate. *Feminist economics*, *9*(2/3), 263–299.

Kynch, J., & Sen, A. (1983). Indian women: Well-being and survival. *Cambridge Journal of Economics*, *7*, 363–380.

Mahieu, F. R. (2016). *Une Anthropologie Economique*. Paris: l'Harmattan.

Malthus, T. (1798). *Essays on the principle of population*. London: J. Johnson.

Marx, K. (1978). Letters on historical materialism. In R. Tucker (Ed.), *The Marx-Engels reader*. New York, NY: W.W. Norton.

Miller, B. (1992). Collective action and rational choice: Place, community, and the limits to individual self-interest. *Economic Geography*, *68*(1), 22–42. Rational Choice, Collective Action, Technological Learning (January 1992).

Nussbaum, M. (1995). Human capabilities, female human beings. In M. Nussbaum & J. Glover (Eds.), *Women, culture and development: A study of human capabilities*. Oxford: Clarendon Press.

Nussbaum, M. (2000). *Women and human development. The capabilities approach*. Cambridge: Cambridge University Press.

Nussbaum, M. (2003). Capabilities as fundamental entitlements: Sen and social justice. *Feminist Economics*, *9*(2–3), 33–59.

Overvold, M. C. (1980). Self-interest and the concept of self-sacrifice. *Canadian Journal of Philosophy*, *10*(1), 105–118.

Qizilbash, M. (2016). Capability, objectivity and "false consciousness": On Sen, Marx and J.S. Mill. *International Journal of Social Economics*, *43*(12), 1207–1218.

Robeyns, I. (2003). Sen's capability approach and gender inequality: Selecting relevant capabilities. *Feminist Economics*, *9*(2–3), 61–92.

Sen, A. (1977). Rational fools: A critique of the behavioural foundations of economic theory. *Philosophy & Public Affairs*, *6*(4), 317–344.

Sen, A. (1980). *Equality of what? The Tanner lecture on human values* (vol. 1, pp. 195–220). Cambridge: Cambridge University Press.

Sen, A. (1983). Economics and the family. *Asian Development Review*, *1*(2), 14–26.

Sen, A. (1985). Goals, commitment and identity. *Journal of Law, Economics & Organization*, *1*(2), 341–355.

Sen, A. (1987). *Gender and cooperative conflicts*. World Institute for Development Economics Research, Helsinki, Working paper no. 18.

Sen, A. (1989). Cooperation, inequality, and the family. *Population and Development Review*, *15*, 61–76.

Sen, A. (1990a). Gender and cooperative conflict. In I. Tinker (Ed.), *Persistent inequalities – Women and world development* (pp. 123–149). Oxford: Oxford University Press.

Sen, A. (1990b). More than 100 million women are missing. *The New York Review of Books*.

Sen, A. (1991). The many faces of gender inequality. *The New Republic*, pp. 466–477.

Sen, A. (1992). *Inequality re-examined*. Oxford: Oxford University Press.

Sen, A. (1994). Population: Delusion and reality. *The New York Review of Books*, p. 41.

Sen, A. (1996). Fertility and coercion. *The University of Chicago Law Review*, *63*, pp. 1035–1061.

Sen, A. (1997). Population policy: Authoritanism versus cooperation. *Journal of Population Economics*, *10*, 3–22.

Sen, A. (2000). *Reason before identity*. Oxford, Oxford University Press.

Sen, A. (2002). *Rationality and freedom*. Cambridge, MA: Belknap Press.

Sen, A. (2006). *Identity and violence*. W. W. Norton & Company.

Sen, A. (2021). *Home in the world: A memoir*. London: Allen Lane.

Sen, A., & Sengupta, S. (1983). Malnutrition or rural children and the sex bias. *Economic and Political Weekly*, *18*, 855–864.

Sumner, L. W. (1996). *Welfare, happiness, & ethics*. Oxford: Clarendon Press.

CHAPTER 5

WITCHES AND EXORCISTS: A CASE STUDY OF AN UNDER-STUDIED INFORMAL ECONOMY IN POST-COLONIAL LATIN AMERICA

Cynthia Hawkinson

ABSTRACT

Witchcraft in Honduras is an unprotected marginalized woman's efforts to gain social, economic, and political power through an informal economy by utilizing the cultural belief in the witches' supernatural power. The Honduran postcolonial Latin American culture allows for a persistent informal economy, in part, based on the commoditization of witchcraft and exorcism. The case study provides a specific example through ethnographic interviews of this underresearched informal economy driven by fear and economic desperation. Further research and analysis of these poorly understood and rarely recorded modern phenomena and the associated informal economy is needed.

Keywords: Witches; exorcists; informal economy; Latin American; commoditization of culture; modern phenomena

INTRODUCTION

Hollywood movie makers have successfully employed the topics of witchcraft and exorcisms into a myriad of box office hits, for example, *The Conjuring* (Wan, 2013)

Research in the History of Economic Thought and Methodology: Including a Selection of Papers Presented at the First History of Economics Diversity Caucus Conference
Research in the History of Economic Thought and Methodology, Volume 41B, 83–96
Copyright © 2023 by Cynthia Hawkinson
All rights of reproduction in any form reserved
ISSN: 0743-4154/doi:10.1108/S0743-41542023000041B005

and *The Happening* (Shyamalan, 2008). Modern Western popular culture seems morbidly curious about these phenomena. These curiosities are, however, publicly shunned across Western society as superstitions that only the primitive, naive, or uneducated believe in, and yet, many US citizens privately admit to belief (Barna, 2009). Modern Western popular culture leaves little space for extensive, in-depth public discussion of witchcraft, exorcisms, and the associated informal economy.

> The temptation to dismiss as superstition or mental illness is founded on a logical worldview based on science, evidence, and modernism. However, religion has always existed outside that realm. (Parsons, 2012)

The theoretical framework for this research is based squarely on the important work of Michael T. Taussig (2010) in which he found that among the South American mining and plantation peasantry stories of the devil and spirits of evil had remarkable power to shape their understanding of their lived social and economic realities within the European post-colonial market economy. Peter Geschiere's (1997) work has shown a direct relationship between modern witchcraft and wealth-power structures and the intensely disruptive impact of colonial socio-economic structures in Africa. Like Taussig's South American peasantry and Geschiere's African people, the belief in supernatural phenomena plays a large role in the daily lives and the social-economic-political status of many impoverished Hondurans. The post-colonial Honduran culture allows for a persistent informal economy based, in part, on the oppressive general belief in witchcraft and exorcism, which provides the witch and exorcist some degree of social, economic, and political power.

Designed around a singular demonic possession and exorcism event, this research presents a case study. The case study is limited to one event because such events are not only rare (Cushman, 2019) but in Honduras, they are even more rarely discussed in public or shared with researchers. This study provides a detailed description of a modern Latin American witchcraft-exorcism event, which is an important step in the study of these practices and the associated economic impact. The intent here is to enrich the groundwork for such economic anthropologic studies, plus call for additional work around the informal capitalistic economies and socio-political structures of witchcraft and exorcism in post-colonial Latin America.

METHODS

Because of the tabooed nature of witchcraft and exorcisms, it is difficult to gather significant data and information on these complex phenomena. Thus, the research methods utilized here include a general analysis of the post-colonial Honduran culture, plus an illustrative case study through ethnographic interviews as a specific event example of the phenomena within the Latin American cultural framework. The researcher has spent 10 years developing a trusted friendship with the subject family living with them for extended periods. Within six months of the actual exorcism event, the researcher was privileged to be included in the retelling of their terrifying story and then interview five adult family members for further details. The setting of the storytelling and interviews was their private Honduran home compound where the researcher was housed.

DISCUSSION AND ANALYSIS

Honduras is an amazingly beautiful, mountainous Central American country. However, according to the World Bank (2020), Honduras is a

> low middle-income country that faces major challenges with more than 66 percent of the population living in poverty in 2016, according to official data. In rural areas, approximately one out of five Hondurans live in extreme poverty, or on less than US$1.90 per day.

And though economic growth rates in the 10 years prior to the COVID-19 pandemic were encouraging, the country continues to experience high levels of poverty which has produced "one of the smallest middle classes in Latin America (11 percent in 2015)." Honduras is also plagued with

> high levels of violence, with over 38 homicides per 100,000 inhabitants. Moreover, Honduras is vastly exposed to adverse natural events and climate change, especially heavy rainfall and drought that occur regularly and disproportionately affect the poor. (World Bank, 2020)

Complicating the situation even further, the Honduran national government is considered only weakly democratic because of the government's poor economic effectiveness with a significant degree of corruption (Marshall & Elzinga-Marshall, 2017) producing persistent political instability and social inequity (The Association of Religion Data Archives, 2020). And thus, within Honduras' unstable society, only the most elite citizens enjoy large amounts of social, economic, or political power.

Within Honduras' impoverished society, particularly in the rural areas, witchcraft, and exorcisms exist hand-in-hand, typically only discussed behind closed doors in whispered voices among extended family units. This tabooed cultural attitude differs greatly from that recorded by E. E. Evans-Pritchard (1979) in the overt witch population of central Africa. Honduran witches are secretly blamed for a wide variety of problems, including financial difficulties, crop failure, marital problems, unquenchable love, unexplained illness, alcohol/drug addiction, mental illness, and unexpected death. Hondurans subscribe to Lucy Mair's (1969, p. 222) fear-based statement, "As servants of the devil, witches are believed to be capable of producing all the many types of misfortune that can be assigned to no other cause."

As shown in the written records of witch hunts and witch trails in early modern Europe, witches were typically treated with fear and suspicion and lived on the margins of society.

> Poor women were the weakest and most vulnerable members of society. They were most readily chosen as scapegoats for the ills of society. As individuals in dire financial straits, moreover, they were the persons most likely to resort to selling of magical cures in order to survive or to use sorcery as a means of revenge against those who threatened to deprive them of their already

meager resources. Even if they did not actually practice maleficent magic, they would be the ones most readily suspected by their neighbors of doing so .... Poor people, being dependent upon the community, easily arouse feelings of resentment.

The witch was

responding to social and economic pressures when she cursed her enemies or used sorcery against them, but her neighbors by denouncing the witch and testifying against her [in the witch trials] were being no less responsive to the social conditions in which they lived. (Levack, 1987, pp. 116, 134–135)

Europe's historical understanding and treatment of witches inform the modern Western definition.

Modern Western popular culture interpretation of a witch is

a woman, believing herself a witch, has made a friendly pact with an evil spirit, which enables her to perform strange deeds by means of a variety of objects, words, or formulas ... [Clients] place faith in the power of such women to do good or evil – whenever, of course, she is paid a fee or reward which she expects in return for handing out magic. (de Lys, 1948, pp. 344–346)

In essence, those in modern Western society, including Honduran society, perceive a witch to be like the historic European witch in that she is a marginalized woman using supernatural powers, typically evil, to perform witchcraft. She utilizes her supernatural powers and reputation to gain economic and social power through the economic exchange of the commodity of witchcraft, typically bringing calamity to her intended victims.

The Honduran culture adds another layer to the depth of the modern Western definition of a witch through its machismo culture which provides few women, especially those without a male protector, with civil rights and protection from violence. According to the United Nations Human Rights Council (Manjoo, 2015), 629 women in 2013 (averaging 52 women per month) were murdered in Honduras resulting from domestic violence or organized crime. However, Honduran women who are believed to be witches are uniquely treated with fear-based respect and reverence not offered to the average woman. This respect is offered typically without the witch having graduated from high school, built a successful business, or marrying into a wealthy family. Out of fear and respect, Honduran witches are consulted on local political issues, are asked for their publicly announced approval on events, and are paid generously for their assistance in bringing wealth, marriages, and success. Also, those Hondurans who are truly desperate are sometimes willing to do desperate things, including seeking out these women to invoke the power of demons into the lives of their enemies or rivals. As a result, witchcraft in Honduras is an unprotected marginalized woman's effort to gain social, economic, and political power through an informal economy by utilizing the genuine cultural belief and fear in the witches' supernatural power. The modern Honduran witch, her paying customers, and her victims are attempting to respond to their poor socio-economic conditions within the limits of their socialized expectations.

Since Spanish colonial times, the Catholic Church in Latin America has been at the center of cultural and religious life blending its culture with existing indigenous Mesoamerican cultures, including the Mayan culture in Honduras. And though the Catholic Church in Honduras has lost some of its membership in the past 30 years (down to 43.6 percent in 2015), it still holds a strong cultural position and significant social and political influence (The Association of Religion Data Archives, 2020). "The components of a myth of evil conspiracy lie deep in culture – hard-wired, as it were, to society and self" (Frankfurter, 2006, p. 209), and as a result, the Catholic Church in Latin America plays a large socialization role in the belief in witchcraft, demons, and exorcisms. Childhood socialization in homes, schools, the media, and the Catholic Church encourages the transmission of belief in witchcraft and demons from generation to generation (Adinkrah, 2017). The modern Catholic Church defines witchcraft as the production of "effects beyond the natural powers of men by agencies other than the Divine" through a "diabolical pact or at least an appeal to the intervention of the spirits of evil" (Thurston, 2020). A demon is defined by the modern Catholic Church as an evil spirit or fallen angel (Kent, 2020).

Most Christian churches, including Catholic and Protestant, teach that "Satan and demons are real and a very dangerous threat" (Harris, 2019), and therefore, the negative opinion of witchcraft and the strong belief in demons are not unique to modern rural Honduras, but also includes modern, self-identified Christians in the United States. In a 2009 Barna survey, 55 percent of self-identified US Christians had negative opinions of organized forms of witchcraft, and two out of three believed that "a person can be under the influence of spiritual forces, such as demon or evil spirits." In this case, however, the difference between US citizens and Hondurans is that the Honduran rural poor are, out of desperation, much more willing to tap into the witches' demonic power.

The use of a witch's power to bring a demon into a victim's life, whether real or perceived, may place the victim in grave danger necessitating an exorcism.

> The work of exorcism carries significant [Western] cultural baggage, whether due to misperceptions gleaned from movies or the many real-life cases where possession had been faked or confused with mental illness. (Jackson, 2019)

Hondurans look to the Catholic Church for clarification. Exorcism is defined by the modern Catholic Church as

> the act of driving out or warding off demons or evil spirits from persons, places, or things which are or are believed to be possessed or infested by them or are liable to become victims or instruments of their malice. (Toner, 2020a)

And though in Honduras as of 2015, 43.6 percent of the population were Catholic Christian, 37.1 percent were Protestant Christian, and 6.3 percent were Pentecostal Christian (The Association of Religion Data Archives, 2020), all three religious groups appear to be willing participants in exorcisms (Rio, MacCarthy, & Blanes, 2017).

An exorcism is a specific form of prayer that the Catholic Church uses against the power of the devil based on the recorded ministry of Jesus Christ (United States Conference of Catholic Bishops, 2020 and see Matthew 17:18, Mark 1:34-39, and Luke 4:35 [ESV]). In 2014, the rite of exorcism was formally recognized by the Vatican along with the International Association of Exorcists, a select group of priests trained at the Vatican to preform exorcisms (Brockhaus, 2020; Toner, 2020b). The priests are trained to look for four things in the possessed victim, including

> the ability to speak and understand languages otherwise unknown to the individual, superhuman strength, elevated perception with knowledge about things the person shouldn't otherwise know, and an aversion to anything of a sacred nature such as being blessed with holy water. (Lampert, 2020)

Rituals of exorcism are "rare because cases of demonic possession are rare" (Cushman, 2019). And yet, though exorcisms are rare, they tend to follow an organized prescription. The Catholic major exorcism ritual (also known as "solemn exorcism") includes a specific series of events: (1) readings from Psalms and the Gospel, (2) recitation of the exorcistic prayers, (3) sprinkling of blessed water, (4) laying on of hands, (5) breathing on the victim's face, (6) showing of the Lord's Cross, and (7) making of the Sign of the Cross over the victim (United States Conference of Catholic Bishops, 2020).

When a person believes themselves to be a victim cursed by a witch and possessed by a demon, that person is likely to be willing to pay generously and to pledge loyalty in an effort to be freed from that situation. Within the cultural expectations of a Honduran victims, their only choice is to seek out the assistance of their local religious leader. On a societal level,

> religious centers claim authority for themselves in the landscape not only architecturally – with imposing temples and splendid iconology – but also through appropriating and recasting local beliefs so as to make the temple priests and their rituals indispensable. (Frankfurter, 2006, p. 15)

A priest's or religious leader's

> ability to see the activity of evil behind misfortune, or to articulate anxiety in terms of evil, has a reciprocal effect on that person's authority. Perceiving what others cannot, he becomes an expert in evil, and his clairvoyance becomes essential for people in their anxiety to avert misfortune. In his ability to show the evil system behind inchoate misfortune, he offers his audiences the tangible hope of purging it. And in conjuring a counter realm of demon, witches, or subversives, the expert in evil grows into a heroic, solitary warrior against evil. As he lays out the nomenclature and intentions of the demonic, as he projects order onto incomprehensible current events, he himself gains a preternatural power. (Frankfurter, 2006, p. 32)

And so, if witchcraft is a play for social, economic, and political power by marginalized women and if the priest is indispensable to religious life because he is capable of exorcism, it seems logical that so too might the exorcism of demons by priests be, in part, a play for power. The church-at-large and individual exorcists gain locally recognized social, economic, and political power through providing a heroic resolution to the feared unknown of witchcraft and demonic possession.

Within Honduras, the cultural belief in the supernatural power of witches and exorcists plus the desire for economic gain has set up a somewhat symbiotic, though contentious, relationship between the witch and the exorcist producing a thriving witchcraft-exorcist informal economy. Because of the tabooed nature and the depth of fear involved in witchcraft and exorcisms, it is difficult to measure the pervasiveness and economic value of this unregulated and unmonitored economy. However, it is not difficult to find examples of exorcism-for-sale in the

United States news media. The following examples hint at the potential economic value of the witchcraft-exorcism informal economy in the United States and may imply, at least to some lesser extent, the economic value in Honduras. In January 2020, NBC Boston reported that police had arrested a woman who "faces charges of larceny, intimidation of a witness, and multiple counts of obtaining property over $250 by trick" through telling her palm-reading client that the client's "daughter was possessed by a demon, and she needed the money to relocate the spirit into a Barbie doll" (Klein & Sotnik, 2020). In January 2018, Reuters reported that

> a self-proclaimed psychic was sentenced to 26 months in prison after admitting that she tried to avoid paying taxes on over $3.5 million that she received from an elderly Massachusetts woman seeking to cleanse herself of demons .... The evidence suggested the psychic took advantage of the Martha's Vineyard resident as the woman began to suffer from dementia. (Raymond, 2018)

In May 2011, CBS News reported that US federal prosecutors in Fort Lauderdale, Florida, had arrested three women who were accessed of "scamming thousands of dollars from unsuspecting people looking to cleanse the evil spirits from their lives." The women "falsely represented themselves as having powers to detect and rid the victims of evil spirits through a religious cleansing" (Martinez, 2011).

Though some individuals in the United States are willing to fraudulently practice exorcism for profit, "it should be noted that the vast majority of ministers and priests perform the [exorcism] rite as a public service, free of charge" (Parsons, 2012). The modern Catholic Church insists that exorcism is a "ministry filled with light, peace and joy" (Brockhaus, 2020) and is a special blessings ministry of the "regular pastoral care of souls" through the name of Jesus Christ. This blessing may be extended to anyone, including non-Christians, who are "in sincere desire to be free of demonic influence" (United States Conference of Catholic Bishops, 2020).

The Catholic Church clearly states that the medical and psychological health of a person needs to be determined prior to moving forward with an exorcism (United States Conference of Catholic Bishops, 2020). Psychological and medical illnesses should be handled through medical science, and not through exorcism (Cushman, 2019; Lampert, 2020; Toner, 2020b). Possession by a demon is difficult to determine because "symptoms associated with demonic possession – convulsion, hysteria, erased memories – can look very similar to the symptoms of conditions like epilepsy and schizophrenia" (Cushman, 2019). It is

> not a hard and fast category in which, if a person fits x out of y symptoms, he can be deemed possessed. Rather, it is an extensive triangulation of medical reports, psychiatric reports, along with the paranormal symptoms and religious distress which lay the foundation for suspicion of possession. (Parsons, 2012)

The Catholic Church wishes to "exercise caution when evaluating such individuals for fear of unnecessarily drawing attention to the machinations of the devil or giving credit where no credit is due" (United States Conference of Catholic Bishops, 2020).

The dangers of misdiagnosing mental illness for demonic possession, and vice versa, are real, and the dangers of the rite of exorcism are also real. Physical, mental, and spiritual trauma are possible. In fact, examples of death because of exorcism have occurred over the centuries and even in the past 20 years (Cushman, 2019; Parsons, 2012; Radford, 2013).

> Children and the weak are often in the most danger during a practical exorcism, as the event by its very nature is highly stressful .... The entire concept surrounding exorcism is fraught with high emotion; people are confronted with what they believe is a life-or-death situation. Further, that life or death is not simply physical life or death, but also ownership of the eternal soul. (Parsons, 2012)

The high stakes of exorcism include the physical, mental, and spiritual health of the possessed, but also the social, economic, and political well-being of all those involved, including the witch, the witch's client, the exorcist, the church-at-large, and the victim's family.

Case Study: Ana's Exorcism

Ana lives in her large extended family's compound near Pena Blanca, Honduras. Prior to Ana's demonic attack, an extended battle had raged for economic resources between her brother-in-law, Lorenzo, and Lorenzo's parents. Lorenzo had built a modest, yet modern house for his wife (Ana's sister) and daughters near the family compound, but instead of being pleased that Lorenzo was providing a good life for his young family, his parents demanded that Lorenzo allow them to move into the house and that Lorenzo build a second house for his wife and children. The parents also demanded that Lorenzo pay off their extensive debts. Honduran culture encourages a son to provide for his parents' needs, especially if he has a well-paying job. However, these demands were beyond Lorenzo's economic capacity, so he refused. This battle raged to such a violent level that Lorenzo had his father arrested for attacking and strangling Lorenzo's wife leaving her badly bruised. Lorenzo's father spent two weeks in jail with a stern warning from the local judge that further attacks would produce much longer jail time. Also, Ana's extended family experienced several other tragic events around this time, including the suicide by one of her teenage nephews, a still birth of another nephew, and the murder of her eldest brother.

The family blames Ana's demonic possession and the additional family misfortune, at least in part, to the cursing of Lorenzo's aunt, who is a community-acknowledged witch-for-hire. It is believed that through attacking Ana the aunt was attempting to assist Lorenzo's parents in obtaining their desired housing and financial assistance from their son. This situation differs greatly from that recorded by E. E. Evans-Pritchard (1979) where central African witches specifically do not exercise witchcraft against family members. Of course, it has not been possible to determine the true role, if any, of Lorenzo's witch-aunt in these events. Nor has it been possible to determine if an economic exchange occurred to purchase the witch-aunt's apparent supernatural evil powers. Ana's family, however, adamantly believes that a demon sent by the witch-aunt invaded her body. This was a singular event, having not occurred previously or since. It should be noted that

> a common notation among exorcists is that the possessed individual does not go about all day under attack; rather, these are acute episodes, and after they pass, the individual is able to resume his or her normal life – at least, until the next episode. (Parsons, 2012)

The evening of the demonic attack, Ana, a small-framed, soft-spoken, yet energetic young woman, had finished cleaning up after dinner and she had walked across the courtyard to check on her children when she was struck as though she had been hit in the stomach by a baseball. Ana was found by the family sitting limply on her bed with her eyes closed, respiration calm, and with a peaceful expression, but completely unresponsive. A catatonic-like state is often described in the demonic possessed (Parsons, 2012). Ana's father called her name with the authority of a Honduran father but received no response from her. So, even though it was a difficult 45 minute, dirt road drive to the local emergency hospital, Ana's limp and unresponsive condition was so concerning that she was loaded into a pick-up truck and rushed to the hospital.

That evening, the local doctor was not on duty, so the hospital nurses evaluated Ana's condition and found nothing medically wrong other than she continued to be limp and unresponsive. The nurses called the doctor, and based on their evaluation, the doctor recommended that Ana be taken to a psychiatric hospital an additional hour's drive away. Superficially, there appeared to be nothing medically wrong with Ana, so her condition was deemed to be a mental illness. It is likely that if Ana had been brought to an emergency room in the United States in such a condition without a history of mental illness, she would have received a CT scan for possible neurological abnormality (epilepsy, stroke, brain tumor, Parkinson's disease, or brain swelling/injury), toxicity tests (drug/alcohol overdose or insect/snake bite), plus tests for autoimmune, blood sugar, kidney, and thyroid problems (Miller, 2010; Nall, 2018; Novac, Bota, Witkowski, Lipiz, & Bota, 2014).

The doctor's recommendation increased the family's concern, and so, they knelt at Ana's bedside and began praying for her healing. Within minutes, Ana's eyes opened, but her unseeing eyes began moving rhythmically as did her hands. Lorenzo called his Protestant church elder, and upon arriving at the emergency room, the elder placed his hands over Ana's stomach and began praying. With the church elder's words, a lump the size of a man's fist rose up from Ana's belly, and as he moved his hand over the lump, it moved away from the elder's hand. Ana's eyes rolled back, and she heaved a deep, dreadful laugh. In horror, the church elder declared that Ana was possessed by a demon and that the Protestant church's pastor was needed to exorcise the demon. It should be noted that twitching or rhythmic movements of the victim's hands or face, physical distortions, the rolling of eyes, and altered voice are all commonly known to occur during an exorcism (Coffin, 2013; Cushman, 2019; Lampert, 2020; Parsons, 2012).

All thoughts of medical or psychiatric care for Ana evaporated, and the family loaded Ana back into the truck and drove her to the pastor's home. The church elder explained the situation to the pastor, and Ana was carried into the house where chairs for the family were placed in a semi-circle around Ana. The Catholic Church particularly prescribes the family's presence, or at least one other female, when the victim is a woman (Toner, 2020b; United States Conference of Catholic Bishops, 2020). Ana sat slumped in a chair while the pastor purified and protected himself with prayer and by pouring water over his head. The pastor explained that a mixture of blessed water and blessed salt – holy water – has "a supernatural power of protecting those who use them with faith against all the attacks of the devil" (Toner, 2020a). The pastor also warned the family that Ana might not survive the exorcism because she had a very strong demon. Holy water was given to Ana to drink, and the pastor asked the family to pray. The pastor got down on his knees and began screaming at Ana's stomach for the demon to come out. He screamed for three extended periods of time while Ana also screamed. Ana's family admits that the pastor's screaming would have seemed rather silly and theatrical if they hadn't also had to listen to Ana's painful screams. After the third set of screams, Ana's father feared that the exorcism would not work, so he prayed a father's desperate prayer, "God, I am your vessel poured out as you see fit. Please heal her!" (see 2 Timothy 2:21 [ESV]). Immediately from the small of his back, Ana's father felt energy surge upward hitting the base of his skull, and then flow out his head, chest, and hands toward Ana. He clenched his eyes shut while pure energy flowed out of him into his daughter. When the energy stopped, it stopped instantly, and Ana suddenly woke up and stood up. The pastor pronounced that all that could be done for Ana that evening had been done but that Ana needed to be brought to church the next evening or else Ana's situation could be terminal. Exhausted and afraid, the family drove Ana home.

The following morning, Ana seemed back to normal, even smiling and making eye contact with family members. However, as evening came, Ana became more and more withdrawn. By the time the family arrived at the church, Ana was once again limp and unresponsive. At the sound of the pastor's voice, Ana began convulsing and thrashing about the truck. The family carried Ana inside and laid her on the church floor, while the church pews were moved out of the way and the door was closed and locked – a common exorcism practice (Coffin, 2013). The family was instructed to form a large circle around Ana's limp body and to pray, and the pastor began loudly praying for Ana to get up, and she responded by slowly and stiffly standing up with her head bowed and arms straight to her sides. Suddenly, Ana looked up, and with straight arms to her sides, she ran full speed into the locked church doors. She fell back onto the floor but oddly was uninjured. The pastor carried her back to the center of the family circle and Ana spit up what appeared to be a ball of human hair. The pastor declared the hair ball to be a link between the living and the dead (Walker, 1977) and demanded that the family not touch it. The pastor continued the exorcism by throwing Ana over his shoulder like a sack of potatoes and running around the family circle. Once again, the family has admitted that this seemed to be rather silly and theatrical, but they were afraid to stop the proceedings. Eventually, Ana came to consciousness, and so, the pastor asked Ana who had healed her. In a clear voice, Ana responded with a declaration that Christ Jesus was her healer, Lord, and Savior. The family knelt and prayed thanking God for Ana's healing.

Theatrics aside, this experience was very traumatic for Ana and her family. They are, however, very thankful that Ana now is well and has not experienced such an attack since. Lorenzo acknowledges that he paid cash money to the exorcist pastor for his services, but Lorenzo refused to disclose the exact amount. It is understandable that the family does not wish to anger God, the pastor, or the witch. Fearing the next attack from the witch and her demon, the family remains generous and loyal members of the pastor's church.

CONCLUSION

Ana's terrifying exorcism occurred within the socio-economic-political framework of the post-colonial Honduran culture. In this impoverished culture which carries significant influence from the historic Catholic Church, witches and the exorcism of demons are part of the enduring landscape. Witches and their invoked demons are quietly blamed for a wide variety of unexplained and unexpected problems. Witches are typically impoverished women who do not have the immediate protection of a male family member. And consequently, witchcraft in Honduras is an unprotected marginalized woman's effort to gain social and economic power through genuine fear and cultural beliefs within the population.

The practice of exorcism of demons by priests and pastors appears to also be, at least in part, an effort to also gain economic, social, and political power within this impoverished environment. Religious centers have historically claimed authority for themselves in Latin America through the recasting of local, indigenous beliefs to make church leaders and their rituals appear indispensable to individual spiritual health and public religious life. If the Church has the exclusive authority to exorcise demons, then the church leaders consequentially gain their own power and therefore benefit economically, socially, and politically.

The culturally inherited fear and belief in witches, demons, and exorcists are at the core of the post-colonial Honduran witchcraft-exorcist informal economy. Within this informal economy, money, goods, services, and socio-political power are exchanged through the capitalistic commoditization of witchcraft and exorcisms. Ana's exorcism included a confirmed payment to the exorcist pastor, and her demonic possession may have included payments to a witch-for-hire, though this was not confirmed by the researcher. The witch, whether she gained economically or not, certainly gained social and political power through the secretive retelling of "stories of terror and extremity" (Taussig, 2010).

Additional research has been delayed because of COVID-19 travel restrictions. And though these restrictions have been lifted, the US State Department issued a Level 3: Reconsider Travel Advisory on October 5, 2022, citing violent crime and insufficient police and emergency resources. Once travel restrictions are removed, interviews to further detail the socio-economic power structure present within the local witchcraft-exorcism informal economy are planned. This researcher will attempt to interview religious leaders (particularly those who have participated in an exorcism including Lorenzo's elder and paster), police, judges, governmental officials, medical professionals, businesspeople, educators, community leaders, news reporters, and witches (or at least, those women who are suspected of witchcraft including Lorenzo's aunt), plus follow-up interviews of Ana and her family are planned. It would be useful to determine the degree of influence each actor has on the local witchcraft-exorcism informal economy and what role each individual plays, if any, so that broader conclusions about the socio-political structure can be made.

Like Parsons (2012), this author is not advocating for the truth or the falsehood of witchcraft, demonic possession, or exorcisms. Nor is the author advocating for a specific religious practice or ritual. The author is, however, advocating for research and analysis of these poorly understood and rarely recorded modern phenomena and the associated informal economy. This is particularly important considering the intense belief and the extensive physical, spiritual, and social-economic-political impact such phenomena have on the individuals and societies involved.

REFERENCES

2 Timothy 2:21. (n.d.) *The Holy Bible: English Standard Version*. Retrieved from https://biblia.com/bible/esv/2-timothy/2/21.

Adinkrah, M. (2015). *Witchcraft, witches, and violence in Ghana*. New York, NY: Berghahn Books.

Barna. (2009). Most American Christians do not believe that satan or the holy spirit exists. Barna Research Release in Faith & Christianity. Retrieved from https://www.barna.com/research/most-american-christians-do-not-believe-that-satan-or-the-holy-spirit-exist/. Accessed on April 13, 2009.

Brockhaus, H. (2020). Exorcism is a ministry of joy, light, and peace new guide says. *Catholic News Agency*, July 30. Retrieved from https://www.catholicnewsagency.com/news/exorcism-is-a-ministry-of-joy-light-and-peace-new-guide-says-70338

Coffin, P. (2013). Interview with an exorcist. *Catholic Answers*, May 1. Retrieved from https://www.catholic.com/magazine/print-edition/interview-with-an-exorcist

Cushman, P. (2019). I could see the demons: An exorcism in Arkansas. *ABC7 on Your Side: KATV*, October 29 Retrieved from https://www.katv.com/news/local/i-could-see-the-demons-an-exorcism-in-arkansas

de Lys, C. (1948). *A treasury of American superstitions*. New York, NY: The Philosophical Library.

Evans-Pritchard, E. (1979). *Witchcraft, oracles and magic amount the Azande*. Oxford: Clarendon Paperbacks.

Frankfurter, D. (2006). *Evil incarnate: Rumors of demonic conspiracy and ritual abuse in history*. Princeton, NJ: Princeton University Press.

Geschiere, P. (1997). *The modernity of witchcraft: Politics and the occult in Postcolonial Africa*. Charlottesville, VA: University Press of Virginia.

Harris, E. (2019, August 29). *Jesuit devil debacle draws fire from exorcist across ecumenical lines*. Crux: Taking the catholic pulse. Retrieved from https://www.cruxnow.com/vatican/2019/08/Jesuit-devil-debacle-draws-fire-from-exorcist-across-ecumenical-lines/

Jackson, G. P. (2019). Meet the protestant exorcist: How fighting the devil became an ecumenical pursuit. *Christianity Today*, September 18. Retrieved from https://www.christianitytoday.com/ct/2019/october/exorcism-vatican-training-protestants.html

Kent, W. H. (2020). Demon. *Catholic Answers: Encyclopedia*. Retrieved from https://www.catholic.com/encyclopedia/demon. Accessed on December 19, 2020.

Klein, A., & Kathryn, S. (2020). Mass: Palm reader stole over $70,000 from client in exorcism scheme, police say. *NBC Boston*, January 2. Retrieved from https://www.nbcboston.com/news/local/mass-palm-reader-stole-over-70000-from-client-in-exorcism-scheme-police-say/2056506/

Lampert, V. (2020). Catholic answers focus: The truth about exorcism. Cy Kellett: *Catholic Answers*, October 5. Retrieved from https://www.catholic.com/audio/caf/the-truth-about-exorcism

Levack, B. P. (1987). *The witch hunt in early modern Europe*. New York, NY: Longman.

Luke 4:35. (n.d.) *The Holy Bible: English Standard Version*. Retrieved from https://biblia.com/bible/esv/luke/4/35

Mair, L. (1969). *Witchcraft*. New York, NY: McGraw-Hill Book.

Manjoo, R. (2015). *Report of the special rapporteur on violence against women, its causes, and consequences, addendum: Mission to Honduras*. Global Database on Violence against Women, United Nations General Assembly, Human Rights Council, March 31. Retrieved from https://evaw-global-database.unwomen.org/-/media/files/un%20women/vaw/country%20report/america/honduras/honduras%20srvaw.pdf?vs=3000

Mark 1:34-39. The Holy Bible: English Standard Version. Retrieved from https://biblia.com/bible/esv/mark/1/34-39

Marshall, M. G., & Elzinga-Marshall, G. (2017). *Global report 2017: Conflict, governance, and state fragility*. Vienna, VA: Center for Systemic Peace. Retrieved from https://www.systemicpeace.org/vlibrary/GlobalReport2017.pdf

Martinez, E. (2011). Polly, Bridgette and Olivia Evans arrested in $59,000 Fla. sorcery scam. *CBS News*, May 10. Retrieved from https://www.cbsnews.com/news/polly-bridgette-and-olivia-evans-arrested-in-59000-fla-sorcery-scam/. Accessed on May 10, 2011.

Matthew 17:18. The Holy Bible: English Standard Version. Retrieved fromhttps://biblia.com/bible/esv/matthew/17/18

Miller, M. C. (2010, September). *Ask the doctor: What is catatonia?* Harvard Health Publishing. Harvard Medical School. Retrieved from https://www.health.harvard.edu/newsletter_article/what-is-catatonia

Nall, R. (2018). Catatonic depression: What to know. *Medical News Today Newsletter*, June 18. Retrieved from https://www.medicalnewstoday.com/articles/322199. Accessed on June 18, 2018.

Novac, A. A., Bota, D., Witkowski, J., Lipiz, J., & Bota, R. G. (2014). Special medical conditions associated with catatonia in the internal medicine setting: Hyponatremia-inducing psychosis and subsequent catatonia. *The Permanente Journal*, *18*(3), 78–81. https://www.doi.org/10.7812/TPP/13-143.

Parsons, J. H. (2012). *The manifest darkness: Exorcism and possession in the Christian tradition*. Master's thesis, University of Georgia. Retrieved from https://getd.libs.uga.edu/pdfs/parsons_jamie_h_201205_ma.pdf

Radford, B. (2013). Exorcism: Facts and fiction about demonic possession. *Live Science*, March 7. Retrieved from https://www.livescience.com/27727-exorcism-facts-and-fiction.html

Raymond, N. (2018). Psychic paid $3.5 million for exorcisms gets prison for evading U.S. taxes. *Reuters*, January 17. Retrieved from https://www.reuters.com/article/us-usa-crime-pyschic/psychic-paid-3-5-million-for-exorcisms-gets-prison-for-evading-u-s-taxes-idUSKBN1F633N

Rio, K., MacCarthy, M., & Blanes, R. (2017). *Pentecostalism and witchcraft: Spiritual warfare in Africa and Melanesia*. Open Access: Cham-Palgrave Macmillan.

Shyamalan, M. (2008). Night, Director. *The Happening*. Dune Entertainment, 1 hr., 30 min.

Taussig, M. T. (2010). *The devil and commodity fetishism in South America* (13th ed.). Chapel Hill, NC: University of North Carolina Press.

The Association of Religion Data Archives. (2020). Honduras. Retrieved from https://www.thearda.com/internationalData/countries/Country_105_1.asp. Accessed on December 4, 2020.

Thurston, H. (2020). Witchcraft. *Catholic Answers: Encyclopedia*, December 28. Retrieved from https://www.catholic.com/encyclopedia/witchcraft

Toner, P. J. (2020a). Exorcism. *Catholic answers: Encyclopedia*, December 15. Retrieved from https://www.catholic.com/encyclopedia/exorcism

Toner, P. J. (2020b). Exorcist. *Catholic Answers: Encyclopedia*, December 15. Retrieved from https://www.catholic.com/encyclopedia/exorcist

United States Conference of Catholic Bishops. (2020, December 21). *Exorcism Catholic Answers: Encyclopedia*. Retrieved from https://www.usccb.org/prayer-and-worship/sacraments-and-sacramentals/sacramentals-blessings/exorcism

United States Department of State. (2022, October 5). Honduras international travel information. Retrieved from https://travel.state.gov/content/travel/en/international-travel/International-Travel-Country-Information-Pages/Honduras.html

Walker, B. (1977). *The encyclopedia of the occult, the esoteric, and the supernatural*. New York, NY: Scarborough House.

Wan, J. (2013). Director. *The Conjuring*. New Line Cinema. 1 hr., 52 min.

World Bank. (2020, October 9). The World Bank in Honduras. Retrieved from https://www.worldbank.org/en/country/honduras/

CHAPTER 6

HELEN LAURA SUMNER AND THE WOMAN SUFFRAGE MOVEMENT

Vibha Kapuria-Foreman and Charles R. McCann, Jr.

ABSTRACT

Prior to the passage of the 20th amendment to the US Constitution in 1920, several states had extended the suffrage to women. Helen Laura Sumner (later Woodbury), a student of John R. Commons at Wisconsin, undertook a statistical study of the political, economic, and social impacts of the granting of voting rights to women in the state of Colorado, and subsequently defended the results against numerous attacks. In this paper, we present a brief account of the struggle for women's equality in the extension of the suffrage and examine Sumner's critical analysis of the evidence as to its effects, as well as the counterarguments to which she responded.

Keywords: Helen Sumner; *Equal Suffrage*; woman suffrage; Colorado; Emma Goldman; Richard Barry

JEL classification: B15; B31

INTRODUCTION

The history of the woman suffrage[1] movement in the United States has been the subject of numerous books and essays, serious scholarly studies as well as political polemics, so a detailed presentation is perhaps unnecessary. Briefly, one may begin with the Seneca Falls Conference of 1848, which ended with a Declaration of Sentiments that included calls for greater educational and employment

Research in the History of Economic Thought and Methodology: Including a Selection of Papers Presented at the First History of Economics Diversity Caucus Conference
Research in the History of Economic Thought and Methodology, Volume 41B, 97–117
Copyright © 2023 by Vibha Kapuria-Foreman and Charles R. McCann, Jr.
All rights of reproduction in any form reserved
ISSN: 0743-4154/doi:10.1108/S0743-41542023000041B006

opportunities for women as well as legal protections respecting property rights and the right of contract; in addition, they acknowledged the duty of women to secure the right to vote. Nearly two decades later, following the Civil War, the issue gained momentum. The American Equal Rights Association was founded in 1866, dedicated to securing voting rights for blacks and women. However, given the political environment of the time, such a proposal seemed far too radical; extending the franchise to black men only seemed a more reasonable alternative to universal suffrage, with an extension to women perhaps possible at some later date, when the political climate might be more favorable.[2]

The decision not to pursue an extension of the suffrage to women caused a rift in the suffragist movement between two competing organizations, the National Woman Suffrage Association, founded in 1869 and led by Elizabeth Cady Stanton and Susan B. Anthony, and the American Woman Suffrage Association, also founded in 1869 and led by Lucy Stone, Julia Ward Howe, and Thomas Higginson. The former expressed opposition to the passage of the 15th Amendment to the US Constitution on the ground that it excluded women from the extension of the suffrage, while the latter supported the Amendment in principle while keeping alive the possibility for universal suffrage at some later date. By 1890, the two Associations had overcome their differences and formed the National American Woman Suffrage Association, which would later (1919) become the League of Women Voters.

The issue of woman's suffrage could not be separated from the fight for labor rights and equal rights in general. Achievement of this goal required the full commitment of the legislative, executive, and judicial branches of government at all levels, in conjunction with the resources of religious and community groups, the media, and academia. In academia specifically, the Faculty of the University of Wisconsin at Madison was deeply committed in seeking legislative solutions designed to ameliorate social, political, and economic disparities they associated with what they regarded as unregulated capitalism. Their efforts came to be known as the "Wisconsin idea,"[3] the notion that the mission of institutions of higher learning should be to devise rational solutions to social problems, for the betterment of society.[4] Economists such as Richard T. Ely, John R. Commons, and others in the progressive movement were profoundly committed to the idea and sought to provide expertise to legislators in the crafting of laws and regulations aimed at improving the working of the capitalist market economy and promoting social objectives.

Among those involved in these efforts was a student of Commons, Helen Laura Sumner.[5] Sumner's career exemplified the "Wisconsin idea," the close collaboration of the University of Wisconsin students and faculty with legislatures, and their engagement in direct service to the government as well as organizations devoted to advancing social causes. This active engagement with progressive politics and legislative action was a hallmark of her academic and social work, which included such topics as child labor legislation (Sumner & Hanks, 1915; Sumner & Merritt, 1915; Woodbury, 1922, 1924), the rights of labor (Adams & Sumner, 1905), the place of women in the industrial labor force (Sumner, 1910), and woman suffrage (1909).

This essay will explore one aspect of Sumner's crusading activities, one that has been too often neglected – her investigation of the political and social factors behind the campaign for the establishment of voting rights for women and the impact on society of the extension of the suffrage. Her statistical study of the issue with respect to Colorado was influential in framing the national debate, yet much recent scholarship on the subject of woman suffrage and the women's rights movement, in general, takes little note of her work or her role in the fight for equality.[6] Even respecting her personal biography, the emphasis has typically been on her contributions to the study of labor, industrial concerns, and children's rights, with a brief (if any) mention of her role in extending the suffrage.[7] This is perhaps understandable, given that, by the time of her death in 1933, the suffrage issue had been settled and she had long before moved on to other concerns of more immediate, pressing interest. Still, at the time, few issues were of such paramount importance than the right to participate in the political process, and Sumner was one of the few women who had the academic training and the financial support to approach the subject from the perspective of the social scientist. That her role in this regard has been minimized in both the academic and the popular literature must be acknowledged. This essay is an effort to remedy this oversight and resurrect interest in the work of a pioneer of women's rights.

THE EXTENSION OF THE SUFFRAGE IN THE STATES

The movement for a constitutional amendment granting women the right to vote in 1920 followed the enactment, to varying degrees of inclusion, of woman suffrage legislation in several states decades earlier, the vast majority of the successful efforts being in the West. The New Jersey Constitution of 1776 had in essence granted women the right to vote,[8] the first of the colonies to do so, but this was overturned in 1807, thereafter limiting the franchise to "free, white, male" citizens of the state; Kentucky passed in 1837 a law allowing women the limited right to vote on matters pertaining to Common Schools.[9] Wyoming, while still a territory, enacted legislation in 1869 extending the suffrage. Colorado in 1893, after a protracted battle, became the first *state* to enact such reform and did so with the support of men.

Throughout the mid-nineteenth century and the first decades of the twentieth, the debate on the question of the extension of the franchise to women raged unabated, with the proliferation of polemics disguised as dispassionate studies giving support to arguments on both sides. What was missing was a critical examination of the impact of woman suffrage on the labor market and on efforts at political reform. It was in part from her interest in the study of labor problems that Helen Sumner, who possessed a keen interest in and aptitude for quantitative analysis, undertook a study of the effect of the extension of the suffrage on the women and the general economic conditions of the state of Colorado, and the impact of women voters and office holders on the politics of the state. Sumner's work represents an early attempt to apply economic and statistical analysis to an important social issue.

The Suffrage Question in Colorado

The fight to extend the suffrage in Colorado began as early as 1868 before Colorado entered the Union as a state; these efforts failed to garner much interest among the electorate. In 1870, Edward McCook, governor of the territory, recommended granting the vote to women, citing the passage of a similar measure in Wyoming territory. A proposition calling for a popular vote on the measure was defeated "in the council chamber by a majority of one, and in the house by a two-thirds vote against it," opposition is said to have been "not so much because of antagonism to the women as it was a means of retaliation upon the governor for his course in the matter" (Brown, 1898, pp. 6–7). Similar efforts were made in 1876–1877, but all came to naught; attempts to secure voting rights throughout the 1880s failed as well.

The turning point occurred in 1893, principally through the efforts of the Non-Partisan Equal Suffrage Association of Colorado. The Colorado General Assembly, after an initial failed attempt, on 8 March passed a bill authorizing a vote on the question of the extension of the suffrage (34–27); on April 3, the Senate did so as well, by a vote of 20–10. Governor Davis Hanson Waite signed the bill, placing the question on the November ballot. Section I of the Act (H.B.118) reads as follows:

> That every female person shall be entitled to vote at all elections in the same manner in all respects as male persons are, or shall be entitled to vote by the constitution and laws of this state, and the same qualification as to age, citizenship and the time of residence in the state, county, city, ward and precinct and all other qualifications required by law to entitle male persons to vote, shall be required to entitle female persons to vote. (Brown, 1898, p. 24)

On November 7, 1893, the measure passed by popular vote, primarily due to the support in counties with Populist majorities.[10] As Joseph Brown expresses it,

> The seventh of November was election day, and a day that will long be remembered by Colorado women as the date of their admission to true and full citizenship in their beloved state; for the men, conceding in both just and generous fashion to the wishes of the women, gave a good majority vote in favor of the amendment that was to make Colorado government in very truth a government of the people, for the people and by the people. (Brown, 1898, pp. 22–23)

THE GENESIS OF SUMNER'S EQUAL SUFFRAGE

The extension of the franchise in Colorado had created an ideal environment in which to examine the social, political, and economic effects of granting women the right to vote. In September 1906, Sumner traveled to Colorado under contract with the Collegiate Equal Suffrage League of New York State to investigate the conditions of woman suffrage, the franchise having been extended there little more than a decade before. The investigation was concluded in December 1907, with another six months "needed to sift results, prepare summaries, and formulate conclusions" (Sumner, 1909, p. x). This comprehensive study, which included a wealth of supporting empirical data, resulted in a book, *Equal Suffrage* (1909), which established Sumner as a social activist.

In the Preface to this work, Sumner reports that her contract with the Collegiate Equal Suffrage League of New York required that the investigation be conducted "in an impartial and scientific manner." Its purpose, after all, was to be that

> of assisting toward a rational conclusion those fair-minded, impartial men and women who, without possessing a political theory as a touchstone, wish to determine, in the light of evidence rather than of assertion, whether equal suffrage is a sound and helpful measure under our present political system. (Sumner, 1909, p. ix)

There is no pretense as to questions of natural rights, no desire to justify equal suffrage by resort to the philosophical argument; this study "has no direct bearing upon the abstract right of women to the ballot, but is concerned merely with the political, economic, and social expediency of allowing them to vote" (Sumner, 1909, p. 1). Thus, her stated goal is to determine whether the acquisition by the women of Colorado of the right to vote in 1893 had negative or positive consequences by examining "the good or evil results of equal suffrage in practice" (p. 2).

Sumner acknowledges at the outset the divergence of opinion on the question of woman suffrage, in its political, economic, and social dimensions. Those favoring the reform note the positive impacts throughout society brought about by the emancipation of women, while those opposed insist that, were the franchise to be extended, women would be sullied by their association with politics, and their involvement in the process would adversely affect family life, leading to "divorce, neglect of home and children, and general loss in womanliness."[11] While it may result in better economic opportunities for women – better job opportunities, better pay, a greater role in the governing of the state – the critics were quick to respond that such advances would be at the expense of men, such displacement ultimately resulting in "a weakening of the forces that hold human society together in families, and a strengthening of the forces that make bitter the competitive struggle" (Sumner, 1909, p. 2).[12]

Why Colorado?

There were many available locations within which a study such as this could be undertaken. Colorado was chosen as the test case "in the belief that this state furnishes the best example of the practical working of equal suffrage and the best indication at present obtainable of its probable results if introduced into other communities" (Sumner, 1909, p. 5). In addition, Colorado was possessed of certain "special and peculiar conditions." For one, while there were few large industrial centers (which would bode well for the success of an extension of the voting franchise), there were a substantial number of mining camps (the effect of which on the suffrage question would have been negative). On the whole, however, considering employment in the industrial, mining, and agricultural sectors of the state economy, Sumner finds Colorado to have been not dissimilar to states in the eastern part of the country (pp. 18–19).

Likewise in terms of politics, Colorado "is a typical corporation, machine-politician-ruled state, with the addition, perhaps, of a degree of wild Western recklessness and contempt for law." Politics is controlled to a great extent by corporations – notably "[t]he Smelter Trust, the Colorado Fuel and Iron Company, the railroads, and the public-service corporations of Denver, including the telephone company." Of special significance is the fact that Colorado politics seems not to have developed a sense of "civic righteousness." There seems to have been no real appetite for social, political, or economic reform. The people appear comfortable with the existing state of affairs, as the status quo has led to rapid economic growth and prosperity (Sumner, 1909, pp. 21–22).[13]

Thus, while the suffrage movement greatly benefited from the Populist sentiment at the end of the nineteenth century, that desire for dramatic political and economic reforms had since waned, leaving Colorado in essentially the same position as other states, "an approximately representative community" (Sumner, 1909, p. 22).

THE ECONOMIC ARGUMENT FOR EQUAL SUFFRAGE

While Sumner spends much of *Equal Suffrage* detailing the political climate in Colorado – describing the electoral process, the structure of committees, and even political corruption; examining the statistics of elections, with specific reference to questions of qualifications for voting and holding office; and identifying the status of women in state and local office – what is of interest here is her study of the *economic* aspects of equal suffrage. To this end, she considers two questions respecting the effects of the extension of the franchise on women's employment and wages: (1) "Has equal suffrage brought enlarged opportunities for employment?"; (2) "Has it tended in any way to increase women's wages or to establish for women as compared with men 'equal pay for equal work'?" A third question follows from the second: How much, if any, effect on wages has been the result of the suffrage, and how much is the result of labor unions? To this question, however, she confesses that "it is impossible to distinguish, in private employment at least, the influence exerted by equal suffrage from that exerted by other forces, such as trade-unionism" (Sumner, 1909, p. 150).

Public Sector Employment
In addressing these questions, Sumner considers separately the influence of woman suffrage on private and public employment. In the public sector, the predominant areas of female employment were teaching and clerical work (clerks and stenographers). Of the latter category, the paucity of data makes difficult any definite conclusions as to the impact of the extension of the franchise. Based on the data available, Sumner concludes that, with respect to state, county, and municipal clerical employees, the stated goal of "equal pay for equal work" holds only for very "minutely classified positions." This distinction within otherwise identical positions – which Sumner describes as "overstepping the bounds of a reasonable classification" – allows for rather considerable differences in remuneration between the sexes (Sumner, 1909, p. 155).

With respect to teachers, the data are more plentiful, but the same conclusions can be drawn. While it is true that women and men employed in the same positions receive comparable wages, the fact remains that men tend to be hired for those positions promising higher salaries.[14] Comparing teacher salaries across states, Sumner finds that the average monthly salaries of Colorado teachers exceed those in every state except Massachusetts (for men) and California (for women), but that "the difference in the salaries of men and women teachers in Colorado, instead of being unusually small, is unusually large," attributable, she notes, most likely to the predominance of men in higher positions (Sumner, 1909, p. 157). In this respect, therefore, one may conclude that the passage of equal suffrage had little impact on the economic situation of women in Colorado.

Private Sector Employment
As to private employment, Sumner asserts that no solid conclusion can be reached: "Such a large number of complicated factors enter into changes in wages during periods of time that comparisons of women's wages in Colorado before and since the adoption of equal suffrage are of no value" (Sumner, 1909, p. 164). In respect of the proportion of men's average yearly wages in manufacturing to women's in 1905, Colorado's position *vis-à-vis* 16 other states[15] (chosen as points of reference) is squarely in the middle. Men's wages in Colorado, however, are the highest among these states, and women's wages are second-highest (after Wyoming). In fact, three of the top five states in which women's wages in manufacturing are highest are states with equal suffrage – Wyoming, Colorado, and Utah (pp. 165–166). The meaning of all this, however, is less than clear, for, as Sumner notes, "[w]hether equal suffrage has anything to do with this is a matter of conjecture" (p. 166). It may simply all have been the result of market forces. While she acknowledges that "[t]he natural conclusion from these facts and figures seems to be that in Denver wages in some lines of employment are higher than in many other places," she accepts the judgment of a Denver employer, who suggests that "suffrage had nothing to do with the wages of either men or women. The wages of men and women in all fields of industry are governed by economic conditions" (p. 170).

Trade Unions
Trade unionists, according to Sumner, have been generally favorable toward equal suffrage. But this endorsement has come alongside their endorsement of "the rest of the Socialist platform" (Sumner, 1909, p. 172). Sumner concludes that, in general, women tend to take a greater role in labor union affairs when they are dominant – women-only unions are the most effective in this regard. Compared with the situation in 1892, when no women-only trade unions existed in Colorado, by 1900, "there were two exclusively or primarily women's unions, both in Denver and twenty-five or thirty unions to which women were eligible in eight or ten towns and cities" (p. 176).

Even here, however, Sumner would not credit the suffrage "as a separate factor," as the expansion of women's involvement in the union movement was not "materially" different from the situation in other states in which the franchise had not been extended (Sumner, 1909, p. 178).

The Economic Impact of Equal Suffrage
In the end, Sumner concludes that the economic impact of equal suffrage has been "slight." While there has been an "opening-up to women of a few new avenues of employment, such as political canvassing and elective offices, their employment in somewhat greater numbers as clerks and stenographers in public offices, and the equalizing in most public positions of their salaries with those of men doing the same work," the fact remains that men are still granted the better positions and receive the higher pay (Sumner, 1909, pp. 178–179). In the private arena, though, the advancement has been much greater than in the public sector in terms of employment opportunities for women, although not in regard to pay, where similar disparities remain.

EQUAL SUFFRAGE AND LEGISLATION

Protections of Women and Children
"The first concern of women in the matter of legislation ... is naturally to promote the interests of their own sex and of children" (Sumner, 1909, p. 181). So contends Sumner in discussing the impact of equal suffrage on the legislative process. Thus, legislation respecting the interests of women and children may be cataloged within six classes. In the first, property rights protection, Colorado had prior to the passage of equal suffrage, in many cases even before Colorado had entered the Union as a state, passed legislation granting women "well recognized and protected" rights of property, including rights of contract (pp. 182–183). The only significant changes since the passage of equal suffrage concerned guardianship of children, equality in inheritance following the death of a child, and remedies for failure to provide for the family.

The situation was markedly different in respect of factory legislation, most likely, maintains Sumner, due to the relative lack of a manufacturing base as compared to Eastern states. Thus, the need for legal protection had not become manifest. The exceptions were in the mining sector, where worker protections aimed specifically at women and children had been instituted prior to the extension of the suffrage, and in those businesses deemed corrupting of or dangerous to children (Sumner, 1909, pp. 185–186).

Since the passage of the suffrage, educational reform had become a priority; school attendance of children between the ages of eight and fourteen was made mandatory. In addition, a Juvenile Court system was introduced, thus establishing a separate judicial structure for the disposition of cases involving delinquent children (Sumner, 1909, pp. 188–190). For the protection of girls under the age of 18 years, an age-of-consent law was passed as well and revised in 1907 (p. 193). As to the legal protection of women and children, in 1901 legislation was passed creating the Bureau of Child and Animal Protection. In addition, the Home for

Dependent Children and the Industrial School for Girls were established, and laws enacted regulating private charities (p. 194).

General Reforms and Municipal Regulations
In the area of general reform measures, those endorsed by the Colorado Federation of Women's Clubs included progressive measures such as a pure food law, a school for the blind, the establishment of free employment bureaus, the grading of criminal activity (establishing different degrees of severity) and the setting of degrees of punishment, civil service reforms, the regulation of expense payments for members of boards of control, and an appropriation for a traveling library (Sumner, 1909, p. 202).

As to municipal regulations, the primary interest was in the securing of the general welfare, but the record of success is mixed. Sumner concludes, therefore:

> that the most conspicuous effect of equal suffrage has been upon legislation, and, though it is impossible to prove beyond the possibility of a doubt that the woman's club movement alone would not have brought about the passage of the same laws, it seems probable that the votes of women have effected the desired end with less effort and in less time than would have been required in non-suffrage states. (Sumner, 1909, p. 211)

In large part owing to the passage of equal suffrage, Colorado is somewhat unique in the protection afforded women and children. In Sumner's opinion, "no state has a code of laws better adapted to its immediate need for the protection of women and children." This is not due merely to the activists but is indirectly indicative of the

> influence of the merely voting woman, [who] by materially strengthening the backing of the men who have stood for reform measures in the interest of women and children, has been even more powerful. (Sumner, 1909, p. 212)

OVERALL IMPACT OF EQUAL SUFFRAGE IN COLORADO
Sumner admits that, while the economic impact of extending the franchise had been "slight," still there had been a "considerable" impact with respect to "legislation in the interest of women, children, and dumb animals, and against the free conduct of the liquor business" (Sumner, 1909, p. 214). Having explored the impact of women on the political process, it remained to examine the reciprocal relation, the impact of the suffrage on women. In addressing this issue, she attempts to deal directly and in a preemptive manner with the criticisms that would most assuredly arise, as it appears obvious that "the arguments for woman's enfranchisement as a measure of political expediency are not strong enough to counterbalance any considerable degree of injury to the woman or to the home" (p. 215).

To judge of the effects of the suffrage on women, woman suffrage has undoubtedly resulted in an increase in political participation, "due largely," notes Sumner, "to their increased sense of responsibility in public affairs" (Sumner, 1909, p. 225). Political participation is a means to an end. With the increase in participation came an increase in influence. On the question of the moral character and public spiritedness of women since the extension of the suffrage, the sentiment seems to have been that there was little or no impact, "nor is there any reason," offers Sumner, "why it should have had" (p. 238). While the impact on the moral character of women is inconclusive, Sumner argues that the impact on public spirit and intelligence has been "distinctly good" (p. 240). Women have demonstrated remarkable public spiritedness and shown a great deal of intelligence in their political decision-making. Borrowing a line from Joseph Brown without attribution (asserting it was a statement frequently made), Sumner offers as evidence the increase in sales of books on political economy (p. 243).

Finally, there is the question of the effect of woman suffrage on the home and family. The majority of those surveyed expressed the view that equal suffrage had either a positive effect or none at all; those who felt the effect was negative typically pointed to the "political woman" as the negative influence, not women in general (Sumner, 1909, pp. 244–246). Sumner argues that political work is generally used to supplement family income, as the work is irregular, instead of being viewed as permanent and secure employment. There is, thus,

> a strong economic motive for political service, and if, occasionally, young children are neglected for a few days while the mother is out canvassing a precinct or attending a convention, this is in a measure compensated for by the additional comforts which she is able to furnish them with the money earned. (p. 250)

Additionally, the irregular nature of the work does not lower the wages of men, as it "is scattered through a mixed industrial population, and is done probably as often by the wives of small tradesmen as by the wives of wage-earners" (p. 250).

In sum, then, the extension of the franchise to women appears to have had the greatest impact in the passage of legislation of particular interest to women, such as the temperance laws, age of consent laws, and laws for the protection of working men and women; the most profound impact was therefore on women themselves. Participation in voting led to a broadening of their interests and perspectives,

> enlarged their interests, quickened their civic consciousness, and developed in many cases the ability of a high order which has been of service to the city, the county, and the state. (Sumner, 1909, p. 260)

THE REACTION, EMMA GOLDMAN, AND RICHARD BARRY'S ANTI-SUFFRAGIST ARGUMENT

Helen Sumner's *Equal Suffrage* had, very shortly after its publication, an impact on public policy and public discourse[16] – it was cited in hearings on the subject before the United States Congress[17] and in anti-suffrage writings as well.[18] It was even cited with its statistical evidence in a debate on the subject of woman suffrage in 1914 at Yale University in support of the resolution – "Resolved: That the Women of the United States Should Be Given the Suffrage on Equal Terms with Men." No one in opposition refuted her evidence (Yale University Debating Association, 1914).

The book also received positive reviews on the basis of its author's acknowledged scientific and unbiased approach to the subject (Fenton, 1910; Nearing,

1910; Philips, 1910). Thus, Nellie Marguerite Seeds Nearing opines that the book presents "an impartial record of the effect of equal suffrage in Colorado," concluding that "[t]he investigation as a whole is careful and thoroughly scientific, and it gives a non-partisan yet conclusive sketch of equal suffrage at work" (Nearing, 1910, p. 260). That the results of the investigation would be unsatisfactory to both the anti-suffragist and the suffragists was taken as evidence of its non-partisan approach. Although reviewers highlighted the scientific nature of the study (based as it was on the analysis of survey responses, the study of newspaper accounts, voter registration, and state, county, and city records), there was also criticism of the tenuous basis of some of the book's conclusions. While acknowledging that Sumner's book "is distinctly a non-partisan study in the methods used and in the conclusions drawn from the evidence," Frances Fenton, of the University of Chicago, notes that "one gets the impression that the writer has tried to be perfectly *fair* to the cause of woman's suffrage and in so doing has added an argument or explanation which often does not hold" (Fenton, 1910, p. 845; emphasis in original). In addition, the Introduction betrays a bias in that "Miss Sumner's facts and conclusions are interpreted beforehand for the reader," and thus "a distinctly partisan argument in favor of woman's suffrage is advanced," reflecting poorly "upon an otherwise impartial and valuable study" (p. 846). Lastly, John B. Phillips, of the University of Colorado, offers that

> [s]tudents of political and social science will be gratified by a perusal of this work, as it is the first scientific attempt by a well-trained investigator to ascertain the results of equal suffrage in Colorado. (Phillips, 1910, pp. 306–307)

Emma Goldman's Attack

Opposition to woman suffrage as a general policy came from all quarters, and so cannot be said to have been limited to any particular political or party affiliation. The anarchist Emma Goldman (1869–1940) addressed the issues of women's emancipation and woman suffrage and made special reference to Sumner's work in *Anarchism and Other Essays* (1910). In *The Tragedy of Woman's Emancipation*, originally published in 1906,[19] Goldman first presents her argument against woman's emancipation. In her view,

> Emancipation should make it possible for woman to be human in the truest sense. Everything within her that craves assertion and activity should reach its fullest expression; all artificial barriers should be broken, and the road towards greater freedom cleared of every trace of centuries of submission and slavery. (Goldman, 1910, p. 220)

This she regards as "the original aim of the movement for woman's emancipation," which nonetheless had, instead of being a solution, only "isolated woman and ... robbed her of the fountain springs of that happiness which is so essential to her." It had "made of the modern woman an artificial being," remindful "of the products of French arboriculture, ... anything, except the forms which would be reached by the expression of her own inner qualities." This she suggests is especially so "in the so-called intellectual sphere of our life" (Goldman, 1910, pp. 220–221).

The movement for equal suffrage and emancipation, in general, had not, as promised, "purified our political life," for political corruption is the product of the material society, "the reflex of the business and industrial world" (Goldman, 1910, p. 221). While emancipation had indeed succeeded in producing economic equality between the sexes, women she sees as ill-equipped to compete on an equal footing with men; the woman "is often compelled to exhaust all her energy, use up her vitality, and strain every nerve in order to reach the market value." Independence, which was the promise of emancipation, instead had become "but a slow process of dulling and stifling woman's nature, her love instinct, and her mother instinct" (pp. 222–223).

In "Woman Suffrage" Goldman addresses the issue is greater specificity. Here she argues, in opposition to Sumner:

> Woman's demand for equal suffrage is based largely on the contention that woman must have the equal right in all affairs of society. No one could, possibly, refute that, if suffrage were a right. Alas, for the ignorance of the human mind, which can see a right in an imposition. Or is it not the most brutal imposition for one set of people to make laws that another set is coerced by force to obey? Yet woman clamors for that "golden opportunity" that has wrought so much misery in the world, and robbed man of his integrity and self-reliance; an imposition which has thoroughly corrupted the people, and made them absolute prey in the hands of unscrupulous politicians. (Goldman, 1910, pp. 203–204)

Universal (male) suffrage is a "fetich" that has had "disastrous results" for the "poor, stupid, free American citizen," including the passage of "stringent labor laws prohibiting the right of boycott, of picketing, in fact, of everything, except the right to be robbed of the fruits of his labor." Worse yet, this outcome had little impact on women's desires, for they continue to assert that their entry into the political realm will serve a purifying role (p. 204).

Yet Goldman is not opposed to the extension of the suffrage because she believes women are "not equal to it." On the contrary, she perceives "neither physical, psychological, nor mental reasons why woman should not have the equal right to vote with man." The reality lies with the political system itself (Goldman, 1910, p. 204). It is simply an "absurd notion that woman will accomplish that wherein man has failed" (Goldman, 1910, pp. 204–205).

Goldman did express some agreement with Sumner. *Equal Suffrage*, an "able work," highlighted the evils of the current political system, exposing its "rottenness and degrading character."[20] While Sumner may have focused on "a particular system of voting," it is evident that such a conclusion applies "with equal force to the entire machinery of the representative system" (Goldman, 1910, p. 205).

Goldman did not think woman suffrage could or would accomplish much to improve the condition of those without property or "the thousands of wage workers, who live from hand to mouth," a conclusion she insists Sumner reached as well (Goldman, 1910, p. 207). The empirical evidence, she insists, is clear on this point:

> As to our own States where women vote, and which are constantly being pointed out as examples of marvels, what has been accomplished there through the ballot that women do not to a large extent enjoy in other States; or that they could not achieve through energetic efforts without the ballot? (Goldman, 1910, p. 207)

As Sumner, "an ardent suffragist," had herself admitted, woman suffrage had a slight economic impact. Goldman points to census data showing fifteen thousand defective school children in Denver, despite the fact that "women have had school suffrage for thirty-four years, and equal suffrage since 1894." This is evidence of a failure of woman's suffrage *and* school suffrage. Woman suffrage also failed to bring a sense of justice to labor, as their votes could not protect mine workers against mine owners or prevent the election of "the tool of the mine kings, Governor Peabody, the enemy of labor, the Tsar of Colorado" (Goldman, 1910, pp. 208–209). No advantage to women or to society has sprung from equal suffrage.

Richard Barry's Essay

The journalist Richard Barry (1881–1958), a noted anti-suffragist, presented an argument purporting to demonstrate the negative impact of woman suffrage, but without explicit reference to Sumner's comprehensive study. Barry's essay, "What Women Have Actually Done Where They Vote," published in the *Ladies' Home Journal* in November 1910,[21] professed to be a "personal investigation into the laws, records and results of the four equal suffrage states: Colorado, Idaho, Utah, and Wyoming." As the Editor of the *Journal* attests in his Foreword to the essay,

> Those in favor of 'votes for women' have repeatedly said that if the ballot were given women the following results could be counted upon as inevitable: (1) higher wages and better hours for working-women; (2) great reforms in child-labor laws; (3) a decided decrease in divorce, and better marriage laws; and (4) a positive regulation of the social evil. (Bok, 1910, p. 15)[22]

While the *Journal*'s editorial stance was opposition to the extension of the franchise, the editor nonetheless commissioned Barry to undertake the investigation and to do so in a dispassionate and impartial manner, reviewing state records and state laws and interviewing officials, in an effort to ascertain the credibility of such claims.

In setting the parameters of his investigation, Barry determined to assess the impact of suffrage by examining the fate of legislation relating to child labor, child literacy, child protection, juvenile crime, protective legislation for women, prostitution, divorce, segregated toilets for women on railroads, and the economic conditions of women generally. With regard to child labor legislation, Barry begins by arguing the ineffectiveness of women in the legislative process – two states in which women voted (Wyoming and Utah) had much weaker child labor laws than states in which only men voted.[23] This apparent lack of concern for the welfare of children could not be ascribed to the absence of factories in the mountain west, since Montana (where only men vote) prohibited work by *all* children under the age of 16, whereas Wyoming, Utah, and Idaho (all states with the extended franchise) did not. Furthermore, the 4 suffrage states required no proof of age in employment, whereas 19 states in which women did not have the right to vote required documentary proof of age. Barry further notes that, of seven bills (all introduced by women) affecting the Juvenile Court of Colorado, four that were of great significance "never got out of committee," while three merely procedural bills passed. In contrast, California, Illinois, and Massachusetts, which still had voting restrictions in place, "found no difficulty in passing similar laws." As evidence of the ineffectiveness of women in this regard, he cites the testimony of an "old State Senator," who proclaimed,

> The legislature has nothing against children, ... and if some sensible man had presented those bills and explained their need in simple, forceful language, they would have been passed. (Barry, 1910c, p. 15)

Similarly with legislation limiting hours of work and the security of the earnings of working women. The 8-hour law, for instance, failed in Colorado, while a 10-hour law passed in Illinois; 20 states had passed legislation limiting the hours for women, but not one of the suffrage states had done so (Barry, 1910c, p. 16).

With respect to the subject of juvenile crime in Colorado, Barry finds there has been an "alarming increase" since the extension of the suffrage. In addition, child illiteracy rates were higher, and provisions for destitute children were worse in states in which women were granted the privilege to vote. Similar results were reported in respect of the "social evils," including prostitution, alcoholism, and divorce. Prostitution appeared to be condoned in Denver and Salt Lake City, albeit restricted to certain "segregated" areas, while the "political women" of Denver rallied to overturn regulations on the sale of liquor to women in cafes and restaurants after 8 p.m., on the grounds that such restrictions violated their rights (Barry, 1910c, p. 16).

As to divorce laws in the suffrage states, they "are as lax as anywhere in the Union" (Barry, 1910c, p. 16). As well with marriage laws requiring physical examination before the issuance of a license – none of the suffrage states had to that time passed such laws! Nor had they sought to abolish common-law marriage, while eight states restricting the vote to men had done so (p. 68).

As to the economic situation of women, wage disparities remained as great as before the extension of the franchise, opportunities for advancement have not materialized, and segregation still exists with respect to positions in both the public and private domains (Barry, 1910c, p. 68).

Finally, woman suffrage had not been shown to have led to a purification of politics in those states in which it had been legislated. Bribery was still rampant, with the "political women" the recipient of special-interest largesse, often accepting money to vote against the interests of the average woman constituent. The economic status of women has not risen and politics had remained as coarse and corrupt as before suffrage. Barry concludes by quoting a political manager who argued that women had lost their fineness, "that indefinable something that ought to set her apart" by mingling in politics (Barry, 1910c, p. 69).

A "Refutation"

The charges leveled by Richard Barry were serious, indeed, and brought forth a quick response in the form of a point-by-point refutation. The National American Woman Suffrage Association, in New York, published a pamphlet, *The Truth versus Richard Barry*, which reprinted the text of Barry's article alongside passages from Helen Sumner's *Equal Suffrage* in an effort to correct what they perceived to be Barry's "false, misleading and inaccurate statements in essential matters" (*Truth*, p. 3).[24]

To the question of child-labor legislation – that Montana passed more comprehensive legislation than the states that had extended the suffrage has no bearing on the matter – the laws of Colorado, Wyoming, and Utah are more than adequate to protect both women and children in the dominant occupations in those states. In addition, Utah, a suffrage state, indeed has a proof-of-age requirement, a fact Barry conveniently ignored (*Truth*, pp. 5–6). Further, with respect to the seven bills affecting the Juvenile Court of Colorado, four were introduced by a woman, Alma V. Lafferty, of which three passed, while the others were introduced by men, with only a single success! (p. 6).

As to laws regulating hours of work for women, the 10-hour law in Illinois mentioned by Barry passed only through the efforts of suffragists, and "was finally secured only by the most unremitting care and watchfulness" of their numbers (*Truth*, p. 7). Another point ignored by Barry is a comparison of the comprehensiveness of labor regulations relative to the importance of manufacturing in the suffrage states – the greater the number of women employed in factory work, the more advanced the legal protections (p. 7).

With respect to juvenile crime, the "alarming increase" to which Barry alludes simply does not exist – in fact, the crime rate had *decreased* over the period considered, and the vast majority of reported acts were of a primarily "trivial" nature. The reason for the *apparent* increase is that more accommodations were made to house the children (*Truth*, p. 9). Likewise, Barry's statistics on child illiteracy appear not to have existed, as the Census notes only that "illiterates are found chiefly among foreigners, Chinese and Japanese largely, and among the Indians" (p. 10).

Barry also overstated the case in respect of prostitution and the sale of alcoholic beverages – the legislature of Colorado passed laws directed at curbing prostitution, with the support and encouragement of women voters, and the Denver statute prohibiting women from entering cafes and restaurants in which liquor was served after 8 p.m. had been enacted to benefit a single resort, and was inconsistently enforced (*Truth*, pp. 10–14).

Finally, as to the "purification" of politics, there is overwhelming evidence that the involvement of women in electoral fraud is "infinitesimal," with women voters responsible for defeating the extension of the monopoly previously enjoyed by the water company, on the grounds of both economy and morality and for passing statutes leading to the restriction of the sale of alcoholic beverages (*Truth*, pp. 16–17).

CONCLUSION

Following the publication of *Equal Suffrage*, Helen Sumner received requests from around the country for comments relating to the issue of the suffrage, as well as for political endorsements. Edward Parsons, Dean of the College of Arts and Sciences at Colorado College, inquired, on behalf of "a friend," as to her opinions on a number of questions, including whether the votes of "disreputable women" were important in an election, whether the extension of the franchise improved life in the slums, and whether the women's vote has proven beneficial "to the individual and the state" (Edward Parsons to Helen Sumner, 3 March 1909; MSS 158, Woodbury Papers, Box 1, Folder 13).[25] The debate team of Commercial High School in Brooklyn, New York, requested her opinions on a number of questions, including whether "granting the vote to women is a step toward taking it away from the indifferent and ignorant voters both men and women" (William Fairley, Principal, Commercial High School, to Helen Sumner, 6 December 1915; MSS 158, Woodbury Papers, Box 1, Folder 13). Her response – "I believe the duty of the community is to educate ignorant voters, to enable them to earn a decent living, and to see that they have sufficient leisure to consider public questions, and not to disfranchise them" (Helen Sumner to William Fairley, 30 December 1915; MSS 158, Woodbury Papers, Box 1, Folder 13). The National American Woman Suffrage Association enlisted her support in its political work, requesting she provides "a list of prominent Democrats (men and women) in Colorado" (Lucy Burns to Helen Sumner, 17 July 1913; MSS 158, Woodbury Papers, Box 1, Folder 13). The Congressional Union for Woman Suffrage queried whether she would agree to "be one of a Committee of One Hundred to provide the expenses of maintaining the headquarters of the Congressional Union at Washington for the ensuing year" (Elizabeth Kent to Helen Sumner, 28 December 1914; MSS 158, Woodbury Papers, Box 1, Folder 13). (Unfortunately, no reply is to be found among the papers.)

Sumner's investigation revealed that many of the positive outcomes predicted to flow from the passage of woman suffrage did not come to pass. On the other hand, neither did the dire predictions of the anti-suffragists come true. In the end, the true worth of the study lay in the attempt to analyze social problems in a dispassionate, scientific manner, to collect data, and to present the findings in as objective a manner as possible. Helen Sumner's contribution to *Equal Suffrage* may then be seen as having been of significance in introducing statistical evidence into a discussion that had been up to then almost entirely dominated by emotion. Still, as the study itself was confined to a specific social, political, and economic context, it is perhaps little wonder that it has been neglected, while the focus has instead been on her later efforts at social reform.

As mentioned at the outset, Sumner's interests centered on the advancement of social, economic, and political equality for all, the fulfillment of the promise stated in the Declaration of Independence – that all men are created equal, and "endowed by their Creator with certain unalienable rights." Voting rights, children's rights, and labor rights were all *human* rights. Without the security of the rights guaranteed in that founding document, democracy itself would be imperiled. That the government, the academy, and other institutions might combine resources so as to promote those reforms conducive to the advancement of liberty and the security of those rights essential to the functioning of a truly democratic state was the stated purpose of the Progressive philosophy and the socialist ideals to which Sumner expressed fealty. Her use of the scientific method and statistical analysis would serve to facilitate the move to a more just and equitable social order.

NOTES

1. The term "woman suffrage" was common at the time, and is still accepted, but "women's suffrage" has also gained currency.
2. See Philip S. Foner (1982, pp. 57–58).
3. The name appears to have been coined by Charles McCarthy, political scientist and chief of the Wisconsin Legislative Reference Department, in his book *The Wisconsin Idea*.
4. These solutions often included eugenics measures as a cleansing mechanism.
5. Helen Laura Sumner Woodbury (1876–1933) was born in Sheboygan, Wisconsin, the daughter of George Sumner and Katherine Marsh. In 1881, the family moved to Colorado, first to Durango and later to Denver. She attended Wellesley College in Massachusetts (A. B. 1898); among her professors were such notable intellectual influences as Vida Scudder, Katharine Coman, Emily Greene Balch, and Mary Whiton Calkins, from whom she developed a passion for political and social reform. A member of the Socialist Party and co-founder of the Wisconsin Socialist Club (1902), she later became associated with the Intercollegiate Socialist Society (later, 1921, the League for Industrial Democracy) and in 1910 attended the Copenhagen Conference of the Socialist International. Sumner began graduate study in economics at the University of Wisconsin Madison in February 1902. Having been named by Commons an honorary fellow in political economy (1904–1906), she contributed a chapter to Commons' *Trade Unionism and Labor Problems* (1905), entitled "The Benefit System of the Cigar Makers' Union." In 1908, she earned her Ph.D. from Wisconsin, only the third woman to have earned this degree in the history of that program (Lampman, 1993, p. 305). Her dissertation, "The Labor Movement in America, 1827–1837," became a major part of Commons et al. *History of Labour in the United States* (1918) – revised and renamed "Citizenship (1827–1833)," it constituted Part II of that work. With Thomas Sewell Adams she published a widely-used textbook, *Labor Problems* (1905). As a member of the US Children's Bureau, she published, with Ella Merritt, *Child Labor Legislation in the United States* (1915) and, with Ethel Edna Hanks, *Administration of Child Labor Laws, Part 1, Employment Certificate System Connecticut* (1915). Later, she published *The Working Children of Boston: A Study of Child Labor Under a Modern System of Legal Regulation* (1922) and *Administration of Child Labor Laws, Part 5, Standards Applicable to the Administration of Employment-Certificate Systems* (1924). In 1918, she resigned from the Children's Bureau and married Robert Morse Woodbury; both began work at the Institute of Economics (later to become the Brookings Institution) in Washington, DC, in 1924. Biographical information may be found in Emily Balch (1915), Frederick Olson (1971), Richard Lobdell (2000), and Sandra Opdycke (2000).
6. To mention only two examples: Neither Holly McCammon and Karen Campbell (2001) nor Carolyn Moehling and Melissa Thomasson (2020) mention Sumner's *Equal Suffrage*, nor do they acknowledge her campaign for women's voting rights. Giandomenica Becchio (2020) does, however, acknowledge Sumner's role in the women's rights movement.
7. The headline in her obituary in *The New York Times*, for instance, stated merely that she was a "Labor Expert," "Noted for Industrial Research," and had authored "Several Books" (R. M. Woodbury, 1933, p. 39).
8. Article IV states, "That all Inhabitants of this Colony of full Age, who are worth Fifty Pounds proclamation Money clear Estate in the same, & have resided within the County in which they claim a Vote for twelve Months immediately preceding the Election, shall be entitled to vote for Representatives in Council & Assembly; and also for all other publick Officers that shall be elected by the People of the County at Large" (https://www.nj.gov/state/archives/docconst76.html#page3).

The legislature on February 22, 1797, passed an Act explicitly acknowledging the right of women to vote: Section XI states, "AND BE IT ENACTED, That all free inhabitants of this State, of full age, who are worth fifty pounds, proclamation money, and have resided within the county in which they claim a vote, for twelve12 months immediately preceding the election, shall be entitled to vote for all public officers, which shall be elected by virtue of this act; and no person shall be entitled to vote in any other township or precinct, than that in which he or she doth actually reside at the time of the election" (http://www.njwom-enshistory.org/Period_2/voting.htm).

9. Chapter 898 – An act to establish a system of Common Schools in the State of Kentucky. Section 37 of the Act states: "*Be it further enacted*, That any widow or *feme sole*, over twenty-one years of age, residing and owning property subject to taxation for school purposes, according to the provisions of this act, in any school district, shall have the right to vote in person or by written proxy; ..." (Acts of the General Assembly of the Commonwealth of Kentucky, 1838, p. 282). This was amended in 1902 as it was construed to have applied to "colored women" who were said to support Republican candidates.

10. "In the popular vote, the twenty-five Republican and Democratic counties gave a majority of 471 against, while the thirty-one counties giving Populist pluralities in the election, gave a majority of 6,818 in favor of equal suffrage" (Brown, 1898, p. 24).

11. Mrs Gilbert E. Jones of the National League for the Civic Education of Women in New York City concludes that "The real truth is that woman suffrage is absolutely *futile*, neither good nor bad, but unnecessary. What women accomplish in all other States *without* the votes, that denotes progress, reforms and betterment of conditions for women, children and humanity, is solely attributed to the ballot in the States where women vote. The franchise granted to women, means a doubling of all the evils now existing in manhood suffrage and this cannot mean progress" (Jones, 1910, p. 21; emphasis in original). In rebuttal, Maud (Mrs Frederick) Nathan offers that, with respect to state labor laws, especially the equal pay for equal work laws, "the four states in which women are enfranchised have the best laws for the protection of women and children of any four states in the Union" (Nathan, 1910, p. 35).

12. The opposition to women's suffrage emphasized that women would not vote; that bad women would vote; that women would vote in the same manner as their husbands or fathers and when they did not, this would lead to disharmony; and that association with politics would contaminate women. See *Woman Suffrage Leaflet* published by the American Woman Suffrage Association (1888) and Bradford (1909). Anne Spencer, of the Society for Ethical Culture in New York City, suggests that there are only two arguments that might be employed in opposition: "that women are not human beings," or "that they are a kind of human beings so different from men that general principles of right and wrong proved expedient as a basis of action in the development of men do not apply to them" (Spencer, 1910, p. 11).

13. "The shibboleth of rapid development of natural resources, regardless of future interests, has ruled the history of Colorado as completely as it has ruled the history of other Western commonwealths, and the dominant sentiment, in spite of grumblings, ominous for the future, is probably still honestly friendly to the great corporations which, by exploiting the natural resources, are making the state industrially a 'going concern'" (Sumner, 1909, p. 22).

14. In 1906, among teachers at "graded" schools, men earned 146.4 percent of the salary of women, with the percentage being 120.2 among teachers at "ungraded" schools (Data from Table XIX of Sumner, 1909, p. 156).

15. These states are: California, Georgia, Idaho, Illinois, Kansas, Massachusetts, Minnesota, Nebraska, New York, Ohio, Oregon, Pennsylvania, Tennessee, Utah, Washington, and Wyoming.

16. *Equal Suffrage* is included in Lutie Eugenia Stearns' *List of Books for Girls and Young Women*, Madison: Wisconsin Free Library Commission, 1911.

17. Woman Suffrage, United States House of Representatives, Sixty-First Congress, Hearings Before the Committee on the Judiciary, April 19, 1910; Woman Suffrage, United States Senate, Sixty-Third Congress, First Session, Hearings Before the Committee on Woman Suffrage, April 1913.

18. See, in particular, Goodwin (1912).

19. Originally published in *Mother Earth*, volume 1, issue 1, March 1906, pp. 9–18. *Mother Earth* was a journal published by Goldman.

20. Here Goldman quotes Sumner.

21. Barry published two additional essays on woman suffrage in *Pearson's Magazine* in 1910, "A Political Promise from Women" (1910a) and "Why Women Oppose Woman's Suffrage" (1910b).

22. The editor's note reads: "Mr. Barry spent several weeks in the four States, and although the Ladies' Home Journal is, from policy, opposed to woman suffrage, it stood prepared and ready impartially to print the results of Mr. Barry's investigations no matter which side the investigation favored. What the Ladies' Home Journal wanted was to get at the actual truth from the actual authoritative records of the States. And these, it believes, are presented in Mr. Barry's article" (Bok, 1910, p. 15).

23. "I found that Wyoming and Utah, where women vote, prohibit the employment of children in mines only, while the states of Nebraska, Oregon, New York, Wisconsin, and Illinois, as well as several others, where men only vote, prohibit the working of children under fourteen years of age in twelve specified employments during school hours" (Barry, 1910c, p. 15).

24. It has been suggested that Sumner was the author of the pamphlet, but there is no attribution.

25. She responded by letting him know the book would soon be published and was thanked for her response (Edward Parsons to Helen Sumner, 28 July 1909; MSS 158, Woodbury Papers, Box 1, Folder 13).

REFERENCES

Acts of the General Assembly of the Commonwealth of Kentucky. (1838). *December session 1837.* Frankfort, KY: A. G. Hodges.

Adams, T. S., & Sumner, H. L. (1905). *Labor problems: A text book.* London: Macmillan Co.

Balch, E. G. (1915). The Wellesley who's who. *The Wellesley College News, 24*(11), 7.

Barry, R. (1910a). A political promise from women. *Pearson's Magazine, 23*(2), 143–158.

Barry, R. (1910b). Why women oppose woman's suffrage. *Pearson's Magazine, 23*(3), 319–331.

Barry, R. (1910c). What women have actually done where they vote. *Ladies Home Journal, 15–16*(11), 68–69.

Becchio, G. (2020). *A history of feminist and gender economics.* London: Routledge.

Bok, E. W. (1910). Editor's note. *Ladies Home Journal.*

Bradford, M. C. C. (1909). *Equal suffrage in Colorado from 1893–1908.* Colorado Equal Suffrage Association.

Brown, J. G. (1898). *The history of equal suffrage in Colorado 1868–1898.* Denver, CO: News Job Publishing Co.

Commons, J. R., Phillips, U. B., Gilmore, E. A., Sumner, H. L., & Andrews, J. B. (1910–1911). *A documentary history of American industrial society.* Cleveland: A. H. Clark Company.

Commons, J. R. Saposs, D. J., Sumner, H. L., Mittelman, E. B., Hoagland, H. E., Andrews, J. B., Perlman, S. (1918). *History of labour in the United States.* New York, NY: Macmillan.

Dorfman, J. (1959). *The economic mind in American civilization* (Vols. 4 and 5, pp. 1918–1933). New York, NY: The Viking Press.

Fenton, F. (1910). Review of equal suffrage. *American Journal of Sociology, 15*(6), 843–846.

Foner, P. S. (1982). *Women and the American labor movement: From the first trade unions to the present* (2nd ed.). New York, NY: Free Press.

Foxcroft, F. (1904). The check to woman suffrage in the United States. *Nineteenth Century and After, 56*(333), 833–841.

Goldman, E. (1910). *Anarchism and other essays.* New York, NY: Mother Earth Publishing Association.

Goodwin, G. D. (1912). *Anti-suffrage: Ten good reasons.* New York, NY: Duffield and Co.

Helen Sumner Woodbury Papers. Box 1, Folder 13. Madison, WI: Wisconsin Historical Society.

Jones, G. E. (1910). The position of the anti-suffragists. Significance of the woman suffrage movement: Session of the American Academy of Political and Social Science, February 9, 1910. Supplement to *The Annals of the American Academy of Political and Social Science*, May 1910 (pp. 16–22). Philadelphia, PA: American Academy of Political and Social Science.

Lampman, R. J. (Ed.). (1993). *Economists at Wisconsin, 1892–1992*. Madison, WI: University of Wisconsin.

Library of Congress. (1893). *H.B.118: An act 'to submit to the qualified electors of the state the question of extending' the right of suffrage to women of lawful age, and otherwise qualified, according to the Provisions of Article Seven, Sec.2, of the Constitution of Colorado*. Laws Passed at the Ninth Session of the General Assembly of the State of Colorado, Chapter 83 (pp. 256–258). Retrieved from http://memory.loc.gov/cgi-bin/ampage?collId=awh_llmisc&fileName=awh/awh0001/awh0001page.db&recNum=0&itemLink=S?ammem/awhbib:@FIELD%28SUBJ+@od1%28+women+suffrage++colorado+%29%29

Lobdell, R. A. (2000). Helen Laura Sumner Woodbury. In R. W. Dimand, M. A. Dimand, & E. Forget (Eds.), *A biographical dictionary of women economists*. Northampton, MA: Edward Elgar.

McCammon, H. J., & Campbell, K. E. (2001). Winning the vote in the west: The political successes of the women's suffrage movements, 1866–1919. *Gender and Society, 15*(1), 55–82.

McCarthy, C. (1912). *The Wisconsin idea*. New York, NY: Macmillan Co.

Moehling, C. M., & Thomasson, M. A. (2020). Votes for women: An economic perspective on women's enfranchisement. *Journal of Economic Perspectives, 34*(2), 3–23.

"Mrs. R. M. Woodbury, Labor Expert, Dead; Noted for Industrial Research, She was the Author of Several Books," *New York Times*, March 12, 1933, Section F, 39.

Nathan, M. (Mrs. Frederick). (1910). Woman suffrage—An aid to social reform. *Significance of the Woman Suffrage Movement: Session of the American Academy of Political and Social Science, February 9, 1910*. Supplement to *Annals of the American Academy of Political and Social Science*, May 1910 (pp. 33–35). Philadelphia, PA: American Academy of Political and Social Science.

Nearing, N. M. (1910). Review of equal suffrage. *Annals of the American Academy of Political and Social Science, 35*(2), 259–260.

Olson, F. I. (1971). Woodbury: Helen Laura Sumner. In E. T. James, J. W. James, & P. S. Boyer (Eds.), *Notable American women, 1607–1950* (Vol. III: P-Z). Cambridge, MA: Harvard University Press.

Opdycke, S. (2000). Sumner, Helen. *American National Biography online*. Accessed on May 13, 2012. https://www.anb.org/view/10.1093/anb/9780198606697.001.0001/anb-9780198606697-e-1500770

Phillips, J. B. (1910). Review of equal suffrage. *The Economic Bulletin, 3*(3), 306–308.

Rutherford, M. (2006). "Wisconsin institutionalism: John R. Commons and his Students. *Labor History, 47*(2), 161–188.

Rutherford, M. (2011). *The institutionalist movement in American economics, 1918–1947*. Cambridge, MA: Cambridge University Press.

Spencer, A. G. (1910). The logical basis of woman suffrage. *Significance of the Woman Suffrage Movement: Session of the American Academy of Political and Social Science, February 9, 1910*. Supplement to *Annals of the American Academy of Political and Social Science, May 1910* (pp. 10–15). Philadelphia, PA: American Academy of Political and Social Science.

Stearns, L. E. (1911). *List of books for girls and young women*. Madison, WI: Wisconsin Free Library Commission.

Sumner, H. L. (1905). The benefit system of the Cigar makers' union. In J. R. Commons (Ed.), *Trade unionism and labor problems*. Boston, MA: Ginn and Company.

Sumner, H. L. (1909). *Equal suffrage*. New York, NY: Harper and Brothers.

Sumner, H. L. (1910). The historical development of women's work in the United States. *Proceedings of the Academy of Political Science, 1*(1), 11–26. (Republished in 1971, *30*(3), 101–113).

Sumner, H. L., & Hanks, E. E. (1915). *Administration of child labor laws, Part 1, Employment Certificate System Connecticut*. U. S. Department of Labor Children's Bureau Publication No. 12. Washington, DC: Government Printing Office.

Sumner, H. L., & Merritt, E. A. (1915). *Child Labor Legislation in the United States*. U. S. Department of Labor Children's Bureau Publication No. 10. Washington, DC: Government Printing Office.

Truth versus Richard Barry, The. (1910). New York, NY: National American Woman Suffrage Association.

Wellesley Magazine. (1896, November 21). *College notes, 5*(2), 111.

Woman Suffrage Leaflet. Vol. I, no. 3 (September 1, 1888) and vol. III, no. 6 (May 1, 1890). Springs, CO: American Woman Suffrage Association, Colorado College Special Collections.

Woodbury, H. L. S. (1922). *The working children of Boston: A study of child labor under a modern system of legal regulation.* US Department of Labor Children's Bureau Publication No. 89. Government Printing Office, Washington, DC.

Woodbury, H. L. S. (1924). *Administration of child labor laws, Part 5: Standards applicable to the administration of employment-certificate systems.* U. S. Department of Labor Children's Bureau Publication No. 133. Government Printing Office, Washington, DC.

Yale University Debating Association. *Handbook No. 1: A discussion of woman suffrage by the Yale University debating teams, in the 1914 triangular debates with Harvard and Princeton.* New Haven, CT: Yale Co-operative Corporation.

CHAPTER 7

GRASSROOTS FEMINIST ECONOMIC THOUGHT: A RECONSTRUCTION FROM THE WORKING-CLASS WOMEN'S LIBERATION MOVEMENT IN 1970s BRITAIN

Toru Yamamori

ABSTRACT

Can we broaden the boundaries of the history of economic thought to include positionalities articulated by grassroots movements? Following Keynes's famous remark from General Theory that 'practical men [...] are usually the slaves of some defunct economist,' we might be wont to dismiss such a push from below. While it is sometimes true that grassroots movements channel pre-existing economic thought, I wish to argue that grassroots economic thought can also precede developments subsequently elaborated by economists. This paper considers such a case: by women at the intersection of the women's liberation movement and the claimants' unions movement in 1970s Britain. Oral historical and archival work on these working-class women and on achievements such as their succeeding to establish unconditional basic income as an official demand of the British Women's Liberation Movement forms the springboard for my reconstruction of the grassroots feminist economic thought underpinning the women's basic income demand. I hope to demonstrate, firstly, how

Research in the History of Economic Thought and Methodology: Including a Selection of Papers Presented at the First History of Economics Diversity Caucus Conference
Research in the History of Economic Thought and Methodology, Volume 41B, 119–146
Copyright © 2023 by Toru Yamamori
ISSN: 0743-4154/doi:10.1108/S0743-41542023000041B007

this was a prefiguration of ideas later developed by feminist economists and philosophers; secondly, how unique it was for its time and a consequence of the intersectionality of class, gender, race, and disiability. Thirdly, I should like to suggest that bringing into the fold this particular grassroots feminist economic thought on basic income would widen the mainstream understanding and historiography of the idea of basic income. Lastly, I hope to make the point that, within the history of economic thought, grassroots economic thought ought to be heeded far more than it currently is.

Keywords: Basic income; feminist thought; intersectionality; social movements; welfare rights; women's liberation

1. INTRODUCTION

The history of economic thought, as a discipline, has concentrated on the thoughts of professional economists. Recently, there have been some admirable efforts to broaden the scope of whose thoughts should be considered as appropriate to the discipline. *Economics in the Public Sphere* is one such project by Tiago Mata (forthcoming) in which the authors shift their focus from academic output to economic journalism. Another endeavour has been the shifting of the focus away from male economists, recent examples of which have been the publications of *History of Women's Economic Thought* by Kirsten Madden et al. (Madden & Dimand, 2018) and of *A Herstory of Economics* by Edith Kuiper (Kuiper, 2022). Encouraged by these attempts, here I wish to broaden the discipline's boundaries even further by suggesting that we ought to also be considering in earnest economic thought articulated by grassroots movements.

One might dismiss such a move by following Keynes' famous remark that 'practical men [*sic.*] […] are usually the slaves of some defunct economist' (Keynes, 1936). While it is sometimes true that grassroots movements channel preexisting economic thought, I wish to argue the case for grassroots economic thought at times preceding ideas and concepts only subsequently developed by economists or academics from other disciplines. The case study presented in this paper is one at the intersection of the Women's Liberation Movement (WLM) and the Claimants Union movement.

I have previously conducted extensive oral historical research on women who organised the Claimants Union movement and joined the WLM in the long 1970s Britain. These women, alongside also men, articulated the concept of what now we know as basic income, drawing on a broader concept of a guaranteed income a decade before academics did the same. At a National WLM Conference, they made the feminist case for basic income and succeeded in passing a resolution to make basic income an official demand of the British WLM. While my previous paper dealt in detail with historiographical particulars (Yamamori, 2014), here I would like to reconstruct the grassroots feminist economic thought that underpins the women's basic income demand. In this paper, I hope to demonstrate, firstly, that their grassroots economic thought prefigured ideas, some of which were subsequently developed by feminist economists and philosophers (as well as other ideas that have yet to gain traction in academia); secondly, how their grassroots economic thought was unique at that time and a product of the inter-sectionality of class, gender, race, and dis/ability; thirdly, that including this grass-roots feminist economic thought on basic income would widen (if not change) the mainstream understanding and historiography of the idea of basic income. Thus finally, I wish to suggest, grassroots economic thought ought to be properly acknowledged within the history of economic thought.

In the upcoming section, I will briefly try to outline the dominant historiogra-phy of basic income. Then I will hazard to pinpoint the historical moment when basic income became a demand of the British WLM, situating this moment in a wider historical context. In order to do all this, I will start by giving a brief overview of the British WLM – focusing on its national conferences and on the demands discussed at these as well as on the activism and economic thought of the women at the intersection of the British WLM and the Claimants Union movement of the long 1970s, particularly with a view to the economic demands they made. Then I will try to show how reclaiming one of these forgotten demands could be a conduit to diversifying feminist economics. My eventual wish in this undertaking would be to try and resurrect this erased demand and the thought behind it – as 'grassroots feminist economic thought'. Finally, I will offer my comments as to how this could also enrich the history of economic thought on basic income.

2. THE DOMINANT DISCOURSE AND HISTORIOGRAPHY OF BASIC INCOME

In 1986, academics (and activists) gathered in Louvain-la-Neuve to discuss basic income. They came to an agreement establishing the foundation of the Basic Income European Network (BIEN). In 1988, the network saw its statute written and in it basic income is described as *an income unconditionally granted to all on an individual basis, without means test or work requirement* (BIEN, 1988). In a sem-inal book *Arguing for Basic Income* (van Parijs, 1992), Belgian analytical political philosopher Philippe van Parijs, who was a major driving force in the foundation of the BIEN, defined basic income using the exact same wording as the BIEN. The foundation of the BIEN in 1986 is widely recognised as the beginning of the 'modern' debate on basic income. Walter van Trier, a Belgian economist who was secretary of the BIEN at its early stage, wrote:

> If the present phase in the history of basic income needs to be given a starting date, an obvious event to mark it would be the formation of the Basic Income European Network in September 1986 as a result of the First International Conference on Basic Income, held at the Université Catholique de Louvain-la-Neuve. The conference not only inaugurated the first real 'reflexive' phase in the history of the concept, but it also consolidated the use of the name 'basic income' for this category of proposals. (van Trier, 2002)

What might be making this 'present phase' different from previous phases in history?

Firstly, it is during this phase that basic income was given a clear academic definition following a consensus that came out from communal efforts, not from individual advocates. It was all done by placing 'unconditionality' at the centre of the concept. The BIEN's primary focus on unconditionality made it possible to distinguish such a conception of basic income from the broader concept that had circulated widely at that time under various names – be it 'basic income', 'minimum income' or 'guaranteed income'. One of the earliest steps in this direction in academic literature is namely the canonical paper by Philippe van Parijs and Robert J. van der Veen (1986).[1]

Secondly, this relative consensus on a clear definition has occasioned the subsequent numerous attempts to produce the definitive history of basic income. Some in academia have tackled the task by trying to spot ideas in history which could be counted as falling within this definition of basic income. van Trier wrote a monograph on the history of economic thought of basic income (van Trier, 1995). It focused on the debate in inter-war period Britain, when famous economists like G. D. H. Cole and James E. Meade played a pivotal role with their advocation of a 'social dividend', which van Trier identifies it as being in essence basic income.[2] van Trier also shed light on the work of advocates who were not economists, such as Denis Milner, C. H. Douglas, and Juliet Rhys-Williams. Milner was a Quaker social reformist who proposed 'the state bonus scheme' in 1918, which again van Trier identified as basic income. Douglas was the originator of the Social Credit Movement, which advocated for a 'national dividend' as a major component of its new economic system in the 1920s – a 'national dividend', which, again, van Trier retrospectively identified as basic income.[3] Rhy-Williams was a British politician, starting in the Liberal camp, then becoming a Conservative, who in 1943 advocated 'the same benefit to all of its citizens' against William Beveridge's famous report for the blueprint of the welfare state. van Trier provides an intricate explication of whether and how the concepts of economists such as Cole and Meade were influenced by these non-economist intellectuals.

Another Belgian economist, Guido Erreygers, and a British political philosopher, John Cunliffe, edited an anthology titled *The Origins of Universal Grants: An Anthology of Historical Writings on Basic Capital and Basic Income* (Cunliffe & Erreygers, 2004). Cunliffe and Erreygers dated back the history of basic income to Thomas Spence's *The Rights of Infants* (1797) and included Belgian Fourierist Joseph Charlier's proposal of 1848, which, in my inference, could qualify as one of the possible candidates of the Fourierist proposal testified to in John Stuart Mill's second edition of *Principles of Political Economy* (Mill, 1849). What Cunliffe and Erreygers then chose from the twentieth century nearly overlaps with the choices made by van Trier (1995). These early attempts set the historiographic paradigm for basic income – resting on the names of theorists (philosophers, economists, policy experts) and their proposals and all recent literature on the history of basic income has inserted itself within this paradigm (Torry, 2021; van Parijs & Vanderborght, 2017).

In the following section, I will venture the introduction of a novel historical moment which had not appeared in the hitherto dominant discourse and history of basic income. I will then try to show how taking this forgotten moment seriously could contribute to diversifying the history of economic thought on basic income.

3. A FORGOTTEN HISTORICAL MOMENT: BASIC INCOME BECOMES A DEMAND OF THE BRITISH WLM

A Sunday afternoon – the 3rd of April, 1977. It was a rather chilly day as far as spring days go in London, but inside the hall of the City of London Polytechnic, it was warm; not just because the hall was packed full of people, but also because of their enthusiasm. Thousands of women across the UK gathered for the ninth National WLM Conference.

The conference began on Saturday, 2nd April, with numerous workshops and social events, and was already approaching its finale, the plenary session, when a resolution was raised proposing the right to what we now know as 'basic income' – an adequate income paid to every person without any conditions. The resolution was passed with a majority vote. Basic income was one of the democratically and officially endorsed demands of the British WLM. But unfortunately, this fact has become steeped in collective amnesia. An amnesia that may have started at the very moment of the resolution's passing.

Spare Rib magazine, the British women's liberation periodical reported the resolution passed, but in a lopsided way.[4] The report lacked vital information, such as who raised the resolution, what exactly the proposed income scheme was, and why it was raised as a demand. Instead, *Spare Rib* reported who opposed it and why. I have provided elsewhere a supplementary account of this unreported side of the information and have stressed the contemporary, global resonance of this demand (Yamamori, 2014). The demand was raised by women in the Claimants Union movement and in the sections that follow I would like to situate this demand in a wider historical context, by interweaving an overview of the British WLM with one of the Claimants Union movement, and then by investigating how a feminist demand emerged out of the interaction between the female claimants' everyday experiences with the preceding economic thought/institutions.

4. A SHORT HISTORICAL OVERVIEW OF THE BRITISH WLM AND ITS DEMANDS[5]

In the early spring of 1970, hundreds of women gathered for 'women's weekend' at Ruskin College in Oxford. This gathering eventually became the first National WLM Conference and is widely considered and described as 'the beginning of a movement' for Women's Liberation in the UK (Condon, 1990). As is the case with many other grassroots movements, it is very difficult to pick one event and designate it as 'the beginning'.[6] Here I am simply following the dominant feminist historiography, which has tended to give a relative importance to the National WLM conferences running from 1970 to 1978, and to the demands approved there.[7]

Around half a year later, the existence of these women's liberationists became known to the wider general public during the Miss World Contest held in Royal Albert Hall. As millions were watching it on TV in their sitting rooms at home, it was suddenly disrupted by flour bombs and voices shouting: 'We're not beautiful, we're not ugly, we're angry!' (Finch, Fortune, Grant, Robinson, & Wilson, 2020).

Another half a year later, the first women's liberation demonstration in London happened (International Women's Day march on the 6th of March 1971).[8] On the posters announcing the demonstration and on the banners and placards during the march itself, there appeared the famous four demands of the WLM – namely:

1. Equal pay.
2. Equal educational and job opportunities.
3. Free contraception and abortion on demand.
4. Free 24-hour nurseries.

These four demands emerged around 1970–1971 and were formally approved at the second conference in Skegness in October 1971 (Rowbotham, 2010).[9]

1972 was the only year when two national conferences were held: the Third National Conference in Manchester, in March, and the Fourth National Conference in London, in November. At the former, Selma James (and the 'wages for housework' campaign which she led) asked to replace the four demands with a programme that consisted of six demands. It was the demand for 'wages for housework' that was at the centre of James' programme and also prompted intense discussions. While James's proposal was rejected at the conference, it was the beginning of a long discussion on this issue, both theoretical and practical.

Selma James was born in the United States, and became a left-wing activist in her teenage years. She moved to London during the mid-1950s and settled down after living in Trinidad for several years around 1960. In June 1971, she met in London Mariarosa Dalla Costa, an Italian radical left-wing activist. This led to two developments: one theoretical and the other political. James and Dalla Costa cowrote a seminal work titled '*The Power of Women and the Subversion of the Community*', which was published in 1972. Together with several other radical left-wing feminists, they formed the International Feminist Collective, which then gave birth to the International Wages for Housework Campaign. This campaign spread to several countries, including Canada, France, Italy, the UK, and the USA.[10] Everywhere, the campaign and its demand for 'wages for housework' succeeded to garner attention among feminists. This brought the so-called 'domestic labour' debate, which had been initiated by several intellectual endeavours in the 1960s (Such as Mitchell, 1966), into wider public discussions. James's intervention at the second National WLM Conference mentioned above, was followed by heated discussions in many corners of the British WLM scene. The Marxist feminist magazine *Red Rag*, founded in 1972, published papers on this issue (Bazin, 2021).

The Fifth National Conference took place in Bristol in March of 1973. The Sixth National Conference was then hosted by Edinburgh in July 1974 and the following two demands were approved:

5. Legal and financial independence for all women.
6. The right to self-defined sexuality. An end to discrimination against lesbians.

There was 'a very antagonistic debate' over the first part of the sixth demand – the right to self-defined sexuality (Delmar, 2010). The fifth demand appears not to have caused such a stir yet the precise meaning of that demand remains a point of contention. In order to actualise this demand, groups were set up: like the Women's Liberation Campaign for Legal and Financial Independence (the so-called 'the Fifth Demand group') and the Rights of Women.[11] The former was founded by Mary McIntosh and other women who raised this fifth demand, in order to address 'tax, benefit and pension policies that treated husband and wife as a breadwinner-dependent couple with no need of separate incomes' (McIntosh, 2001, p. 147).[12] Their focus seems to have been on 'legal' rather than on 'financial' independence. Some even dropped the word 'financial' from their poster of WLM demands.[13]

The Seventh National Conference was held in Manchester in March 1975 and the Sex Discrimination Act received a Royal Assent in November 1975. The Eighth National Conference was held in Newcastle upon Tyne in 1976. The Ninth was in London in 1977, where, as mentioned in Section 2, the demand for basic income was passed. At the Tenth National Conference, in Birmingham in April 1978, the following demand was added:

7. Freedom for all women from intimidation by the threat or use of violence or sexual coercion regardless of marital status; and an end to the laws, assumptions and institutions which perpetuate male dominance and aggression to women.

In the course of eight years of National WLM Conferences, the movement grew significantly and the conferences functioned as a venue for socialising, discussions, and peer-empowerment. 'The most fantastic day of my life' – this was a voice of an attendee at the Ninth Conference, which was on the front cover of issue 58 of *Spare Rib*. On the other hand, the enthusiasm of sisterhood that marked the earlier years gradually ceded to the recognition of differences within the movement. A women's liberation group that attended the Eighth Conference reported 'very real splits' on sexual orientation, class divide, political divide and so on (Ross & Bearse, 1996). The Tenth Conference eventually came to be the last conference, as it 'ended in chaos and no-one dared organise another one after such an experience' (Binard, 2017, p. 7).

5. A FEMINIST BASIC INCOME OUT OF THE CLAIMANTS UNION MOVEMENT

In almost all of the existing literature on the British WLM, it is hard to find the name of Claimants Unions as an intellectually viable subject contributing to the WLM's demands. However, if we were to look at archival materials and oral historical testimonies, we are going to notice plentiful intersections between the WLM and the Claimants Union movement, and we are also going to witness, verily, feminist economic thought emerging from this intersection.

A Claimants Union was first formed in Birmingham in late 1968 by claimants of means-tested benefits. The union afforded membership to claimants and ex-claimants. Many other such unions were formed spontaneously, which led to the formation of the National Federation of Claimants Unions (NFCU) in March 1970. The demand for 'the right to an adequate income without any means test' had been on the banner of the Birmingham Claimants Union from the beginning.[14] It then transmogrified into the first of fourth components of 'the claimants charter' of the NFCU, as decided upon at its first national conference.[15]

To the Oxford 'Women's Weekend', the Birmingham Claimants Union sent a delegate with a statement, in which it was argued that '[t]he claimants struggle is a struggle for women's rights', and three demands for 'economic emancipation' were laid out (Birmingham Claimants Union, 1970b). The first was 'Personal Allowances', that is, 'a demand to be free from obligation to work for capitalists', whereupon it was also mentioned that '[w]omen have been making this demand for years'.[16] The second demand, the delegate made was 'Universal Welfare', which was meant to refer to social services such as creches 'as of right'. The third demand was one for an increase in Family Allowances. Family Allowances were introduced in 1945 and were paid to a mother who took care of two or more children.

We have no record of whether these demands for 'economic emancipation' by the Birmingham Claimants Union were discussed during the first National WLM Conference. While the Birmingham Claimants Union's demand for 'Universal Welfare' (such as the provision of creches) resonated with the WLM's fourth demand, the Claimants Union's other two demands had no counterparts in WLM's 'four demands'.

Where did the Birmingham Claimants Union's demand for 'the right to adequate income without means test' come from? The idea of 'the right to an adequate income' itself was not new. For them, it seemed to come from – as it were – 'the spirit of "45"'.[17] The Birmingham Claimants Union frequently referred to the principles of the welfare state and the Beverage report that was a blueprint for the former.[18] What was new is the latter part of the demand, namely – the addition 'without any means test'. Their idea of doing away with the means test came from their everyday experiences of claiming benefits. The criteria for eligibility for these benefits were not shared with the claimants. The latter perceived the decisions as discretionary, which made them feel humiliated and disgraced. The most notorious among various aspects of means testing was the so-called 'cohabitation rule'. Obviously, if one would like to make means-tested benefit fair, one would need to identify the boundary of the unit of 'household' sharing the financial resources and responsibilities. At the time in the UK, a married couple and its minor dependent(s) were considered to be one such unit, and the 'cohabitation rule' was the rule, when claiming benefits, to treat a cohabitating couple just as one would a legally married couple. Combining this written rule with the unwritten yet prevailing 'morality' and sexism, meant that female claimants were effectively being spied upon as to the nature of their personal relationships, and even a neighbour's kind visit (say, to repair a kitchen pipe) resulted in discontinuation of the benefits.[19] The Birmingham Claimants Union tried to bring the problem of means-testing and its nefarious consequences to the attention of the wider public. A Claimants Union pamphlet soliciting the solidarity of labor, trade unions, and cooperative organisations stated: 'Treatment of claimants can be scandalous: perhaps seen at its worst in the harassment of unsupported mothers, who are being continually spied on to see if they are being supported' (Birmingham Claimants Union, 1970a).

At the second national conference of the NFCU in the summer of 1970, there was a lengthy discussion on what was meant by 'the right to an adequate income without any means test'.[20] At this stage, there were diverging opinions on the matter. The core members of the Birmingham Claimants Union took their opposition to means testing seriously and logically so that their vision of this right was an adequate income that is unconditional and individual (④ in Fig. 1). If we were to abolish means-testing, while still having a fair income transfer, there would be no other way.[21] Some thought that this purist version would not be practically achievable. Their understanding of this right thus tended to accommodate the idea that only people who not having access to wages, such as single mothers, unemployed, sick, and disabled people would have non-means tested (or less-means tested) benefits (③ in Fig. 1). This understanding corresponded with concepts circulating in the media under several names such as 'basic income', 'minimum income' or 'guaranteed income'.[22]

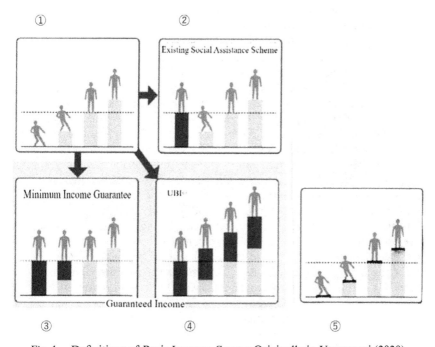

Fig. 1. Definitions of Basic Income. *Source*: Originally in Yamamori (2020). Slightly modified by the author.

In early 1972, the NFCU decided to have a national campaign for 'Guaranteed Adequate Income'. The demand was thought to be a good one, with which claimants could be in solidarity with the trade union movement and the WLM. Some women in the NFCU went to the Third National WLM Conference held in March 1972 in Manchester, where Selma James proposed the 'wages for housework'. Women in the NFCU saw that there was the danger of trapping women at home through this demand, while their own demand for Guaranteed Adequate Income remained free from this danger on account of its unconditionality, as these women understood their version of guaranteed income as ④ in Fig. 1 (Author(s) Anonymous, 1972). The campaign no doubt contributed to facilitating the discussion (at least inside the NFCU) about 'Guaranteed Adequate Income' and helped clarify the term. A clear distinction was made between ③ and ④ in Fig. 1 during this campaign.[23] However, in light of their organisational goal of establishing solidarity with the trade unions movement and the WLM under the banner of 'Guaranteed Adequate Income', this campaign utterly failed.

With this recognition of failure, the NFCU decided to have a campaign on the more concrete issue behind their demand for Guaranteed Adequate Income. The national campaign against the 'cohabitation rule' was held in August 1972.[24] Monica Sjöö, who was active in the Bristol Claimants Union, explained that Guaranteed Adequate Income is the reason 'why the Claimants' Union nationally decided to have a campaign against cohabitation ruling' (Sjöö, 1972). According to Sjöö, this struggle against the cohabitation rule was vital not only for single mothers, who were directly affected by this rule but also for married women, because this ruling was a part of the system making women dependent on men – meaning – this struggle was a step for 'every woman's right to an independent income whether she is married or not' (Sjöö, 1972).

This time they succeeded in attracting more attention from the WLM, as compared to the campaign for basic income or other issues the Claimants Union movement had campaigned for.[25] *Spare Rib* reported on their campaign and used a photo of the claimants protesting in front of the headquarters of the Department for Health and Social Security. The same photo was then used to create the poster for the International Women's Day demonstration in London the following year. The image of militant female claimants became one of the representative images of the WLM.[26]

Mary McIntosh of the Fifth Demand group recalled that '[t]he Anti-Cohabitation [rule] Campaign was quite big' and the group 'had a lot of liaison with the Anti-Cohabitation Campaign which was focused on the cohabitation rule assessment for benefits'. Also, Julia Mainwaring, who was a founding member of the Birmingham Claimants Union and later raised the motion for basic income at the national WLM conference, would attend from time to time the meetings of the fifth demand group.[27]

The Fifth Demand group started in 1974, but let's turn the clock back to 1972 again. In October, the Conservative government published 'the Green Paper on Proposals for a Tax-Credit system'. This was a proposal for tax-rationalisation based on the idea of Negative Income Tax.[28] Thus in a sense, it was a slight step forward to a guaranteed income. In this proposal, family allowances, which are paid out to mothers, would be replaced by refundable tax credits – paid to the head of the household: almost exclusively a man. Immediately after the government's announcement, the campaign to defend family allowances was prepared and soon enough launched – at the start of 1973. Women in the Claimants Union movement and the 'wages for housework' campaign were at the centre of this campaign. On the day of the International Women's Day march, in Mach 1973, they occupied a post office in London as a symbolic act of the campaign.[29]

Family allowances were, for many stay-at-home working-class mothers, the only income of their own at that time. Unlike means-tested benefits, family allowances were reliable, in the sense that women could be sure that money was coming, every Tuesday. Julia Mainwaring recalls that this universal and guaranteed income for mothers was an inspiration for their articulation of basic income. As we've already shown, the Birmingham Claimants Union advocated 'personal allowances', which combined with the increase in family allowances would probably come to constitute a kind of basic income. It is reasonable to believe that the founding members of the Birmingham Claimants Union, including Mainwaring, had realised this from the very beginning (1968–1970), but this campaign for defending family allowances in 1973 made it easier for the women joining the campaign to arrive at the selfsame or similar articulations of the concept. The fact that this government's proposal was not actualised and the succeeding Labor government introduced a universal child benefit (which mothers could get as soon as their first child was born and which in a sense could be said to be an expanded version of the family allowances) gave from 1975 onwards a more consolidated material basis, from which women could imagine basic income as a reasonable demand.

As shown in the previous section, the Sex Discrimination Act received a Royal Assent in November 1975. While it tried to prohibit sex discrimination in education or the workplace, it did not cover the realm of social security, which led claimant's women disappointed and incensed. Their response against the government' neglect of sex discrimination in social security was to demand a Guaranteed Minimum Income, which is an individual and unconditional income. Women in the Claimants Union movement published a leaflet titled 'Women and Social Security'. This was primarily a practical guide for women (either single, single mother, or married) on how to claim the benefit, but contains also the invitation to think together as to why women have been subjected to harassment and dependence. It pointed out sexism in the social security system and reasoned that this sexism was necessary for maintaining the capitalist order and the structure of the nuclear family – one based on the gendered division of labour. Their strategic and pragmatic stance against sexism and its causes was the demand for Guaranteed Minimum Income (FCU, 1987; NFCU, 1975, 1977): 'A minimum income, paid at an adequate level, to every individual member of society', 'individually based', 'automatic payments ... without a means-test' and 'guaranteed for people in and out of employment' (FCU, 1983).

According to testimonies by Julia Mainwaring and Jane Downey who was active in East London Claimants Union, claimant's women raised the motion asking the British WLM to endorse the demand of Guaranteed Minimum Income prior to the 1977 National WLM Conference (quite plausibly at the 1976 National WLM Conference in Newcastle). It was passed but then erased by the chair of the plenary session (Yamamori, 2014).[30] Women claimants came back to the National WLM Conference to raise the same motion again, and once again the motion passed – with the crucial difference that this time it was recorded, as we have seen in Section 3.

6. DIVERSIFYING FEMINIST ECONOMICS

It has been more than two decades since both feminist economists and other feminist scholars started arguing for or against basic income.[31] In 2021, during the pandemic, the *International Association for Feminist Economics* did, in fact, call for basic income.[32] However, the fact that basic income had been formulated as a demand of the British WLM in the 1970s has been entirely ignored in feminist academia. It had been completely ignored at least up until my previous paper (Yamamori, 2014), and I am sad to report that not much has changed since.

This is perplexing on several counts. First of all, feminist economics and other feminist disciplines, generally speaking, have tried to emphasise women's experiences ordinarily dismissed by male-oriented academia. Then how could feminist arguments on basic income manage to ignore the women who articulated and demanded basic income?

Second, it has been widely recognised that the WLM in the long 1970s – a.k.a. 'second-wave feminism' has had relevance to the birth of feminist economics. For example, Giandomenica Becchio has recently stated that one of the two phenomena connected to '[t]he genesis of feminist economics' was 'the introduction of women's studies in academic departments, which was a consequence of the so-called second-wave feminism' (Becchio, 2020, p. 122). Elsewhere we could find literature depicting the relationship between the two more directly (Hewitson, 2001).[33] Basic income was not just demanded by a minority of women – it had been a formal demand of the British *WLM*, democratically and officially endorsed. How could this fact have gone unheeded?

My third and final point of perplexity is that while academic literature on feminism is often criticised for being Eurocentric or Anglocentric, this is the *British* WLM we are talking about – how could even its demand for basic income have been so sidelined?

In the rest of this section, I would like to lay out my conjecture regarding the possible reasons for the historical erasure of a documented demand for basic income. They would constitute, at the same time, the reasons why we ought to reclaim it as a step forward towards diversifying economics.

An unrealistic or unrealisable demand – there was certainly a feeling that basic income is much too utopian, and cannot be a practical demand. Indeed, one of the two objections recorded by *Spare Rib* ran: 'it was not a tactical demand as we couldn't expect to get it at the moment'.[34] The objection had been made by the Fifth Demand group. Mary McIntosh lays out the criticism more fully:

> It is a demand that the need to sell one's labour power in order to survive should be abolished. So it is nothing less than a demand that socialism be introduced: but a demand ostensibly made of the capitalist state and a demand that socialism should enter through the back door, the relations of distribution; rather than the front door, the relations of production. It is thus, as *its proponents are well aware, an unrealisable demand* under capitalism, since it negates the wage relation which lies at the heart of capitalism. Any of their *supporters* who join the ranks because they think they might actually gain the demand have been *sadly deceived*. (McIntosh, 1981, p. 36. The italics are mine)

Thinking of basic income or any other form of guaranteed income as 'unrealisable' is not unique to McIntosh. It is echoed by the jibe below, in a national newspaper:

> When Claimants Unions demand a decent minimum income ... they are asking for the moon. (*Sunday Times supplement*, 26th November 1972, cited in North London Claimants Union, 1977)

However, women in the Claimants Union movement, at least Mainwaring, Downey, and other interviewees of my oral history research, thought differently. Mainwaring considered it in line with the idea of Beveridge's welfare state, with the only difference being the removal of his sexist assumption. An already-existing family allowance scheme was the main source of her inspiration. Downey recalls that she didn't think their guaranteed basic income was something radical.

Moreover, it was not only women in the Claimants Unions who deemed basic income realisable, but also a Cambridge economist did. James E. Meade argued for a 'social dividend', the description of which is similar to what we now call basic income, as realisable and desirable in a paper in the *Oxford Economic Papers* published in 1972 (Meade, 1972). The difference between the ideas by Claimants Unions and by the Cambridge economist was that the former was an individual basis while the latter seemed to be a household basis. McIntosh's criticism would not be affected by this difference and thus would apply to Meade's idea as well.

Thus Downey, Mainwaring and Meade were, according to McIntosh, 'sadly deceived'. But if they were 'supporters' who were 'sadly deceived', who were the 'proponents' who deceived them? As shown in Yamamori (2014), Downey and Mainwaring were, with other claimants, the very people who articulated basic income by themselves from a broader concept of guaranteed income. And as the history of economic thought confirms, Meade had advocated a 'social dividend', something similar to basic income since the 1930s (van Trier, 1995).

Further, McIntosh seems not to be distinguishing basic income from guaranteed income in general, and her as 'unrealisable' seems to apply to the latter as well. Thus other economists, politicians, and activists at that time who advocated or considered some forms of guaranteed income as a 'realisable' policy (such as Milton Freedman, Martin Luther King, Richard Nixon, James Tobin, and James K. Galbraith) were also 'sadly deceived'. But again, by who? And why and how did such an 'unrealisable' idea become '*the* welfare reform strategy of the late 1960s and 1970s (Steensland, 2008, p. ix)'?

As apparent from the citation above from McIntosh's paper, her judgement came from a particular interpretation of Marxian theory, in which almost all of the advances of social policies would be dismissed as illusionary because real progress would be impossible under capitalism.[35] However, if we were to follow this type of theoretical perspective, the fifth demand itself would be 'unrealisable'. Because if the demand for 'financial independence of all women' were not to presuppose any "trade off" (such as other parts of the population losing their financial independence), then we would not have any 'reserve army of labour', which is essential to capitalism according to the theory McIntosh relied on.

In light of all this, it would not be unreasonable to think that perhaps this peculiar interpretation of Marxian theory and the ensuing negative judgement of guaranteed income could have been one of the reasons for the historical erasure.

The *Spare Rib* report of the Ninth National WLM conference records one other reason for the 'Fifth Demand group's objection to basic income, namely, that 'it would amount to implicit support for the wages for housework'.[36] Indeed, it was not only *Spare Rib*, but also other feminists who conflated basic income with the wages for housework. Michèle Barrett's *Women's Oppression Today* (1980), while one of the few precious works that recorded the fact of the Claimants Union's demand for 'guaranteed minimum income', almost equated it with the wages for housework, and dismissed it as 'tending to reinforce women's role in the household and as not providing a fundamental challenge to the state's assumptions concerning women's dependence'.[37] Many of the claimant's women themselves shared this criticism of the wages for housework, but thought the case for basic income was different (Yamamori, 2014).

In its early stage, the 'wages for housework' campaign tried to recruit women from the Claimants Union movement, and there were some women who joined both. For example, Monica Sjöö was active not only in Bristol's Claimants Union and Bristol Women's Liberation Group but also in the 'wages for housework' campaign until she was excommunicated from the latter on the grounds of her 'anarchist feminist' leanings (Honeybourne & Singer, 2003). However, the two demands were ostensibly not alike, and the two organisations were different in many ways, as explained in detail in Yamamori (2014).

Different as the two were in reality, mainstream feminists such as Barrett were still at liberty to conflate the two. But even this could not explain basic income's erasure from the historiography of the WLM. The wages for housework have been well documented, from contemporaries in the 1970s (with many criticisms against the demand, for instance, reprinted in Malos, 1980) to today (Ferguson, 2020; Toupin, 2018; not to mention writings by and interviews with founders of the campaign such as Mariarosa Dalla Costa, Silvia Federici, and Selma James).

A possible inference as to why claimant-women's basic income ended up erased from history despite being a formal demand of the British WLM, while no such thing befell the wages for housework, is that the former case was one of a purely collective voice, without single authorship. Including these kinds of voices and recognising them as economic thought can be done by diversifying the respective disciplines (be it feminist economics, history of feminism, or history of economic thought) with a methodology that would allow such collective voices to be included.[38]

7. GRASSROOTS FEMINIST ECONOMIC THOUGHT

Taking Claimants Unions' economic thought seriously would rewrite some of the dominant discourses in feminist literature. The feminist philosopher Nancy Fraser has put out a 'Universal Caregiver' model, in which she argued against what she has charted as most US feminists' and liberalists' goal for a 'Universal Breadwinner' and as most Western European feminists' and social democrats' goal for 'Caregiver Parity'. The 'Universal Breadwinner' model aims 'to foster gender equity by promoting women's employment', 'the centerpiece' of which is 'state provision of employment-enabling services such as day care' (Fraser, 1997, p. 43). The 'Caregiver Parity' model 'aims to promote gender equity chiefly by supporting informal carework', 'the centerpiece' of which is the 'state provision of caregiver allowances' (Fraser, 1997, p. 43). In contrast to these two models, Fraser's new model for a 'Universal Caregiver' aims to 'promote gender equity by effectively dismantling the gendered opposition between breadwinning and caregiving' (Fraser, 1997, p. 61). It permits everyone to be a caregiver without falling into disadvantages, or without what feminist economist Nancy Folbre has called the 'care penalty' (Fraser, 1997; Folbre, 2001). In fact, the historiography outlined in this paper demonstrates that this 'Universal Caregiver' model already existed within working-class feminist discourse in the long 1970s Britain, more than a decade prior to this philosophical reinvention.[39]

Claimants Unions were not professional campaigners or policy advocates. They were neighbourhood community organisations. Lyn Boyd and Annette Mckay, both of whom were born to working-class families and were active at the Newcastle Claimants Union, recall:

> It taught us how to work together with other people to support without prejudice... It's about actually thinking about other people as well as yourself and actually trying to develop the community which is good for your kids. (Interview on the 12th of September, 2009)

Supporting each other without prejudice wasn't something that came easy – especially taking into consideration the diverse and intersectional composition of Claimants Unions: single mothers, the disabled, old-age pensioners, strikers, unemployed; women and men; transgender and cisgender; working-class and middle class; Black, Asian, and White. But they tried their best. The minutes of the East London Claimants Union record Julia Mainwaring's warning regarding the welfare officers' tactic to divide the claimants, and her remark: 'We reiterate that we support all claimants without condition'. Demanding an unconditional income echoes this unconditional solidarity they collectively tried to seek. Both the spirit of unconditional solidarity and the demand of unconditional income was hard learnt through an everyday struggle in their diverse and intersectional circumstances. None of the other similar organisations in 1970s Britain, whose composition was less intersectional than the Claimants Union movement, seemed to articulate unconditional income.

The Claimants Union movement also problematised the gender division of labour, and the nature of 'work' itself (Yamamori, 2014). People saw their demand for basic income as a transitional demand, one that would lead to a better society free from the impositions of gendered labour and from harmful 'work', such as in the military, or meaningless work; what David Graeber would later call 'bullshit jobs' (Graeber, 2018). This was also a result of the Claimants Unions' diverse and intersectional composition. While the Claimants Union Movement was one of several organisations representing single mothers, it was possibly the only one of these that dared to call out the gendered division of labour and to call into question the very conceptualisation of 'work'. Also, the membership of claimants' unions was not limited to single mothers but included also trans-gender claimants, whom the Department of Health and Social Security considered fit to work, but who were eventually unable to find a job owing to the transphobia of the employers. In so far as unemployment itself is concerned, there were of course many other organisations for the unemployed other than the Claimants Unions – for instance, trade unions. These protested under the banner of the 'right to work', with which Claimants Unions vociferously disagreed and instead demanded basic income together with free social services. Again, it was thanks to the intersectional and diverse composition that Claimants Unions enjoyed in comparison to the customary trade unions or the other organisations that mobilised the unemployed.

The demands of the Claimants Unions are determined at National Federation conferences held 3–4 times a year and the agenda at these reflects the everyday struggles and discussions from local weekly meetings at each union. These substantively intersectional and always grassroots aspects and the perspectives they have afforded on basic income are thus rather unique.

The Claimants Unions' disagreement with the 'right to work' slogan popular with the trade unions movement, and their distancing from what Nancy Fraser later termed the 'universal breadwinner model' popular with the WLM, have anticipated the following remarks of twenty-first century feminist economists:

> As Charusheela has pointed out, the notion that paid work results in autonomy, self-realization, and choice is a culturally specific understanding of work that reflects the experiences of relatively privileged women. Paid work has a different meaning for the descendants of enslaved persons, for immigrants, and for others on the bottom rung of the labor market. Rather than liberating, work for these people is often 'demeaning, undignified, and oppressive'. (Barker, 2005, p. 2202; Charusheela, 2003, p. 298)

8. DIVERSIFYING THE DOMINANT DISCOURSE AND HISTORIOGRAPHY OF BASIC INCOME

As we have seen in Section 6, one of the reasons why feminist scholars have neglected the fact that basic income was a demand of the British WLM is because they thought the demand is too utopian to actualise, or not radical enough from their feminist perspective. Then we could expect that it must be recorded in the history of basic income, either within or outside of the history of economic thought, because there is such an endeavour to depict the history of basic income, and the above reasons would not apply to this case. However, it had been totally ignored at least until 2014 my previous paper (Yamamori, 2014) was published.[40] Here I would like to point out four points about how including this erased grassroots feminist economic thought would urge us to rewrite the historiography of basic income.

Before going to these four points, let me first layout the methodology of the history of ideas that I am going to adopt here. First, the standard historiography of basic income, as we have seen in Section 2, usually starts with adopting the current definition of basic income by the Basic Income Earth Network or by Philippe van Parijs.[41] Then it tries to find proposals that seem to fit this definition in the past. Those historiographies have been valuable on their own, and especially useful in an earlier stage of research on the idea when almost of those economic thoughts had been 'hidden in dark corners of our knowledge, or even (almost) completely forgotten' (Cunliffe & Erreygers, 2004, p. vii). And women in the Claimants Unions and their thought could fit in this type of historiography well.[42] But I myself would not repeat with the same methodology here for the following three reasons.

It is firstly because this type of historiography is difficult to avoid the 'mythologies' that Quentin Skinner warned against: 'mythologies of doctrines', of 'proplesis', and of 'parochialism' (Skinner, 1969).

It is secondly because it seems to be almost impossible to be loyal to its own methodology. Torry (2021) seems to be the best and purest work based on this methodology, by declaring his as 'a history of basic income: an unconditional and non-withdrawable income for every individual' (p. 26), and van Parijs and Torry have made major contributions to try to establish this particular definition as authoritative (Yamamori, 2022). Nonetheless, both of their works (Torry, 2021; van Parijs & Vanderborght, 2017) include proposals that do not fit their definition of basic income. For example, G. D. H. Cole's proposal for social dividends is treated as basic income. However, it is clearly conditional as Cole wrote:

> the social dividend would be payable to able-bodied persons only on condition that they were ready to work, and there would have to be means whereby a man's receipt of the social dividend could be questioned on grounds of proved unwillingness to perform his part in the common service. (Cole, 1935, p. 263)

It is rather strange because neither van Parijs, Vanderborght, or Torry would not call such a conditional income as basic income if it were to be proposed in 2022. We need something more than their methodology in order to justify their inclusion of Cole's proposal. This case itself can be dealt within their methodology, by simply removing Cole's social dividend from their lists of basic income. But there are more harder cases, such as John Stuart Mill's case where a certain minimum is distributed to 'every member of the community' (Mill, 1849). It is not known whether it means 'every individual' – not 'every household'.

It is thirdly because the definition of basic income is not in agreement, despite their treatment as it is in the definite consensus in van Parijs and Vanderborght (2017) and Torry (2021). There are competing definitions, such as whether it should come with some notion of a threshold or level to be taken as a minimum or as adequate, or whether it could include income in kind (Yamamori, 2022). And if we were to adopt any of competing definitions different from the one adopted by van Parijs and Vanderborght (2017) and Torry (2021), what is to be included in its historiography might be different.

Recognising these issues, I would like to adopt here the following methodology. First, I respect the plurality of several competing definitions that exists today among respected scholars and organisations (Yamamori, 2022). Second, by not only focusing on abstract characteristics of basic income such as 'unconditional', 'individual', etc., but also taking the reason why contemporary discussions take these characteristics seriously – such as why unconditionality is important (or harmful), etc., our historiographical endeavour would be to trace the historical roots of such discussions. It would be beneficial both to understand the current idea of basic income and its historical connection. Third, here I pay attention to the difference between 'income' and 'dividend'. The terms such as 'basic income', 'guaranteed income', and 'minimum income' were almost interchangeably used, and in almost cases meant an income, the level of which would be equal to or above a threshold or level to be taken as a minimum or as adequate (Yamamori, 2022). It was also widely used not only in academia but also in media and in social movements in the 1960s and 1970s. The usage of the term 'social dividend' was relatively limited to scholars or policy experts, and what was included in this labelling was not identical to 'basic income', though there were cases it was used interchangeably with 'basic (guaranteed or minimum) income'. A dividend could be quite small and occasionally zero (Yamamori, 2022, pp. 45–46). The following is, in principle, from a perspective of the history of the term basic income or similar, which corresponds to the perspective I used more in detail elsewhere (Yamamori, 2022, pp. 36–40).

Now, let me mark the more concrete points arrived at thanks to the inclusion of the Claimants Unions' economic thought. First, the Claimants Unions' articulation of 'Guaranteed Minimum Income' as purely unconditional income preceded the academic articulation. As we have seen in Section 5, the Claimants Union movement collectively discussed guaranteed income around 1970, and by 1972 distilled a definition of unconditional income from various types of guaranteed income proposals that had circulated up until then. By 1975, they had collectively reached a consensus that their version of Guaranteed Minimum Income is unconditional individual income, and when Mainwaring, Downey and other women turned up with the resolution at the National WLM Conferences, what was meant by Guaranteed Minimum Income was this version – basic income.

These arguments and elucidation of unconditional income among the broader concept of guaranteed income prefigures the later academic elucidation which distinguishes basic income from guaranteed income in general. One such later academic clarification can be found in van Parijs and van der Veen (1986, pp. 161–163). 1986 is the year marking both this publication and the foundation of the BIEN.

Second, and related to the above first point, I would like to suggest that including the Claimants Unions' thoughts on basic income could help solve the current confusion in the definition of basic income. As Yamamori (2022) shows, among both academics and activisms, there are two competing definitions. One is 'an unconditional income to every person' that allows a penny a month to be thought of as basic income (⑤ in Fig. 1). The other comes with a threshold concept, the wording of which typically take such forms as 'covering basic needs', 'minimum', 'adequate', or 'high enough to ensure X', etc. The academic elucidation of the definition of basic income was attempted in the mid-1980s, and it came with a threshold. Then around the end of the 1980s and the beginning of the 1990s, the definition without a threshold was invented. This issue was problematised in the BIEN in 2016, and revisited there again in 2021 (Yamamori, 2022). The economic thought of Claimants Unions is rather relevant in providing a discussion far earlier than this academic version. One internal document of the NFCU voiced the merits of an unconditional income even if its amount were to be low, but still, it maintained in the definition of basic income a threshold of adequacy.[43]

Third, the Claimants Union movement, by the mid-1970s, clearly connected their demand for basic income with their demand for free social services (Yamamori, 2014). This is not isolated in the history of basic income or similar ideas. For example, possibly the first usage of the exact term 'basic income (basis-inkomen)' in the sense of universal income explicitly includes 'inkomen' in kind (van Tuyll van Serooskerken, 1932). This was followed by Van Parijs' 'basic income in kind' (van Parijs, 1995, pp. 42–45). On this point, a picture would not be that different, even if we were to broaden our scope from the history of the term basic income to include the history of the term social dividend: G. D. H. Cole's ' "social dividend" in kind' (Cole, 1944, p. 144). This tradition is almost in amnesia, but the grassroots feminist economic thought of the Claimants Unions makes us recall it. With this recollection, we could shed a different light on the current debate between advocates for basic income and advocates for 'Universal Basic Services', which seems to presume as if those two are incompatible with each other and we have to choose either (Coote & Percy, 2020; Gough, 2021).

Fourth, the Claimants Union's economic thought is almost the first occasion that clearly elucidates the need and merit of an individual income, not of a household income. The concept of guaranteed income circulated in the 1960s and 1970s was vague not only on unconditionality but also on individuality. There were many cases of guaranteed income proposals which were not individual basis. To name a few, Nixon's Family Assistance Plan, almost of Negative Income Tax proposals, and Meade's idea in 1972 if we were to broad our scope to 'social dividend'.[44] The importance of individual income was not widely recognised not only in the general discourses on income transfer but also in the particular circle that was in favour or sympathetic to a guaranteed income.[45] Here let me pick an example by Thomas Balogh, an Oxford economist. In his pamphlet for the Fabian Society in 1970, he mentioned a guaranteed minimum income positively, and recommend a reform that integrates family allowances into the tax system, as 'the most important step' in line with a guaranteed minimum income. Then he added:

> There is very little doubt that an enormous effort in education and propaganda is needed if that system is to be acceptable, especially among Labour supporters, because it is normally the woman who gets money and the man who pays the tax. (Balogh, 1970, p. 46)

Three years later it was proved that his worry was right. When the Tory government tried to implement this, which was a bit ironical because it wasn't by Labour as Balogh recommended to, but by the Conservatives, women liberationists had a successful campaign 'hands off family allowances', which women in the

Claimants Unions took a significant part. While the oxford economist would see those women's opposition was due to the lack of their education, those women thought they were fighting against sexist 'reform'.

As Yamamori (2022) indicates, the existence of the two major competing definitions of basic income partially reflects two different ways to see the idea of basic income, one that sees it as philosophers' invention, and the other that sees it as an idea that evolved from collective practices and movements. The exclusion or sideline status of the economic thought of the Claimants Unions in the historiography of basic income is a consequence of the dominant view that see basic income as philosophers' (and economists') invention. With a novel methodology that diversifies the dominant narrow view, we could take Claimants Unions' grassroots feminist economic thought seriously.

9. CONCLUSION

I hope to have effectively made a case here for why we ought to take grassroots feminist economic thought seriously. It would give us a different picture regarding the history of economic thought on basic income, and more broadly regarding the idea of feminist economic thought.

The collective amnesia that has befallen the women in the Claimants Unions movement can be partially explained because of the broad intersectionality of their composition and thought. If I am allowed to borrow the words of Louise Toupin in her description of the Canadian branch of the 'wages for housework' campaign (Toupin, 2018), we can say that the Claimants Unions' economic thought is 'an intersectional perspective before its time'.

The Claimants Unions' interrogation of the gendered division of labour and of the nature of 'work' has a heightened relevance, now more than ever. During the current pandemic, feminists have reclaimed this feminist tradition of basic income. In April 2020, The Hawaii State Commission on the Status of Women made the first feminist economic recovery plan for COVID-19, where one of the policy proposals was basic income (Hawai'i State Commission on the Status of Women, 2020). Khara Jabola-Carolus of the Commission notes:

> Some of the key elements are full economic self-sufficiency regardless of work. And that sounds really neutral at first. But if you think about it, many of us, especially women, women with disabilities, women who are caregiving and don't have the same ability to access employment, and will never have that same value as workers. And so making sure that universal basic income, which has been a long intergenerational rallying cry of feminists is at the center was really important. (Blackwell, Jabola-Carolus, & Smith-Johnson, 2020)

Several weeks later, the International Association for Feminist Economics made a statement calling for 'the immediate and urgent implementation of a gender-equitable universal basic income', as we have seen before.

Yet despite the centrality of women's activism, then and now, written history and research on basic income have been overwhelmingly white and male-dominated. It is my hope that the current exposé, which sought to reclaim an erased history, could come to constitute a small contribution to what the Hawaiians who collectively composed the feminist recovery plan have called 'a transnational feminist future' (Mahelona, Heine, Jabola-Carolus, & Shaw, 2021). I equally hope that it would find a readership in this special issue aiming to 'diversify history of economic thought'.

ACKNOWLEDGEMENTS

The empirical part of this paper was based on oral historical research on the Claimants Union movement in Britain in the long 1970s. I am grateful to all interviewees. Constraints of space preclude including here everyone by name, but especially to Lyn Boyd, Susan Carlyle, Roger Clipsham, Susan Cooper, Jane Downey, Mary Issitt, Bill Jordan, Julia Mainwaring, Annette McKay, Rosemary Robson, Margaret, and Chris Tyrrell for their encouragement and friendship. Boyd, Clipsham, Cooper, Issitt and Mainwaring kindly dug out from their attic internal documents of and photos related to the Claimants Unions movement. Phillipe Van Parijs and Walter van Trier generously sent me scanned copies of historical materials related to BIEN. I am also grateful to Barb Jacobson and Ellen Malos for their generous answers to my questions. Regarding the Dutch usage of 'basis-inkomen', I am indebted to van Trier and Anton Jäger for their enlightening correspondences, and to Liza Silvius at the Jan Tinbergen Archive of Erasmus University Rotterdam for her generous assistance. I am also grateful to Guido Erreygers for his kind reply to my enquiry. An earlier version of this paper was presented at the 1st History of Economic Thought Diversity Caucus Conference, held 24–25 May 2021. (In its call for papers, the title of the conference was given as 'history of economic thought', not 'history of economics'). I am encouraged by the warm reception of participants there. The discussions with Clem Davies, Chloe Halpenny, Jessica Schulz, and Almaz Zelleke at the 'UBI and gender' research team at the Freiburg Institute for Basic Income Studies have been encouraging. Rositza Alexandrova and Zelleke kindly read the draft and gave me several suggestions, for which I am grateful. Work underlying parts of this paper were supported by grants from the Japan Society for the Promotion of Science (JP19K12621, JP26360054, JP22710266), which is gratefully acknowledged. I am also grateful to the editor and anonymous reviewers of this journal for their constructive comments. Any mistakes belong to me.

NOTES

1. Both van Parijs and van der Veen are introduced as 'political economist' in the introductory paper in the same issue of the journal (Aya & Tromp, 1986, p. 632). They were members of the September Group, which was the group of so-called analytical Marxists.

2. Both G. D. H. Cole (1889–1959) and James E. Meade (1907–1995) were British economists who theorised and advocated for a 'social dividend'. Cole was an Oxford economist famous for his work on guild socialism. Meade taught both at Cambridge and at Oxford, winning in 1977 the Nobel Memorial Prize in Economic Sciences.

3. Douglas was referred by J. M. Keynes in his General Theory as 'the most famous' among under-consumption theorists: 'Major Douglas is entitled to claim, as against some of his orthodox adversaries, that he at least has not been wholly oblivious of the outstanding problem of our economic system' (Keynes, 1936, chapter 23).

4. *Spare Rib*, no. 58, p. 11.

5. Obviously, a proper overview would need a book-length space and could not be accomplished in just this short section. The intention here is to provide the minimum of information necessary for readers to make sense of the rest of the paper. Moreover, there already exist many good overviews – examples of which: Coote and Cambell (1982), Rowbotham (1989), and Jolly (2019).

6. To give but two examples, women who were working as sewing machinists at the Ford Dagenham plant took a strike action demanding equal pay in 1968 (Cohen, 2012) and the London Women's Liberation Workshop and its monthly journal *Shrew* started posing the demand in 1969 (Setch, 2002).

7. For example, Philips (2010) and Sisterhood and After Research Team (2013). The former reports on the 40th anniversary of the first conference as 'the women's liberation movement at forty'. This also corresponds to the popular perception of the WLM. Calvini-Lefebvre et al. (2010) records media coverage of the first national WLM conference as the 'birth of feminism'.

8. We already discussed the difficulty in pinpointing a single moment at the originary one. Similarly, it is contestable which women's liberation demonstration in the UK was the 'first'. Here, I follow Ferguson (2018).

9. There have been competing testimonies concerning when these four demands were proposed. One of the claims is that this happened at the first conference (Bruley, 2013; Fairbairns, 2002; Jolly, 2019; Rees, 2010), the other claim is that it was during the process of preparing the International Women's Day march on 6 March 1971 (Setch, 2002). Sheila Rowbotham, a leading socialist feminist who played a major role in making the Oxford 'women's weekend' happen, gives us an interesting anecdote on how WLM decided to have its demands in the first place: at first, 'many people in the Women's Movement thought it would be reducing you if you had demands, because obviously we needed to transform everything and, you know, there was a sort of resistance to have demands, they were thought to be a bit reformist'. Then on the counsel of a Leninist-Maoist man that it would, indeed, be imperative to have them, 'we had our minimum demands' (Rowbotham, 2010).

10. See Bracke (2013), Toupin (2018), and Zelleke (2022) for more detail on the International Wages for Housework Campaign. However, in the majority of cases when 'the wages for housework' campaign is referred to in the paper, the reference is not to the international campaign as a whole, but to the British one in particular.

11. London Women's Liberation Campaign for Legal and Financial Independence and Rights of Women (1979).

12. Mary McIntosh (1936–2013) was one of the founders of the London Gay Liberation Front and also active in the WLM. A leading scholar of the emergent feminist scholarship, she has left a rich archive of WLM materials from which the study has inestimably benefited. The archive is held at the Women's Library in LSE.

13. A poster by See Red Women's Workshop for Women's Liberation's seven demands erased 'economic independence of women' from the fifth demand. What it had instead was: 'Abolition of the legal definition of women as dependent on men' (Stevenson et al., 2016, pp. 46–47).

14. The Birmingham Claimants Union adopted its policy that consisted of 'right to an adequate income' and 'welfare-state controlled by who use it'. It said that the former should be 'universal' and 'no means test' (Birmingham Claimants Union, 1969). Also the testimonies from two founding member of the union: Julia Mainwaring and Roger Clipsham.

15. The overview of the history, structure, and daily activities of the Claimants Union movement is depicted in Yamamori (2014).

16. What was exactly meant by 'Personal Allowances' is not entirely known? Given the Claimants Union's opposition to means-testing, what was probably meant was a universal benefit. And inferring from its depiction as a long-term demand of women, it could be interpreted to have been a benefit paid out only to women. However, given the fact that they already endorsed a universal right for adequate income, and shortly after articulated what we now call basic income (Yamamori, 2014), the benefit in question could be interpreted as being paid to *every* adult. While the term 'personal allowances' was generally used for and understood as a tax exemption in the UK tax system, some used this term to refer to an

idea of Juliet Rhys-Williams, not dissimilar to basic income (Meade, 1948). It is not impossible that Rhys-Williams's idea might have influenced the Birmingham Claimants Union's articulation of basic income.

17. cf. The 2013 Ken Loach's film of the same name.

18. Birmingham Claimants Union (1970a, 1970c). Julia Mainwaring, who is from a small mining village in Wales and was one of the founders of the union, was at the time doing her studies at Birmingham University on the British Welfare State.

19. Testimonies by several women in Birmingham CU and Newcastle upon Tyne CU.

20. Testimony by a claimant who was active at the West London CU at the time.

21. Testimonies by two claimants who were active at the Birmingham CU at the time.

22. At the other side of the Atlantic, the National Welfare Rights Organisation demanded guaranteed income in this vague sense (Kornbluh, 2007; Nadasen, 2005).

23. Brapstacks (1972). The name was a pseudonym. The document was written by one of the founding members of the Birmingham Claimants Union (according to three testimonies by founding members of the Birmingham Claimants Union).

24. Women in the Claimants Union movement continued to organise similar campaigns under various names throughout the 1970s.

25. Still the WLM's attention was not high enough *vis-à-vis* the Claimants women's expectations. Monica Sjöö recalls: 'I found to my disappointment that there wasn't much support forthcoming, this time, from the Women's movement itself. I thought at first that perhaps the reason for this was that quite a few women in the movement came from relatively well-off middle-class backgrounds, & had an above average education, & so have never had to suffer the humiliations of the S.S. or Dole offices' (Sjöö, 1975).

26. However, what was written on the placard ('End the Cohabitation Rule – Fight with the Claimants Union') was erased. See Yamamori (2014).

27. According to the interview on April 5th, 2014. Mainwaring kindly also showed materials distributed at the meetings of the Fifth Demand group and which she had kept in her attic.

28. Negative Income Tax has its intellectual origin in the 1940s Chicago School economists – people like George Stigler and Milton Freedman – and was popularised by the latter in 1960s (Friedman, 1962; Stigler, 1946). It would fall under ③ in Fig. 1.

29. Family allowances were paid to mothers via the post offices.

30. As for the reason of the erasure, it is Julia Mainwaring's opinion that it was based on class prejudice. Mainwaring recalls that the chair of the plenary at the National WLM conference when the resolution for basic income was first raised saw claimant's women as scum, below the working-class (Yamamori, 2014).

31. For examples from an earlier period in feminist economics, see Robeyns (2001) and McKay (2005). For examples in other feminist disciplines, see Pateman (1988) and Withorn (1993).

32. The text of the statement is: 'IAFFE, the largest academic association for feminist economists, champions universal social provisioning as both a fundamental value and the only way to lay a strong foundation for sustained and ecologically-attuned social life. In light of the coronavirus, IAFFE calls for the immediate and urgent implementation of a gender-equitable universal *basic income* and the provision of essential services, ensuring that individuals are not marginalized or excluded because of their race, ethnicity, or caste. Essential services such as food and housing should be accompanied by universal healthcare, public care services including child and elder care and education, strengthened labor protections, and rigorous safeguarding of the public interest. These measures will recover the purchasing power of individuals and households, particularly those in vulnerable situations, boosting aggregate demand. Through international collaboration and appropriate macroeconomic policies, national governments should be enabled to expand their fiscal space and finance these investments' (http://www.iaffe.org/news/126/, Italics are mine. Last accessed on May 20, 2021).

33. One of the earliest examples of such a connection would be Barbara Bergman's 'The Economics of Women's Liberation' (Bergmann, 1973).

34. *Spare Rib*, no. 58, p.11.

35. This particular adaptation of Marxist theory against the welfare state was criticised around the same time, notably in Ian Gough's canonical book (Gough, 1979).

36. *Spare Rib*, no. 58, p. 11.

37. Barrett (1980 [1988], pp. 244–245). It is a bit ironical that Claimants Union's basic income was criticised here as not radical enough to make 'a fundamental challenge' while at the same time being criticised as too radical to be actualised by others, such as McIntosh, as we seen earlier. Another interesting point here is that Barrett noted the failed attempts to make 'wages for housework' as a formal demand of the British WLM while she kept silent about the successful attempt to establish basic income as a formal demand.

38. Another, more apparent reason is class prejudice, as we have seen in footnote 30. And McIntosh and Barrett are rather the best part among the WLM, because they think 'economic independence of women' seriously, and at least paid attention to Claimants Unions' demand for basic income. At some other corners of the British WLM, the demand for economic independence of women itself was erased, as shown in footnote 13.

39. With the overview provided by this paper, one might be tempted to chart the following trajectory: 1. Mainstream feminists such as Mary McIntosh, Michèle Barrett, or the Fifth Demand group, which was for the 'financial independence' of women, but against basic income could be said to correspond to Fraser's 'Universal Breadwinner' model. 2. The wages for housework (at least in their usual reception) could be said to correspond to Fraser's 'Caregiver Parity' model 3. Basic income by women in the Claimants Union movement, with which they envisioned to put an end to the sexual division of labour and to the nuclear family tout court, could rightfully be mapped onto Fraser's 'Universal Caregiver' model. I fully agree on this third point – the Claimants Unions' feminist basic income corresponding to the 'Universal Caregiver' model. However, I must withhold sanction of the first two correspondences. Yes, there has been apparent 'workerism' among some of mainstream feminists, but not all. There was a placard that said 'Equal Pay is not enough. We want the moon!' at the first WLM demonstration in London in 1971 (Rowbotham, 2021). And yes, there is an apparent 'caregiver parity' aspect to the 'wages for housework' campaign. However, some of leading advocates such as Silvia Federici clearly used the term the 'wages for housework' in a rhetorical way, while envisioning something similar to the 'Universal Caregiver' model (Federici, 1974).

40. After the publication of Yamamori (2014), there emerged literature mentioning the Claimants women's basic income proposal. See van Parijs and Vanderborght (2017) and Sloman (2019). Malcolm Torry included the chapter mentioning the Claimants women's basic income proposal in *The Palgrave International Handbook of Basic Income*, which he edited (Miller, Yamamori, & Zelleke, 2019).

41. The Basic Income European Network (BIEN) changed its name to Basic Income Earth Network in 2004.

42. Van Parijs and Vanderborght (2017) referred to them based on Yamamori (2014), as mentioned in footnote 40.

43. Brapsstacks (1972) and testimonies by Susan Carlyle, Roger Clipsham, Jane Downey, Mary Issitt, Julia Mainwaring and Margaret Tyrrell (all were active in the Claimants Union movement in the 1970s).

44. See, for example, Steensland (2008), Friedman and Friedman (1980), Tobin et al. (1967), Minsky (1969), and Meade (1972).

45. This conflation of an individual with a household existed not only in 1970s. It has still been almost every corner of the basic income discussion in the world. For example, Tony Fitzpatrick wrote in 1999: '[A]lthough BI [basic income] is usually portrayed as a benefit paid out on an individual basis, it is possible to envisage forms of BI which are based upon calculations of *household* income (Fitzpatrick, 1999, p. 35)'.

REFERENCES

Author(s) Anonymous. (1972, May 27/28). *Minutes of conference on guaranteed adequate income campaign. Swansea*. (Internal document of NFCU).

Aya, R., & Tromp, B. (1986). Taking the capitalist road: An immodest proposal. *Theory and Society*, *15*(5), 631–634.

Balogh, T. (1970). Labour and inflation. *Fabian Tract*, 403 London: Fabian Society.

Barker, D. K. (2005). Beyond women and economics: Rereading "women's work". *Signs: Journal of Women in Culture and Society*, *30*(4), 2189–2209.

Barrett, M. (1980). *Women's oppression today: The Marxist/feminist encounter*. London: Verso.

Bazin, V. (2021). Red Rag magazine, feminist economics and the domestic labour pains of liberation. *Women: A Cultural Review*, *32*(3–4), 295–317.

Becchio, G. (2020). *A history of feminist and gender economics*. Oxfordshire: Routledge.

Bergmann, B. (1973). The economics of women's liberation. *Challenge*, *16*(2), 11–17.

BIEN. (1988). Basic Income European Network Statutes (Internal document of BIEN).

Birmingham Claimants Union. (1969). *United Claimants News*, No. 5.

Birmingham Claimants Union. (1970a). *Support the Birmingham Claimants Union Campaign for a new welfare state*.

Birmingham Claimants Union. (1970b). Female liberation statement, in NFCU (1970). *Journal of the National Federation of Claimants Unions*, *1*, 24.

Birmingham Claimants Union. (1970c). *United Claimants News*, No. 8.

Binard, F. (2017). The British women's liberation movement in the 1970s: Redefining the personal and the political. *Revue Française de Civilisation Britannique*, *22*.

Blackwell, G., K., Jabola-Carolus, & Smith-Johnson, T. (2020). Hawaii's feminist recovery plan: Host Angela Glover Blackwell in conversation with Khara Jabola-Carolus and Tanya Smith-Johnson. Retrieved from https://radicalimagination.us/episodes/feminist-recovery-plan. Accessed on March 18, 2022.

Bracke, M. A. (2013). Between the transnational and the local: Mapping the trajectories and contexts of the wages for housework campaign in 1970s Italian feminism. *Women's History Review*, *22*(4), 625–642.

Brapsstacks, B. (pseudonym). (1972). The Confusion of Swansea: A little light on the G.A.I. (Internal document of NFCU)

Bruley, S. (2013). Consciousness-raising in Clapham: Women's liberation as 'lived experience' in South London in the 1970s. *Women's History Review*, *22*(5), 717–738.

Calvini-Lefebvre, M., Cleall, E., Grey, D. J. R., Grainger, A., Hetherington, N., & Schwartz, L. (2010). Rethinking the history of feminism. *Women: A Cultural Review*, *21*(3), 247–250.

Cohen, S. (2012). Equal pay: Or what? Economics, politics and the 1968 Ford sewing machinists' strike. *Labor History*, *53*(1), 51–68.

Cole, G. D. H. (1935). *Principles of economic planning*. New York, NY: Macmillan.

Cole, G. D. H. (1944). *Money: Its present and future*. London: Cassell and Company.

Condon, J. (1990). The women's weekend: The beginning of a movement. *Women: A Cultural Review*, *1*(1), 25–28.

Coote, A., & Campbell, B. (1982). *Sweet freedom: The struggle for women's liberation*. London: Picador.

Coote, A., & Percy, A. (2020). *The Case for universal basic services*. Cambridge: Polity.

Cunliffe, J., & Erreygers, G. (Eds.). (2004). *The origins of universal grants: An anthology of historical writings on basic capital and basic income*. London: Palgrave Macmillan.

Delmar, R. (2010). *Rosalind Delmar discusses the WLM sixth demand*. British Library. Retrieved from https://www.bl.uk/collection-items/rosalind-delmar-the-wlm-sixth-demand. Accessed October 23, 2022.

Fairbairns, Z. (2002). *Saying what we want: Women's demands in the feminist seventies and now*. York: Raw Nerve Books.

FCU. (1983). *On the dole: A claimants union guide to social security benefit*.

FCU. (1987). *Social security and women*.

Federici, S. (1975). *Wages against housework*. Bristol: The Power of Women Collective and the Falling Wall Press.

Ferguson, D. (2018). The day that feminists took 'women's lib' to the streets. *The Guardian*, March 3. Retrieved from https://www.theguardian.com/world/2018/mar/03/women-liberation-movement-first-march-remembered. Accessed October 23, 2022.

Ferguson, S. (2020). *Women and work: Feminism, labour, and social reproduction*. London: Pluto Press.

Finch, S., Fortune, J., Grant, J., Robinson, J., & Wilson, S. (Eds.). (2020). *Misbehaving: Stories of protest against the Miss World contest and the beauty industry*. London: Merlin Press.

Fitzpatrick, T. (1999). *Freedom and security: An introduction to the basic income debate*. New York, NY: Macmillan Press.

Folbre, N. (2001). *The invisible heart: Economics and family values*. New York, NY: The New Press.

Fraser, N. (1997). *Justice interrupt us: Critical reflections on the 'postsocialist' condition*. Oxfordshire: Routledge.

Friedman, M. (1962). *Capitalism and freedom*. Chicago, IL: University of Chicago Press.

Friedman, M., & Friedman, R. (1980). *Free to choose: A personal statement*. San Diego, CA: Harcourt Brace Jovanovich.

Gough, I. (1979). *The political economy of the welfare state*. New York, NY: Macmillan.

Gough, I. (2021). *Move the debate from universal basic income to universal basic services*. UNESCO Inclusive Policy Lab. Retrieved from https://en.unesco.org/inclusivepolicylab/analytics/move-debate-universal-basic-income-universal-basic-services. Accessed March 18, 2022.

Graeber, D. (2019). *Bullshit jobs: The rise of pointless work, and what we can do about it*. London: Penguin Books.

Hawai'i State Commission on the Status of Women. (2020). Building bridges, not walking on backs: A feminist economic recovery plan for COVID-19. Retrieved from https://humanservices.hawaii.gov/wp-content/uploads/2020/04/4.13.20-Final-Cover-D2-Feminist-Economic-Recovery-D1.pdf. Accessed May 20, 2021.

Hewitson, G. (2001). *A survey of feminist economics*. Working Papers. School of Economics, La Trobe University.

Honeybourne, V., & Singer, I. (2013). *Personal histories of the second wave of feminism: Feminist archive oral history project, summarised from interviews* (Vols. 1 and 2). Bristol: Feminist Archive South, Bristol University Special Collections.

Jolly, M. (2019). *Sisterhood and after: An oral history of the UK women's liberation movement, 1968-present*. Oxford: Oxford University Press.

Keynes, J. M. (1936). *The general theory of employment, interest and money*. New York, NY: Macmillan.

Kornbluh, F. (2007). *The battle for welfare rights: Politics and poverty in modern America*. Philadelphia, PA: University of Pennsylvania Press.

Kuiper, E. (2022). *A herstory of economics*. Polity.

London Women's Liberation Campaign for Legal and Financial Independence and Rights of Women. (1979). Disaggregation now! Another battle for women's independence. *Feminist Review, 2*(1), 19–31.

Mahelona, Y., Heine, T., Jabola-Carolus, K., & Shaw, A. (2021). The story and sisterhood behind the world's first feminist economic recovery plan for COVID-19. In N. Goodyear-Ka'ōpua, C. Howes, J. K. Kamakawiwo'ole Osorio, & A. Yamashiro (eds.), *The value of Hawai'i 3: Hulihia, the turning*. Honolulu, Hawaii: University of Hawaii Press

McKay, A. (2005). *The future of social security policy: Women, work and a citizens' basic income*. Oxfordshire: Routledge.

Madden, K., & Dimand, R. W. (Eds.). (2018). *Routledge handbook of the history of women's economic thought*. Oxfordshire: Routledge.

Malos, E. (1980 [1995]). *The politics of housework*. New York, NY: New Clarion Press.

Mata, T. (Ed.). (forthcoming). *The economist in history: The political economy of liberal journalism*. Cambridge: Cambridge University Press.

McIntosh, M. (1981). Feminism and social policy. *Critical Social Policy, 1*(1), 32–42.

McIntosh, M. (2001). Engendering economic policy: The women's budget group. *Women: A Cultural Review, 12*(2), 147–157.

Meade, J. E. (1948 [1994]). *Planning and the price mechanism*. William Pickering.

Meade, J. E. (1972). Poverty in the welfare state. *Oxford Economic Papers, 24*(3), 289–326.

Mill, J. S. (1849). *Principles of political economy* (2nd ed.). Cambridge: John W. Parker.

Miller, A., Yamamori, T., & Zelleke, A. (2019). The gender effects of a basic income. In M. Torry (ed.), *The Palgrave international handbook of basic income* (pp. 133–153). New York, NY: Palgrave Macmillan.

Minsky, H. (1969). *The macroeconomics of a negative income tax*. Hyman P. Minsky Archive. Paper 429.

Mitchell, J. (1966). Women: The longest revolution. *New Left Review, 1*(40), 11–37.

Nadasen, P. (2005). *Welfare warriors: The welfare rights movement in the United States.* Oxfordshire: Routledge.

NFCU. (1975). *Social security and women.*

NFCU. (1977). *Social security and women.*

North London Claimants Union. (1977). Claimants unions. In J. Cowley, A. Kaye, M. Mayo, & M. Thompson (Eds.), *Community or class struggle?* Stage One.

Pateman, C. (1988). The patriarchal welfare state: Women and democracy. In A. Gutmann (Ed.), *Democracy and the welfare state.* Princeton, NJ: Princeton University Press.

Philips, D. (2010). The women's liberation movement at forty. *History Workshop Journal, 70*(1), 293–297.

Rees, J. (2010). A look back at anger: The women's liberation movement in 1978. *Women's History Review, 19*(3), 337–356.

Robeyns, I. (2001). An income of one's own: A radical vision of welfare policies in Europe and beyond. *Gender & Development, 9*(1), 82–89.

Ross, E. A., & Bearse, M. L. (edited by K. E. Boyle with the Oral History Project Advisory Group). (1996). *Chronology of the Women's Liberation Movement in Britain: Organisations, Conferences, Journals and Events, with a Focus on Leeds and Bradford 1969–1979.*

Rowbotham, S. (1989). *The Past is before us: Feminism in action since the 1960s.* Kitchener: Pandora Press.

Rowbotham, S. (2010). *Sheila Rowbotham discusses the origin of the WLM demands.* British Liberary. Retrieved from https://www.bl.uk/collection-items/sheila-rowbotham-the-origin-of-the-wlm-demands. Accessed October 23, 2022.

Rowbotham, S. (2021). *Daring to hope: My life in the 1970s.* Verso.

Setch, E. (2002). The face of metropolitan feminism: The London women's liberation workshop, 1969–79. *Twentieth Century British History, 13*(2), 171–190.

Sisterhood and After Research Team. (2013). *Women's liberation: A national movement.* British Liberary. Retrieved from https://www.bl.uk/sisterhood/articles/womens-liberation-a-national-movement. Accessed November 1, 2021.

Sjöö, M. (1972). Women, claimants unions and the cohabitation ruling. *Red Rag, 2*, 2011–220.

Sjöö, M. (1975). *Unsupported mothers & the C. Us: My experience.* Feminist Archive South, Bristol University Special Collections.

Skinner, Q. (1969). Meaning and understanding in the history of ideas. *History and Theory, 8*(1), 3–53.

Sloman, P. (2019). *Transfer state: The idea of a guaranteed income and the politics of redistribution in modern Britain.* Oxford: Oxford University Press.

Steensland, B. (2008). *The failed welfare revolution: America's struggle over guaranteed income policy.* Princeton, NJ: Princeton University Press.

Stevenson, P., Mackie, S., Robinson, A., & Baines, J. (2016). *See Red Women's Workshop: Feminist Posters 1974–1990.* London: Four Corners Books.

Stigler, G. (1946). The economics of minimum wage legislation. *American Economic Review, 36*(3), 358–365.

Tobin, J., Pechman, J. A., & Mieszkowski, P. M. (1967). Is a negative income tax practical? *The Yale Law Journal, 77*(1), 1–27.

Torry, M. (2021). *Basic income: A history.* London: Edward Elgar.

Toupin, L. (2018). *Wages for housework: A history of an international feminist movement, 1972–77.* London: Pluto Press.

van Parijs, P. (Ed.). (1992). *Arguing for basic income: Ethical foundation for a radical reform.* Verso.

van Parijs, P. (1995). *Real freedom for all: What (if anything) can justify capitalism?* Oxford: Oxford University Press.

van Parijs, P., & van der Veen, R. J. (1986). A capitalist road to communism. (Reprinted in van Parijs, Philippe (1993). *Marxism Recycled.* Cambridge: Cambridge University Press.)

van Parijs, P., & Vanderborght, Y. (2017). *Basic income: A radical proposal for a free society and a sane economy.* Cambridge, MA: Harvard University Press.

van Trier, W. (1995). *Every one a king.* Leuven: Katholieke Universiteit Leuven.

van Trier, W. (2002). Who framed 'social dividend'? USBIG Discussion Paper, No. 26.

van Tuyll van Serooskerke, H. P. (1932). Letter from H.P. van Tuyll van Serooskerke. Inventory number: NL-RtEUR_TBCOR01_ 002T007, Jan Tinbergen Archive. Rotterdam, Netherlands: Erasmus University Rotterdam University Library.

Withorn, A. (1993). Women and basic income in the US. *Journal of Progressive Human Services*, *4*(1), 29–43.

Yamamori, T. (2014). A feminist way to unconditional basic income: Claimants unions and women's liberation movements in 1970s Britain. *Basic Income Studies*, *9*(1–2), 1–24.

Yamamori, T. (2020). The pandemic makes inequality visible, *Nikkei*, 16th October, 29.

Yamamori, T. (2022). Is a penny a month basic income? A historiography of the concept of a threshold in basic income. *Basic Income Studies*, *17*(1), 29–51.

Zelleke, A. (2022). Wages for housework: The Marxist-feminist case for basic income. *Política y Sociedad*, *59*(2).

PART II

ESSAYS

CHAPTER 8

ALBERT HIRSCHMAN, LAUCHLIN CURRIE, "LINKAGES" THEORY, AND PAUL ROSENSTEIN RODAN'S "BIG PUSH"[1]

Roger J. Sandilands

ABSTRACT

This paper introduces a hitherto unpublished 1970 paper written by Lauchlin Currie (1902–1993) on Paul Rosenstein Rodan's famous 1943 paper on the "Big Push" which led to the balanced-unbalanced growth debate to which Albert Hirschman (1915–2012) was an important contributor. Both Currie and Hirschman had been key economic advisers to the Colombian government, and their respective views on development planning are contrasted. In particular, it is shown how Currie's 1970 paper illuminates the theory behind the 1971–1974 national plan for Colombia that he prepared and helped deliver, and how the related institutional innovations have had an enduring impact on Colombia's recent economic history.

Keywords: Lauchlin Currie; Paul Rosenstein-Rodan; Big Push; balanced growth; Albert Hirschman; development planning

This paper introduces Chapter 19, "The Big Push and Balanced and Unbalanced Growth," of a hitherto unpublished manuscript of a book on economic development that Lauchlin Currie (1902–1993) wrote in 1969–1971 at Simon Fraser

Research in the History of Economic Thought and Methodology: Including a Selection of Papers Presented at the First History of Economics Diversity Caucus Conference
Research in the History of Economic Thought and Methodology, Volume 41B, 149–175
Copyright © 2023 by Roger J. Sandilands
ISSN: 0743-4154/doi:10.1108/S0743-41542023000041B008

University, Canada.[2] This book and especially Chapter 19 on Paul Rosenstein Rodan's (1943) theory of the "Big Push," offer insights into a significant period in Colombia's recent economic development that was heavily influenced by Currie's role as a top policy adviser.

I was Currie's research assistant at SFU from June to September 1970. In April 1971, Currie, who had been resident in Colombia for all but five years since 1949, returned there at the urgent behest of President Misael Pastrana to advise Roberto Arenas, the new director of the Departamento Nacional de Planeación (DNP).[3] Currie thereupon shelved his book project to concentrate on *Guidelines for a New Strategy of Development* (Currie, 1971) which Pastrana outlined in his Presidential Message to Congress in July 1971.

This was followed by *The Plan of the Four Strategies (El Plan de las Cuatro Estrategias)*, launched in December with Currie as its driving force. This emphasised (i) a new index-linked housing finance system to encourage a big increase in non-inflationary savings and a corresponding increase in real demand for (mainly urban) housing and related infrastructure; (ii) realistic exchange rates to promote exports; (iii) incentives for increased agricultural output and productivity (reduced unit costs), based on an expected increase in demand for food and raw materials; and (iv) a resultant improved income distribution from the creation of higher paying urban jobs for migrant rural workers who were previously disguisedly unemployed, along with higher incomes for the smaller rural workforce that consequently could earn higher average incomes than before.

Currie had long been concerned with the issues that motivated Paul Rosenstein Rodan's seminal 1943 paper that argued the need for a "Big Push" industrialisation plan to break the interlocking vicious circles of underdevelopment that appeared to be trapping millions of disguisedly unemployed workers in extreme rural poverty. He had first visited Colombia in 1949 as director of the World Bank's first comprehensive country mission. Rosenstein Rodan had himself been at the World Bank since 1947 and was the organiser of a preliminary survey of available information about Colombia, ahead of the Currie mission. Lionel Robbins, whom Currie knew (but did not warm to) from his undergraduate days at the LSE, 1922–1925, was one of those approached to direct the Colombia mission but he declined.[4]

A native of Nova Scotia, Currie studied for two years at St Francis Xavier University, but then transferred to the LSE in 1922, followed in 1925 by Harvard. There Allyn Young had a profound influence on his subsequent work. Rosenstein Rodan, Ragnar Nurkse and others such as Hans W. Arndt (1955) and Maiju Perälä (2006) also acknowledged Young's influence on their thinking about the "Big Push" and the "balanced-unbalanced growth" debate.[5]

After Young's departure for the LSE in 1927, Currie completed his PhD dissertation on "Bank Assets and Banking Theory" (January 1931) under John H Williams, but kept in touch with Young, including through a visit to London in 1928 in connection with his PhD work. There, Young spoke of his satisfaction with his upcoming (September 1928) presidential address to the British Association on "Increasing Returns and Economic Progress" (published in *The Economic Journal* in December 1928, just three months before his untimely death).

At Harvard, Currie was a teaching assistant for Ralph Hawtrey and Joseph Schumpeter (both of whom were replacements for Young while he was on leave in London). In the summer of 1934 Jacob Viner, a special adviser at the US Treasury, recruited him for his "Freshman Brain Trust" to propose reforms to the Federal Reserve System that would strengthen monetary control. At the Treasury, he teamed up with Marriner Eccles, another special adviser who shortly after was appointed chairman of the Federal Reserve Board. He took Currie with him and the 1935 Banking Act followed soon after, reflecting reforms Currie had recommended at the Treasury.

Currie led the spending wing of the New Deal (Herbert Stein, 1969, p. 165), and from 1939 to 1945 was based in the White House as President Franklin Roosevelt's adviser on economic affairs. During this time he was involved in lend-lease operations for war-torn China which he visited in 1941 and 1942 as FDR's emissary to Chungking for talks with Chiang Kai-shek and Zhou En-lai. In 1943–1944, he was acting head of the Foreign Economic Administration; and in February 1945 headed a tripartite mission to neutral Switzerland to persuade them to freeze Nazi gold in Swiss banks and to halt supplies passing through Switzerland to Nazi forces in Italy.

When the World Bank survey mission arrived in Bogotá in July 1949 they found that many city-centre building were still burnt-out shells from the recent "Bogotazo" that followed the assassination of a popular political leader, Jorge Eliécir Gaitan. Currie's report, published in September 1950, found the same conditions that underlay Rosenstein Rodan's 1943 paper on the need for a "big push" to absorb a mass of disguisedly unemployed rural poor. Currie's report stressed the poor transport and communications links between what were essentially four relatively isolated regions. Improving those links was a priority in a programme to boost overall productivity by extending the effective size of the Colombian market, along Adam Smithian (and Allyn Youngian) anti-mercantilist lines.

Traditional labour-intensive agricultural practices underlay low productivity, and high birth rates were exacerbating this low productivity by putting population pressure on land, while discouraging more productive, capital-intensive techniques. This was one of the vicious circles of underdevelopment later stressed by Ragnar Nurkse (1963) and Harvey Leibenstein (1957), for example.[6] Much of the country's best land, notably the relatively flat, fertile Sabana de Bogotá was being used for extensive cattle grazing instead of intensive cultivation of crops. A land tax was one solution recommended.

Over time, however, the Green Revolution greatly increased agricultural productivity. This reduced labour inputs (per ton of output) much faster than the growth of (relatively inelastic) demand, even after allowing for export opportunities. Too few observers understood that in these conditions an increase in *productivity* is not the same as an increase in *production*, still less an increase in rural employment. Instead, the net result is labour displacement, more disguised unemployment and more rural poverty. This is true even in the face of so-called labour-intensive innovations such as new seeds and fertilisers (as opposed to capital-intensive tractors). To believe otherwise is to commit a fallacy of composition: that what is true of some innovating farmers – who need more workers to bring in a bigger harvest – is supposedly also true if all farmers are innovating. Increased supply with a much smaller increase in demand results in smaller farm incomes and substantial overall labour displacement.

Currie found little of this in his survey of big push literature (including Hirschman's), but it was central to Currie's own perceptions ever since he arrived in Colombia in 1949 and especially in the 1960s when he launched a concerted political campaign in favour of a massive "breakthrough" plan, *Operación Colombia* (Currie, 1961), elaborated in his award-winning *Accelerating Development: The necessity and the means* (1966).[7]

In his paper below, Currie appraised Hirschman's critique of Rosenstein Rodan's Big Push that would involve comprehensive planning across many industries to overcome indivisibilities and complementarities through a simultaneous investment programme, underwritten by foreign aid. This could ensure that while a small number of investments may not generate sufficient demand for firms to operate at a technically efficient scale, a "Big Push" would overcome this problem and make modern industry competitive against traditional low-wage, low-productivity, labour-intensive handicrafts.[8] Currie believed Hirschman and others had distracted attention from the issue of whether a Big Push was necessary or feasible towards what Currie saw as a separate issue, namely whether Rosenstein Rodan's Big Push would involve a "balanced" or an "unbalanced" approach, with those terms not clearly defined.

He also criticised as "a completely false issue," Hirschman's argument (1958, p. 63) that

> the advantage of a see-saw advance over "balanced growth," where every activity expands perfectly in step with every other, is that it leaves considerable scope to *induced* investment decisions and therefore economizes our principal scarce resource, namely genuine decision-making.

For, wrote Currie, "the possibility of an expansion where every activity is perfectly in step with every other in any underdeveloped country (or developed!) is ludicrous." In a growing economy, disequilibrium exists wherever prices are moving ahead of costs. The exploitation of those profit opportunities generates pecuniary external economies for the rest of the economy (see Scitovsky, 1954). Unsettling, countervailing forces thus ensure that disequilibrium rather than equilibrium is *characteristic* of a freely functioning market economy. Currie wanted to promote those growth-enhancing disequilibria by removing unnatural blocks to free market forces of competition and mobility. He did not seek to create tensions and disequilibria that go against those benign forces.

By contrast, Hirschman, in order to economise on the underdeveloped economy's "principal scarce resource," advocated the deliberate creation of bottlenecks, tensions and disequilibria that he considered could more powerfully provoke induced investments. This could be helped along by the "Principle of the Hiding Hand": the deliberate concealment of the true costs and benefits of projects so that industrialists would undertake projects on which they otherwise would not risk their money. Hirschman suggests that in this way the strategy would produce net benefits to the economy as a whole even if the initial investors lose their money (not the planners'). It also ignores the adverse incentive effects of those losses on future investors. Hence Currie's rebuke that the Hiding Hand principle is "not only dubious economics but even more dubious morality."[9]

Hirschman goes on to suggest that those benefits would be greatest, the greater the net external economies generated. And the gain would be best achieved by identifying industries most connected to others through the greatest number of "backward and forward linkages," or technical input–output coefficients. Hirschman (1958, pp. 106–107) has a chart that ranks different industries according to this criterion, with interdependence and complementarities measured by the ratio of their backward and forward inter-industry purchases and sales. These are given as percentage measures that would be greater or lesser *irrespective of the absolute value of sales output.*[10] Furthermore, (a) those sales would have been measured on the basis of past output, *not on the basis of the future demand potential* (which Hirschman nowhere discusses in this context); and (b) input–output tables usually assume fixed coefficients, whereas in reality, the ratios vary as the size of the market increases.

However, what struck Hirschman was that

> the industry with highest combined linkages score is iron and steel. Perhaps the underdeveloped countries are not so foolish and so exclusively prestige-motivated in attributing prime importance to this industry! (1958, p. 108)

Thus, Hirschman (1957), supported a decision in 1950 to accede to pressure groups, against the strong advice of the World Bank (and Currie), in approving a highly subsidised integrated steel mill in a poor and remote region of Colombia. However, this is to neglect negative linkage effects. In this steel project, the negatives were due to the poor quality of the local iron ore, exorbitant transport and mining costs, and a ban on much cheaper and higher-quality steel previously imported from Venezuela. User industries, taxpayers and final consumers suffered the consequences for decades. But politics and regional interests prevailed and Hirschman too optimistically wrote that this project

> will probably turn out to be ... an effective development move compared with any program to provide such an area with plentiful social overhead capital whose capacity may go *begging* for many years. (Hirschman, 1957)

Alacevich (2007, pp. 9–14; 2009, pp. 98–102, 176–177) gave a detailed history of this project (see also Currie, 1981a, ch.12) and suggested there were "hidden rationalities" in both Hirschman's unbalanced, incrementalist "project loan approach" and Currie's balanced, comprehensive "programme loan approach." The steel industry eventually developed more incrementally than first planned, and thus Alacevich thought the protagonists were not so far apart. In this connection, Adelman (2013, p. 401) also emphasised the "centrality of side effects" in the form of linkages and tensions. Thus, effectively, even though Colombia's steel mill was unprofitable for decades, failure may be counted as success – by ignoring the negatives.

However, there is a fundamental difference in the implications of Hirschman's and Currie's complementarities and side effects. A domestic iron and steel industry may have the greatest number of interdependencies but the main issue is whether it also enjoys a large demand, at unsubsidised competitive prices, currently and prospectively. Even with subsidies, Colombia's steel industry still imports only half of the local demand for steel, and itself accounts for only a very small proportion of Colombia's GDP, despite its linkages to other industries. For Currie, this means it is not an industry that could play a significant leading role in boosting the economy's overall growth rate. Instead, it would be a "follower," more dependent on growth of the overall economy and the demand arising from that.[11]

In other words, it is not only the industrial or sectoral *composition* of GDP that matters. *Size* matters too, currently and potentially, as does the size of the overall economy. They are of course interrelated. Thus, while Currie favoured a Big Push, he also sought balance between supply and demand potentials at the sectoral levels. Effort should be concentrated rather than diffused, with focus on a very few strategic sectors chosen not according to input–output coefficients but by the size of their potential demand and the resultant impact of that size on the overall economy through reciprocal demand and supply elasticities. His approach follows Young's (1928) conception of the interrelations that potentially produce self-sustaining, cumulative increasing returns, best achieved to the extent that competitive market forces successfully balance supply with demand at both the sectoral and overall levels:

> In an inclusive view, considering the market not as an outlet for the products of a particular industry, and therefore external to that industry, but as the outlet for goods in general, the size of the market is determined and defined by the volume of production. If this statement needs any qualification, it is that the conception of a market in this inclusive sense – an aggregate of productive activities, tied together by trade – carries with it the notion that there must be some sort of balance, that different productive activities must be proportioned one to another.
>
> Modified, then, in the light of this broader conception of the market, Adam Smith's dictum amounts to the theorem that the division of labour depends in large part upon the division of labour. (Young, 1928, p. 533)

The question, however, is whether market forces, especially in less developed countries, operate sufficiently freely for the fullest possible degree of this kind of cumulative causation.

Currie's answer was that the volume of rural labour displaced by the Green Revolution (in all of its revolutionary manifestations) has been imposing too great a burden on the mobility mechanism in Colombia (and many other countries) *under current institutions*. Too much of the displaced labour was retiring into subsistence farming or migrating to towns and cities unable to provide enough well-paying jobs for the numbers arriving. Unemployment, open and disguised, was burgeoning. Overall income growth, especially in per capita terms, was anaemic.

Currie's view was that the mobility mechanism was severely weakened by particular market distortions associated with a history of chronically high and variable inflation rates. Money was not neutral. Instead, monetary inflation severely discriminated against two major sectors for which demand had been repressed much more than elsewhere, namely in the market for long-term mortgage finance and for exports.

In housing finance, double-digit inflation had caused nominal interest rates in Colombia to average 16 percent. This creates a severe cash-flow (or front-end loading) problem for new borrowers, even if in real terms the rate was some-times negative. At the same time, with the main provider of mortgages being the monopolistic Banco Central Hipotecario, savers would receive perhaps only 10 percent which was severely negative in real terms. This deterred savers from plac-ing their savings in banks; they preferred to hold gold, dollars or jewels. Since most people rely on mortgages to finance home purchases, the reduced volume of savings further reduced the effective demand for housing. In addition, the risk to banks from the high nominal interest rates (as well as the equally serious problem of highly variable rates that mirrored volatile inflation rates), meant they would demand high down-payments and maximum terms of 15 years instead of 25 or 30 years as in other countries. All of these considerations had a serious repressive effect on demand for housing – as well as for government borrowing for large infrastructure projects associated with housing.

These inflation-related problems are far less serious for short-term finance – industrialists' commercial loans for "working capital" or for consumer credit. The discrimination was mainly against long-term finance. This clearly restrained the mobility of labour from low-paying agriculture into higher paying urban jobs, to the severe detriment not only of growth but also of better income distribution.

At the same time, and closely related to the housing problem, exports were being artificially repressed by inflation because of a mistaken but too commonly held belief that inflation was a structural rather than a monetary phenomenon, and that a depreciating exchange rate was a cause rather than a symptom. Thus the central bank would prefer to control the exchange rate than the money supply and deficit spending. A chronically overvalued exchange rate then made exports uncompetitive (along with import-substitutes). All of this reduced urban employ-ment and homes for actual and potential migrants in search of a better life. It also meant that real incomes were below potential. This impacted real demand for consumer goods and services across the board. Where in the Big Push and balanced-growth literature was this so forcibly explained as in Currie's publica-tions and innumerable briefings and memoranda for policy-makers?

That was theory. The main institutional reforms needed to make the dif-ference in practice consisted in (i) the introduction of a new, competitive, index-linked housing finance system; (ii) an exchange rate regime that was also adjustable with inflation to maintain export competitiveness; and (iii) Currie's tireless education of ministers, the central bank, and the country's brightest stu-dents in monetary theory and policy, of which he was a leading world author-ity (see Sandilands, 2004). All this aimed at separating central banking from development banking. The central bank needed to concentrate on monetary control, with expansion of the money supply kept closely in line with the growth of the real economy (which largely determines the non-inflationary real demand for money). So long as central bank management was dominated by spending ministers, monetary control was at risk. And with monetary control at risk, so too was inflation, housing, exports, jobs and economic growth generally. Meanwhile, development banking – and especially long-term finance, including mortgages – needed to rely on real savings out of real incomes (not new money) for non-inflationary lending.

How did index-linked housing finance help? The basic principle was to set a real interest rate at, say, four percent on index-linked savings accounts and six percent on borrowers' index-linked mortgages. This would do two things. Firstly, it would encourage real saving in ten newly established, competitive private housing finance corporations known as Savings and Housing Corporations (*Corporaciones de Ahorro y Vivienda* [CAVs]) that would invite deposits in units of constant purchasing power (*unidades de poder de compra constante,* UPACs) that would earn interest fixed in real terms though daily adjustment in line with the consumer price index.[12]

Secondly, the great increase in savings in no way saturated an equal (or greater) increase in demand for them, thanks to the great easing of borrowers' "front-end loading" problem despite the increase in the real interest rate they paid on their outstanding mortgages.

Though some of the increased savings captured by the CAVs diverted savings from other financial institutions that then had to cut back on consumer credit, for example, there was no fall in consumer demand or business investment because wages and profits increased as the economy moved to a higher growth rate. This higher rate could have been sustained for a longer period – Young's endogenous "increasing returns" effect – had growth not been slowed by exogenous policy mistakes by the monetary and fiscal authorities. There was also acquiescence to interest groups. These were mainly borrowers who, once they had obtained their mortgages (previously very hard to get), then lobbied for relaxation of the index linking, to the detriment of savers. This then reduced funding for future mortgage applicants and a weakening of the leading sector's economic dynamo effect.

One may conclude that a critical minimum effort is not enough. The effort and understanding on the part of policy-makers must be sustained. However, there is an *underlying tendency* for a higher growth rate to sustain itself, endogenously. If so, as Currie (1981b) explained, the main source of growth could be growth itself – through the ever-increasing opportunities to increase specialisation as the market expands – and in this way be capable of reducing the damage from policy mistakes, natural disasters and other exogenous events. Much can be learned from the debate sparked by Rosenstein Rodan's seminal paper in 1943; even more from Allyn Young's seminal paper on macroeconomic increasing returns; from the provocative encounters between Albert Hirschman and Lauchlin Currie on related ideas; and from the institutional reforms that in Colombia were driven by Currie as a top economic adviser. Ideas were not just there to play with. They were for policy-makers to use.

In contrast, a recurring theme in Adelman's (2013) biography, as highlighted in Sandilands' (2015b) review, is Hirschman's microeconomic focus as a development economist on the "backward and forward linkages" criterion for project selection and his related "principle of the hiding hand." Adelman showed how Hirschman delighted in filling his notebooks with *petites idées* and Flaubertian and Montaignesque aphorisms. These added up to one *grande idée*: that big ideas are bad. This, at least, was Hirschman's view of Rosenstein Rodan's "Big Push" that Currie defended for its insights into how the interlocking vicious circles could be most effectively overcome. It was an inspiration for Currie's (1971) *Guidelines for a New Strategy of Development*, the basis of an overall Colombian national plan actually implemented during 1971–1974. It was theory converted into a successful reality.

Currie's commentary on Hirschman and Rosenstein Rodan is in the accompanying paper below.

REFERENCES

Adelman, J. (2013). *Worldly philosopher: The Odyssey of Albert O*. Hirschman. Princeton, NJ: Princeton University Press.

Alacevich, M. (2007). *Early development economics debates revisited*. World Bank Working Paper 4441. Washington, DC. Retrieved from http://documents.worldbank.org/

Alacevich, M. (2009). *The political economy of the World Bank: The early years*. Stanford University Press, Stanford, CA.

Álvarez, A., Andrés M. G.-I., & Jimena, H. (2020). The quarrel of policy advisers that became development experts: Currie and Hirschman in Colombia. *History of Political Economy 52*(2), 275–306.

Arndt, H. W. (1955). External economies in economic growth. *Economic Record*, Novemer 31, 192–214.

Chandra, R. (2006). Currie's "leading sector" strategy of growth: An appraisal. *Journal of Development Studies, 42*(3), 490–508.

Chandra, R. (2022). *Endogenous growth in historical perspective: From Adam Smith to Paul Romer*. London: Palgrave Macmillan.

Chandra, R., & Sandilands, R. J. (2006). The role of pecuniary external economies and increasing returns to scale in the theory of increasing returns. *Review of Political Economy, 18*(2, April), 193–208.

Currie, L. (1961). *Operación Colombia: Un Programa Nacional de Desarrollo Económico y Social*. Barranquilla: Cámara Colombiana de la Construcción.

Currie, L. (1971). *Guidelines for a new strategy of development*. Bogotá: National Planning Department.

Currie, L. (1974). The leading sector model of growth in developing countries. *Journal of Economic Studies*, N.S., *1*(1) (May), 1–16.

Currie, L. (1976). *Taming the megalopolis: A design for urban growth*. Oxford: Pergamon Press.

Currie, L. (1981a). *The role of economic advisers in developing countries*. Westport CT: Greenwood Press.

Currie, L. (1981b). Allyn Young and the development of growth theory. *Journal of Economic Studies, 8*(1), 52–60 [Spanish version in *Revista de Planeación y Desarrollo* (1981), *12*:1–2].

Currie, L. (1983). The 'multiplier' in economic literature. *Journal of Economic Studies, 10*(3), 42–48.

Currie, L. (1997). Implications of an endogenous theory of growth in Allyn Young's macroeconomic concept of increasing returns. *History of Political Economy, 29*(3, Fall), 413–444. [Published in Spanish in *Revista de Economía Institucional* (2013), *15*(1), pp. 95–126.]

Flybjerg, B. (2017). Did megaproject research pioneer behavioural economics? The case of Albert O. Hirschman. In F. Bent (Ed.),. *The oxford handbook of megaproject management* (Ch. 8, pp. 155–193). Oxford: Oxford University Press.

Hirschman, A. O. (1957). Investment policy and 'Dualism' in underdeveloped countries. *American Economic Review, 47*(5), (September), 550–570.

Hirschman, A. O. (1958). *The strategy of economic development*. New Haven, CT: Yale University Press.

Hirschman, A. O. (1963). *Development projects observed*. Washington, DC: The Brookings Institution.

Hirschman, A. O. (1967). Review of accelerating development: The necessity and the means, by Lauchlin Currie. *American Economic Review, 57*(3, June), 611–613.

Krugman, P. (1993). Toward a counter-counterrevolution in development theory. *Proceedings of the World Bank conference on development economics, 1992*. Washington, DC: World Bank.

Leibenstein, H. (1957). *Economic backwardness and economic growth*. New York, NY: Wiley.

Nurkse, R. (1953). *Problems of capital formation in underdeveloped countries*. Oxford: Oxford University Press.
Perälä, M. (2006). "Looking at the other side of the coin": Allyn Young and the early development theory. *Journal of the History of Economic Thought, 28*(4), 461–488.
Rosenstein-Rodan, P. N. (1943). Problems of industrialisation of Eastern and South-eastern Europe. *Economic Journal, 53*(June–September), 202–211.
Rosenstein-Rodan, P. N. (1984). Natura Fecit Saltum: Analysis of the disequilibrium growth process. In M. M. Gerald & S. Dudley S. (Eds.). *Pioneers in development* (pp. 205–221). Oxford: Oxford University Press for the World Bank.
Sandilands, R. J. (1990). *The life and political economy of Lauchlin Currie: New dealer, presidential adviser, and development economist*. Durham, NC: Duke University Press.
Sandilands, R. J. (1999). New evidence on Allyn Young's style and influence as a teacher. *Journal of Economic Studies, 26*(6), 453–479.
Sandilands, R. J. (2004). New light on Lauchlin Currie's monetary economics in the new deal and beyond. *Special issue of Journal of Economic Studies, 31*(3/4), 170–403.
Sandilands, R. J. (2009). Solovian and new growth theory from the perspective of Allyn Young on macroeconomic increasing returns. *History of Political Economy, 41*(annual supplement), 285–303.
Sandilands, R. J. (2015a). The 1949 World Bank mission to Colombia and the competing visions of Lauchlin Currie and Albert Hirschman. *History of Economic Thought and Policy*, 2015(1), 21–38. [Also in Spanish: *Revista de Economía Institucional, 17*(32), 213–232.]
Sandilands, R. J. (2015b). Jeremy Adelman, Worldly Philosopher: The Odyssey of Albert O. Hirschman. *Journal of the History of Economic Thought, 37*(4), 674–680.
Scitovsky, T. (1954). Two concepts of external economies. *Journal of Political Economy, 62*, 143–151.
Stein, H. (1969). *Fiscal revolution in America*. Chicago, IL: Chicago University Press.
Sunstein, C. R. (2015a). Albert Hirschman's hiding hand. Foreword to Albert O. Hirschman, Development Projects Observed (3rd ed.). Washington, DC: Brookings Institution.
Young, A. A. (1928). Increasing returns and economic progress. *Economic Journal, 38*, 527–542.

THE BIG PUSH AND BALANCED AND UNBALANCED
GROWTH: LAUCHLIN CURRIE[13]

The need for a massive effort to activate or accelerate the growth process, to achieve the take-off, to escape from the vicious circle of poverty or the trap of under-development, to make the critical minimum effort for sustained growth, to make a big push, to achieve the breakthrough or transition to the developed category, and the means by which this might be done, which should have been the main issues with which underdevelopment literature and policy are concerned, have never been given adequate consideration. Part, at least, of the reason can be found in the creation of a false issue – that of balance versus unbalance – and the absorption of the real issue underlying the big push into this false issue, or the identification of the big push proposal with a particular theory of growth.

Hence the necessity and character of the critical minimum effort never received the attention its importance merited. For this reason, attention is devoted here to the question of balanced versus unbalanced growth, as in reality the subject appears to have run into the ground and is disappearing from current literature (though not from collections of readings and graduate examination requirements).

It is a very curious story as in retrospect it does not appear that there ever was a real issue. At least, no prominent writer[14] ever elaborated a theory of balanced growth in the sense of explaining growth in terms of balance, unless it can be said that the idea of balance is implicit and inherent in the functioning of the free enterprise or market economy and the pricing mechanism. At bottom the concepts of balance, equilibrium and efficiency are indistinguishable – the allocation of factors in response to or in anticipation of demand, and the relation to marginal costs, so that there is a tendency for equalisation of returns. The concepts of maximum output and social welfare are concepts of striving toward (though never attaining) a condition of equilibrium or balance. As Scitovsky (1954) has said, the existence of profits is in itself an indication of disequilibrium; in a condition of perfect equilibrium, profits would disappear. But this, it hardly needs saying, is only a concept which no one expects to be realised. In short, just as equilibrium implies an allocation or "balancing" of productive effort according to demand, or equating marginal costs with marginal utilities as reflected in demand, so it implies simultaneously disequilibrium or unbalance since we never attain equilibrium.

Thus a "theory" of balanced growth, if offered as an explanation of the growth process, would be only that the concepts of profit maximization, of incentives to improve one's condition or to "succeed," of mobility, of competition and of the operation of the pricing mechanism would, in a suitable physical and social environment, lead to development or growth. Actually, this appeared to be what had happened in the case of the non-socialist developed countries in their earlier history. Attempts to explain their development in terms of state intervention – of non-market forces – are unconvincing except possibly in the case of Japan. Even in this case, however, the matter was treated as a case of the state intervening not to create disequilibrium or unbalance but rather to make the environment more favourable for the functioning of the market forces. The other type of state intervention – to correct deficiencies in distribution and to provide services not adequately provided by the market mechanism – could be explained and defended on these grounds and not as a means of creating "unbalance" leading to "decision making."

Generally, the "doctrine" or "theory" of balanced growth is attributed to three writers – Rosenstein-Rodan, Scitovsky and Nurkse. It is interesting to return to the original sources and consider what these writers actually said.

The pertinent article of Rosenstein-Rodan was published in 1943 under the title of "Problems of Industrialisation of Eastern and South-Eastern Europe." The main thrust of the article was a proposal to accelerate the post-war industrialization of South-Eastern Europe by a massive programme of foreign aid utilizing the super-abundant labour resources, or the disguised agricultural unemployment, in a widely diversified expansion of wage good industries. It was most definitely not presented as a "theory of growth," but as a specific proposal to meet what the author thought would be an emergency situation (and was) just as the Marshall Plan was proposed and adopted a few years later to accelerate the reconstruction of Western Europe.

In its support, however, Rosenstein-Rodan used two arguments that were seized upon by his critics. One related to the external economies that would follow a large-scale spending programme. Doubtless some internal and external economies of scale would follow from an increase in the size of the market, as Allyn Young (1928) had earlier argued, but this was not really necessary to Rosenstein-Rodan's point. All he needed to demonstrate was that *a growth in the overall market itself* would justify or induce many investments not otherwise justified. He conceived the problem as one of assuring that consumer demand increased sufficiently to provide a market for the product of the new consumer goods industries he proposed so that there would be a continuing market for the production of the currently underemployed. For this purpose, he should have been more concerned to make more explicit the implications of inelasticity of demand for individual consumer goods and with the necessity of continuing offsets to leakages or growth in savings than with the reduction in per unit costs that might result. It was as though Keynes had sought to justify his proposal for an expansion of aggregate demand in the depths of the depression by citing the economies of scale that would follow such an expansion, rather than in concentrating on the direct growth in output and employment resulting from the spending. The introduction of the argument for external economies, while valid, tended to divert attention from the main issue.

The concept of balance was implied in the idea that "the industries producing the bulk of the wage goods can be said to be complementary" (p. 206) in the sense of creating a demand for each other's products which in turn suggests that in allocating the investment funds attention be paid to indicated varying income elasticities of demand, which is surely a reasonable suggestion if such an investment programme were to be undertaken. The stumbling block of inelasticity of demand for goods of mass consumption is not mentioned explicitly, but is clearly implied in the often-cited shoe factory example and the idea of complementarity which in turn rested in the idea that for all consumer goods the income elasticity of demand is unity. (He was clearly aware of Keynesian leakages but did not suggest how they might be offset – a lack easily remedied.) Nurkse applied the concept of inelasticity of demand for any one good more clearly later, but failed to grasp its far-reaching implications for the nature and rapidity of the growth process and for policy purposes.

One can imagine that Rosenstein-Rodan must have been startled to find later that his bold suggestion of state intervention to accomplish quickly what the market mechanisms would accomplish only slowly, if at all, should have been transformed into a statement of a theory or doctrine of growth – and not only of growth but of balanced growth or development. It was a policy proposal and it would just as reasonably have been cited as a suggestion for unbalanced growth – the deliberate expansion of the non-agricultural consumer good sector of the economy to correct the unbalance caused by excessive numbers in the agricultural sector, and a shortage of external sources of capital. The anticipated expansion of the market, in turn, was expected to create "disequilibrium," tensions and profit possibilities" and have "horizontal and vertical linkages," all of which would act to induce further investment and further absorption of the redundant agricultural forces and the growth of certain sectors relative to others. One could, in other words, just as plausibly list Rosenstein-Rodan as a protagonist of unbalanced as of balanced growth. Neither characterization would be apt as what he was really concerned with was the desirability, in the circumstances then prevailing, of a deliberately large effort to accelerate industrialization.

Nurkse (1953) can with more justice be credited with a more generalized and more extended treatment of balanced growth, though again it was not his central thesis. It appeared not as a theory of growth but rather as an explanation of the functioning or faulty functioning of Say's Law and the pricing mechanism. Again in the statement, "The difficulty vanishes, at least in principle, in the case of a more or less synchronized application of capital to a wide range of different industries" (Nurkse, 1953, p. 11), the idea of balance in the sense of expanding output and hence investment in accordance with varying effective demands appeared as an implication of different ways of escaping from the underdevelopment trap arising from the inelasticity of demand for any one consumer good. The greater the production, provided no miscalculation is made, the greater the demand for other people's products, and the better Say's Law functions. This is where the idea of "balance," that is, balance between additional production and income elasticities of demand at a profitable level, enters.

It is important to note that in his 1953 book Nurkse did not place much emphasis on the matter of balance. He spoke of "more or less synchronized application" and he cited with approval Schumpeter's concept of waves or outbursts of innovations and investments and was not in the slightest perturbed by the idea of growth proceeding in oscillations above and below a trend line. If he subscribed to any particular theory of growth, it was that of Schumpeter. He was also, however, prepared to accept the desirability of governmental intervention to promote growth. "It may be that ... the forces that are to defeat the grip of economic stagnation have to be deliberately organized to some extent, at any rate initially" (Nurkse, 1953, p. 15), and cited with approval the early economic intervention of the Japanese government. He warned that such intervention may result in mistakes – "unbalance" – but went on to remark that "[d]isproportionalities of one kind or another have also been a feature of the cyclical booms through which economic progress was achieved by private enterprise" (Nurkse, 1953, p. 16). The fact is that he was not here really concerned with the *methods* of accelerating development or with a theory or explanation of development but rather with the key or central role he conceived capital formation or its lack plays in the process. Indeed, it was this insistence, which I considered excessive, which led me to consider that the influence of his work was not as constructive as it might have been, and to neglect the constructive passages on the possibilities and desirability of large scale but "more or less" synchronised methods of enlarging the market, output and employment mentioned above.[15]

The third writer generally cited as a proponent of the theory of balance is Scitovsky (1954). In his well-known article on external economies he repeated the observations of Rosenstein-Rodan and Nurkse on the problems posed by a small market. He extended the concept of external economies to cover all the benefits of larger markets so that when a firm's operations make other firms' operations more profitable, its calculations of private profitability understate its social desirability, the difference being accredited to external economies. After dealing with the two-industry model, he concluded that limitations on investment arising from the smallness of the market "can be fully removed only by a simultaneous expansion of both industries." To this extent he supported the policy of the big push, stating that "profits in a mixed economy are a bad guide to economic optimum so far as investment and industrial expansion are concerned, and they are worse the more decentralized and differentiated the economy" (Scitovsky, 1954, p. 149).

Is this, then, an argument for balanced growth? Again it is a matter of semantics. Scitovsky (1954) himself identified balance with equilibrium and equilibrium as the antithesis of growth. Later, Scitovsky (1959) wrote an article setting forth this view at length. In his earlier piece, he stated that the analysis of an equilibrium theory becomes applicable when there are no profits. He gave even less consideration to the implementation of planned expansion than did Rosenstein-Rodan. To place him in the balanced growth camp would necessitate placing all the emphasis on his casual use of the words "simultaneous" and "integrated." In short, his interest and concern lay in extending a concept of external economies and not in elaborating a "theory" of growth – balanced or otherwise. He believed, however, that the concept of pecuniary external economies gave support to a *planned* expansion of investment in an underdeveloped economy, which would be a *development policy*.

It is interesting to note that none of the three writers commonly credited with holding or elaborating a "theory of balanced growth" regarded themselves as doing so. They were all, in more or less degree, concerned with the problem of accelerating development (or with current inadequate rates of growth) and stressed the obstacle imposed by an initial small market in inducing investment. They all believed that success breeds success or that growth breeds growth, that the more widely based the development movement, the more likely is it to beget demand, employment, profits, investment and further growth. If investment, whether private or public, is planned, it should, they believed, be in relation to anticipated demands so that losses or unutilised capacity may be minimised. It is this last feature that was singled out as the essential characteristic and to which the label "balanced growth" was attached. Actually, however, Rosenstein-Rodan was mainly concerned with accelerating post-war industrialisation and employing excess agricultural labour, Nurkse with ways and means of stimulating the demand for and the supply of capital, and Scitovsky with clarification of concepts of external economies.

Fleming's writing (1955) with the title "External economies and the doctrine of balanced growth," remarked that "the argument that the adoption of investment projects, which, though unprofitable individually would be profitable collectively, and hence is a good thing," is frequently referred to as the doctrine of balanced growth. So by this date, one feature of Rosenstein-Rodan's proposal, via Nurkse's (1953) discussion of the underdevelopment trap and the incentive to invest, and Scitovsky's (1954) discussion of external economies, had become identified in the literature as the doctrine of balanced growth. The merits of the original proposal became bound up with Nurkse's discussion of the circle of poverty. One of the strange things in this strange episode in the history of economic thought is that Nurkse did not really appear to be much interested in Rosenstein-Rodan's proposal, and in his exposition of the underdevelopment trap made assumptions directly counter to those of the latter. For example, it was fundamental to the validity of the latter's proposal that there should be virtually unlimited supplies of "surplus" labour. In his discussion of the case for a widely diversified range of investments, Nurkse assumed, on the contrary, as Fleming brought out, an elastic supply of capital and a given labour supply.

By 1957, however, Nurkse (1957) had accepted the designation of the balanced-growth "principle," "doctrine," "notion," but saw the issue more in terms of international specialization versus internal industrial or agricultural development for under-developed countries. Scant attention was paid to the big push in *The Problems of Capital Formation* (1954) and none at all in the 1957 article.

In short, Nurkse, in the chapter that received so much attention, never set forth "balance" as a principle or doctrine of growth, but rather as a limiting factor or a condition. He states this explicitly: "Balanced growth may be a good thing for its own sake, but here it interests us mainly for the sake of its effects on the demand for capital" (p. 12). As an economist, he would doubtless have preferred that investments, if made, should be utilized and profitable. However, the main concern of his book was in increasing the output of under-developed countries by increasing their capital formation. Balance was not something to be sought for its own sake, but only as a condition of growth – the acceleration of growth through the inducement to invest and the goodness of investment. It is a pity that Nurkse did not wrestle more with the problem of "the underdevelopment equilibrium" (p. 10) on the side of the inducement to produce, rather than on the conditions of the supply of capital, as he ended up stressing the importance of capital formation

in growth, but not in setting forth any very positive policy of achieving larger
investment and neglecting other factors in the growth process. Whether or not the
existence of Schumpeter's innovation waves is valid history, they hardly constitute
the basis of a conscious and deliberate policy of development, and this is what
is evidently needed, unless, of course, it is felt that the forces of the marketplace
can be relied upon to enable the rapidly growing population of underdeveloped
countries to take full advantage of modern technology.

It is tempting to review the subsequent literature to which many distinguished
writers contributed, including Fleming, Singer, Streeten, Sheahan, Scitovsky,
Montias, Lipton and Mathur among others, but this would take me too far afield
from the main argument of this work. I shall limit myself, therefore, to a discussion of Hirschman's treatment as I feel that much of the unfortunate confusion
stemmed from his work, which was widely cited, and which Hirschman attempted
to develop into a theory of growth and a basis for policy.

In Hirschman's (1958) treatment of the issues, he succeeded in confusing it
thoroughly by identifying the big push with the discussion of balance, and lumped
the two together as a "theory of development," which most assuredly it never was.
Having created something that never existed, he then proceeded to demolish it.

As we have seen, Rosenstein-Rodan mentioned the necessity of producing
what people wanted as a condition of planned large-scale expansion. He was concerned with a specific suggestion to accelerate industrialization in a specific group
of countries under specific circumstances. Nurkse's earlier discussion of balance,
to which Hirschman devoted his attention, occurred, as was remarked previously,
in a discussion of the vicious circle of poverty, in which "balance" – the necessity
of investing in the production of things for which there is a demand – appeared,
in conjunction with indivisibility of capital and inelasticity of demand, as conditions limiting the rate of growth rather than explaining it. Nurkse's formulation
of the vicious circle or trap is open to criticism, as I have attempted to show, but
these were not the bases of Hirschman's criticisms. Nurkse's rather casual remark
that the requirement of balance could be met by increased investment in a "number of different industries" over a "wide range of activities" as Rosenstein-Rodan
had advocated or by the Japanese government type of intervention or, as Nurkse
evidently preferred, by Schumpeter's waves of innovation, hardly seems sufficient
grounds for setting forth Nurkse's "theory of growth" as one of "balance" and
even less for identifying this with Rosenstein-Rodan's big push, as Hirschman
proceeded to do.

In the latter's treatment, the doctrine of "balanced growth" becomes a particular form of the big push wherein "a people" or a government is to set up
"a whole flock of industries that are going to take each others' output." Having
transformed the big push into a theory of balanced growth, he proceeded to criti-
cise balanced growth by insisting that Rosenstein-Rodan's version of the big push
required skills an underdeveloped country does not possess.

> For this is of course the major bone that I have to pick with the *balanced growth theory*: its
> application requires huge amounts of precisely those abilities which we have identified as likely
> to be in very limited supply in underdeveloped countries. (Hirschman, 1958, p. 53. Italics mine)

For the sake of clarity, it is useful to separate out the various elements that have been lumped together and combined as the doctrine of balanced growth:

There is first the diagnosis of inadequate growth that stresses the impediments arising from small and slowly growing markets and "lumpy" capital requirements and rapid growth in population. This concerns problems centering around lack of sufficient inducements to invest, of factor proportions, of investment criteria, and of the use and allocation of resources. It cannot be accurately described as a theory or doctrine of balance. It has already been discussed in Chapter XVII.

Secondly, there are the repercussions of one investment on others, or of one demand on others. This is an extension of the concept of external economies of scale to the impact on the demand for the product of an individual project arising from the growth of the market in general. Allyn Young linked the old concept of the advantages of the division of labour to the Marshallian concept of internal and external economies and Rosenstein-Rodan and Scitovsky extended this to economies arising from any growth in demand. The latter distinguished between technical economies and pecuniary external economies. The widely pervasive nature of the repercussions of one type of activity on another was made much of by Schumpeter. In this catch-all category, therefore, are repercussions that range from the Keynesian multiplier effect of an initial expansion in expenditures through induced investments to "true" economies of scale resulting in lower cost per unit of production resulting from the growth in the market – again taking in much of economics.

Thirdly, there are the various senses in which the word "balance" is used, ranging from the allocation of resources to meet the effective demand resulting from a given distribution of income – the general sense in which Rosenstein-Rodan and Nurkse use the term – to the strict sense of perfect equilibrium in which profits disappear, which Scitovsky pointed out. Or one can speak of a "balance" between full employment savings and voluntary investment, or of "unbalance" in which excess or deficient capacity is conceived to have a stimulating or induced effect on other investment, so that the meeting of demand over time is consistent with short run losses resulting from (temporary) overshooting or undershooting of current demand. There is also the popular sense in which the term is used as synonymous with constant relations of employment or output such as "balance" between agriculture and industry, which must result in "unbalance" if relative demand and relative technological progress are changing.

Finally, there is the uncertainly as to whether "balance" occurs by itself and is therefore a theory of growth in response to the forces of the market, or whether growth is something that has to be induced or stimulated, and if so whether stimulation is by creating and meeting demands, or by stimulating investment by not meeting demands, and the role of the state in the acceleration of development in a non-socialist underdeveloped country. This discussion, in turn, touches on another related issue, whether rapid growth has to proceed by steps or requires simultaneity in investment in a number of fields.

It is apparent that the theme has become very broad and diffused and can mean all things to all men, which suggests that the subject of development cannot be usefully discussed in terms of balance and unbalance. As a case in point, again consider the treatment of the subject by Hirschman (1958). Although he refers constantly to the "theory" or "doctrine" of balanced growth, he directs his principal criticisms against the "big push," or a specific policy proposal to accelerate development. On what actually causes development in the absence of intervention he is not clear. On the one hand, he speaks of "the ubiquitous poverty and inefficiency, the immensity of the task and the interlocking vicious circles" which suggest the necessity of vigorous countervailing measures. On the other hand, the big push proposal is dismissed as "escapist" and "defeatist" since an underdeveloped country is by definition incapable of undertaking simultaneous development on many fronts (1958, p. 53), and those who suggest the need neglect "the abundant historical evidence about the piecemeal penetration by industry that competes successfully with local handicraft and by new products which are first imported and then manufactured locally" (Hirschman, 1958). Yet he himself apparently does not rely on this evidence either, as he advocates a deliberate policy of "unbalanced growth."

Thus we are left without a theory or explanation of development, but with the need for intervention. It is never satisfactorily explained why an underdeveloped country is capable of a deliberate policy of unbalanced but not of balanced development, perhaps because the term unbalance as used by Hirschman implies production without reference to the market and the certainty of losses and/or bottlenecks over a more or less extended period and it is easier to produce at a loss than at a profit. Thus a condition which earlier writers treated as an impediment to growth – the possibility of losses – becomes a positive benefit. Support for this interpretation is afforded by his claim that an underdeveloped country lacks the skills to undertake a number of projects simultaneously (Hirschman, 1958, p. 55). Either the unbalanced projects do not require skills since they are expected to result in losses or they are taken up piecemeal and successively. But then what happens to the numerous projects made possible by the "linkages"? The greater the linkages the greater the skills and decision-making qualities required in order to realize the anticipated profits, which expectation gives rise to the linkages that lead to further investment.

Hirschman argues that

the advantage of see-saw advance over "balanced growth," where every activity expands perfectly in step with every other, is that it leaves considerable scope to induced investment decisions and therefore economizes ... genuine decision-making. (Hirschman, 1958, p. 63)

This is a completely false issue. The possibility of an expansion where every activity is perfectly in step with every other in any underdeveloped country (or developed!) is ludicrous. Underdeveloped countries need not be restrained from making "correct" investment decisions on the grounds of the possible disappearance of profits or because the tendency of profits to equalise would discourage further investment. As Adolph Lowe (1965, p. 310) dryly observes, "When we face up to the limited success which even the strongest efforts of balancing economic development are likely to achieve in most of the regions concerned we need hardly worry about too little disequilibrium." It appears more likely that the greater the number of unprofitable investments, the less incentive there would be to make new investments. Moreover, the distinction between an "induced" decision to invest and genuine decision-making does not exist.

This, then, is Hirschman's answer to the possibility of "the underdevelopment equilibrium," or a too slow rate of growth. It does not exist, since developed countries experienced piecemeal industrial advances, but if it does it can be broken by inducing international lenders and local capitalists and governments to make unbalanced ("mistaken" in terms of current effective demand) investments which create disequilibrium and tensions, which induce further investments to correct the mistakes, and so economises decision making! This might be called the strategy of lurching development as the progress would somewhat resemble that made by the efforts of a drunk to recover equilibrium and get ahead as he lurches from side to side. Even population pressure is conceived to provoke counter pressures and these latter then aid the cause of development. Thus, Hirschman is led to take a "calmer view" of the population explosion (Hirschman, 1958, p. 182) since it "qualifies as an inducement mechanism ..." (Hirschman, 1958, p. 181).

On the other hand, the insistence on the shortage of decision-making ability in underdeveloped countries suggests that he is not satisfied with the rate of growth actually being experienced by piecemeal efforts since a "shortage" must be in relation to some condition. It is difficult to believe that Hirschman actually means a shortage of "decision making ability," even though he uses this term frequently. What he must surely have in mind is insufficient inducement to invest rather than ability to make a decision. If the former is the case this would suggest that his diagnosis differs little from that of Nurkse and numerous other writers who have stressed the point of insufficient inducements. His real quarrel is not with a "theory of development" but with a specific proposal to accelerate development which he has named the "theory of balanced growth." He does not rely on market forces as he thinks there is a "shortage" of "decision making ability"; he believes that state or other intervention to stimulate investment, output and employment, if designed to meet actual and newly created effective demand, is unrealistic and naïve but that intervention to stimulate investment that will not meet effective demand is realistic. For some unexplained reason, the latter type of intervention is expected to generate "linkages" (forward, backward, vertical, horizontal and sideways) with repercussions on other firms and on demands and so create other investment (balanced?) opportunities, whereas interventions to induce investments to meet demands do not have such linkages. Finally, one learns by making mistakes but not by doing the right things.

It is interesting to note the stress Hirschman places on linkages, as the very concept of linkage rests on the efforts or response of the economic system to restore balance or equilibrium created by a profit opportunity (disequilibrium or unbalance) or the desire to minimize loss by overcoming bottlenecks (disequilibrium). Having cast out the desire to make profits by anticipating effective demands as a motivating force, he then relies upon it for the investments that are expected to follow original mistaken (unbalanced) investments "induced" by linkages. One might ask why attempts to anticipate demands are unrealistic in one case but realistic in the other or why skills are lacking for the projects designed to accelerate development by anticipating created demands but are amply available for the projects that result from other initial efforts to increase output and demand. There is no discussion of the point, which is a rather vital one, as Hirschman's main criticism of the big push type of approach lies precisely in the alleged lack of adequate skills to initiate and carry it out. One might even unkindly point out that it would be consistent with Hirschman's argument if skills to make profitable investments were lacking, as in this case losses would be incurred and "disequilibria, pressures and tensions" would be created whose solution would result in a "learning" process. Hence Hirschman's main criticism of the big push type of approach is not consistent with the approach he favours. He would doubtless retort that he does not favour any project but only those particular ones which entail the maximum linkages or repercussive value or in which a country learns the most. However, this argument does not enable him to escape the charge of inconsistency as both their selection and execution require "decision making ability" and "skills" which he has argued are lacking to carry out a balanced type of development.

Hirschman was not content to set up and then demolish a theory of balanced growth. He proceeded to espouse a policy of unbalanced growth. At the beginning of the exposition of his positive theory, he distinguishes between the "pure" theory of balanced growth and the less rigorous one that allows for a "see-saw" effect, a balance only over time and considerable scope for induced investment. This sounds like Nurkse's position except that Nurkse allowed for temporary unbalance arising from forces on both the supply and demand side, and Hirschman has restricted the statement to forces on the supply side. Two questions immediately arise: who espoused the "pure" theory of balanced growth, and wherein does "unbalanced" growth differ from the "less rigorous" statement of balanced growth just cited?

In answer to the first question, Hirschman quotes Scitovsky who, after remarking upon the actual see-saw characteristic of growth, wrote, "equilibrium is reached only when successive doses of investment and expansion in the two industries have led to the simultaneous elimination of investment in both" (quoted by Hirschman, 1958, p. 66), and only when there are no further pecuniary external economies does private profitability corresponds with social desirability. This will be recognized by any fair-minded reader as simply an academic device of exposition of the striving of the pricing mechanism toward the attainment of an ultimate goal of equilibrium that is never reached, and will be related to Scitovsky's concern with the nature of external economies. Hirschman, however, chooses to interpret it as *advocacy* of a theory on the part of Scitovsky, charging that he proposes "to short-circuit" the process of investments inducing other investments and "to reach in a single jump a new point of equilibrium where 'the elimination of investment' has been accomplished" (Hirschman, 1958). He continues, "development policy must concern itself with the judicious setting up of the kind of sequences and repercussions so well described by Scitovsky, *rather than with any attempt to suppress them*" (Hirschman, 1958, p. 66, italics added). It was possibly this grotesque charge that led Scitovsky (1959) much later to write an article specifically espousing the fast growth attainable through "unbalanced" growth (which, however, he pointed out is compatible with balanced growth in other contexts). In other words, it appears highly questionable whether any writer espoused the "pure theory of balanced growth."

We are then left with the interesting question of wherein the "unbalanced theory" differs from the "less rigorous balance theory" presumably attributed to Nurkse. It is a difficult question to answer. Both would appear to be concerned with inducements to invest. In Hirschman's view "the task of development policy is to maintain tensions, disproportions and disequilibrium" (Scitovsky, 1959, p. 66) whereas Nurkse sees "disproportionalities" as a necessary consequence of government intervention or Schumpeter-type waves of innovations. It appears to be a matter of emphasis. Scitovsky and Nurkse looked upon the desire to make profits as an incentive to investment. But Hirschman does not appear to dispute this. In discussing "complementarity" and "entrained want" he remarks that complementarity exists in "any situation where an increase in the demand for commodity A and the consequent increase in its output calls forth an increased demand for commodity B at its existing price" (Scitovsky, 1959, pp. 67–68). Rosenstein-Rodan, Nurkse and Scitovsky could have subscribed to this. Hence, Hirschman's apparently paradoxical statement that "the sequence that 'leads away from equilibrium' is precisely an ideal pattern of development" (Scitovsky, 1959, pp. 66–67), appears to be no more than a play on words. He seeks to create an issue here by asserting that the conventional meaning of "induced investment" is that investment which is directly related to past increases in output (Scitovsky, 1959, p. 70), whereas his concept of induced investment is restricted to those investments which are expected to benefit more from external economies than they will benefit other industries by creating external economies, that is, they "must be *net beneficiaries* of external economics" (Scitovsky, 1959, p. 71). This tortuous bit of reasoning is promptly abandoned by saying "we shall continue to speak of investment inducing other investments and shall simply be aware that there are widely varying degrees of 'inducements'" (Scitovsky, 1959). In thus extricating himself he neglected to point out that he was also abandoning his attempt to distinguish his treatment of inducements from that of the writers he was criticising.

Another attempt at a distinction between his "unbalanced" growth position and the "less rigorous" balanced growth position is made in his concept of the major constraint on development – the scarcity of "decision making ability." But if this is to make any sense, it must surely be a curious way of referring to lack of sufficient inducement to invest. Anyone who has worked in underdeveloped countries will attest to the fact that there is no lack of grandiose projects and proposals – that is, no lack of ability to "make decision" – but rather the lack is the ability to make "good" decisions; that is, good from the point of view of development, and the lack of adequate inducements to invest because of an unfavourable environment, lumpiness of many investment processes, the smallness of the market, the exchange constraint and so forth. However, it is possible that Hirschman actually does mean what he says – lack of ability to make decisions – as in a later work (Hirschman, 1967) he appears to come dangerously close to advocating concealing discouraging facts while exaggerating expected benefits in order to encourage decision making. This piece of dubious economics and even more dubious morality is exalted into "the Principle of the Hiding Hand" – "a way of inducing action through error, the error being an under-estimate of the project's costs or difficulties" (Hirschman, 1967, p. 29).

It might be thought that because of his emphasis on complementarity, linkages and induced investment, Hirschman might be expected to espouse the big push approach to the acceleration of development. His main reason for not doing so – the underdeveloped countries' alleged lack of ability to plan and the lack of requisite skills – has nothing to do with balanced or unbalanced growth and is equally present in the type of projects he advocates. He surely cannot reject the approach because of the danger that it may be so superbly successful as to result in perfect equilibrium and no further inducement to invest. Since he feels that underdeveloped countries are completely incapable of a more or less synchronized big effort, he should logically advocate it for the "tensions, disproportions and disequilibria" it would create and the valuable learning that would arise from efforts to correct the disequilibria that would result:

The conclusion that would appear to emerge from this examination is that the balanced vs unbalanced theory of growth issue does not exist and much valuable time and effort was dissipated in dealing with it. Worse, it diverted attention from real and pressing issues, which were consequently neglected. The main issue raised by Rosenstein-Rodan, Scitovsky and Nurkse and later by Nelson, Leibenstein and Myrdal was that of the underdevelopment trap or vicious circle or more simply and generally, the inability of the forces of the market to make adequate headway against the depressant factors. Different writers stressed different degrees of the nature and strength of the depressant factors and hence the solutions, which were probably natural, but all writers mentioned concurred on the central point that conscious and deliberate action was probably necessary to break out of the trap and accelerate development. Even Hirschman recognized a specific impediment and proposed means to alleviate it. However, this identification of the big push with balanced development and his general condemnation of both undoubtedly had influenced causing the main issue that concerned the writers he criticized to be ignored or slighted. The identification of growth with a positive rise in the GNP per capita and the statistical demonstration that virtually all underdeveloped countries were experiencing such a rise, and possibly the substitution of the terms "developing" or "lesser developed" for "underdeveloped" countries, all conspired to create a feeling that an underdevelopment trap does not exist, that growth is proceeding slowly but surely, and that therefore no big push or heroic measures of any sort are called for. But this is another story.

Here it only remains to appraise Hirschman's positive proposals. That all economic phenomena are related and that every price change, innovation, investment, change in demand and factor supplies have far-reaching repercussions on other economic phenomena is the core of equilibrium theory, pricing theory and the growth process. One can hardly make a useful theory out of disequilibria and advocate disequilibrating as a conscious policy. What one can do is to appraise the relative strength of the income-stimulating and depressant factors, the forces making for innovation, technical progress and investment against the forces making for continuance of dualism which leaves a major sector of the economy advancing little if at all, and advocate measures to strengthen the former and weaken the latter. The idea that underdeveloped countries and lending agencies should concentrate their efforts on particular projects selected deliberately because they create tensions and disproportionalities and attempt to compare them by calculating the possible extent and nature of the probable repercussions or linkages appears to be a completely impractical one. What, for example, is likely to be the net outcome of the repercussions set up by deliberately undershooting or overshooting the demand for electric power as contrasted with trying to estimate the probable demand and build it? As Michael Lipton (1962) later pointed out, Hirschman ends up with a frighteningly involved model with distinctions between social overhead and directly productive activities, compelled and induced activity, state and private activity, and in basic and consumer goods activities. Not only must projects be classified in these categories, but the subsequent linkages are unknown. Moreover, the approach, while involved, omits many of the more important income stimulating and depressant forces. The sequence that leads away from equilibrium as an ideal pattern and the espousal of unbalanced growth may be intriguing ideas to some academic writers but hardly furnish workable investment criteria to attain better factor proportions.

It is interesting to note Rosenstein-Rodan's (1961) brief further discussion of the theory or, more properly speaking, the policy of the big push, delivered in a paper presented at a meeting of the International Economic Association in Rio de Janeiro in 1957, but not published until 1961. This was entitled "Notes on the Theory of the Big Push" and was a brief, highly condensed statement. He had not read Hirschman but had been, I should judge, influenced by Nurkse as he remarked that "the theory of growth is very largely a theory of investment" (Rosenstein-Rodan, 1961, p. 57). With the passage of time and the emergence of new conditions, the treatment shows some interesting changes. The most significant modifications appear to be the much greater stress placed on indivisibilities in supply, especially in social overhead capital, and in external economies. There is still the basic argument that a number of simultaneous investments – the Big Push – will create the requisite demand for their output. But this is related in the later (1961) version more directly to an increase in the incentives to invest rather than to employment and output, and the necessity and indivisibility of social overhead capital appears as the first and major hurdles that must be overcome, perhaps amounting in terms of investment, in a closed society, to three-quarters of the whole.[16] He finds the explanation for Nineteenth Century lack of growth in underdeveloped countries in the deficiency of social overhead capital. International trade reduced the size of the minimum quantum of investment but does not dispense with the need for a big push. An interesting additional point is added on the psychological impact of speed and size of development and the probability that a number of isolated and small efforts may not add up to a sufficient impact on growth (Rosenstein-Rodan, 1961, p. 66). "Balance" is not mentioned except by implication when reference is made to the fact that "low elasticities of demand make it much more difficult to fit supplies to demand" (Rosenstein-Rodan, 1961, p. 63), a point earlier made by Nurkse.

Nurkse was a discussant of Rosenstein-Rodan's paper. The latter's change of emphasis to social overhead capital apparently was entirely acceptable to the former. He stated that to him "the more important substantive point, stressed in the paper before us, is that public overhead investment creates investment opportunities in directly productive activities" and that "overhead capital may have to be built ahead of demand" (Nurkse, 1961, p. 75). So the writer characterised as the leading exponent of a "theory of balanced growth" found no difficulty or inconsistency in advocating the creation of capacity in certain circumstances in advance of demand. Again, there was no mention of balance. However, Rosenstein-Rodan's change of emphasis to social overhead capital, while it made the theory of the Big Push more acceptable, also diminished the force and impact of the earlier presentation. Nurkse queried why the label "Big Push"?

> Is there a competing theory of the little push? We are nearly all agreed on the importance of public overhead investments, on the complementarity of consumers' wants, on the need for large savings and the vital role of enterprize, private and public, i.e. the drive for development. (Nurkse, 1961, p. 74)

Even though later he conceded that "to rely solely on the price system for the structural changes that constitute development may not be enough" (Nurkse, 1961, p. 75), the basic issue of the necessity or desirability of a critical minimum effort was blurred and lost sight of. Disguised unemployment or grossly underutilized manpower drops out of the picture. Balanced growth was introduced into the discussion in the summary of Alexandre Kafka (1961), who attributed to Nurkse the thought that "the principle of balanced growth did not seem to him to be a necessary component of the big push theory" (p. 78). On the whole, the discussion was rather unsatisfactory and failed to center on what should have been the key issue, whether a big push or a critical minimum effort was necessary or desirable to accelerate development. It did indicate, however, that as late as 1957 neither Rosenstein-Rodan nor Nurkse thought there was any real issue between balanced and unbalanced growth, nor did they identify the proposal to accelerate development by a massive effort with "the theory of balanced growth."

If "balance" is understood in the sense of the basic motivation and drive of the free enterprise system, it constitutes a defensible "theory" of growth in explaining the historical sequences in most currently developed countries. But this is only another way of saying that in certain favourable environments, the system has within itself a sufficient drive toward innovation and cost reduction. It hardly appears appropriate or descriptive to characterize this as "the theory of balanced growth." Writers who directed their criticisms at balanced growth were aiming at the wrong target.

An integral part of the argument of the present work is that the changing environment has worsened the chances that the system can perform for the underdeveloped countries as it performed for the developed, except in increasingly rare cases where the environment is favourable. Hence what needs examination is not so much the basic forces of economic change as the changing conditions and circumstances under which they operate. The balance versus unbalance issue was a red herring which served only to distract attention from more important problems.

It is tempting to bypass the balanced-unbalanced growth discussion as having only interest for the historian of economic thought. The reason for dwelling on it at some length is the unfortunate impact it had on proposals for a massive attack on the problem of underdevelopment. The "big push" appeared to pre-empt this field and it, in turn, became identified with balanced growth and became the target of many criticisms directed at this concept. No writer so far as I know attempted to separate the issues or to reformulate Rosenstein-Rodan's proposal to meet the valid criticisms. He himself did not attempt to push it beyond the idea stage stating that "attention is confirmed here to what ought to be done rather than how it is to be done." He did not even defend the idea for a period of fourteen years (18 if we go by the date of publications) and then settled for an infrastructure programme of public works which all governments and international agencies were actually pushing. Nurkse remained convinced of the inadequacy of the price mechanism, unaided, to achieve sufficiently rapid growth, but settled for an eclectic and diffused programme. For some inexplicable reason, Leibenstein's (1957) masterly argument for the necessity of a critical minimum effort was not identified with the necessity of a big push and was not spelled out in specific terms for specific countries. My own attempt (Currie, 1966) undoubtedly suffered from its somewhat hasty and unconventional presentation.

Nevertheless, the need for a big push or critical minimum effort is daily becoming more urgent in most underdeveloped countries. Conventional aid programmes and the reported steady growth in the meaningless reported GNP per capita figures only serve to conceal the alarming deterioration in the demographic and political environmental, the widening gap in consumption levels and the growing deprivation effect that make the possibility that the functioning of the price system will prove adequate less and less promising. Underutilized and poorly utilized domestic resources, poor mobility, inadequate and misused exchange resources, technical indivisibilities, inelasticity of demand, poorly functioning price and competitive systems, worsening ability to compete in international trade, rapidly growing populations and unfavourable political and social environments – all these in varying degrees and combinations must be taken into account if a new attack on the problem of underdevelopment is to be effective. If not, the job may well go by default to different economic systems better equipped to mobilize economies for a breakthrough on this front.

NOTES

1. An earlier version of this paper was presented on my behalf by Mario Garcia Molina at the Latin American History of Economic Thought (ALAHPE) conference, University of the Andes, Bogotá, 1 December 2017.
2. Reprinted by kind permission of Currie's daughter, Elizabeth Currie. The original manuscript is in the Currie archive, Rubenstein Library, Duke University, Durham, NC.
3. Arenas was previously head of the Centro de Investigaciones para el Desarrollo (CID) at the Universidad Nacional, having replaced Currie when he left for Canada in 1967.
4. Michele Alacevich (2009, ch. 2) gives the recruitment details and a balanced account of the tensions between Currie and Hirschman in 1952–1956 when both were in Colombia. A somewhat less-balanced account is in Jeremy Adelman's (2013) Hirschman biography,

reviewed in Sandilands (2015b). See also Sandilands (1990, 2015a) and Álvarez, Guiot-Isaac and Hurtado (2020).

5. Allyn Abbott Young (1876–1929) was president of the American Economic Association, the American Statistical Association and the British Association, a unique record. It was his 1928 presidential address to the British Association on "increasing returns" that was seminal for the "Big Push" debate and continues to influence modern "endogenous growth" theory (Chandra, 2022; Sandilands, 2009). Currie devoted much of his later career to explaining its theoretical and policy implications, including in a posthumous publication (Currie, 1997). His tribute to Young as a teacher is in Sandilands (1999).

6. Thus Currie supported Leibenstein against Hirschman's "calmer view" of population growth. He also criticised Hirschman's interpretation of Nurkse and Rosenstein Rodan (who both acknowledged Young's influence) as "balanced-growth" theorists, though elsewhere Currie criticised Nurske for excessive emphasis on the supply of savings and capital as (autonomous) causal constraints on growth. He instead stressed the (endogenous) dependence of savings and investment on demand-side constraints capable of being relaxed in non-inflationary ways, including through action to remove market imperfections that repress demand for key sectors (see below).

7. In Hirschman's (1967) review of this book, he questioned Currie's belief in elastic agricultural supply; rejected his claim that land redistribution would not help; and criticised his "breakthrough" plan as requiring emergency controls at peak efficiency "for at least a generation" before the rural labour force could fall below ten percent of the total – another case of an unrealistic big push. However, he did applaud Currie's "commendable desire to tackle the present situation with the means at hand instead of waiting for some *deus ex machina* – be it large-scale foreign aid, improved terms of trade, an interregional common market, or revolution."

8. This is the focus of Paul Krugman's (1993) reformulation of Big Push theory, with particular reference to Hirschman (1958). Alacevich (2007, p. 13, n. 32) also discusses Krugman in the context of Hirschman's defence of the decision to build an integrated steel plant in Colombia, on the basis of technical input–output linkages (rather than on its likely absolute size which depends on the potential size of demand for the industry's own output).

9. Bent Flybjerg (2017) reviewed Hirschman's *Development Projects Observed* (1963) and concluded that empirical support for a benevolent "Hiding Hand" was weak, being subject to "optimism and sample biases". It was more often a *malevolent* Hiding Hand. He thus disputed Cass Sunstein's (2015) suggestion that the Hiding Hand supported his own "nudge" theory in behavioural economics.

10. In this, Hirschman differs from Nurkse (1953) whose "horizontal" and "vertical" inter-industry complementarities allowed for individual sectors to grow at different rates according to differing elasticities of demand; that is, he called for a balance of sectoral supply with the *unequal* growth of sectoral demand. It did *not* mean that all sectors should be expanded at the same rate or according to input-output coefficients. This is consistent with Currie's leading sectors model of growth, spelled out in Currie (1974) to explain the theory behind the 1972–1974 Colombian national plan. See also Chandra (2006) and Chandra and Sandilands (2006).

11. Currie (1974) specifies the conditions that would qualify a sector as a *significant* potential leader rather than follower. Currie (1983) discusses these in the context of different "multiplier" concepts, including the "input–output multiplier". He believed the latter cannot be computed independently of price and income elasticities of demand in the real or "reciprocal" sense of J B Say and Allyn Young.

12. Rosenstein Rodan (1984, p. 214) worried about "an indivisibility in the supply of saving" needed for a "high minimum quantum of investment". He thought there was a "zero (or very low) *price* elasticity of the supply of savings," but a high *income* elasticity with a higher growth rate once a critical minimum effort was achieved. Currie was much more confident about the response of savings to a higher real return – the price elasticity – as well as the income elasticity. The results amply justified Currie's optimism (see Sandilands 1990, ch. 10). Furthermore, Rodan (1984, ch. 11) and Currie (1976)

describe his role in influencing more efficient urban design and the public capture of unearned land values as cities grew in size and scope.

13. This is Chapter 19 of an unpublished book on economic development that Lauchlin Currie (1902–1993) wrote in 1969–1971 at Simon Fraser University, Canada. Reprinted by kind permission of his daughter, Elizabeth Currie.

14. Nurske (1961 [1957]) came close to doing this in his 1957 lectures at Istanbul which were relatively unknown but not, I shall argue, in his well-known *Problems of Capital Formation in Under-Developed Countries* (1953) on which the attacks were levelled.

15. See also my discussion of Nurkse's views in Currie (1966, ch. 9).

16. Currie (1966, p. 60). It was this emphasis on social overhead capital that caused me to give too scanty recognition to the value of Rosenstein-Rodan's contribution and the close relation of the Big Push to my own Breakthrough, in *Accelerating Development* (Currie, 1966, pp. 74–75).

REFERENCES

Currie, L. (1966). *Accelerating development: The necessity and the means.* New York, NY: McGraw-Hill.

Fleming, M. (1955). External economies and the doctrine of balanced growth. *The Economic Journal, 65*(June), 241–256.

Hirschman, A. O. (1958). *The strategy of economic development.* New Haven: Yale University Press.

Hirschman, A. O. (1963). *Development projects observed.* Washington, DC: The Brookings Institution.

Kafka, A. (1961). The theoretical interpretation of Latin American economic development. In H. S. Ellis & H. C. Wallich (Eds.), *Economic development of Latin America* (pp. 1–28). London: Macmillan.

Leibenstein, H. (1957). *Economic backwardness and economic growth.* New York, NY: Wiley.

Lowe, A. (1965). *On economic knowledge.* New York, NY: Harper & Rowe.

Nurkse, R. (1953). *Problems of capital formation in underdeveloped countries.* Oxford: Oxford University Press.

Nurkse, R. (1961 [1957]). "The conflict between 'balanced growth' and international specialization," and "some reflections on the international financing of public overhead investments." *Lectures on Economic Development.* Istanbul University. Reprinted as "Balanced and unbalanced growth" in G. Haberler & R. M. Stern (Eds.), *Equilibrium and growth in the world economy: Economic essays by Ragnar Nurkse* (pp. 241–278). Cambridge, MA: Harvard University Press.

Rosenstein-Rodan, P. N. (1943). Problems of industrialisation of Eastern and south-eastern Europe, *Economic Journal, 53*(June–September), 202–211.

Rosenstein-Rodan, P. N. (1961). Notes on the theory of the "big push." In H. S. Ellis & H. C. Wallich (Eds.), *Economic development of Latin America* (pp. 57–81). London: Macmillan.

Scitovsky, T. (1954). Two concepts of external economies. *Journal of Political Economy, 62*, 143–151.

Scitovsky, T. (1959). Growth, balanced or unbalanced? In M. Abramovitz et al. (Eds.), *The allocation of economic resources: Essays in honor of Bernard Francis Haley.* Stanford, CA: Stanford University Press.

Young, A. A. (1928). Increasing returns and economic progress. *Economic Journal, 38*(December), 527–542.

CHAPTER 9

AN AMERICAN ECONOMIST IN A DEVELOPMENTAL STATE: MARION CLAWSON AND ISRAELI AGRICULTURAL POLICY, 1953–1955

Daniel Schiffman and Eli Goldstein

ABSTRACT

The American agricultural economist Marion Clawson advised the Israeli government during 1953–1955. Clawson, a protégé of John D. Black and Mordecai Ezekiel, criticized the government for ignoring economic considerations, and stated that Israel's national goals – defense, Negev Desert irrigation, immigrant absorption via new agricultural settlements, and economic independence – were mutually contradictory. His major recommendations were to improve the realism of Israel's agricultural plan; end expensive Negev irrigation; enlarge irrigated farms eightfold; freeze new settlements until the number of semi-developed settlements falls from 300 to 100; and limit new Negev settlements to 10 over 5–7 years. Thus, Clawson ignored political feasibility and made value judgments. Minister of Finance Levi Eshkol and Minister of Agriculture Peretz Naphtali rejected Clawson's recommendations because they ignored Israel's national goals. By September 1954, Clawson shifted towards greater pragmatism: He acknowledged that foreign advisors should not question the national goals or make value judgments, and sought common ground with the Ministry of Agriculture. At his initiative, he wrote Israel Agriculture 1953/54 in collaboration with the Ministry of Agriculture. Israel Agriculture was a consensus document: Clawson eschewed recommendations and accepted

Research in the History of Economic Thought and Methodology: Including a Selection of Papers Presented at the First History of Economics Diversity Caucus Conference
Research in the History of Economic Thought and Methodology, Volume 41B, 177–219
Copyright © 2023 by Daniel Schiffman and Eli Goldstein
ISSN: 0743-4154/doi:10.1108/S0743-41542023000041B009

that the government might prioritize non-economic goals. In proposing Israel Agriculture, Clawson made a pragmatic decision to relinquish some independence for (potentially) greater influence. Ultimately, Clawson was largely unsuccessful as an advisor. Clawson's failure was part of a general pattern: Over 1950–1985, the Israeli government always rejected foreign advisors' recommendations unless it was facing a severe crisis.

Keywords: Foreign economic advisors; economic development; economic planning; agriculture; irrigation; Israel

I. INTRODUCTION

The role of development advising in the exchange of ideas between developed and developing nations is a fruitful field of inquiry (Alacevich & Boianovsky, 2018). The role of American agricultural economists in development advising is a particularly intriguing topic. As Burnett (2011) explains

> Agricultural economists ... were in the first rank of American development efforts abroad for a reason. As an administrative science, agricultural economics was a preestablished body of academic expertise in technology transfer. Agricultural economists also brought with them their political experience as policy experts.

The global activities of American agricultural economists have been documented in studies of international institutions such as the FAO, World Bank and Ford and Rockefeller Foundations (e.g., Loveridge, 2017; White, 2013). However, detailed studies of development missions by American agricultural economists, as individuals, are lacking, with the notable exception of Stross (1986, Ch. 7) on John L. Buck in China.

This paper documents the activities of the American agricultural economist Marion Clawson in Israel during June 1953–July 1955. Clawson served as a member of the Economic Advisory Staff, a group of American economists that was invited and funded by the Government of Israel. A protégé of John D. Black and Mordecai Ezekiel, Clawson brought to Israel extensive US government experience in agricultural economics and land management.

Clawson quickly discovered that Israeli agriculture and irrigation were highly inefficient, and that agricultural and irrigation planning almost completely ignored economic considerations.[1] We tell the story of Clawson's valiant but largely unsuccessful effort to change this reality, using archival documents from Israel State Archives and the Marion Clawson Papers (MCP) at the Forest History Society.[2]

The remainder of the paper is organized as follows: Section II describes the Economic Advisory Staff, Section III presents Clawson's biography and professional orientation, Section IV introduces Israel's national goals and describes the challenge of immigrant absorption, Section V presents a primer on Israeli agriculture and irrigation, Section VI describes the institutional environment, Section VII sets out Clawson's conception of his advisory role and early views,

Section VIII sets out Clawson's findings and recommendations, Section IX documents the government's response to Clawson's recommendations, Section X documents Clawson's shift from purism towards greater pragmatism, and Section XI concludes.

II. THE ECONOMIC ADVISORY STAFF[3]

Why was the Economic Advisory Staff established? Beginning in April 1952, Israel repeatedly requested emergency US aid to pay down short-term foreign debt. The Truman administration provided just enough aid to avert default; concurrently, it sent Raymond Mikesell to Israel in July 1952 to investigate Israel's financial condition and make recommendations regarding aid conditionality. The government accepted Mikesell's conditions and received the aid, but Israel's financial condition remained dire. In December 1952, Ben-Gurion decided to form an economic advisory unit that would formulate policies to move Israel towards economic independence – that is, ending Israel's chronic dependence on foreign debt. Ben-Gurion sought economists with US government experience; he understood that the Truman-Eisenhower transition created a brief window of opportunity to recruit them. Ben-Gurion asked Oscar Gass, Israel's economic advisor in Washington, to organize and lead the Economic Advisory Staff.

The Economic Advisory Staff was formed as a unit within the Prime Minister's Office, and was fully funded by the government under contract with Gass' economic consulting firm. The Economic Advisory Staff had six senior members:

1. Oscar Gass (Director), formerly an economist in the office of the Treasury Secretary (1938–1943) and the War Production Board (1943–1944), and Israel's economic advisor in Washington (1946–1953).
2. Bernard Bell (Deputy Director, Acting Director from June 1954), formerly chief economist of the Export-Import Bank (1946–1953).
3. Bertram Gross, formerly Executive Secretary of the Council of Economic Advisers (1946–1952), and a drafter of the 1946 Employment Act.
4. Abba Lerner, the world-renowned theoretical economist.[4]
5. Clawson, whose official title was Senior Officer for Agriculture.
6. Arye Gaathon, the government's chief economic planner.

After an auspicious beginning, the Economic Advisory Staff developed a contentious relationship with Minister of Finance Levi Eshkol, and the government ignored much of the Economic Advisory Staff's advice. This was almost inevitable because the Economic Advisory Staff and the government had divergent policy goals: The Economic Advisory Staff prioritized efficient resource allocation and cost control while the government prioritized state building – national security, regional development and full employment.

Nevertheless, the Economic Advisory Staff made several important contributions: (a) It produced 120 policy memoranda of which 50 were authored by Clawson (see the Appendix for a complete listing); (b) It more than paid for itself through project evaluation (in this field, the government generally accepted its recommendations); (c) It developed good working relationships with four ministries, including the Ministry of Agriculture; (d) It trained young Israelis in applied economics.

III. MARION CLAWSON

Biography

Marion Clawson (1905–1998) was the son of a Nevada miner, rancher and farmer. After completing his B.A. and M.A. at the University of Nevada-Reno, Clawson joined the University of Nevada's Agricultural Experiment Station in 1926. There, he met the future institutionalist luminary Mordecai Ezekiel.[5] Ezekiel recruited Clawson to the USDA's Bureau of Agricultural Economics in 1929 (Clawson, 1987, pp. 86–87); at the time, the Bureau of Agricultural Economics "had more social scientists than the rest of the federal government combined" (Banzhaf, 2006). Clawson remained there through 1946; his supervisors were Oris V. Wells, a future Director of the Bureau of Agricultural Economics (1946–1953), and Sherman E. Johnson (5509/14-Gimmel). Clawson also came to know Bureau of Agricultural Economics Director Howard R. Tolley (1938–1946), an institutionalist (Gilbert, 2015, pp. 47–48) who had originally recruited Ezekiel (McDean, 1983); Louis H. Bean, Ezekiel's close colleague and fellow institutionalist; and Walter W. Wilcox, a future coauthor and future USDA Director of Agricultural Economics (Clawson, 1987, pp. 100–102).[6] Unlike Ezekiel, Tolley and other Bureau of Agricultural Economics/USDA institutionalists, Clawson was not directly involved in New Deal agricultural reforms[7] (Clawson, 1987, pp. 119–120), including the cooperative land-use planning effort of 1938–1942 (documented by Gilbert, 2015).

In 1936, Clawson, at the urging of his supervisors (Clawson, 1987, p. 92), enrolled at Harvard's Graduate School of Public Administration where he completed his Ph.D. in Economics in 1943 under John D. Black. At Harvard, Clawson was strongly influenced by Black and by the economic historian Abbott P. Usher. Black taught Clawson "how to bridge the gap between the economics of the individual farm and the economics of overall land use for a whole area," while Usher taught Clawson how to study institutional change using both qualitative and quantitative methods (Vaughn, 1995).[8]

During 1940–1942, Clawson was research coordinator of the Columbia Basin Joint Investigations, a massive Bureau of Reclamation project based in Spokane, Washington. There, Clawson played a leading role in the "difficult and tricky" endeavor of agricultural planning in an undeveloped area. World War II caused a 10-year delay that rendered Clawson's plans obsolete (Clawson, 1987, pp. 140–150). From 1942, Clawson participated in the Bureau of Reclamation's Central Valley (California) project, which was so highly politicized that US Senator Sheridan Downey (Democrat-California) publicly attacked Clawson's integrity (Clawson, 1987, pp. 150–160). At Central Valley, Clawson collaborated with Paul S. Taylor on research and policy advocacy (Kirkendall, 1964). Clawson was completely uninvolved with the USDA's contributions to the war effort (Clawson, 1987, p. 137). In 1946, Clawson coauthored a report on the Central Valley project with his future wife, Mary Montgomery (married 1947). During 1945–1946, Clawson taught at the USDA Graduate School (Inventory of the MCP) (where he had studied statistics before enrolling at Harvard; Clawson, 1987, p. 96), which had shifted away from institutionalism by then (Rutherford, 2011b).

In March 1948, Clawson became Director of the Bureau of Land Management. Clawson reorganized the Bureau of Land Management, dealt extensively with Congress, and managed a snow emergency in the West (Clawson, 1987, pp. 196–248; Muhn & Stuart, 1988, pp. 58–76). As a Truman appointee, Clawson was forced out by Eisenhower's Interior Secretary, Douglas McKay, in April 1953. Clawson immediately joined the Economic Advisory Staff (Clawson, 1987, pp. 244–245); this was the first time that he advised a foreign government.[9]

A prolific writer, Clawson published three books (two as sole author, one coauthored with Black and two others), 21 academic journal articles (16 as sole author), and numerous reports by 1953. As we shall see, Clawson continued to write prolifically while in Israel.

After returning from Israel in 1955, Clawson spent the rest of his career at Resources for the Future. There, he made major contributions to forestry (Sedjo, 2000) and cost-benefit analysis of outdoor recreation (Banzhaf, 2006, 2010).

Ideology and Methodology

Although Clawson came of age during the heyday of the institutionalist movement and was associated with some of its leading lights, he was a neoclassical economist at his core. As Banzhaf (2010) writes:

> Although fundamentally a marginalist, Clawson reflected the pluralism of American economics in the 1920s and 1930s, with interests covering wide ground, from the psychology of preference formation to the historical evolution of social institutions. First coming to government work in the New Deal years, Clawson was also a strong believer in planning. ... [In 1951, he wrote] that all future water development should be done by the federal government. ... In Balisciano's (1998) taxonomy, Clawson was a technical-industrial planner [a proponent of industrial planning by government experts, with emphasis on scientific management]

Clawson favored free markets, but accepted government intervention where necessary:

> I recognize that economic forces and processes are interfered with in the agriculture of many countries in the world today, including the United States. ... I do not quarrel with subsidies, controls, etc. as such; but ... they should be reexamined frequently and critically, to be sure they produce the desired results more cheaply and effectively than any alternative methods. ... Controls and subsidies should be eliminated, simplified or modified. Unless there is a clear-out gain from a particular control ... it should be eliminated. (#13)

In summary, Clawson advocated combining state planning with the price mechanism; thus, he was ideologically close to Ezekiel and Theodore W. Schultz (regarding Schultz, see Burnett, 2011).

Like most agricultural economists (including Black; Cochrane, 1989), Clawson sought to solve practical problems using existing tools, and had little use for formal theory (Banzhaf, 2006) or econometrics (unlike Ezekiel – see Fox, 1989). At Columbia Basin, Clawson learned to value realistic/up-to-date assumptions over theoretical elegance:

> All too often, an economist … gets absorbed by the details within his studies … and neglects the larger [economic, social, and political] framework within which they are set. His results may be impeccable for the economy and society he … assumed but completely unrealistic for the economy and society which exists or is developed. … Elaborate models are no more likely to be realistic than are simpler ones. (Clawson 1987, p. 150)

IV. ISRAEL'S NATIONAL GOALS CA. 1953[10]

National Goals

Israel's national goals, as defined by Ben-Gurion and his Mapai ruling party, were as follows: strong national defense; immigrant absorption, with no limit on Jewish immigration[11] (Gross, 1990; Krampf, 2009, 2018, p. 77); rapid economic development through large-scale investment in physical and human capital (Gross, 1990, 1995); full employment (like most Western governments at the time; Gross, 1990; Krampf, 2018, pp. 78, 92–93) and a rising standard of living to maximize net immigration, to be provided by a welfare state regime (Gross, 1990, 1995); equality of incomes (Bareli & Cohen, 2008; Gross, 1995) and equality in distribution of essential goods (Barkai, 1990, p. 36; Gross, 1995); attainment of economic independence (Krampf, 2009, 2018, Ch. 4); population dispersal for strategic reasons (Evans, 2006)[12]; food security and self-sufficiency[13]; and "return to the land" – maximizing Jewish employment in agriculture at the expense of bourgeois occupations (Metzer, 1998, pp. 195–196; Karlinsky, 2000)[14] while eschewing hired labor in agriculture (Kislev, 2015).[15] According to Mapai's worldview, these goals could be attained only through a planned economy with a preference for public and semi-public (labor managed) enterprises (Gross, 1990; Krampf, 2018, p. 99).

The Challenge of Immigrant Absorption

Immigrant absorption was a challenge of historic proportions. The mass immigration of 1948–1951 increased the population from 873,000 to 1,494,000; by 1953 the population had increased to 1,650,000 (Barkai, 1990, p. 99). The government had to provide the immigrants with food, housing, and employment and integrate them culturally, while defending the country from its Arab enemies (Gross, 1990; Hacohen, 2003; Lissak, 2003). To meet this challenge, the Israeli economy functioned on a wartime footing during the first years of statehood (Barkai, 1990, p. 38; Gross, 1990).

In 1949, Israel suffered severe shortages of food, fuel and foreign currency (Barkai, 1990, p. 37); that year, almost two thirds of the food supply was imported (Clawson, 1955a). To deal with these shortages, the government adopted an austerity and rationing regime that was modeled in many respects on the UK's

WWII rationing regime. As in other countries, Israel's austerity and rationing regime caused repressed inflation and black markets (Barkai, 1990, pp. 38–39). Because the regime failed to supply food of adequate quantity and quality, it was highly unpopular and widely disobeyed (Rozin, 2011, Ch. 1–2). In early 1951, global price increases due to the Korean War forced the government to increase official prices, which further eroded the public's faith (Barkai, 1990, pp. 39–40; Rozin, 2011, p. 97). Mapai finally bowed to public pressure in February 1952: It almost completely abolished austerity and rationing as part of the "New Economic Policy." CPI inflation was 14% in 1951, 58% in 1952 and 28% in 1953.

In mid-1952, 250,000 immigrants – one-sixth of Israel's Jewish population – lived in transit camps (*ma'abarot*) under extremely primitive conditions.[16] The transit camps "remained an ugly blot on the Israeli landscape and eliminating them [by constructing permanent housing] was an ordeal that continued for years to come" (Hacohen, 2003, pp. 231–232).

In 1950 the unemployment rate among immigrants was at least 14% versus 6.9% overall. The overall unemployment rate rose sharply from 7.2% in 1952 to 11.3% in 1953 (Barkai, 1990, pp. 41 and 99). Unemployment was disproportionately concentrated among immigrants born in Muslim countries who were less educated than veteran Israelis and immigrants from Western countries (Lissak, 2003; Patinkin, 1967, Ch. 1). To ameliorate structural unemployment among immigrants, the government established public works projects (Barkai, 1990, pp. 42–43; Gross, 1990; Hacohen, 2003, p. 135; Patinkin, 1967, pp. 34–35).[17] By the late 1950s, most immigrants had left public works for regular employment, leaving behind only the least-skilled (Barkai, 1990, p. 43).

Sociocultural integration was extremely difficult due to enormous cultural differences between immigrants from Muslim countries and the European-born ruling elite (Lissak, 2003). When Mapai functionaries forced religious immigrants to send their children to secular schools, a severe coalition crisis ensued, resulting in Ben-Gurion's resignation as Prime Minister in October 1950 and new elections in July 1951.

V. A PRIMER ON ISRAELI AGRICULTURE AND IRRIGATION CA. 1953[18]

Agriculture accounted for 11.4% of NDP, 17.2% of total employment (Michaely, 1975, p. 193) and 25% of Israel's Gross Domestic Fixed Capital Formation (vs. 18.3% in 1952) (Patinkin, 1967).

During 1948–1953, real agricultural output increased by 2.5 times; the area of irrigated crops increased by almost 2.5 times. New settlements accounted for 56% of the increase in irrigated area. Israel had 4 million dunams of "fairly good" arable land that could be cultivated with reasonably-priced irrigation water. Clawson classified these lands as Priority A – none in the Negev Desert; Priority B – over half in the Negev Desert. The government leased land to farmers very cheaply; thus, farmers felt like owners rather than tenants (Clawson, 1961).[19]

Over 1948–1954, the Jewish Agency, an international quasi-governmental organization that was responsible for Jewish immigration and settlement,[20] established approximately 20,000 new one-family farm units in approximately 400 new settlements. The new settlements, which were partially completed, accounted for approximately half of all agricultural settlements and 40% of all farm units. Due to lack of capital and experience, farmers on new settlements were highly dependent on Jewish Agency assistance (financial and otherwise). At the end of 1954, no new settlements had been weaned off Jewish Agency assistance, and only 53 of 400 were "mature" – potentially self-supporting via proposed investments. Many new farmers suffered from poor living conditions and were forced to take (non-agricultural) second jobs in order to make a living.

In June 1954, 95,000 individuals were mainly occupied in agriculture, of which 21,000 were self-employed, 40,000 were hired workers, 12,000 were members of kibbutzim (communes) and moshavim (semi-cooperative villages),[21,22] and 15,000 were family members. Although the government idealized the establishment of new family farms without hired labor ("self-labor"), hired labor comprised approximately 40% of agricultural employment, with the citrus sector accounting for approximately half of hired labor.

Farmers suffered greatly from the threat of terrorism (Clawson, 1955b):

> [...] A man works all day on his farm, and then several nights a month stands guard half the night[23]. ... Infiltrations, thefts, and assaults by individuals or groups from across the border are all too common. Livestock is stolen frequently. ... Farm tools and machines must always be brought ... home each night. ... Along the frontier, men and women in the fields may be fired upon at any time. Within settlements, a house may be bombed or fired upon at night. Far more serious than the physical losses ... is the constant watchfulness necessary, a watchfulness that places many people under a constant tension.

Marketing and distribution were carried out under abnormal conditions. Although rationing was almost completely abolished in February 1952, food and agriculture markets were very far from free. Marketing was transitioning from scarcity to abundance.

Agricultural exports were $23 million in 1953. In every year since 1948, citrus accounted for at least 75% of agricultural exports. In 1953, citrus fruits and citrus products accounted for 37.5% and 4.3% of Israel's exports, respectively (Table 1). Agricultural imports were $74 million in 1953. The share of imports in the food supply fell from almost 2/3 in 1949 to 47% in 1953, while per capita food consumption rose. In 1953, 96% of wheat for human consumption was imported; grain and flour accounted for 12.7% of all commodity imports (Stanford Research Institute, 1955, pp. 136–138, 310).

The largest subsidy items were imported animal fodder (subsidized indirectly via artificially low exchange rates) and milk production/marketing. Credit was also subsidized: For example, farmers in new settlements received interest-free loans for five years. Irrigation water was somewhat subsidized, but many farmers were unable to pay their water bills.

In June 1953, Bruce McDaniel, director of the US Technical Cooperation Administration in Israel, urged Eshkol (in Mikesell's presence) to draw up

Table 1. Composition of Israeli Exports, 1950–1960, %.

Year	Citrus Fruit	Other Agricultural Products	Citrus Products	Industrial Products (Excluding Citrus)	Diamonds	Mine and Quarry Products
1951	47.2	0.6	3.9	23.4	24.7	0.3
1952	35.5	0.4	7.1	30.5	26.1	0.2
1953	37.9	0.5	7.1	27.1	26.4	0.9
1954	37.5	0.9	4.3	32.5	22.2	2.6
1955	38.8	2.7	3.2	33.5	18.2	3.6
1956	35.5	2.9	2.4	33.3	22.8	3.3
1957	37.7	3.2	3.6	29.0	23.2	3.5
1958	34.5	4.3	2.7	30.5	25.2	2.9
1959	34.8	6.0	4.1	29.6	23.9	1.7
1960	26.0	6.9	3.0	34.8	25.6	3.7

Source: Michaely (1975, p. 197).

seven-year plans for agriculture, industry and natural resources (5364/11-Gimmel). The Joint Planning Center for Agriculture and Colonization (formed by the Ministry of Agriculture and the Jewish Agency's Colonization Department) was already preparing a seven-year agricultural plan (#12); Eshkol, the head of the Jewish Agency's Colonization Department (1948–1963) and a former Minister of Agriculture (1951–1952), adopted the third version of that plan – "Plan C."[24] Clawson was not consulted regarding Plan C.

Eshkol founded the national water carrier, Mekorot, in 1937, and led it through 1951. Thereafter, Eshkol "was the minister of water de facto" (Blass, 1973, p. 258). Mekorot was a semi-private company (ownership: Histadrut – General Federation of Labor 50%, Jewish National Fund 25%, Jewish Agency 25%; Herzog, 2019, p. 190). Tahal (=Water Planning for Israel) was founded in 1952 as a government company (until 1956, its shares were divided as follows: government 52%, Jewish Agency 24%, Jewish National Fund 24%; Herzog, 2019, p. 157); it oversaw planning, management and construction until 1956. Tahal's Director-General, Simcha Blass, had an acrimonious relationship with Eshkol that led to Blass' resignation from Tahal in 1956 (Blass, 1973, Introduction; Herzog, 2019, p. 198). Tahal's Deputy Director-General, Aharon Weiner, doubled as Mekorot's chief engineer and often clashed with Blass (Feitelson, 2013).[25] Israel's major water projects were the first (Eastern) Yarkon-Negev pipeline that opened July 19, 1955, and became fully operational ca. July 1956,[26] and the second (Western) Yarkon-Negev pipeline that was under planning in 1953 and was constructed ca. August 1955–1961 (see Fig. 1).[27] Herzog (2019, p. 151) describes the post-1948 development of the national water carrier as follows:

> Over the course of the 16 years from Israeli statehood to the completion of the national water carrier, the project was mired in ideological conflicts and debates between experts, governmental agencies vying for control over the planning and control of Israel's water, and a continuous reformulation of how to determine water rights, prices for water, and legal ownership of water.

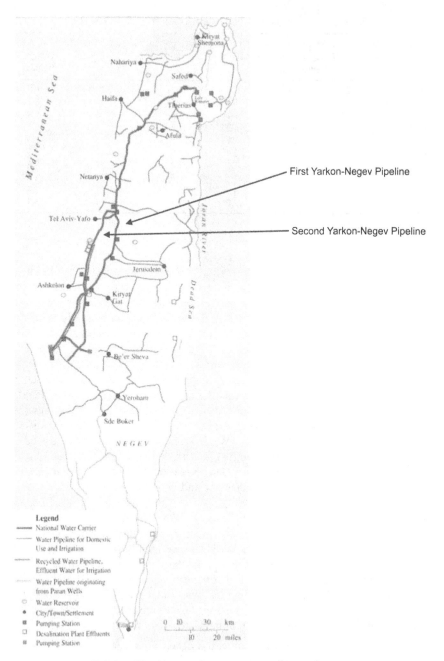

Fig. 1. Water Map of Israel. *Source*: Sitton (2000).

VI. THE INSTITUTIONAL ENVIRONMENT CA. 1953

Clawson came to Israel with his wife Mary and their two sons. The Clawsons resided in West Jerusalem, educated their sons in regular Israeli schools, took a keen interest in Israeli culture, socialized with Israeli political leaders and traveled all over the country (Clawson, 1957).

Clawson's deputy, Uri Ariav,[28] provided Clawson with indispensable assistance (Clawson, 1955b). Because Clawson did not know Hebrew, Ariav interpreted for Clawson and sometimes went to meetings in his place. Ariav must have been well-regarded in government circles: He met with Eshkol twice (including a private meeting) in July 1954 (4914/7-Peh).

Government personnel routinely leaked Economic Advisory Staff memoranda to the newspapers. The newspapers gladly published the memoranda (in summary), accompanied by sensationalized, politicized reporting that made rational discussion difficult (Schiffman & Goldstein, 2019).

The FAO's permanent representative, Albert G. Black, was John D. Black's student and coauthor and a former director of the Bureau of Agricultural Economics (1935–1938). Despite these connections, Clawson and A.G. Black never formed a significant relationship.[29]

The Ford Foundation made its first grant to Israel in 1953 (Sutton, 1987). Some of the funds were designated for agricultural development (Jewish Telegraphic Agency, May 5, 1953).[30]

Blass was advised by a group of American water engineers with extensive US government experience. Its leading members were James B. Hays (died October 1953), John S. Cotton, Abel Wollman, Harry Bashore and John Savage (Blass, 1973, pp. 227–236; 7144/4-Chet Tzadi). Until Blass' resignation from Tahal in 1956, his advisory group strongly influenced Israel's master plan for irrigation and hydroelectric power.

There was a sharp debate regarding the quantity of Israel's water supply. Like most Israeli politicians and experts before ca. 1955, Blass belonged to "the abundance school." He estimated Israel's water supply at over 3,000 million m^3 per year, above the Cotton-Hays estimate of 2,691 m^3 per year in July 1952. Weiner belonged to the "scarcity school;" his estimates were 2,415 million m^3 per year in February 1954 and 2,200 million m^3 per year in December 1955. The "scarcity school" was gaining influence; it would become the predominant school of thought by the late 1950s (Alatout, 2008a).[31]

In Israel's institutions of higher education, the academic fields of economics, agricultural economics and business administration were in their infancy (at best). In 1949, Don Patinkin brought US-style analytical economics to the Hebrew University. The Hebrew University's Faculty of Agriculture lacked an analytical agricultural economist until Yair Mundlak (Ph.D., UC-Berkeley) arrived in 1957 (Michaely, 2014). Thus, it is not surprising that Clawson taught two courses at the Hebrew University (Clawson, 1987, p. 186). Hebrew University's Department of Business Administration was founded in 1952.

The government had three PhD-level agricultural economists:[32] Ludwig Samuel (Ministry of Agriculture), Yehuda Lowe (Joint Planning Center) and Ludwig Yehuda Oppenheimer (Agricultural Research Station-Rehovot through 1954, Ministry of Agriculture thereafter). All three had been trained at German universities. Samuel and Lowe had served as Israeli agricultural attachés in Washington and Israeli representatives to the FAO. Lowe had also taken a three-month study tour of nine US states, arranged by the USDA and the Bureau of Reclamation (Jewish Telegraphic Agency, November 13, 1950, August 1, 1952). Clawson genuinely respected many of the government's agricultural policymakers (Gass to Ben-Gurion, November 19, 1953, 5486/1-Gimmel).

VII. CLAWSON'S CONCEPTION OF HIS ADVISORY ROLE AND EARLY CRITICISM OF ISRAELI ECONOMIC POLICY

Economic advisors often face two fundamental (interrelated) dilemmas:

a. If the advisor disapproves of the government's basic values and goals, should he say so openly? Should he remain or resign?
b. Should the advisor recommend policies regardless of political feasibility?

There are two schools of thought regarding these dilemmas that we shall call "pragmatist" and "purist":

a. Pragmatist – If an advisor cannot accept the government's basic values and goals, he should resign (Fischer, 2001; Seers, 1962). An advisor should not recommend policies that are politically infeasible (Brunetti, 2018; Fischer, 2001; Galbraith, 1979; Pigou, Macmillan Committee testimony, May 28, 1931; Seers, 1962).
b. Purist – an advisor should recommend economically efficient policies, regardless of political feasibility (Keynes, Macmillan Committee testimony, May 28, 1931; Milton Friedman, E. A. Goldenweiser and Edwin Nourse – Fishman & Fishman, 1957).

How did Clawson envision his advisory role? Before September 1954, Clawson was a purist: He believed that advisors should communicate "frankly" with policymakers (#13) without fear of controversy (Clawson, 1987, pp. 159–160) and asserted that the Economic Advisory Staff must criticize conventional wisdom and "speak up on unpopular issues" without hesitation (#35). Most importantly, Clawson reserved the right to "question or comment" on Israel's national goals (#13). But for diplomacy's sake, he declared that he accepted the national goals and was "chiefly concerned with means, timing, and cost of reaching those goals" (#14).

In January 1954, Clawson criticized Israel's rejection of economic analysis as a basis for policy-making, the phenomena of inflation and speculation, and the

Israeli tendency to pay lip service to economic independence (Clawson, 1957, pp. 96–99):

> [...] the experiences of the past thirty years or more ... have been the worst possible training ground for any critical-economic analysis today. ... Things had to be done for policy or political reasons and cost was not considered. Land had to be bought wherever and whenever Jews could get it, immigrants had to be helped to come in, and settlements had to be established. ... Two important economic forces have been hard at work: rising prices and gifts from abroad. ... For over thirty years speculation has been more profitable than efficiency in production. ... Since the earliest Jewish settlements here, financial aid from abroad has been essential ... .[As a] result. ... it [is] almost impossible for so-called foreign experts to present a careful economic analysis which points out the best course of action, based on Israel's income. The men in authority in the government, and also Israelis as a whole, say on the one hand they must be independent, but when presented with a plan to live within their income ... they are apt to exclaim in horror that the country must have more than that and if they had spent the past thirty years being sensible, Israel would never be a full-fledged [politically] independent country. The foreign experts say that is fine, but the government should make up its mind what it wants; to be independent or to continue the old course. If the former, act as if you meant it; if the latter, say so; but do not give lip service to the former and act on the latter basis. ...

> Marion has ... suggested that [agricultural planning] must include some consideration of demand for agricultural commodities, costs of producing them, and economic considerations generally. All present plans are utterly devoid of such mundane and boring details. Some top agricultural officials have told Marion that [economic considerations] will be considered once the country gets on a self-sufficient basis agriculturally. Marion says that is sheer nonsense.

Throughout his stay in Israel, Clawson avoided political statements and media interviews as stipulated in his Economic Advisory Staff contract, with one notable exception: In mid-1954, Ariav published two lengthy opinion pieces that castigated the government's agricultural and irrigation policies, based on Clawson's views (*Haaretz*, June 23 and July 7, 1954). Although Ariav did not mention Clawson's name, it was reasonable to assume that Clawson had approved publication. Fortunately for Clawson, Ariav's op-eds did not provoke a negative reaction from Eshkol.[33]

VIII: FINDINGS AND RECOMMENDATIONS

Agriculture: Major Weaknesses

Although Clawson praised Israeli agriculture for its "outstanding" development since 1948 (#13), he identified several major weaknesses (#13, unless otherwise stated):

Settlement and farming are generally not geared to land characteristics. Irrigation water costs are least three times US irrigation water costs (#37), and 5–10 times irrigation water costs in comparable countries (#6). Furthermore,

> [...] the timing of regional irrigation development has been almost exactly backwards – expensive and dubiously feasible projects are built first, while cheaper projects that might [at least] pay for themselves ... are delayed.

Israeli agriculture is too capital intensive[34] and capital is used wastefully (#25). Israel, a country with scarce capital but plentiful labor, often uses more capital than would be used in the US.[35] Human capital is low: "Many settlers are still unskilled in farming and are reluctant entrepreneurs" (Clawson, 1955b). Output per worker is just 37.5% of the US level (#37).

Production and consumption are distorted by subsidies, price ceilings and supports, various controls, exchange rate variations, and the like. The government extends or withholds credits, supplies and equipment, in order to artificially stimulate production of certain commodities in high-cost regions. Marketing and processing are poorly organized.

The government completely disregards costs – both direct costs and opportunity costs. Policymakers are unaware of the costs of their decisions and planners do not inform them.

The process of policy formation is "weak and inefficient." The Cabinet and Knesset adopt misguided policies because they fail to realize that Israel's national goals are mutually incompatible:

> [...] national ideals of full irrigation development of the entire country, independent farmers on their own land hiring little or no labor, permanent agriculture based on continued use of the soil in each locality, ample food supply at reasonable cost for non-farm people, and farm living on an essentially Western standard, are mutually incompatible. ... Likewise, the drive for economic self-sufficiency in agriculture without regard to costs is inconsistent, because maximum production can be achieved only by lowering costs. ... The ideals are not abandoned or modified, but instead programs mutually inconsistent among themselves and with these ideals are approved and financed. (#11)

A major consequence of the weakness in policy formation is that policymakers make wasteful expenditures in the name of security, without consulting the military:

> In almost every agricultural and irrigation program various actions are taken, often at relatively great cost, for 'security.' The magic word 'security' seems to justify anything and everything. ... On questioning the nature of the national hazard in the event of war shows [great] diversity; it seems that in Israel every man is, if not his own general, at least his own chief of staff. ... Very substantial sums are being expended in the name of security, and some of them, at least, are being wasted, for some contradict, or offset others. ... In our discussions with military officials they have rejected the security benefits imputed to certain actions by those responsible for them. There may well be instances in which the military will overlook some important factor, or in which its judgment should be overridden. But it is clearly one thing to consider their judgment and overrule it, and a very different matter never to consider their views at all. (#11)

Agricultural Employment

Clawson excoriated the government's policy of creating new agricultural jobs for the long-term unemployed.

> [Some] argue that ... it would be better to have some of [the long-term unemployed] partially employed in agriculture than to have them wholly unemployed in the cities. [This implies] a program of consciously trying to place more people into agriculture than necessary [in order to] ... keep unemployment concealed. ... That is a philosophy of despair that I am not yet ready to accept. ... Even if one grants that there will be many unemployed for many years, is agriculture the best place to put them? (#35)

Clawson asserted that agriculture could not absorb many more workers, at least for several years.

Agricultural Planning

Clawson rejected Plan C as unrealistic, because government planners failed to consider demands and costs (#15). Plan C projected a 134% increase in real agricultural output (Eshkol, 1954), and increases of 37% and 81% in per capita fruit and vegetable consumption, respectively. Clawson pointed out that supply curves slope upwards: The planned quantities would only be produced if consumers would be able to pay sufficiently high prices. Was this realistic?

To answer that question, Clawson performed the following exercise: Assuming that the quantities specified in Plan C would be produced in 1960, what would be the percentage changes in prices of various commodities over 1953–1960, conditional on per capita income growth? Assuming zero per capita income growth, Clawson projected price declines of 7.5–37.2% for vegetables, potatoes, legumes, fruit, wheat, milk/milk products and fish. On the other hand, Clawson projected increases of 69.4% and 92.8% in the (official) prices of eggs and meat, respectively, because their per capita outputs were projected to decrease (Table 2) (#34).

Based on this exercise, Clawson concluded that Plan C's projections for agricultural income, farm units and employment in 1960 were extremely over-optimistic. He estimated that no more than 65,000–70,000 farm units would be necessary in 1960 (vs. 43,000 in 1953; #39), assuming zero labor productivity growth versus the 80,000 farm units contemplated by agricultural leaders.

Table 2. Percentage Changes in Agricultural Retail Prices, 1953–1960: Clawson's Projections Based on Plan C Quantities Versus Actual.

Product	Clawson's Projection Assumption: % Change in Per Capita Income = −20%	Clawson's Projection Assumption: % Change in Per Capita Income = 0%[a]	Clawson's Projection Assumption: % Change in Per Capita Income = 20%	Actual % Change in Per Capita Income = 71%
Vegetables	−49.8%	−37.2%	−24.7%	27.5% vegetables and potatoes
Potatoes	−39.0%	−34.3%	−29.6%	27.5% vegetables and potatoes
Fruits	−42.8%	−23.2%	−2.0%	93.9% citrus, 54.7% other fruits
Milk and milk products	−25.9%	−7.5%	10.9%	28.5% Milk
Wheat	−9.1%	−9.1%	−9.1%	21.9% all field crops
Eggs	29.0%	69.4%	109.7%	49.7%
Fish	−26.2%	−7.7%	10.7%	28.8%
Meat	49.4%	92.8%	141.0%	55.6%

Sources: Projected percentage changes–calculated from #34, Table 8. Actual percentage changes–calculated from Mundlak (1964a, p. 57).

[a] According to Clawson, this was the most likely scenario.

If labor productivity growth continued at current (positive) rates or accelerated, only 50,000–55,000 farm units might be necessary. Clawson warned that excessive growth in farm units

> would mean low incomes per farm, possibly lower in many instances than farmers will accept or for which they will produce unless we were willing heavily to subsidize agriculture at the expense of the consumer. And then we would face the problem of how much subsidy the rest of the producers and consumers could afford or would tolerate. (#37)

Because Plan C envisioned 10,000–30,000 superfluous farm units, it "would entrench inefficiency and low earnings in agriculture and hence a poor market for non-agricultural products, and would almost surely lead to higher costs of food and hence higher wages and lower international competitiveness [in] industry." Instead, Clawson advocated maximizing agricultural output per worker and incomes by having less but "higher quality" employment. This would require less capital and higher capital utilization (#41).

The newspapers reported Clawson's objections to Plan C. Clawson was quoted as saying that the Joint Planning Center understood Plan C's shortcomings and would work with the Economic Advisory Staff to remedy them (*Zmanim*, January 24, 1955).

The National Irrigation Plan: Major Weaknesses

In an early memorandum, Clawson questioned Israel's national irrigation goals (#3):

> I recognize that there is strong sentiment and powerful forces pushing for maximum irrigation development in Israel. The idea of dry but fertile land [especially in the Negev] lying more or less unused, and of potential irrigation water wholly unused, impresses many people as unsound...if not downright unmoral. But costs [of irrigating distant lands, against gravity] cannot be escaped. ...Irrigation which cannot pay its own way is equally unproductive. ...I do not mean...to oppose the national irrigation plan unequivocally and completely. But I do argue that a scheme of this magnitude, with obvious serious shortcomings, should not be adopted and begun without the most thorough and serious study and public discussion.

He elaborated:

a. Irrigation costs are prohibitively expensive for low value-per-acre crops such as cotton, sugar beets, irrigated cereals and grains. Unless irrigation costs are reduced, Israel will not achieve international competitiveness in these crops (#6).

b. Government agricultural planners must state openly that excessive irrigation costs (as planned by Mekorot) make current agricultural plans infeasible (#8).

c. Regional irrigation development has lagged in areas where irrigation costs are average or less, and where making water available would facilitate rapid agricultural development. The Eastern Yarkon-Negev pipeline that is under construction will carry water through a region where it is badly needed and can be relatively cheap, to a distant region where it will be expensive even by Israeli standards (#13).

d. The uniform nationwide price for water causes resource misallocation[36] (#45). Water prices should vary by region, to reflect regional differences in irrigation costs.

In the debate regarding Israel's water supply, Clawson sided with Weiner and the scarcity school. He argued that the Cotton-Hays estimate was unrealistically high, and stated that a realistic estimate "might well [be] 2,000 [million m³ per year] or less" (1955a, pp. 4, 28–29). He asserted that current water plans were based on outdated assumptions (1955a, p. 43); this criticism was aimed at Blass and his American advisors (Clawson criticized the Cotton plan by name in #43).

Irrigation Costs

To reduce irrigation costs and/or minimize their deleterious effects, Clawson proposed the following:

a. Shift irrigation development from the Negev to lower-cost areas, thus reducing average central irrigation system costs by up to 20%. Local distribution costs can be halved via drastic farm reorganization, with sprinkler systems for large fields and surface irrigation where possible. Full implementation of these measures will reduce national average irrigation costs by 40% (#6).
b. Tahal should reduce construction and operating costs for the central irrigation system by much as 20% by abolishing needlessly costly construction methods (that are not used in the US) and pumping methods that entail high energy input and low yield per well (#10, 2nd version).
c. Sharply reduce local irrigation distribution costs (=one-third of total costs). Considerable savings are possible even with the current small farms, since the average new settlement farm remains mostly unirrigated. With larger farms, irrigated using gravity methods, labor costs in irrigation could also be sharply reduced (#10, 2nd version).

Agricultural Settlements

In November 1953, Clawson declared that because immigration had slowed, the government should strengthen existing agricultural settlements rather than founding new ones. He proposed freezing new settlements until the number of partially developed post-1948 settlements declines from 300 to 100. He argued that these 300 settlements cannot survive in a competitive market, because they generally have only 5–10 dunams irrigated out of a total farm unit of 28 dunams – which is too small for efficient production even if fully irrigated (#13). The minimum size for efficient production is 40 dunams (#6).[37]

Furthermore, new projects should deliver water only to existing settlements and only to low-cost areas. In the Negev, irrigation projects should be limited to existing settlements until projects in low-cost areas have been completed. The second (Western) Yarkon-Negev pipeline should be cancelled. The planned diversion of the Jordan River through the coastal area to the Negev should wait until low-cost areas are fully developed (#14).

Over time, Clawson moderated his position. In April 1954, he stated that "It will be desirable for the next 5–7 years to limit new [Negev] settlements to at most ten [and] to divert at most 90 million m³ of water to the Negev ... instead of the presently planned 200 million m³" (#33). In September 1954, he presented two options for the next 3–5 years: (a) Establish 50–150 new settlements; (b) Establish fewer than 25 new settlements, and bring existing settlements to maturity as soon as possible (#33).

When Clawson opposed the establishment and irrigation of new settlements and the construction of the second Yarkon-Negev pipeline, he made the value judgment that the non-economic benefits were not worth the costs. This was problematic: As Seers (1962) writes, "to make value judgments about policy in a foreign country seems to me particularly questionable."

IX. THE GOVERNMENT'S REACTION TO CLAWSON'S RECOMMENDATIONS

The following policymakers reacted to Clawson's recommendations: Minister of Finance Levi Eshkol,[38] Minister of Agriculture Peretz Naphtali and Ministry of Agriculture Deputy Director-General Arye Amir – Clawson's closest government contact,[39] and Tahal Director-General Simcha Blass. These policymakers decisively rejected Clawson's recommendations.

Eshkol was predisposed towards rejecting Clawson's recommendations. Eshkol had played a pivotal role in Negev settlement and irrigation, both before and after the founding of the State (Porat, 1991, 1995).[40] He disparaged foreign advisors, and as Mekorot's founder, he was so confident in his own expertise that he tried to dissuade the Economic Advisory Staff from studying irrigation (Schiffman & Goldstein, 2019).[41]

On January 13, 1954, Eshkol told the Knesset that the population must be dispersed throughout the country; therefore, expensive irrigation projects would continue[42] despite the disapproval of certain foreign experts (90/28-Kaf):

> If [certain experts] tell us that raising water to Manara [on the Lebanese border, 188 km north of Tel Aviv] costs a lot, we reply: That is correct. But if they tell us that it is not worthwhile ... we do not accept that. If [an expert] says that the Jordan River waters can be transferred to a close location, up to the Jezreel Valley, then we say that this is a very beautiful plan, but we do not accept it.

Presumably, Eshkol was referring to Clawson. Eshkol also instructed Gass to alter the Economic Advisory Staff's irrigation plan:

> Mr. Gass: According to your plan, Israeli agriculture ends here [Eshkol placed his ruler on the map at Beer Tovia, 50 km south of Tel Aviv[43]]. ... We want it to end here [Eshkol placed his ruler on the map at a point 60 km south of Beer Sheba = 170 km south of Tel Aviv[44]]. ... Please take care of this, expert gentlemen. (undated; Nevo-Eshkol, 1989, p. 80)

Clawson was in frequent contact with the Ministry of Agriculture and Joint Planning Center, especially Ministry of Agriculture Deputy Director-General Amir.[45] After Gass sent memoranda #10, #13 and #15 (with summaries) to Ben-Gurion, Eshkol and Naphtali, Amir told Naphtali that Clawson's advice was "dangerous and misleading," because it was based on two false assumptions (*italicized,* followed by Amir's counterarguments in regular type; Amir to Naphtali, December 18, 1953; 2433/21-Gimmel):

1. *There is no urgent need for new agricultural settlements because mass immigration has ended, and many unemployed refuse to live in settlements.* Although immigration has declined significantly, immigrant absorption is still unsatisfactory – 30,000–40,000 are permanently unemployed. The Jewish occupational structure is worrisome: Agriculture and industry accounted for just 38% of employment in 1952 versus a healthy minimum of 45%.[46]
2. *Current agricultural output is sufficient to provide urgent dietary needs.* Israel is self-sufficient in fruits, vegetables and eggs, but not in wheat, oil, sugar, fish, meat, legumes, milk powder and animal feed (total annual imports = $65 million). Stopping these imports would rapidly cause starvation.

Amir asserted that by making these false assumptions, Clawson demonstrated a failure to understand Israel's basic economic realities. Clawson had a narrow, productivity growth-oriented view, as opposed to government planners who prioritized agricultural settlement expansion and production of the broadest range of commodities as soon as possible.

Amir rejected Clawson's three main recommendations: Freeze new agricultural settlements for the next 3–5 years, cancel the second (Western) Yarkon-Negev pipeline, and cancel the Jordan River diversion project. Amir stated that although Clawson was correct from a purely economic perspective, he erred by ignoring the government's commitment to settling the entire country. As Eshkol had explained (at a meeting on December 2, 1953; Amir implied that Clawson had been present), the only way to settle the entire country was to divert the Yarkon River and coastal wells to the Negev at a high cost.

Amir agreed that existing agriculture must become more efficient (while disputing some of Clawson's numbers), but faulted Clawson for ignoring the fundamental goals of feeding the general population, expanding the agricultural population and settling the land. Amir also agreed that the government must reduce water prices to the extent possible and utilize water resources effectively, but he saw this as a technical problem for engineers. Amir also conceded that Plan C is "far from perfection, is open to criticism and will require various revisions."

Naphtali (who saw Amir's critiques) rejected Clawson's entire approach, because it was based on "pure economic theory," without consideration of essential non-economic factors. Naphtali, who was strongly influenced by German social democracy (Bareli & Cohen, 2008), denounced Clawson's "extreme liberalism": How can Clawson insist on free market agricultural policies, when interventionism is the norm worldwide, even in the US? "Economic policy can stimulate development that is impossible under an abstract liberal regime. … Even the history of the US can prove this" (Naphtali to Bell, July 30, 1954, 2433/21-Gimmel). Naphtali was exaggerating; as we have already seen, Clawson was far from free market extremism, and understood that interventionism was the norm worldwide, even in the United States.

At the same time, Naphtali (like Amir) conceded that Plan C was flawed and suggested that the Joint Planning Center, Tahal and Economic Advisory Staff reevaluate it. The parties worked on reevaluation (Bell to Naphtali, August 6, 1954, 10757/9-Gimmel; *Zmanim*, January 24, 1955) but the outcome is unknown.

Blass vehemently rejected Clawson's recommendations. Although Blass and Clawson never mentioned each other by name, they evidently disdained each other's views. According to Mary Clawson (1957, pp. 98–99, January 14, 1954) "the irrigation people" rejected Clawson's memorandum on irrigation costs (almost certainly #6):

> Everyone agrees cheerfully that [irrigation] costs are too high … But the irrigation people [=Blass] are unwilling to consider any modification in their plans; they wax emotional about suggestions for curtailment and say that is not how the State of Israel came into being. They learned most of their more extravagant ideas in the States from the Bureau of Reclamation, which is not noted for its economical ways of working [=Bashore and Savage, formerly Bureau of Reclamation Commissioner and Bureau of Reclamation chief design engineer, respectively] … the Bureau of Reclamation would never use a Ford when a Lincoln would do.[47]

Blass disparaged Clawson in his autobiography. After lauding his American advisors, Blass wrote: "There were other 'advisors' whose value was zero [=Clawson/Economic Advisory Staff]. I knew [this] from the very beginning" (Blass, 1973, p. 228).

Ultimately, the government ignored almost all of Clawson's recommendations. Farm units increased to 80,500 by 1959, far above Clawson's maximum of 55,000 by 1960, as the government populated new agricultural settlements with unskilled new immigrants. During 1954–1956, 85,000 Jews immigrated from North Africa (accounting for 80% of all immigrants). The government settled 70–90% of North African immigrants in frontier areas under the "Ship to Village" plan, which sent new immigrants directly from ships to frontier areas (sometimes via coercion). Thus, the government succeeded in establishing 45 new moshavim[48] and expanding 50 existing moshavim. By 1956, new immigrants accounted for 92% of the Negev's population (Picard, 2013). The military staunchly supported the population dispersal policy and was highly involved in its planning and implementation (Evans, 2006).[49] This appears to contradict Clawson's assertion that the military was not consulted on agriculture and irrigation planning; apparently, Clawson only had partial information regarding the military's involvement. Regarding irrigation, the government ignored Clawson's recommendations to cancel the second Yarkon-Negev pipeline and the Jordan diversion, and adopted the Cotton water plan in 1955 (Sitton, 2000) despite Clawson's objections (#43).

Despite Clawson's exhortations, the government failed to integrate economic analysis into agricultural policy formation. As A.G. Black lamented in 1956,

Never, or almost never, are the economists ... consulted in advance or their advice sought. Sometimes they are asked to make a "post-mortem" after blunders have been made. This, of course, is the usual process in all inexperienced governments. (8182/12-Gimmel Lamed)

X. CLAWSON'S SHIFT FROM PURISM TO PRAGMATISM

Apparently dissatisfied with his lack of influence, Clawson took a step towards pragmatism in July 1954. In a public lecture before the Farmers' Federation (#37),[50] he acknowledged that it was not his place to question the national goals or make value judgments:

> The professional economist does not have any special competence to decide what the goals of agriculture, or of any other segment of the economy, should be. ... A visitor, like myself, may also have some ideas on the subject, but this is a matter on which the citizens of a country must make their own decision. ... [For] judgements on policy matters ... the guiding consideration must be the broad social ideological objectives of the people of Israel, rather than the views of any one expert. (#37)

However, Clawson did not completely abandon purism: He stated that "an agriculture responsive to economic forces would contribute more toward the goal of economic independence than any other." Thus, "if our resources for helping new settlements are limited, then perhaps we should cease to establish more settlements" until existing settlements are self-supporting. Obviously, this was a political non-starter.

In September 1954, Clawson took a further step towards pragmatism by seeking common ground with Amir. In response to Amir's critique of the Farmers' Federation lecture (#37), Clawson wrote Amir a six-page letter (September 2, 1954; 2433/21-Gimmel) in which he set out their agreements and disagreements on five major issues:

a. Both value *economic independence*, but attaining it is harder than Amir (and the general public) thinks, and "will require some reexamination of non-economic goals and objectives, and some choosing among them."
b. Both agree that *"noneconomic values and criteria* must often supersede purely economic ones." For example, Jewish immigration should not be limited. But Clawson, unlike Amir, believes that one cannot always prioritize non-economic goals and still attain economic goals. For every non-economic goal, we must ask: (a) Is there a less expensive way to attain it? (b) Does attaining it jeopardize the attainment of other non-economic goals?

> [...] there is ... a too uncritical acceptance of the goals of security, Zionism, and return to the land, without questioning their cost, not only in monetary terms but also in their relation to other noneconomic goals. ... As economists ... part of our job is to estimate as accurately as possible ... what the costs of various lines of action may be, so that choice of both economic and non-economic goals may be made as rationally as possible.[51]

c. Clawson, unlike Amir, emphasizes that "much of the *agricultural and irrigation development* now underway is needlessly costly," and some projects will "lead Israel away from economic independence."

d. Like Amir, Clawson values *family farms* without hired labor, "both as an economic and a social goal," and understands that the government opposes "the establishment of a permanent large hired agricultural labor class." But Clawson emphasizes that these farms must be as efficient as possible, and can certainly improve their efficiency substantially over the next few years.

e. Both agree that *public financial assistance* is necessary because private capital is inadequate, but Clawson argues that "the real questions are: How to give such public assistance, how much to give, where, and on what terms?" Two critical points: (a) Israel should not imitate large developed countries, because in Israel, irrigation subsidies and price supports are a much larger percentage of national income. (b) Even with 100% government-financed irrigation (which some have proposed), many farmers will be unable to afford unsubsidized water.

Clawson asked Amir to establish an open dialogue: "Perhaps you can show me ways in which my thinking should be modified, and perhaps I can influence your ideas." Soon afterwards, Clawson and the Economic Advisory Staff proposed a collaborative project with the Ministry of Agriculture and Joint Planning Center (Clawson, 1955a, p. 1). The result was *Israel Agriculture 1953/54* (Clawson, 1955a; p. 254, 104 tables and 31 charts). Clawson wrote the first draft in collaboration with Samuel, Lowe, and D. Dinur (Central Bureau of Statistics), and the second and final draft in collaboration with an 18-member committee chaired by Amir; the final work was "a consensus of the various persons working on it" (Clawson, 1955a, pp. 1–2).

In *Israel Agriculture*, Clawson sought to establish facts and pose policy questions, while eschewing criticism and recommendations (Clawson, 1955a, p. 1). He reframed past recommendations that were anathema to the government as items on a menu of policy options and accepted that the government might prioritize non-economic over economic goals. For example, Clawson (1955a, p. 5) stated that based on "the least favorable reasonable estimates" of the water supply, if the government prioritized the most irrigable lands (Classes A and B), no irrigation water would be available south of Beer Tovia (1955a, p. 5). He emphasized that he was not recommending this policy (without mentioning that he had essentially recommended it in #6 and #14):

> These calculations do not say that it is desirable ... to irrigate [only] all ... Class A and B lands beginning in the North and moving southward [ending at Beer Tovia]. ... The government might, after consideration of these and other facts, make different policy decisions.

At the end of *Israel Agriculture* (Clawson, 1955a, pp. 225–226), Clawson backed away from his earlier view that Israel's national goals were mutually incompatible, and acknowledged once more that state-building might trump economic efficiency:

> What should be the goals for Israel agriculture, and what are the realistic alternatives to the attainment of those goals? Many goals or objectives for agriculture are possible, and they are not all mutually exclusive or at least not completely incompatible in all degrees. There might be a goal of efficiency and economic strength for agriculture; Or a goal of economic independence

...; Or a goal of settling the land, dispersing the population, and promotion of rural life in general; Or a goal of a certain standard of living for the population ...; Or a goal of security in the broadest sense with occupation of the land as a necessary accompaniment to it; or various other goals. ...

[...] At what cost if any, in reduced efficiency must the social goals be chosen; or what social goals must be given up, if any, in order to achieve a desired level of efficiency? It is on questions like these that economic analysis may play a part; by its use it is often possible to estimate the cost, not only in monetary terms but also in terms of other opportunities that must be given up, of a particular course of action. After such economic analysis are available, some people might wish to reconsider their initial choices. ...

If the goal is chosen of maximum efficiency and competitive strength for agriculture, then planning for agriculture can proceed on an objective basis towards this goal. ... If the goal for agriculture is not maximum efficiency, just what goal do we choose, and to what degree and how far and in what ways are we prepared to incur higher costs for other goals?

As the Economic Advisory Staff wound down, the government invited Clawson to stay for another year as advisor to the Ministry of Agriculture. Clawson declined because he wished to continue his career and his children's education in the United States (Clawson, 1987, pp. 252–253). Naphtali hosted a farewell party for Clawson on June 22, 1955 (*Haboker*, June 24, 1955).

XI. CONCLUSION

As an advisor to the Israeli government during 1953–1955, Marion Clawson discovered that Israeli agriculture and irrigation were highly inefficient, and that agricultural planning almost completely ignored economic considerations. Clawson directly criticized Israel's agricultural policy, and stated that Israel's national goals – defense, full irrigation of the Negev Desert, immigrant absorption via new agricultural settlements, and economic independence – were mutually contradictory. He recommended improving the realism of Israel's agricultural plan by reducing projected agricultural prices, ending expensive Negev irrigation, increasing irrigated farm size eightfold, freezing new agricultural settlements until the number of semi-developed agricultural settlements declined from 300 to 100, and limiting new Negev settlements to 10 over 5–7 years.

The Israeli government vehemently rejected Clawson's recommendations: It continued expensive Negev irrigation projects and immigrant absorption via new agricultural settlements, and failed to integrate economic analysis into agricultural policy formation. Only one of Clawson's recommendations was eventually accepted: The Minister of Agriculture initiated the reevaluation of Israel's agricultural plan, but the outcome of that process is unknown.

In July 1954, Clawson, apparently dissatisfied with his lack of influence, took a step towards pragmatism – that is, acceptance of Israel's national goals and respect for considerations of political feasibility. In a public lecture, he acknowledged that as a foreign advisor, it was not his place to question the national goals or make value judgments. In September 1954, he took a further step towards pragmatism by toning down his criticism and seeking common ground with the

Deputy Director-General of the Ministry of Agriculture. Soon afterwards, he initiated a collaboration with the Ministry of Agriculture, which resulted in the publication of *Israel Agriculture 1953/54* (Clawson, 1955a). *Israel Agriculture* was a consensus document – it presented facts and asked questions but did not prescribe policies. In *Israel Agriculture*, Clawson reframed past recommendations that were anathema to the government as items on a menu of policy options, and accepted that the government would likely prioritize state-building over economic efficiency. In proposing *Israel Agriculture* as a collaborative project, Clawson made a pragmatic decision to relinquish some of his independence in return for a chance to gain influence. As a result, Clawson improved his working relationship with the Ministry of Agriculture, but did not gain influence.

Why was Clawson largely unsuccessful as a foreign economic advisor in Israel? That is, why was he unable to persuade the Israeli government to adopt his recommendations? How did Clawson's experience compare to the experiences of other foreign economic advisors in Israel? In the paragraphs that follow, we address these questions using the conceptual framework developed by Mosley and Ingham (2013).

Based on the insights of Seers (1962) and Hirschman (1963, 1984), Mosley and Ingham (2013, pp. 161–165) identify three types of errors that cause visiting economists to fail: Type 1 – personal failings (e.g., Hirschman's "visiting economist syndrome" – making recommendations based on what works in Western countries, without taking local factors into account); Type 2 – technical errors (e.g., changing one's mind suddenly regarding a major public investment project); Type 3 – political errors (e.g., overestimating one's ability to influence policymakers). Mosley and Ingham emphasize that visiting economists may also fail due to contextual factors (e.g., the special circumstances of new post-colonial governments), and/or the absence of a problem-solving intermediary – a credible third party who is willing and able to "translate what the adviser needs into a language that the [policymaker] understands" (Mosley & Ingham, 2013, p. 169).

Accordingly, Mosley and Ingham (2013, pp. 166–168) evaluate Arthur Lewis' experiences as a visiting economist by answering the following questions: Who was Lewis' client? What was Lewis' official role? What were the contextual factors that influenced Lewis' ability to succeed? What was the incidence of Type 1, Type 2 and Type 3 errors? Was there a "problem-solving intermediary?"

We now utilize Mosley and Ingham's framework to evaluate the experiences of Clawson and seven other foreign economic advisors in Israel – Michal Kalecki, Raymond Mikesell, Abba Lerner, Richard Kahn, Milton Friedman, and Stanley Fischer/Herbert Stein (Table 3). Clawson operated in a difficult context: Israel's chief economic policy-maker, Minister of Finance Levi Eshkol, had played a key role in Negev irrigation and settlement, and as the founder of the national water carrier, he was so confident in his own expertise that he denied the need for advice on irrigation. Furthermore, Israel's chief water planner, Simcha Blass, had his own American hydrological advisors whose views were diametrically opposed to Clawson's. Israeli policymakers faced little external pressure to implement reforms: The Eisenhower Administration was indifferent to the EAS and lost interest in Israeli economic policy (from August 1954), and per capita GDP growth and short

(Continued)

Table 3. Foreign Economic Advisors in Israel, 1950–1985.

Advisor	Dates	Role	Major Recommendations	Degree of Success in Getting Recommendations Implemented	Contextual Factors	Incidence of Type 1 Errors (Personal Failings of Advisor), Type 2 Errors (Technical Flaws); and Type 3 Errors (Political Mistakes)	Problem-Solving Intermediaries
Michal Kalecki	Late July–Sept 1950	Advisor to the Ministry of Finance	Retain exchange and price controls. Modernizing industry is an unaffordable luxury. State-organized investment to maximize exports and finance imports of industrial goods and machinery.	Failure	Ben-Gurion commissioned the Kalecki Report to legitimize the statist status quo, but was forced to repudiate it after the electorate rejected austerity and rationing in July 1951.	None[a]	None
Raymond Mikesell	Late June–Late July 1952, June–July 1953	Representative of the US Secretary of State	1952 Mikesell Report – implement a foreign exchange budget, avoid new short term debt. 1952 and 1953 oral recommendations – fiscal and monetary restraint to reduce budget deficits and inflation, maximize investment and minimize consumption, reduce dependence on foreign aid.	Partial Success – after Israel accepted the Mikesell Report, a foreign exchange budget was introduced, and short term debt declined from $124 million in June 1952 to $111 million in June 1953. However, the oral recommendations were vehemently rejected by Ben Gurion and Eshkol in 1953. The short term debt situation improved by March 1954; the short term debt crisis was over by December 1954. Real per capita GNP increased by 19.2% in 1954, vs -1.5% in 1953.	Short term debt crisis. In July 1952, the US permitted Israel to use $25 million in Mutual Security Agency grants for FY 1953 for debt repayment, conditional on acceptance of the Mikesell Report.	Type 3– Mikesell expected Israelis to subsist on local agricultural produce, and to avoid additional capital investment in agriculture; he failed to appreciate their desire for a modern, egalitarian economy.	None

Table 3. (Continued)

			Failure[b]		Type 3– Until Sept.
Marion Clawson	May 1953– July 1955	Senior Officer for Agriculture, Economic Advisory Staff, Prime Minister's Office	Reduce projected commodity prices in Plan C; end expensive Negev irrigation; enlarge irrigated farms eightfold; freeze new settlements until the number of semi-developed settlements falls from 300 to 100; limit new Negev settlements to 10 over 5–7 years.	Finance Minister Eshkol played a key role in Negev settlement and irrigation, and denied the need for advice on irrigation; Israel already had American hydrological consultants, and they disagreed with Clawson. The Eisenhower Administration was completely indifferent to the EAS and lost interest in Israeli economic policy from August 1954. The short term debt situation improved by March 1954; the short term debt crisis was over by December 1954. Real per capita GNP increased by 19.2% in 1953, vs. -1.5% in 1954.	Type 3– Until Sept. 1954, criticized Israel's national goals, made politically infeasible recommendations and made value judgments. None

| Abba Lerner | May 1953–July 1955 | Chief Monetary and Fiscal Officer, Economic Advisory Staff, Prime Minister's Office | Establish an independent central bank with a monetary board. Fully index government loans of over 12 months. Achieve economic independence by increasing labor hours at the same nominal wage, cutting real wages and export prices, and increasing import prices. Achieve zero inflation by limiting credit expansion. | Failure[c] | In 1952, Eshkol asked his friend and economic advisor, David Horowitz, to organize the Bank of Israel and serve as its founding Governor. Eshkol and Horowitz wanted a central bank that was not too independent, with the Governor setting monetary policy alone. The ruling Mapai party refused to pay the political price of implementing Lerner's plan to achieve economic independence.[d] CPI Inflation was 19.1% in 1953 and 7.5% in 1954. | Type 3– Believed that he could persuade the government to reconsider Horowitz's draft Bank of Israel Law, despite Eshkol's close relationship with Horowitz. | None |

(Continued)

Table 3. (Continued)

Abba Lerner	Aug. 1955–Aug. 1956	Advisor to Minister of Finance Levi Eshkol	Cut basic wages by 25%. Abolish the COLA. Allow bankruptcies and efficiency dismissals. Implement anti-cartelization measures. Devalue the currency and compensate firms via subsidies.	Failure / In late 1955, Lerner joined Ben-Gurion and Eshkol to oppose a basic wage increase, and played an important role in wage negotiations. In January 1956, Mapai's central committee and Histadrut approved a 4–8% basic wage increase despite Ben-Gurion and Eshkol's opposition. Lerner's other recommendations were not implemented, with the following exceptions: A limited antitrust law was passed in 1959; over 1955–1960, effective exchange rates for exports and imports increased by 41% and 16% respectively.	The Czech-Egyptian arms deal caused Eshkol and Ben-Gurion to strongly advocate wage restraint. Lerner worked closely with them to prevent an increase in the basic wage.	Type 3– Lerner greatly overestimated the potential for US-style participatory democracy in Israel: On the wage/COLA issue, he went directly to the public via two open letters, in which he argued that Ben-Gurion and Eshkol wished to act responsibly but needed greater public support in order to do so.	None
Richard Kahn	June 24, 1957–July 9, 1957, Dec. 21, 1962–Jan. 6, 1963	No formal appointment	Reform the COLA to reduce its scope and degree of real wage protection (thus, move towards the Swedish COLA system); Accept the reality that the EEC will reject Israel's application for Associate Membership (1957); avoid overoptimism regarding the potential benefits of an Israel-EEC commercial agreement (1962).	Failure		Type 1– Kahn did not meet Prime Minister Ben-Gurion or Finance Minister Eshkol. However, he did meet with Bank of Israel Governor David Horowitz (1957, 1962) and Finance Ministry Director-General Jacob Arnon (1957), among others.	None

| Milton Friedman | July 3–8, 1977 | Invited by Minister of Finance Simha Erlich during his (already planned) visit to Hebrew University | Float the currency and liberalize the capital account, phase out import restrictions and export subsidies. Implement a monetary growth rule and reduce government spending. Privatize nondefense government enterprises. Reform banking regulation, labor markets, industrial subsidies, social welfare and housing. Introduce a negative income tax. | Failure[a] | Erlich was already planning the October 28, 1977 liberalization but he never told Friedman due to a fear of leaks. Erlich and Prime Minister Begin always supported floating and capital account liberalization, and faced IMF pressure to abolish export subsidies. On the other hand, Begin was beholden to previously marginalized groups that opposed fiscal retrenchment; he also feared that fiscal retrenchment would destabilize his coalition and thus harm the Israel-Egypt peace process. | Type 2– "Visiting Economist Syndrome" – Friedman gave virtually identical advice in every country; he justified this by arguing that Israel's problems were identical to those of Italy and the UK. Type 3– Friedman made controversial remarks on unemployment in the Israeli press on May 24, 1977, just before the Histadrut elections. | None |

(Continued)

Table 3. (Continued)

Stanley Fischer and Herbert Stein	Late 1983–Mid-1985	Members of "advisory group" and Joint Economic Development Group, both of which were appointed by US Secretary of State George Shultz	Success	CPI Inflation was 445% in 1984. An alarming decline in foreign reserves (not US pressure) forced Israeli policymakers to finally adopt a serious inflation stabilization program.	The academic economists Michael Bruno and Eitan Berglas, Finance Ministry Director-General Emanuel Sharon

Based on Mosley and Ingham (2013, pp. 166–168).

Sources: Schiffman, Young, and Zelekha (2017), Schiffman and Goldstein (2019), Mikesell (2000, Ch. 7), and Ginzburg (1977, 2009).

[a] Ben-Gurion failed to anticipate public discontent with austerity and rationing. Gauging public opinion is not the responsibility of foreign advisors.

[b] With one exception: The Ministry of Agriculture began to reevaluate Plan C in cooperation with the Economic Advisory Staff, but the outcome is unknown.

[c] Eshkol prevailed, although 32 Knesset members and five ministers supported Lerner's proposed monetary board.

[d] By May 1956, Lerner realized that "in a democratic country, the government cannot move the people more rapidly to economic independence than the people consent to go."

[e] Although some of Friedman's recommendations were implemented, this was not due to Friedman's influence. For example, export subsidies were abolished due to IMF pressure. Other policy measures contradicted Friedman's recommendations.

term debt improved dramatically over 1954. Clawson (and his colleagues on the Economic Advisory Staff) lacked a problem-solving intermediary (Schiffman & Goldstein, 2019). On the other hand, Clawson committed Type 3 errors (before he shifted towards pragmatism): he criticized the national goals; recommended economically efficient policies regardless of their political feasibility; and in opposing new Negev settlements and the second Yarkon-Negev pipeline, he made value judgments that the (non-economic) benefits were not worth the costs.

Clawson's experience was typical for a foreign economic advisor in Israel. As Table 3 shows, the Israeli government always rejected the recommendations of foreign advisors unless it was faced with a severe economic crisis (Mikesell and Fischer/Stein); US government pressure and problem-solving intermediaries were not sufficient conditions for success (Fischer/Stein). Furthermore, Clawson was not the only foreign advisor to make Type 3 errors.

We conclude with Clawson's retrospective self-assessment (Clawson, 1987, pp. 186–187):

> [...] I extensively criticized the irrigation, agricultural, and settlement programs, in terms which I meant to be clear and forceful but diplomatic. I disturbed many people in government and outside of it. ... Shortly before we left Israel ... [a collaborator on *Israel Agriculture* said] that I had taught Israelis that it was possible to apply economic principles and economic analysis to agriculture. My response was, that if in fact I had achieved this, I considered my two years' work as highly successful. ... in the years since, Israel still does not apply economics fully to these problems but does so far more than when I went to Israel. I have always considered [Israel] a good but not great professional experience. ... As an economist I learned an important truth: Much of the world does not value economic efficiency as highly as do most economists.

Postscript

In retrospect, some of Clawson's arguments proved wrong: Some of Clawson's objections to Plan C were unfounded, and Clawson greatly underestimated the Negev's agricultural potential. On the other hand, Clawson's insights regarding restrictive arrangements in agriculture remain relevant to this day.

Plan C: Real agricultural output increased by 161% over 1953–1960 versus Plan C's projection of 134%. Farm units increased to 80,500 by 1959 despite rapid agricultural productivity growth (annual average for 1952–1959 = 10%; Mundlak, 1964a, p. 209). Clawson's price projections were way off the mark (Table 2): Every commodity price increased over 1953–1960, with fruit and vegetables showing the sharpest increases. Clawson's price projections were so wrong because he massively underpredicted real income growth. The actual increase in real (disposable) income was 71% (Mundlak, 1964a, p. 76), whereas Clawson only considered three scenarios: –20%, 0% (which he considered most likely) and 20%.

On the other hand, Clawson correctly predicted that maintaining farm incomes would require "heavily subsidiz[ing] agriculture at the expense of the consumer." In 1960, subsidies as a percentage of production values were 8.4% for vegetables (vs. 5.6% in 1954), 17.3% for milk (vs. 10.1% in 1954), 20.7% for eggs, 2.6% for poultry and 2.0% for beef (vs. 0% for eggs, poultry and beef in 1954). The government used its food subsidy budgets to purchase surplus and thus keep prices high (Mundlak, 1964a, pp. 65–68).

Negev Agriculture: Today, Negev agriculture is a spectacular success, having overcome the weaknesses that Clawson identified. The Negev (including Jerusalem) accounts for 45% of Israel's agricultural crop area (32% for citrus, 56% for vegetables, potatoes and melons and 57% for field crops). The Negev's Central Arava region accounts for 60% of Israel's agricultural exports. Israel is a global leader in water technologies, having solved the water scarcity problem through desalination and wastewater purification.

Restrictive Arrangements in Agriculture: Today, food is expensive by international standards, due to "lack of competition and high non-tariff barriers" (OECD, 2018). The "lack of competition" is due in large part to government-sanctioned restrictive arrangements in agriculture.

Clawson foresaw the harmful effects of such restrictive arrangements [emphasis ours]:

> [...] *Agriculture in Israel might adopt a program of restricted production, regulated marketing, supported prices, and the like, in an attempt to maintain farm income.* Aside from the difficulty, or perhaps impossibility of making them sufficiently effective, such programs would involve heavy costs both in money and in time and energy of important people, *and would be at the expense of the mass non-farm consumers.* ... (#13)

ACKNOWLEDGEMENTS

We thank the staff of the Forest History Society for their gracious hospitality and assistance in locating archival materials. We thank participants at the 2019 History of Economics Society meetings and the 2021 STOREP conference for useful comments and suggestions.

NOTES

1. Douglas North observed the same phenomenon in Brazil in 1961. He lamented the "vast array of government pricing and investment policies which have reflected ineptitude, corruption, and a lack of understanding of the most rudimentary determinants of economic efficiency" (Boianovsky, 2018).

2. We cite Israel State Archives documents by folder number (e.g., 5509/14-Gimmel), and Clawson's memoranda by their numbers in the Appendix (e.g., #13).

3. This section is adapted from Schiffman and Goldstein (2019).

4. On Lerner's Economic Advisory Staff activities, see Schiffman, Young, and Zelekha (2017, chapter 3).

5. On Ezekiel's contributions to institutionalism, see Rutherford (2011a, pp. 179–180).

6. On Bureau of Agricultural Economics research, see Baker and Rasmussen (1975).

7. On the Bureau of Agricultural Economics' contributions to the New Deal, see Skocpol and Finegold (1982) and Gilbert (2015). On Ezekiel's advocacy of statist planning as a solution to the Depression, see Rutherford (2011b). On Ezekiel's conversion to Keynesianism, see Rutherford and Desroches (2008).

8. Neither Black nor Usher identified as institutionalists (Yonay, 1998, pp. 87, 240).

9. Clawson had made his "first real trip abroad" in 1950. At Ezekiel's invitation, he participated in a World Bank-UN-FAO training seminar in Pakistan that had no tangible impact (Clawson, 1987, pp. 179–182).

10. In this section, we discuss policy only in general terms.

11. Free immigration was the State of Israel's raison d'être – an independent state was necessary in order to end the British Mandate's restrictions on Jewish immigration (Gross, 1990).

12. In 1948, 80% of the Jewish population lived between Tel Aviv and Haifa, while the Negev and Galilee had a strong Arab majority. The military saw this concentration as a major strategic liability (Evans, 2006).

13. Food self-sufficiency was seen as critical in light of Israel's existence under siege, massive trade deficit (about 20% of GNP) and acute shortage of foreign currency (Krampf, 2009, 2018, p. 82).

14. "Labor Zionism ... preached the abandonment 'non-productive' branches of employment, such as commerce and banking, which had been traditional occupations of the majority of Jews in the Diaspora, and a return to 'productive' branches of employment, especially farming and rural settlement. This was considered the path to reinstating Jewish land-ownership in the Land of Israel and 'rehabilitating' the Jewish people through the creation of a 'new' Hebrew-cultured person – physically and mentally hardened" (Karlinsky, 2000).

15. This ideal was based on the Socialist principle that using hired labor was inherently exploitative (Kislev, 2015).

16. Mary Clawson (1957, pp. 149–150) described the squalid conditions in a transit camp that she visited in March 1954.

17. There was a broad consensus against unemployment benefits (Barkai, 1990, p. 43).

18. Unless otherwise stated, data in this section are taken from Clawson (1955a).

19. Thus, land reform (which Arthur Lewis and Theodore Schultz strongly advocated; Rashid, 2018) was a nonissue in Israel.

20. The Jewish Agency was founded in 1929 as the executive arm of the World Zionist Organization for the purpose of mobilizing World Jewry to build a Jewish state in Palestine. During the British Mandate, the Jewish Agency was the de facto governing body of Palestine's Jewish community; David Ben-Gurion served as Jewish Agency Chairman during 1935–1948. With the establishment of the State, the Government of Israel assumed all governmental functions. In November 1952, the Knesset passed the Status Law which recognized the historic contributions of the Jewish Agency and World Zionist Organization to the establishment of the State, and authorized those bodies "to continue to act ... for the development and settlement of the Land, for absorption of [Jewish] immigrants ... and for coordination of [Diaspora] Jewish institutions and associations which are active in these fields." For the Jewish Agency's current mission statement, click here: https://www.jewishagency.org/who-we-are/.

21. Kimhi and Tzur-Ilan (2021) defined Kibbutzim and Moshavim as follows: "The Kibbutz was a commune in which each member produced according to his ability and consumed according to his needs. The Moshav was a semicooperative village made of individual family farms, in which certain activities such as purchasing, marketing, and financing were handled jointly in order to exploit economies of scale in these activities."

22. The Kibbutzim were politically influential: "In the 1950s, when they were less than 4% of the population, kibbutz members formed a fifth of the representatives in the early Parliaments and occupied up to six seats in the cabinet. The power base thus created helped to support policies favoring kibbutzim (and often also moshavim) in agriculture and in other economic spheres ..." (Kislev, 2015).

23. Clawson seems to be describing the plight of civilian farmers, although he does not say so explicitly. In reality, many frontier settlements were established or reinforced by soldiers from the Nahal ("Pioneering Fighting Youth") program (Heymont, 1967), which provided new conscripts with combined military and agricultural training before sending them to frontier settlements.

24. We cannot locate the original Plan C. Two summaries of Plan C by Eshkol have survived (October 26, 1953 speech – 702/7-Peh Tzadi; Eshkol, 1954).

25. For further details on the relationships between Mekorot and Tahal and between Blass and Weiner, see Herzog (2019, pp. 156–157) and Alatout (2008b).

26. Blass envisioned bringing water from the Yarkon to the Negev as early as 1939 (Herzog, 2019, p. 107).

27. This is a basic historical fact, and is not taken from Clawson (1955a).

28. Ariav's father was Deputy Knesset Speaker Haim Ariav of the General Zionist party, a former Director-General of the Farmers' Federation (1931–1951).

29. Their only known interaction was service on the Survey of Moshavim (#50) advisory committee.

30. The Rockefeller Foundation made no grants to Israel until 1957.

31. This debate was not new. In 1945, Hays estimated Palestine's water supply at 1,900 million m³ per year, much lower than Mekorot/Blass' 1944 estimate of 4,000. Nathan, Gass, and Creamer (1946) criticized Mekorot/Blass' estimate as "based on extremely optimistic assumptions. ... Many experts have expressed doubt as to the feasibility of [Mekorot/Blass'] figures" (Nathan, Gass, & Creamer, 1946, p. 402). For further details regarding Blass' 1944 estimate, see Herzog (2019, pp. 110–111). On the connection between the abundance narrative and Zionist political objectives before 1948, see Alatout (2009).

32. In September 1953, A.G. Black lamented the shortage of agricultural economists in the government: The Ministry of Agriculture's economists worked on import licensing rather than economics, and the Joint Planning Center had just one well-trained economist (745/7-Peh).

33. Just weeks before, Eshkol had rebuked Gass for holding an unauthorized press conference and making statements that Eshkol saw as damaging to public morale (Schiffman & Goldstein, 2019).

34. This view was shared by Mikesell (Ginzburg, 2009, p. 124), Assistant Secretary of State Henry Byroade (Foreign Relations of the United States 1952–1954, 884A.10/6–1752, No. 445, June 17, 1952) and the 1953 Export-Import Bank mission to Israel (which included Bell; *Haaretz*, February 11, 1953).

35. Clawson implicitly assumed that capital intensity in US agriculture was optimal. Wilcox (1952) thought otherwise: He argued that US agriculture utilized "outmoded technology, too much labor and too little capital."

36. Blass made the same argument (Blass, 1973, pp. 254–255; Herzog, 2019, p. 174). See also Rubner (1958).

37. Cortez, Gadgil, Hakim, Lewis, and Schultz (1951, pp. 26–27) stated that too-small family farms were a widespread problem in developing countries. This contrasts with Berry and Cline (1979), who posited an inverse size-productivity relationship.

38. Prime Minister Moshe Sharett (January 1954–November 1955) was acquainted with Clawson (Mary Clawson 1957, pp. 99, 173–174) and his criticisms of irrigation policy (Sharett 1978, November 4, 1953), but took no position regarding Clawson's recommendations. As the Economic Advisory Staff wound down, Sharett regretted Clawson's impending departure (Sharett, 1978, May 9, 1955).

39. Clawson had much less interaction with Ministry of Agriculture Director-General Haim Gvati.

40. The policy of establishing agricultural settlements all over the country regardless of cost dated back to the interwar period (Metzer, 1978).

41. Eshkol told Bell: "[Regarding] irrigation and Mekorot ... we know pretty well what we want to do. [Instead,] you should ... stress ... those areas where nothing has been done" (Yohanan Beham to Gass, August 12, 1954, 5509/15-Gimmel).

42. The government was so ideologically committed to Negev irrigation that it allowed the Jewish Agency to increase water allocations to Negev agricultural settlements in 1953 despite a general drought and lack of drinking water in other regions (Herzog, 2019, pp. 254–255). Blass' American advisors encouraged this policy because they believed it was necessary for population dispersal: In December 1950, Bashore, Savage and Wollman told Ben-Gurion that the Yarkon-Negev pipelines must receive high priority, because they "will permit [Negev] colonization, thus relieving the [population] congestion in the coastal areas" (Herzog, 2019, p. 174).

43. Clawson contemplated ending irrigation at Beer Tovia (Clawson, 1955a, p. 5).

44. Eshkol may have pointed to Sde Boker, the location of Ben-Gurion's desert home. Ben-Gurion zealously championed Negev settlement and set a personal example by moving to Sde Boker in 1953. Mary Clawson (1957, p. 63) enthusiastically praised Ben-Gurion for moving to Sde Boker.

45. Clawson met with Ministry of Agriculture/Joint Planning Center officials and received data from them. Clawson requested and received Ministry of Agriculture feedback on some memoranda; some of the feedback was translated into English.

46. The average employment share of agriculture and industry in seven European countries was 55%; the lowest was 44.6% in the Netherlands (Patinkin, 1967, p. 41).

47. As noted previously, Blass' American advisors reinforced the government's belief that costly Negev irrigation was essential for population dispersal.

48. Eshkol had declared in January 1951: "...our goal is to establish 500 new agricultural settlements within five years, because we will need the agricultural output of 1000 settlements to feed the [population] in 1955." This goal was never attained; in 2018, Israel had 955 rural settlements (including nonagricultural and Arab settlements) (*Yisrael Hayom*, January 15, 2021).

49. New settlements were planned by the Jewish Agency and the military's Engineering Corps. In 1949, the military strongly opposed an alternative planning approach that would have increased population density on the coast (Evans, 2006). NaHaL soldiers established new military outpost settlements and reinforced existing civilian settlements (Heymont, 1967); in 1948–1949, soldiers established 39 frontier agricultural settlements, and in 1952, demobilized soldiers established 14 more (Evans, 2006).

50. This lecture was reported in the press, sent to Naphtali for comments, and later published in Hebrew.

51. Simon Kuznets, Don Patinkin and Bank of Israel Governor David Horowitz took the same approach. Kuznets (1954) wrote: "...Economic public policy must also consider non-economic calculations. ... However, it is important to establish by means of proper analysis, at least those economic phenomena which are measurable, so that whenever there arises a need to decide against the economic consideration, this will be done not out of ignorance, but from knowledge of the economic aspects that are measurable." Horowitz wrote in 1955: "Economics is a science of setting priorities. What is better: expanding consumption or broadening investment? Broadening production capacity or raising housing standards? Increasing exports or transferring additional goods to the local market? All these [questions] require choices and decisions that are especially acute in a country with limited natural resources and production factors" (*Davar*, June 3, 1955; cited in Mandelkern, 2016). At a 1961 symposium, Patinkin told Ben-Gurion: "...Whatever is done in the economic sphere must be done as efficiently as possible. ...If we deviate from the approach of efficiency, we must know how much it will cost us and if we can pay for it. It is certainly necessary to settle the Negev – there is no question about that. But does it need to be 50,000, 100,000 or 200,000 [people]? On what basis is this number determined? We also need to know the implications of this number regarding agriculture in other regions...and the [general] standard of living. All these are questions that the economist must answer. ...I did not perceive enough awareness [in your remarks today] of whether there is compatibility between all of the goals you enumerated and [our] limited resources. We speak very much about Negev settlement and we are bringing the national water carrier [there], and I ask: How many high schools could we establish with that money? Perhaps I would reach the same conclusion [as you, that Negev settlement is absolutely essential], but there must be consideration [of opportunity costs]" (Ohana, 2003, pp. 230, 234; cited in Mandelkern, 2016). To the best of our knowledge, this was the first time that Patinkin, the renowned monetary economist, commented publicly on agriculture and irrigation policy. See Krampf (2010) regarding Patinkin's contribution to the policy discourse in Israel and the influence of Patinkin and his students on macroeconomic policy in the 1960s.

REFERENCES

Alacevich, M., & Boianovsky, M. (2018). Writing the history of development economics. *History of Political Economy 50*(Suppl. 1), 1–14.

Alatout, S. (2008a). "States" of scarcity: Water, space, and identity politics in Israel., 1948–59. *Environment and Planning D: Society and Space*, 26(6), 959–982.

Alatout, S. (2008b). Locating the fragments of the state and their limits: Water policymaking in Israel during the 1950s. *Israel Studies Forum, 23*(1), 40–65.

Alatout, S. (2009). Bringing abundance into environmental politics: Constructing a Zionist network of water abundance, immigration, and colonization. *Social Studies of Science 39*(3), 363–394.

Baker, G. L., & Rasmussen, W. D. (1975). Economic research in the department of agriculture: A historical perspective. *Agricultural Economics Research, 27*(3–4), 53–72.

Balisciano, M. L. (1998). Hope for America: American notions of economic planning between pluralism and neoclassicism, 1930–1950. *History of Political Economy, 30*(Suppl.), 153–178.

Banzhaf, H. S. (2006). The other economics department: Demand and value theory in early agricultural economics. *History of Political Economy, 38*(Suppl. 1), 9–31.

Banzhaf, H. S. (2010). Consumer surplus with apology: A historical perspective on nonmarket valuation and recreation demand. *Annual Review of Resource Economics, 2*, 183–207.

Bareli, A., & Cohen, U. (2008). The middle class versus the ruling party during the 1950s in Israel: The "engine–coach car" dilemma. *Middle Eastern Studies, 44*(3), 489–510.

Barkai, H. (1990). *The beginnings of the Israeli economy*. (Hebrew). Jerusalem: Bialik Institute.

Berry, R. A., & Cline, W. R. (1979). *Agrarian structure and productivity in developing countries*. Baltimore, MD: Johns Hopkins University Press.

Blass, S. (1973). *Water in strife and action*. (Hebrew). Givatayim: Masada.

Boianovsky, M. (2018). 2017 HES presidential address: Economists and their travels, or the time when JFK sent Douglass North on a mission to Brazil. *Journal of the History of Economic Thought, 40*(2), 149–177.

Burnett, P. (2011). The price is not right: Theodore W. Schultz, policy planning and agricultural economics in the cold-war United States. In V. H. Robert, M. Phillip, & S. Thomas (Eds.), *Building Chicago economics: New perspectives on the history of America's most powerful economics program* (pp. 67–92). Cambridge: Cambridge University Press.

Brunetti, A. (2018). On economists as policy advisors with applications to Switzerland. *Swiss Journal of Economics and Statistics, 154*(2).

Clawson, M. *Clawson papers, Forest History Society*. Durham, NC.

Clawson, M. (1955a). *Israel agriculture 1953/54*. Joint Planning Center for Agriculture and Colonization and Economic Advisory Staff. Jerusalem: Government Printer.

Clawson, M. (1955b). Israel agriculture in recent years. *Agricultural History, 29*(2), 49–65.

Clawson, M. (1957). *Letters from Jerusalem*. London: Abelard-Schuman.

Clawson, M. (1961). Man and land in Israel,. *Agricultural History, 35*(4), 189–192.

Clawson, M. (1987). *From sagebrush to sage: The making of a natural resource economist*. Ana Publications.

Cochrane, W. W. (1989). Remembering John D. Black. *Choices First Quarter*, 30–32.

Cortez, A. B., Gadgil, D. R., Hakim, G., Lewis, W. A., & Schultz, T. W. (1951). *Measures for the economic development of underdeveloped countries: Report by a group of experts appointed by the Secretary-General of the United Nations*. New York, NY: United Nations Department of Economic Affairs.

Eshkol, L. (1954). Foundations for an economic and financial plan, based on an address at the Jerusalem Conference. (Hebrew) *Economic Quarterly, 3*, 163–171.

Evans, M. (2006). Defending territorial sovereignty through civilian settlement: The case of Israel's population dispersal policy. *Israel Affairs, 12*(3), 578–596.

Feitelson, E. (2013). The four eras of Israeli water policies. In B. Nir (Ed.), *Water policy in Israel: Context, issues and options*. Dordrecht: Springer.

Fischer, S. (2001). Beyond the ivory tower: The role of the economist in society. IMF Working Paper.

Fishman, B. G., & Fishman, L. (1957). Public policy and political considerations. *Review of Economics and Statistics, 39*(4), 457–462.

Foreign Relations of the United States, 1952–1954, The Near and Middle East. Vol. IX, Part 1.

Fox, K. A. (1989). Agricultural economists in the econometric revolution: Institutional background, literature and leading figures. *Oxford Economic Papers, 41*(1), 53–70.

Galbraith, J. K. (1979). September seventy-nine: On professor Milton Friedman's disillusionment with the economic policy of the Likud. (Hebrew) *Migvan, 39/40*, 28–29.

Gilbert, J. (2015). *Planning democracy: Agrarian intellectuals and the intended New Deal*. New Haven, CT: Yale University Press.

Ginzburg, E. (1977). *Israel and American Jews: The economic connection*. New York, NY: American Jewish Committee.

Ginzburg, E. (2009). *My brothers' keeper*. London: Routledge.

Gross, N. (1990). Israeli economic policies, 1948-1951: Problems of evaluation. *Journal of Economic History*, *50*(1), 67–83.

Gross, N. (1995). The economic regime during Israel's first decade. In S. Ilan Troen & N. Lucas (Eds.), *Israel: The first decade of independence*. New York, NY: State University of New York Press.

Hacohen, D. (2003). *Immigrants in turmoil: Mass immigration to Israel and its repercussions in the 1950s and after*. Syracuse. NY: Syracuse University Press.

Herzog, D. (2019). *Contested waterscapes: Constructing Israel's national water carrier*. Ph.D. Dissertation. New York University.

Hirschman, A. (1963). *Journeys towards progress*. Washington, DC: Brookings Institution.

Hirschman, A. (1984). A dissenter's confession: "The strategy of economic development" revisited. In M. Gerald & S. Dudley (Eds.), *Pioneers in development*. New York, NY: Oxford University Press.

Heymont, I. (1967). The Israeli Nahal program. *Middle East Journal*, *21*(3), 314–324.

Karlinsky, N. (2000). California dreaming: adapting the 'California model' to the Jewish citrus industry in Palestine, 1917–1939. *Israel Studies*, *5*(1), 24–40.

Kimhi, A., & Tzur-Ilan, N. (2021). Structural changes in Israeli family farms: Long-run trends in the farm size distribution and the role of part-time farming. *Agriculture*, *11*, 518.

Kirkendall, R. S. (1964). Social science in the central valley of California: An episode. *California Historical Society Quarterly*, *43*(3), 195–218.

Kislev, Y. (2015). Agricultural cooperatives in Israel: Past and present. In K. Ayal & L. Zvi (Eds.), *Agricultural transition in post-Soviet Europe and Central Asia after 25 years*. Halle: Leibniz Institute of Agricultural Development in Transition Economies (IAMO).

Krampf, A. (2009). The coining of the expression 'economic independence' in the Israeli economic discourse. (Hebrew). *Iyunim*, *19*, 1–34.

Krampf, A. (2010). Economic planning of the free market in Israel during the first decade: The influence of Don Patinkin on Israeli policy discourse. *Science in Context*, *23*(4), 507–534.

Krampf, A. (2018). *The Israeli path to neoliberalism: The state, continuity and change*. London and New York: Routledge.

Kuznets, S. (1954). Economic policy and its research. (Hebrew). *Economic Quarterly*, *1*(4), 291–294.

Lissak, M. (2003). The demographic-social revolution in Israel in the 1950s: The absorption of the Great Aliyah. *Journal of Israeli History*, *22*(2), 1–31.

Loveridge, J. (2017). *The hungry harvest: Philanthropic science and the making of South Asia's green revolution, 1919–1964*. Ph.D. Dissertation. University of Texas-Austin.

Mandelkern, R. (2016). The new economic policy of 1962: How Israeli economists almost changed the Israeli economy. *Israel Studies Review*, *31*(2), 41–60.

McDean, H. C. (1983). Professionalism, policy, and farm economists in the early Bureau of Agricultural Economics. *Agricultural History*, *57*(1), 64–82.

Metzer, J. (1978). Economic structure and national goals—The Jewish National Home in interwar Palestine. *Journal of Economic History*, *38*(1), 101–119.

Metzer, J. (1998). *The divided economy of mandatory Palestine*. Cambridge: Cambridge University Press.

Michaely, M. (1975). *Foreign trade regimes and economic development: Israel*. New York, NY: National Bureau of Economic Research.

Michaely, M. (2014). The Hebrew University Economics Department: The early days—A personal perspective. *Israel Economic Review*, *12*(1), 1–25.

Mosley, P., & Ingham, B. (2013). *Sir Arthur Lewis: A biography*. London: Palgrave MacMillan.

Muhn, J., & Stuart, H. R. (1988). *Opportunity and challenge: The story of BLM*. Washington, DC: Bureau of Land Management.

Mundlak, Y. (1964a). *Long term projections of supply and demand for agricultural products in Israel*. Jerusalem: Falk Project for Economic Research, Hebrew University.

Mundlak, Y. (1964b). *An economic analysis of established family farms in Israel 1953–1958*. Jerusalem: Falk Project for Economic Research, Hebrew University.

Nathan, R., Gass, O., & Creamer, D. (1946). *Palestine: problem and promise. An economic study.* Washington, DC: Public Affairs Press.

Nevo-Eshkol, O. (1989). *Eshkol shel humor* (Hebrew). Tel Aviv: Idanim.

OECD. (2018). *OECD economic surveys: Israel.*

Ohana, D. (2003). *Messianism and Mamlachtiut: Ben-Gurion and the intellectuals between political vision and political theology.* (Hebrew). Sde Boker: Ben-Gurion Research Institute for the Study of Israel and Zionism and Ben Gurion University Press.

Patinkin, D. (1967). *The Israel economy: The first decade.* Jerusalem: Falk Institute for Economic Research.

Picard, A. (2013). The reluctant soldiers of Israel's settlement project: The Ship to Village Plan in the mid-1950s. *Middle Eastern Studies, 49*(1), 29–46.

Pomfret, R. (1976). *Trade policies and industrialization in a small country: The case of Israel.* Tubingen: J.C.B. Mohr.

Porat, H. (1991). The policy of land acquisition and Negev settlement on the eve of the War of Independence. (Hebrew). *Cathedra, 62,* 123–154.

Porat, H. (1995). The plan for settlement and development of the Negev. (Hebrew). *Cathedra, 78,* 122–145.

Rashid, S. (2018). From anxiety to nonchalance: 'Neoclassical economic development' from 1950 to 2000. *History of Political Economy, 50*(Suppl. 1), 286–302.

Rubner, A. (1958). The 'price-less' land of Israel. *Land Economics, 34*(4), 290–297.

Rutherford, M. (2011a). *The institutionalist movement in American economics, 1918–1947: Science and social control.* New York, NY: Cambridge University Press.

Rutherford, M. (2011b). The USDA Graduate School: Government training in statistics and economics, 1921–1945. *Journal of the History of Economic Thought, 33*(4), 419–444.

Rutherford, M., & Desroches, C. T. (2008). The institutionalist reaction to Keynesian economics. *Journal of the History of Economic Thought, 30*(1), 29–48.

Seers, D. (1962). Why visiting economists fail. *Journal of Political Economy, 70*(4), 325–338.

Schiffman, D., & Goldstein, E. (2019). The Economic Advisory Staff and state-building in Israel, 1953-1955. *Oeconomia–History/Methodology/Philosophy, 9*(3).

Schiffman, D., Young, W., & Zelekha, Y. (2017). *The role of economic advisors in Israel's economic policy: Crises, reform and stabilization.* Cham: Springer.

Sedjo, R. A. (2000). Marion Clawson and America's forests: A lifetime of commitment. In R. A. Sedjo (Ed.), *A vision for the U.S. Foreign Service: Goals for its next century. In Memory of Marion Clawson.* Washington, DC: RFF Press.

Sharett, M. (1978). *Sharett diary 1953–1957* (Y. Sharett, Ed.). Tel Aviv: Maariv Library. Electronic edition.

Sitton, D. (2000). *Development of limited water resources: Historical and technological aspects.* Working Paper, Ben Gurion University. Reproduced by Israel Ministry of Foreign Affairs.

Skocpol, T., & Finegold, K. (1982). State capacity and economic intervention in the early new deal. *Political Science Quarterly, 97*(2), 255–278.

Stanford Research Institute. (1955). *The industrial economy of Israel.* Prepared for US Operations Mission in Israel and Israel Ministry of Trade and Industry. SRI Project 989. Menlo Park, CA.

Stross, R. E. (1986). *The stubborn Earth: American agriculturalists on Chinese soil, 1898–1937.* Berkeley, CA: University of California Press.

Sutton, F. X. (1987). The Ford Foundation: The early years. *Daedalus, 116*(1), 41–91.

Vaughn, G. F. (1995). Policy making for natural resources: An interview with Marion Clawson. *Choices* (Fourth Quarter), 13–15.

White, B. (2013). Software for Asia's green revolution: The Agricultural Development Council, Arthur Mosher and 'getting agriculture moving. Rockefeller Archive Center Research Report.

Wilcox, W. (1952). Social scientists and agricultural policy. *American Journal of Agricultural Economics, 34,* 173–183.

Yonay, Y. (1998). *The struggle over the soul of economics.* Princeton, NJ: Princeton University Press.

APPENDIX: CLAWSON'S MEMORANDA

Memoranda Listed in MCP

The following list (number, title and date) is copied from the document "Memoranda and Brief Reports Prepared by Marion Clawson and Others, June 1953 to December 1954 while Member of Economic Advisory Staff" (MCP Box 8, Folder 1). Notes and location have been compiled by the authors. DNS=Did not survive. Unless otherwise stated, memoranda are located in MCP Box 8, Folder 1.

#	Title	Date	Note	Location
1	Per Capita Food Consumption in Israel and in Other Countries	6/30/53		
2	Progress Report: Training for Agriculture in Israel	8/11/53		
3	Proposed Purchases of Irrigation and Agricultural Equipment under Reparations Program (Shilumim)	9/7/53		
4	Comprehensive Economic Program	9/14/53	Addressed to Bell	
5	General Survey of Agriculture in Israel	9/20/53		
6	Cost of Irrigation Water in Israel, and its Economic Significance	9/20/53		
7	Retail Food Prices in Israel and in United States	9/21/53		
8	Agricultural Planning in Israel	9/30/53		
9	Agriculture and Food in Israel, 1952–1953	10/6/53		
10	Estimated Future Cost of Irrigation Water to be Provided by Mekorot Water Co., and its Economic Significance	10/12/53		Subsequent drafts: 5486/1-Gimmel (undated, sent by Gass to Ben-Gurion (11/19/53), MCP (11/13/53) and 10757/10-Gimmel (11/13/53). Hebrew Translation 2433/21-Gimmel (undated)
11	General Survey of Agriculture in Israel	10/12/53	Revision of #5	
12	Agricultural Planning in Israel	10/16/53	Revision of #8	

(Continued)

#	Title	Date	Note	Location
13	General Survey of Agriculture in Israel	11/12/53	Revision of #11	Sent to Ben-Gurion (cc Naphtali, Eshkol) w/ summary and Gass cover letter
14	Summary of Memorandum "Estimated Future Cost of Irrigation Water to be Provided by Mekorot Water Co., and its Economic Significance"	11/19/53	Summary of #10	Also in 5486/1-Gimmel
15	Agricultural Planning in Israel	11/16/53	A much longer, more detailed version of #12	5486/1-Gimmel has 2nd draft; Sent to Ben-Gurion (cc Naphtali, Eshkol) w/ summary and Gass cover letter
16	Summary of memorandum "Agricultural Planning in Israel"	11/19/53	Summary of #12	Also in 5486/1-Gimmel; Sent to Ben-Gurion (cc Naphtali, Eshkol) w/ summary and Gass cover letter
17	Research Plan for Agricultural Research Station (with Consideration of Economic Aspects)	Undated		
18	Storage of Irrigation Water in the Loessal Soils of the Negev	12/10/53		
19	Use of Reclaimed Sewage from the Tel Aviv Metropolitan Area, in the Negev and on the Coastal Sand Dunes	12/24/53		
20	Farm Organization to Economize Use of Water in the Negev	12/28/53		
21	Study of Livestock and Feed Price, Demand, and Subsidy Problems	1/1/54		
22	Data copied from Irrigation Advisers' Guide, published by Bureau of Reclamation, 1951	Undated		
23	Current Proposals about Grain Import, Feed Prices and Prices of Livestock Products	1/19/54	Based on # 21	
24	Price Relationships Among Agricultural Commodities	1/22/54		

#	Title	Date	Note	Location
25	Amount of Farm Machinery Needed in Israel	1/29/54		Also in 2433/21-Gimmel, with Bell to Eshkol cover letter, cc. Naphtali, Joint Planning Center, Gvati, six others, and Farm Machinery Section of Ministry of Agriculture. Also in 648/8-Peh. Clawson strongly suggested a group discussion including MOF officials. The Ministry of Agriculture held a discussion on March 17, 1954; Amir communicated the main points to Gass (March 29, 1954, 2433/21-Gimmel).
26	Current Status of Irrigation Studies	1/29/54		
27	Suggestions for More Efficient Use of Farm Machinery in Israel	2/5/54		
28	A Program to Subsidize the Cost of Living Index as far as Eggs, Bread and Related Commodities Are Concerned	2/14/54		
29	Use of Reclaimed Sewage from the Tel-Aviv Metropolitan Area, in the Negev and on the Coastal Sand Dunes	2/17/54	Essentially restates #19 and #20	
30	Suggestions for More Efficient Use of Labor and Farm Machinery in Israel	2/22/54	Significantly overlaps with #27	Also 648/8-Peh. The Ministry of Agriculture held a discussion on March 17, 1954. Amir communicated the main points to Gass (March 29, 1954, 2433/21-Gimmel).
31	Some Notes on Marketing of Vegetables in Israel	3/22/54		
32	Alternative Possibilities on Egg and Grain Prices	2/1/54		
33	Irrigation, Agricultural and Settlement Problems and Policy for the Coastal Plain-Negev Regions	4/25/54	With Gass cover letter to P. Naphtali, 5/3/54	
	Appendix: Farm Organization to Economize the Use of Water in the Negev		Cites #10	

(*Continued*)

#	Title	Date	Note	Location
34	Prices at which Agricultural Commodities Estimated in Plan C to be Produced will Sell in 1960	6/8/54		Sent to Naphtali w/ Bell cover letter 10757-9/Gimmel. Also Bell to Naphtali, 10757-9/Gimmel. Also in 2433/21-Gimmel, with Bell cover letter.
35	Manpower for Agriculture	6/23/54		Addressed to Gross. Stimulated by discussions with Gross, and Clawson and Gross' attendance at a meeting of the Aranne Committee on labor productivity.
36	Prospective Prices of Agricultural Commodities, and What to Do About It	6/29/54	Abridged version of #34 with implications	Cover letter Bell to Naphtali, 10757-9/Gimmel.
37	Economic Factors in the Development of Agriculture in Israel. Remarks presented at a Meeting of the Farmers' Federation of Israel, Tel Aviv	7/8/54	Published in Hebrew in *Israel Farmers 5715*, the Farmers' Federation yearbook of 1954/55.	Also 2433/21-Gimmel.
38	Israel Agriculture in Recent Years, article submitted to *Journal of Agricultural History* (sic)	1955	Refers to Clawson (1955b)	
39	Labor Required to Produce Agricultural Commodities in Israel	7/14/54		
40	Major Economic Problems and Policy Issues in Agriculture and in Irrigation	7/18/54		
41	Labor Requirement of Israel Agriculture, and Related Policy Issues	7/29/54	Hebrew translation dated 12/25/54	See Bell to Sapir (cc. Gvati, Amir, Kollek, Horn), October 25, 1954, 5509/15-Gimmel. Also 648/8-Peh.
42	Review of Current Status of Studies on Demand for Agricultural Commodities and Some Further Possible Steps	8/25/54	A restatement of previous memoranda by Clawson and David Dinur.	
43	Cotton Report for the Development and Utilization of the Water Resources of the Jordan and Litani Basins	9/12/54		

#	Title	Date	Note	Location
44	Statement on Settlement Program for Planning Committee/ Formulation of the Best Settlement Program	9/26/54		
45	Letter to D. Kahane on water prices, Min. of Agriculture., Tel Aviv	9/27/54	23 pages	
46	Theoretical Aspects of Milk Marketing in Israel	10/26/54		Also 648/8-Peh.
47	Hebrew translation of milk marketing memorandum	2/14/55	DNS; mentioned in a note from Zvi Neumann to Clawson.	
48	Inducing Farmers to Use Irrigation Water Wisely	12/22/54		

Memoranda Not Listed in MCP

#	Title	Date	Note	Location
49	Inputs of Tractors' Work per Dunam: California Practice by R.L. Adams 1953	3/14/54		2433/21-Gimmel, 434-438
50	Survey of Established Family Farms on Moshavim	Beginning 1953	DNS; Clawson was on the advisory committee.*	
51	Memorandum: Irrigation of the Southern Half of Israel	Ca. March 1954	DNS; With Uri Ariav. A "first rough draft" was circulated for comments within the Ministry of Agriculture (Gass-Naphtali correspondence, March 14 and 23, 1954, 2433/21-Gimmel).	
52	Public lecture on irrigation	Before 7/8/54	DNS; Mentioned in Naphtali to Bell, July 30, 1954, 2433/21-Gimmel.	

*The advisory committee consisted of six Israelis, Clawson, and FAO representative Albert G. Black. The survey was conducted annually over 1953–1961, and resulted in 14 publications through 1962 (Mundlak, 1964b). Clawson's involvement was publicized in *Zmanim*, January 24, 1955. Clawson (1955a, pp. 208–214) extensively cited the (as yet) unpublished Survey of Moshavim for 1952/1953.

PART III

FROM THE VAULT

CHAPTER 10

AN INTERVIEW WITH FRANCIS WILSON

Phillip Magness and Micha Gartz

ABSTRACT

The son of academics Monica and Godfrey Wilson, Francis Wilson (b. 1939) was raised in a Zulu-speaking locale of rural South Africa. Despite a keen interest in history imbued by his anthropologist parents, Wilson completed his undergraduate degree in physics at the University of Cape Town (UCT) before pursuing his doctorate at Cambridge University. Fascinated by the economics of discrimination and their relationship to the Apartheid regime in South Africa, Wilson spent a year in the United States as a visiting graduate fellow at the University of Virginia's Thomas Jefferson Center for Political Economy (TJC) in 1964

JEL classification: B20

After witnessing America's civil rights movement first hand, Wilson worked on his dissertation in residence at the TJC. The finished product was later published in a more accessible form as *Labour in the South African Gold Mines 1911–1969*. From his historical analysis of the gold mining industry's labor market, Wilson concluded that the industry's manipulation of black wages profoundly influenced racial segregation and real wage inequality in South Africa.

Wilson's time at the TJC overlapped with the peak of this storied department's academic acclaim. As he explains in the interview, Wilson came to Virginia on the recommendation of Cambridge's Peter Bauer, who had previously spent a term as

Research in the History of Economic Thought and Methodology: Including a Selection of Papers Presented at the First History of Economics Diversity Caucus Conference
Research in the History of Economic Thought and Methodology, Volume 41B, 223–230
ISSN: 0743-4154/doi:10.1108/S0743-41542023000041B010

a visiting faculty member at the TJC and who returned for a lecture on "African Political Economy" in 1964. Bauer's writings on the subject anticipated the work of UCT economist William H. Hutt, whose *The Economics of the Colour Bar* contained a sweeping economic indictment of the Apartheid regime.[1]

Although Wilson came from the opposite end of the political spectrum as Bauer and Hutt – indeed he never met Hutt during his time at TJC and considered him too much of a free-marketeer for his own tastes – the parallels between their respective interests in the economics of Apartheid were sufficient to strike certain commonalities. Bauer accordingly recommended Wilson for a visiting graduate fellowship at the TJC. A report from the center to the president of the university specifically highlighted Wilson's work, noting that he was "completing research on the economic effects of racial discriminatory policies in South Africa."[2]

During his time in Virginia, Wilson worked directly with G. Warren Nutter and James M. Buchanan, and had opportunities to meet Gary Becker and Kenneth Boulding. A labor economist by training, Wilson recounted his own political differences with Nutter and Buchanan, whom he regarded as conservatives. Their most pronounced area of disagreement concerned the Vietnam War, as exemplified by Nutter's later acceptance of an appointment in the Pentagon during the Nixon administration.

Wilson nonetheless described a welcoming research atmosphere, fostered by his two main hosts – a marked contrast with certain recent accounts of the TJC that have attempted to depict it as a reactionary political project, or even its contemporary critics at UVA who accused it of political one-sidedness.[3] Aside from occasional sparring with the famously acerbic Gordon Tullock, Wilson recalled an extremely supportive research environment at the TJC. The department encouraged his dissertation work on Apartheid in the mining industry, and Nutter secured funding for Wilson's travel to Columbia University to meet with Gary Becker. While Wilson originally expected to adapt Becker's work on racial discrimination to his project, he found its purely mathematical approach unsuitable for the political story he was investigating. Instead, Becker's insights on human capital theory would provide a formative influence on Wilson's own work.

In addition to his scholarly projects, Wilson recounted how he was able to participate in contemporary events such as the U.S. Civil Rights Movement's campaigns to end racial segregation. He witnessed civil rights protests at the University of Virginia, and made an investigative trip across the deep south to study segregation.

After completing his degree, Professor Wilson was appointed a lecturer and researcher at the University of Cape Town and held this position for over 40 years. He became the founder and director of the South African Labour and Development Research Unit (SALDRU), and directed the Second Carnegie Inquiry Into Poverty and Development in Southern Africa alongside prominent South Africans such as Mamphela Ramphele. Wilson retired from UCT in 2004, and resides with his wife Lindy in the Eastern Cape province of South Africa.

Magness: Professor Wilson, I wanted to thank you for joining us in this conversation. I want to explore several topics that I think are interesting for the history of how the economics profession developed, and to get your take because you interacted with a very vibrant moment in the history of the University of Virginia's economics program, including several leading figures that were there. I wanted to ask you to start us off by telling us how you came to the University of Virginia (UVA) and what drew you to that department?

Wilson: Ah, well I got there kind of by accident. I'm a South African and – cutting a long story short – I was writing a PhD in Cambridge and I wanted to work on the economics of discrimination. So I spent a year in Cambridge getting ready for that and in about February – very late in about February I said to my supervisor, "You know, I don't have any money to go on next year in Cambridge, couldn't I go to [...] America for a year?" and he said, "Well, what kind of scholarship have you got?" and I said, "I've got nothing." So he said, "Well, let me talk to my friend Peter Bauer." Who was an economist, you'll know his name – yes – and Peter had run economics in Caius where I was a student and so my supervisor, Michael Farrell, sent me down to London to meet Peter Bauer.[4] And Peter Bauer said he had – he was a Hungarian I think – anyway he had an accent, and he said, "Well, I don't know anything about you, but anybody who Michael Farrell sends to me I'll take seriously." Well that was nice. So he said, "Let me talk to my friends at UVA."

Ah, now the thing is – the funny thing here is that the friends at UVA are probably like you are, they were very much free marketeers, and in a place where I wasn't very familiar or sympathetic – I mean they were quite conservative. In fact very conservative, as you will see.

But he wrote to them and they had had Bill Hutt, William H. Hutt, as a visiting scholar there and they loved William Hutt, who I was hugely critical of because I thought: No, no. Hutt's thinking is no good for what we need in South Africa now.[5]

But on Hutt's ticket I got to UVA because they thought, "Well, if this is a young man from South Africa he must have been influenced by William Hutt and so he's okay with us." So I got to UVA as a protege of William Hutt sent by Peter Bauer, the two of whom I probably disagree [with] more than any other economists I can think of. But that's by the by.

Anyway I got to UVA and they were all incredibly kind and nice to me. I mean particularly Jim Buchanan, Warren Nutter – Gordon Tullock is another story, we'll talk about him in a moment, but they gave me an office; they gave me money (I needed to go and visit Gary Becker in New York) and all that kind of thing. They could not have been nicer to me even though they found my views distinctly unpalatable.

So that's the story of how I got there. And of course it was 1964 and that was the year of Selma. It was the huge civil rights year and so – UVA was right at the heart of the storm really – and we got to know a number of teachers like Paul Gaston (a historian) and others who were deeply immersed in the civil rights campaign.[6] And so we got to know the civil rights movement through UVA – which is not necessarily what Jim Buchanan had planned but that was fine, it worked well.

Magness: Actually I guess we can continue on Buchanan and I want to hear the stories about – any that you have on Gordon Tullock because I had similar interactions of my own with him. He was a character, to put mildly. And then also Warren Nutter, what do you remember distinctly about interacting with him in the department?

Wilson: Well, Warren Nutter and Jim Buchanan were the older men and much more experienced than me and, as I said, could not have been nicer. I mean, my wife and I had meals in their home. And they talked about life with us, you know, and we got on very, very well at a personal level.

Jim Buchanan I remember telling me a story about having grits for breakfast, I suppose he was a Southerner, and he explained to me what grits were. And he never tried to change my views or anything like that. He just was a very decent man.

As was Warren Nutter. Well I knew, or I discovered subsequently, that some of his politics was a bit off the charts – let's put it that way. He became, in the end, Warren Nutter did, he became

Nixon's economic advisor in the Pentagon, which from my student perspective was about as low as you could get.[7] I don't think that's at all a good place to be. But he was lovely to me, and it was he who found me the money. He was head of the department at the time, he found me the money to go down to meet Gary Becker and I didn't know anything then about the amazing work he was doing to analyze the Russian economy – because he kind of unpacked the Russian economy before anybody else did, I seem to remember.[8]

So Warren Nutter sent me down to meet Gary Becker because he'd written a book on the economics of discrimination, and that was the reason I wanted to go. Well, when I went down, I had these fascinating discussions with Gary – who was very kind to me, he was at Columbia then, and we had long discussions about economics of discrimination – whose book was of absolutely no use to me whatsoever because the analysis that he was doing was static: it had no politics in it; political forces didn't play any part. And in the South African context, we did not have large numbers of workers black and white doing the same job, so you couldn't develop a market discrimination coefficient or anything like that. But it helped one to think – you know I did physics as my first degree – and there's a sense in which economics of discrimination is like a physics textbook: you have to go very precisely through the argument. His book on *Human Capital* on the other hand, is *hugely* important on investment in human beings and so on.[9]

And I mean for me, economic discrimination was this kind of plaything really. It was just an intellectual exercise but the economics of human capita, the fundamentally important book, and he came in at a very early stage before a lot of the other people talking about education in economic terms. Now that – I owe all of that to the University of Virginia, to the economic department, and to Warren Nutter in particular.

Gartz: So what was the academic environment at UVA like, did they host any seminars or speakers in the department?

Wilson: Oh well this is interesting you know. It's amazing how fast life has changed, I mean when I was at the University of Virginia we had a march around the Rotunda and this was to [inaudible] and in favor of, you know, to integrate the university properly. This meant black men and white men. It did not mean women. There were no women [there] at the time, and so it was very much a boy's college. And with that atmosphere, and those drawbacks. And it's hard to think of this now but I mean in 1964 even Princeton was men only. And we can't believe that these days, but that was the situation. So in that context Virginia had a reputation as being sort of for the not-so-bright-sons of the wealthy. And Bobby Kennedy was a student there, and so it was not taken very seriously as a university in the way that, say, Harvard was.

At the same time, it had some wonderful staff. I mean the history department which I knew were – well I mean first of all our economics department, even if I disagreed with their views was the tip-top department – I mean some of the best people in the world were there: Nobel Prize winners and all. The history department we got to know because my wife was doing a history course with Paul Gaston. I think he was chairperson of the civil rights movement of Charlottesville, something like that. Anyway we got to know, through him and others, a number of people in the civil rights movement where UVA was very much alive – *very* much alive – and part of the process of that whole deracializing of the South actually, because Virginia is in the South. So there was that kind of combination of fairly conservative economists, but very powerful economists; of very active civil rights people, including academics and historians; plus this kind of gentleman's college environment where no women were allowed. Now that's a strange mixture but it was a pretty lively place.

Magness: And did you participate directly in some of the protests or the integration movement?

Wilson: Er … Yes, well we had the famous well I mean not very for a South African not very marked, but there was a march around the campus to try and integrate the campus properly. I never went down to Selma. I was very tempted to go to Selma, because we could have all gone to the second crossing – the first crossing everybody got beaten to hell.[10] The second crossing I wanted to go – everybody was going down to demonstrate, but I took the view that I needed to keep my powder dry because I was a South African and going to be working in South Africa, which was going to be no less complicated than the United States. Therefore, don't get involved in the United States: leave them to do their own thing. Which I still regret of course, it would have been lovely to go down to Selma. But I didn't, and I think it was the right decision for me at the time.

Gartz: So how did your time in Charlottesville shape your own research in the end with the mining industry and the larger problem of Apartheid?

Wilson: Ah, that's a nice question. Well, as I explained, my conversations with Gary Becker were very fruitful. He couldn't have been nicer, couldn't have been nicer, and took time and we talked a lot about things and I really realized that his approach – however brilliant it was – was not going to take me anywhere in the South African context. I had to find a different kind of way in. And – I always tell my students now that when they're writing a PhD they must take the first year – a whole year – to work out what is the correct question, because once you've got the question right you can begin to move.

Now the question for me was: what are the wages in the gold mines of South Africa, and why are they different for black and for white? Now that is the question that I worked out while I was at UVA reading everything I possibly could about American discrimination; reading about South Africa – and so that interactive process for me was *fundamental*. I don't know if I would have got there if I'd never been down to Charlottesville. But it was a South African question in the end. And so all my life my work has been on labor economics really. I've been looking for these kinds of critical questions that one needs to find the answer to in the South African context. And that means of course that we have to be talking about political *economy* because one is looking at political forces as well as economic forces, if I can make a distinction.

Magness: So let me ask you, I guess a little bit more on the Apartheid question. How did it compare with everything that you saw in the United States – happening in both countries having severe problems with racial segregation but of a different type. Did that impress upon you?

Wilson: Oh yes, because near the end of my trip of my time in the States, the year there we had an old – I think it was a Chev[rolet] station wagon and we drove down, right through the South. We could afford to go either to the South or to California. But we decided to go South, which was a great move. And so we drove down through Alabama all the way to Mississippi, and then up through the middle of Mississippi and back to Charlottesville. Well that was an amazing journey because we were sent from civil rights worker to civil rights worker. We got on kind of the train going backwards, if I can put it that way, and went all the way down South. It's quite an interesting question, the similarities and the differences. I mean I was much more scared in Alabama or Mississippi than I ever was in South Africa.

Now that may have been because I didn't *know* the places, and I was more familiar in South Africa, but there was a kind of violence in the air in the South that was quite … scary. Really quite scary. Having said that I mean your battles at that stage were fairly tame; they were to sort of students going to sit at segregated ice cream parlors and that kind of thing. And we had that in abundance in South Africa, but we had a much bigger political challenge in the sense that you had people going to jail for life for trying to change the government in a fundamental way. So there was that huge difference in the structure of racism in America and the structure of racism in South Africa if I can put it that way.

And in the South of course the civil rights workers had the support of the Kennedys and of the governments and all of that kind of thing – which was not true in the South African context. The other point that is interesting – if I can just go on for a moment – is that black Americans in South African terms would be classed as "colored." Now this doesn't mean anything to you, because the words – you play with the words – but in South Africa a black African is some-body whose family, whose ancestors, go back 10,000 years in Africa. A "colored" person is somebody whose ancestors are partly European and partly African. Now, that is true of most black Americans. And so there's a fairly big difference there, that black Americans their home language is English, which is not their original language. In South Africa we've got *nine* major languages which are African: Xhosa, isiZulu, Tswana, so on and so on. So there are all sorts of similarities and differences, and that we found fascinating.

Magness: I also wanted to ask you a little bit more – I know you mentioned Peter Bauer at Cambridge; William Hutt had a connection to UVA, and this is originally how I found your work. I was noticing the different speakers that came through UVA and did visitations there and I noticed that there was a bit of a South African theme. Because one of Bauer's lectures had been on the problem of Apartheid when he came over, and then I noticed Hutt of course who was writing about Apartheid at that time. Did you interact with either of them much more than just making the connections to come over?

Wilson: Not really, you know. I knew – I met Peter Bauer because he helped me enormously. What was lovely about them was that they helped somebody who they disagreed with, but that's by-the-by. Peter Bauer was notorious should I say – or whatever the right word is in the English-speaking world – for being on the far right of where the economics profession was. I think today one would see him as not necessarily far right at all but with a very lively view about the dangers of the state. Bill Hutt – William Hutt – I didn't know at all: he was older than me, he was my mother's generation at the university, and I don't know if I ever even met him.

Magness: That's a fascinating connection though, just putting it together. And I guess a little bit the follow-up on that, did the others in the department talk about either of their research, or did they reflect on South Africa at all when they were hearing your presentations and your material?

Wilson: No, the conversation you know at lunch time was really about Vietnam because of the war sort of peaking up. So South Africa was very low on anybody's agenda. What I do remember about all of that of course was Gordon Tullock. It was very, way off the charts – I mean Gordon would come away from lunch saying, "Well, the only thing to do now is to drop an atomic bomb on China." And you weren't quite so sure he was just joking. Not necessarily: he was wild, he was very wild.

The other two I didn't really talk about their economics with them. No – to my sadness I should have. I mean I should have engaged with Jim Buchanan on public choice; I should have engaged with Warren Nutter on Russia. It would have been fascinating but I never did. The book that was just being published at the time was *The Calculus of Consent*, which Gordon Tullock had a lot to say about of course, but I wasn't going to listen too much to Gordon Tullock; I never read it.[11]

Magness: Yes, he was a character in my own interactions with him. I think I showed him an article once, and his response was that I had convinced him to have an even lower opinion of the person I was writing about!

Wilson: Yeah, that's a key Gordon Tullock remark .... You know he was very small, very bright – obviously much too bright for his own good – and he liked to take people down. So I never was going to spend a lot of time worrying about that.

Gartz: So Professor Wilson, I do just have one last question. In a 1999 interview you mentioned that growing up you recognized your privilege and you recognized the income discrepancies between black and white South Africans. This issue has recently gained traction here in the US and I was just wondering, what are your views on white privilege and guilt – or "wokeness" – and how should we try and deal with that nowadays?

Wilson: My view is that you don't feel guilty about privilege. Money – it's not your fault – it's not my fault that I've got a reasonable family background but what you must do is to take account of it: recognize that it is a special place and then use it to help eliminate privilege. I mean privilege is a bad thing no question about it and so one's got to do what one can to eliminate it. But you don't feel so guilty that you get paralyzed.

And I had to think that all through when I was in Cambridge because: was I going to go back to South Africa, yes or no? A lot of my friends refused to go back to South Africa because they said, "Hey, there's nothing they can do." And they'll then become part of the issue (and part of the problem) and they will feel very guilty. I took an entirely different view: I felt that there was a lot one could do and that one didn't have to feel guilty about it so long as you were actually doing something to eliminate it. So that's where I stand, and so that all those paralyzed characters in California now who don't quite know what they're doing they get off the[ir] backsides and do something to change it.

Gartz: Right, I think probably the main thing that people see as creating any change is just protesting but at the end of the day, I'm not sure whether or not that actually achieves anything.

Wilson: Well you know that was true in South Africa too – I mean we sat there in the 1950s, 1960s and that had been a racist totalitarian state for 200 years and it wasn't going to change in a hurry. But you know slavery in 1770 had been in existence for a thousand years and then six or seven people got together with a cup of coffee in London and they'd begin to change this thing and in 50 years they eliminated it. So things can change. Yeah, I mean, I do believe that the American dilemma is not that great. I mean we're only talking of 10[%] of the population after all, you know, so to kind of find a way to make everybody feel at home – well it means of course changing the world view of white Americans, which need some significant changing, because it's far too egocentric and violent in my view.

Magness: Thank you. All right. This has been a very fruitful conversation.

Wilson: [inaudible] who were the two Nobel Prize winners?

Magness: So Ronald Coase was there in the late 1950s and I think he left in 1962 and then Buchanan, and then we all there was also a visit at some point by George Stigler so – I think that was in 1961 – that's the record that I've got on that.[12]

Wilson: The big man who came when I was there was Kenneth Boulding.

Magness: Oh yeah, yeah.

Wilson: He's one of my heroes as an economist. I think he's fantastic ….

Many years ago, so when I got to Cambridge in [1960] I went in to see my supervisor for the first time. Now I had done a physics degree in South Africa and was not at all well-read in history, or social, or literature, or anything like that and he said to me, "Well, Wilson," he said, "go out and buy Kenneth Boulding's *Economic Analysis*," which in those days was in one volume (it wasn't two volumes). And he said, "On page 737 you'll find a list of questions and I want you to write an essay about question number five." Well you know I dashed off and put a towel around my head and read the whole thing in about seven days flat because I could barely begin to answer the question. I hadn't the vaguest idea what it was about. But then I met [inaudible] saw a lot more of Kenneth Boulding and his work and he, of course, conceived of that phrase "the spaceship earth" which really says it all.

And so Boulding came through UVA when you were there as well and even came to lunch with us. Yes, no, I was thrilled.

NOTES

1. W. H. Hutt (1964). *The Economics of the Colour Bar*. Institute of Economic Affairs.
2. Report of the Thomas Jefferson Center for Political Economy, 1964–65, p. 9. University of Virginia Special Collections, Papers of the President 1964–65, Box 23.

3. See in particular Nancy MacLean's *Democracy in Chains* (2017), which portrays the TJC as an academic extension of Harry Flood Byrd, Sr.'s political machine. For a corrective account of the errors and misrepresented evidence in MacLean's book, see Magness, Phillip W., Art Carden, and Vincent Geloso. (2019). James M. Buchanan and the political economy of desegregation. *Southern Economic Journal, 85*(3), 715–741. In 1964, the University of Virginia's administration prepared an internal report on the economics department, alleging that its scholarly activities biased in a politically conservative direction.

4. Michael James Farrell (1926–1975) and Peter T. Bauer (1915–2002) were University of Cambridge economists. Bauer visited the University of Virginia's Thomas Jefferson Center for Political Economy in 1958, and hosted James M. Buchanan as a visiting Fulbright professor in 1961–62.

5. William H. Hutt (1899–1988) was an economist at the University of Cape Town, and spent one year at UVA as a Distinguished Visiting Professor in 1966.

6. Paul M. Gaston (1928–2019) was a professor of history at UVA who also served as president of the Southern Regional Council, and was involved in the American Civil Rights movement.

7. Nutter served as Assistant Secretary of Defense for International Security Affairs in the Nixon administration, holding this appointment from 1969 to 1973.

8. G. Warren Nutter. (1957). *Some observations on Soviet industrial growth*. National Bureau of Economic Research.

9. Gary S. Becker (1957). *The economics of discrimination*. University of Chicago Press; Gary S. Becker. (1964). *Human capital: A theoretical and empirical analysis, with special reference to education*. University of Chicago Press.

10. The first crossing, known as "Bloody Sunday," took place on March 7, 1965.

11. James M. Buchanan and Gordon Tullock. (1965). *The calculus of consent: Logical foundations of constitutional democracy*. University of Michigan Press.

12. Other future Nobel laureates affiliated with the TJC during this period included Bertil Ohlin and Maurice Allais, both of whom spent terms in residence as visiting faculty. Milton Friedman delivered a guest lecture at the TJC in 1960, but declined an offer to spend a semester in residence.

Printed in the USA
CPSIA information can be obtained
at www.ICGtesting.com
JSHW050725230324
59678JS00029B/72